POWER

Learning

Strategies for Success in Higher Education and Life

Third Canadian Edition

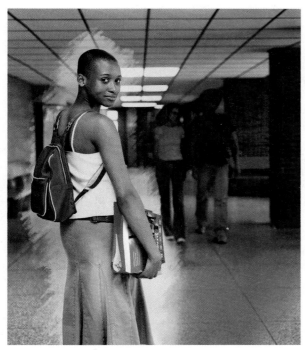

Robert S. Feldman

University of
Massachusetts—Amherst

Sheila Chick

Fanshawe College

Carlos Frewin

Humber Institute of Technology and Advanced Learning

 McGraw-Hill Ryerson

Toronto   Montréal   Boston   Burr Ridge, IL   Dubuque, IA   Madison, WI   New York
San Francisco   St. Louis   Bangkok   Bogotá   Caracas   Kuala Lumpur   Lisbon   London   Madrid
Mexico City   Milan   New Delhi   Santiago   Seoul   Singapore   Sydney   Taipei

The McGraw-Hill Companies

P.O.W.E.R. Learning:
Strategies for Success in Higher Education and Life
Third Canadian Edition

McGraw-Hill
Ryerson

ISBN-13: 978-0-07-097265-0
ISBN-10: 0-07-097265-6

1 2 3 4 5 6 7 8 9 10 TCP 0 9 8

Printed and bound in Canada

Editorial Director: Joanna Cotton
Sponsoring Editor: Lisa Rahn
Marketing Manager: Matthew Busbridge
Senior Developmental Editor: Maria Chu
Editorial Associate: Marina Seguin
Supervising Editor: Graeme Powell
Copy Editor: Evan Turner
Senior Production Coordinator: Madeleine Harrington
Cover Design: Bruce Graham
Interior Design: Bruce Graham
Cover Image: © Getty Images/Digital Vision
Page Layout: Aptara, Inc.
Printer: Transcontinental Interglobe

Library and Archives Canada Cataloguing in Publication

Feldman, Robert S. (Robert Stephen), 1947-
    P.O.W.E.R. learning : strategies for success in higher education and life / Robert S. Feldman, Carlos Frewin. — 3rd Canadian ed.

Includes bibliographical references and index.
ISBN 978-0-07-097265-0

    1. College student orientation.   2. Study skills.   3. College students—Life skills guides.   I. Frewin, Carlos C. (Carlos Cecil), 1945-   II. Title.   III. Title: Power learning.

LB2343.3.F44 2008   378.1'98   C2008-900295-4

Brief Contents

Contents

③ Making the Most of Your Time 57

④ Getting Along with Others 85

5 Taking Notes   113

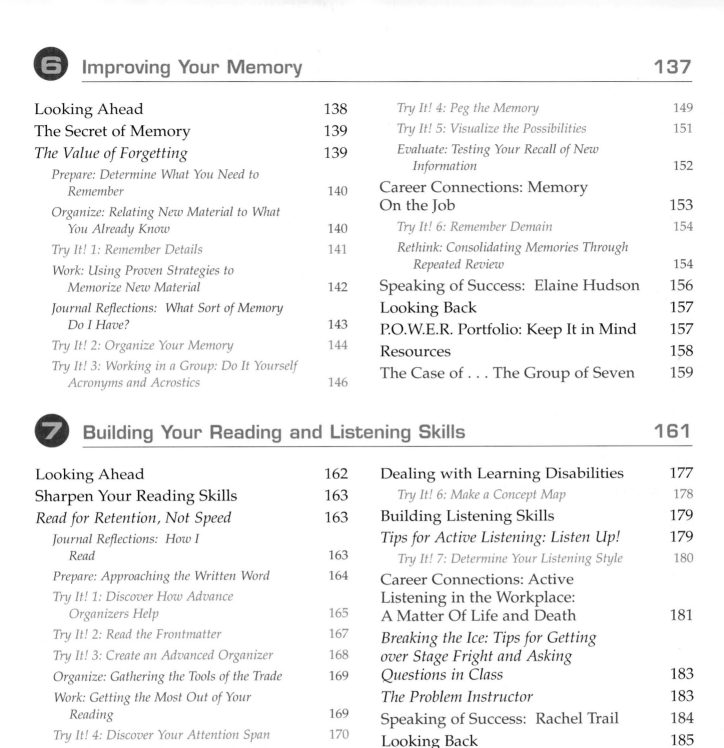

8 Taking Tests

9 Writing

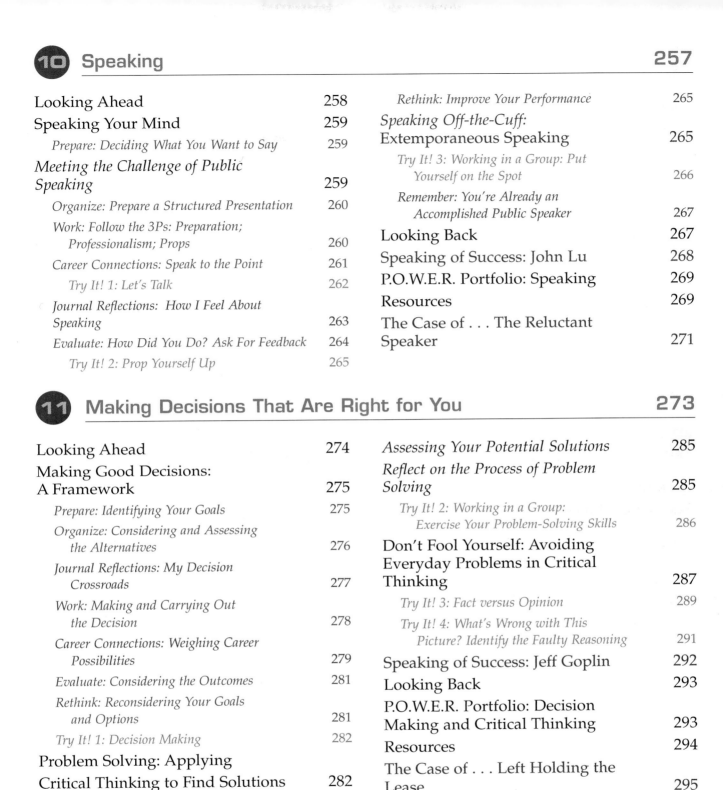

10   Speaking   257

11   Making Decisions That Are Right for You   273

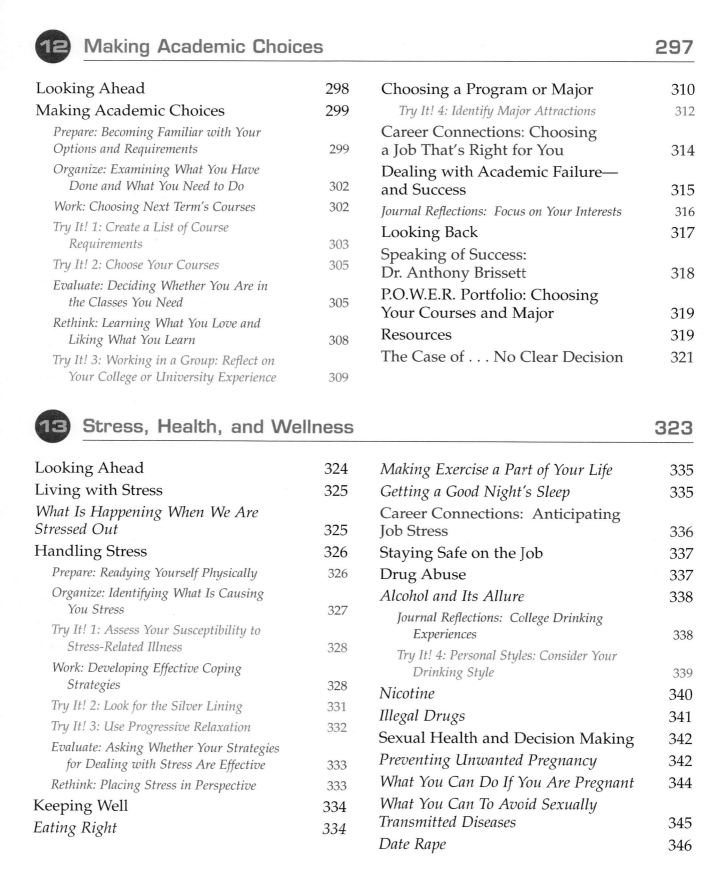

12 Making Academic Choices 297

13 Stress, Health, and Wellness 323

14 Money Matters 353

Introducing *P.O.W.E.R. Learning: Strategies for Success in Higher Education and Life*, Third Canadian Edition

For many students, the student success course is a literal lifeline. It provides the means to learn what it takes to achieve academic success and to make a positive social adjustment to the campus community. If students learn how to do well in their first semester of college or university, they build a foundation that will last a lifetime.

P.O.W.E.R. Learning provides a framework that students can begin to use immediately to become more effective students. Having taught student success courses many times, we know this framework had to meet several important criteria:

- Clear, easy-to-grasp, logical, and compelling, so that students could readily see its merits.

- Effective for a variety of student learning styles—as well as a variety of teaching styles.

- Workable within a variety of course formats.

- Transferable to settings ranging from the classroom to the dorm room to the board room.

- Effective in addressing both the mind *and* the spirit, presenting cognitive strategies and skills, while engaging the natural enthusiasm, motivation, and inclination to succeed that students carry within them.

The Third Canadian Edition of *P.O.W.E.R. Learning: Strategies for Success in Higher Education and Life* helps students confront and master the numerous challenges of the postsecondary experience through use of the P.O.W.E.R. learning approach, embodied in the five steps of the acronym P.O.W.E.R. (Prepare, Organize, Work, Evaluate, and Rethink). Using simple—yet effective—principles, P.O.W.E.R. Learning teaches the skills needed to succeed in college or university and careers beyond.

The Goals of the Book

P.O.W.E.R. Learning: Strategies for Success in Higher Education and Life, Third Canadian Edition **addresses five major goals.**

1. **To provide a systematic framework for organizing the strategies that lead to success.** Using the P.O.W.E.R. framework and relying on proven strategies, *P.O.W.E.R. Learning* provides specific, hands-on techniques for achieving success as a student.

2. **To offer a wide range of skill-building opportunities.** *P.O.W.E.R. Learning* provides a wealth of specific exercises, diagnostic questionnaires, case studies, and journal writing activities, in the text and online, to help students to develop and master the skills and techniques they need to become effective learners and problem solvers. *Readers learn by doing.*

3. **To demonstrate the connection between academic success and success beyond the classroom.** Stressing the importance of *self-reliance* and *self-accountability*, the book demonstrates that the skills required to be a successful student are tied to career and personal success as well.

4. **To develop critical thinking skills.** Whether to evaluate the quality of information found on the Internet or in other types of media, or to judge the merits of a position taken by a friend, colleague, or politician, the ability to think critically is more important than ever in this age of information. Through frequent questionnaires, exercises, journal activities, and guided group work, *P.O.W.E.R. Learning* helps students to develop their capacity to think critically.

5. **To provide an engaging, accessible, and meaningful presentation.** The fifth goal of this book underlies the first four—to write a student-friendly book that is relevant to the needs and interests of its readers and that will promote enthusiasm and interest in the process of becoming a successful student. Learning the strategies needed to become a more effective student should be a stimulating and fulfilling experience. Realizing that these strategies are valuable outside the classroom as well will provide students with an added incentive to master them.

In short, *P.O.W.E.R. Learning: Strategies for Success in Higher Education and Life* is designed to give students a sense of mastery and success as they read the book and work through its exercises. It engages and nurtures students' minds and spirits, stimulating their intellectual curiosity about the world and planting a seed that will grow throughout their lifetime.

Achieving the Goals of the Book

The goals of *P.O.W.E.R. Learning: Strategies for Success in Higher Education and Life,* Third Canadian Edition are achieved through a consistent, carefully devised set of features common to every chapter. They include the following:

Chapter-opening scenarios.

Each chapter begins with a short vignette, describing an individual grappling with a situation that is relevant to the subject matter of the chapter. Readers will be able to relate to these vignettes, which feature students creating positive working relationships (Chapter 4), building their reading and listening skills (Chapter 7), or taking tests (Chapter 8).

Looking Ahead sections.

These sections provide a bridge between the opening vignettes and the remainder of the chapter and include orienting questions that lay out the chapter's objectives.

P.O.W.E.R. Plan.

Every chapter includes a figure that summarizes the key activities related to each step of the P.O.W.E.R. process for the major topic discussed in the chapter. The P.O.W.E.R. Plan figures are especially helpful to visually oriented learners.

Try It! activities.

These sections, interspersed throughout the chapter and available on the text's Online Learning Centre, include written exercises of all types. These activities are keyed to one or more of the steps of P.O.W.E.R.; the relevant steps are indicated by highlighted letters at the top of each *Try It!* There are at least five *Try It!* activities in every chapter, and at least one of these is designated as an in-class, group exercise. Examples of *Try It!* exercises include "Resolve That Conflict" (Chapter 4), "Organize Your Memory" (Chapter 6), "Working in Groups Mark Up a Book Page" (Chapter 7), and "Complete a Test-Preparation Checklist" (Chapter 8).

Speaking of Success.

Every chapter includes interviews with individuals who exemplify academic success. Many of these individuals have struggled to overcome difficulties in their personal lives or in school before achieving academic or career success. Students will be able to relate to or identify with the stories told by the people profiled in these sections; some accounts may inspire readers to realize their goals and aspirations.

Career Connections.

This feature links the material in the chapter to the world of work, demonstrating how the strategies discussed in the chapter are related to career choices and success in the workplace. Topics addressed in these sections include narrowing career choices, applying for jobs, and developing workplace listening skills.

Journal Reflections.

This feature provides students with the opportunity to keep an on-going journal, making entries relevant to the chapter content. You can keep a written journal or use online methods such as the journal exercises on the Online Learning Centre, blogs, or Facebook to post your reflections, but the emphasis is on taking just a few minutes to think about what you are doing now and how you could improve your effectiveness. Students are asked to reflect and think critically about related prior experiences.

Running Glossary.

Key terms appear in boldface in the text and are defined in the margins. Key terms are high-lighted in colour in the index.

End-of-chapter material.

Each chapter ends with a summary (Looking Back), organized around the orienting questions featured in the Looking Ahead section; a P.O.W.E.R. Portfolio section with suggestions for portfolio submissions; and an annotated list of student resources. These resources include campus offices, relevant supplemental readings, and World Wide Web sites. This material helps students study and retain important concepts presented in the chapter, as well as guiding future inquiry.

P.O.W.E.R. Portfolio.

Each section includes suggestions for submissions to a learning or skills portfolio. This feature allows students to compile a portfolio, which can be used as an evaluation tool for the whole course. Some submissions are revised and edited assignments from the chapters, for example, the Personal Mission Statement from Chapter 2. Students will be able to understand and learn the skills of developing a portfolio, an important tool in goal setting, evaluation, and career development.

Case Study.

Each chapter ends with a case study (The Case of . . .) to which the principles described in the chapter can be applied. Case studies are based on situations that students might themselves encounter. Each case provides a series of questions that encourage students to consider what they've learned and to use critical thinking skills in re-sponding to these questions.

What's New and Updated in the Third Canadian Edition?

- While *Power Learning: Becoming a Successful Student* (Chapter 1) continues to set the stage for learning, the sections *Recognizing How You Learn, Who You Are, and What You Value* are now found in Chapter 2.

- *Making the Most of Your Time* (Chapter 3) incorporates personal insights and the *Personal Mission Statement* from Chapter 2 as a foundation for time management.

- *Using Technology for Information Management* (previously Chapter 4) now resides on the Online Learning Centre as most students have the computer skills required to succeed in college and university. The OLC provides an opportunity for assessing computer skills and identifying learning needs where necessary.

- *Getting Along with Others* (new Chapter 4) now appears earlier in the text as the ability to work in teams and to be collaborative is necessary in most college and university courses. Additionally, people skills are a critical workplace competency. These skills need to be taught early and reinforced throughout the course.

- *Taking Notes* (Chapter 5) presents a discussion on how the use of PowerPoint in lectures changes the nature of notetaking in the classroom. Readers will learn how to take notes effectively from PowerPoint slides, and use slide decks to create revision notes for exam preparation.

- *Improving Your Memory* (Chapter 6) has been moved earlier so that students can implement the memory techniques to prepare for the midterm assessments common in many courses.

- *Writing and Speaking* are divided into two separate chapters in response to reviewer feedback. Separating these important topics allowed for much more coverage of both. The *Writing* chapter has an expanded discussion of plagiarism, and now incorporates tips on prevention, evaluation of Internet sources, and a discussion on cheating via electronic media.

- Try It! activities now fully implement the P.O.W.E.R. learning framework, which reinforces the principles and concepts of the material, and provides a thoroughly integrated experience.

P.O.W.E.R. Tools for Instructors and Students

The same philosophy and goals that guided the writing of *P.O.W.E.R. Learning: Strategies for Success in Higher Education and Life,* Third Canadian Edition have informed the development of a *comprehensive, first-rate* set of teaching aids. Through a series of focus groups, questionnaires, and surveys, we asked instructors what they needed to optimize their courses.

As a result of the extensive research that went into devising the teaching aids, we are confident that whether you are an instructor with long experience, or are teaching the course for the first time, this book's instructional package will enhance classroom instruction and provide guidance as you prepare for and teach the course.

For Instructors

Online Learning Centre (OLC) www.mcgrawhill.ca/power The OLC includes a password-protected Web site for instructors. This site offers downloadable supplements and access to PageOut, the McGraw-Hill Ryerson Web site development centre.

Instructor's Manual The Third Canadian edition of the manual contains suggestions for teaching each topic in the text, tips on teaching student success, handouts and transparency masters, audio-visual resources, sample syllabi, tips on the Web, and chapter quizzes.

Computerized Test Bank This test bank contains multiple-choice questions, true-false questions, and short answer questions. The test bank is available on the Instructor's Online Learning Centre in McGraw-Hill's EZ Test testing software. This user friendly program allows instructors to sort questions by format; edit existing questions or add new ones; and scramble questions for multiple versions of the same test.

PowerPoint® Presentation The Microsoft® PowerPoint® Presentation slides contain lecture presentation visuals that may be edited and manipulated to fit a particular course format.

For Students

Online Learning Centre (OLC) www.mcgrawhill.ca/olc/power The site includes quizzes, interactive exercises, web links, videos, and other useful study resources.

Create a custom course Website with **PageOut**, free with every McGraw-Hill Ryerson textbook.

To learn more, contact your McGraw-Hill Ryerson publisher's representative or visit www.mhhe.com/solutions

courses · campus · community

www.blackboard.com

Course Management

PageOut McGraw-Hill Ryerson's course management system, PageOut, is the easiest way to create a website for your student success course. There is no need for HTML coding, graphic design, or a thick how-to book. Just fill in a series of boxes in plain English and click on one of our professional designs. In no time, your course in online!

For the integrated instructor, we offer content for complete online courses. Whatever your needs, you can customize the *P.O.W.E.R. Learning* Online Learning Centre content and author your own online course materials. It is entirely up to you. You can offer online discussion and message boards that will complement your office hours, and reduce the lines outside your door.

Content cartridges are also available for course management systems, such as WebCT and Blackboard. Ask your iLearning Sales Specialist for details.

Superior Service

Service takes on a whole new meaning with McGraw-Hill Ryerson and *P.O.W.E.R. Learning* we have consistently raised the bar in terms of innovation and educational research—both in student success courses and in education on general. These investments in learning and the education community have helped us to understand the needs of students and educators across the country, and allowed us to foster the growth of truly innovative, integrated learning.

Integrated Learning Your Integrated Learning Sales Specialist is a McGraw-Hill Ryerson representative who has the experience, product knowledge, training, and support to help you assess and integrate any of our products, technology, and services into your course for optimum teaching and learning performance. Whether it's using our test bank software, helping your students improve their grades, or putting your entire course online, your *i*Learning Sales Specialist is there to help you do it. Contact your *i*Learning Sales Specialist today to learn how to maximize all of McGraw-Hill Ryerson's resources!

iServices McGraw-Hill Ryerson offers a unique *i*Service package designed for Canadian faculty. Our mission is to equip providers of higher education with superior tools and resources required for excellence in teaching. For additional information, visit *www.mcgrawhill.ca/highereducation/iservices* or contact your local *i*Learning Sales Specialist.

Teaching, Learning & Technology Conference Series The educational environment has changed tremendously in recent years, and McGraw-Hill Ryerson continues to be committed to helping you acquire the skills you need to succeed in this new milieu. Our innovative Teaching, Learning & Technology Conference Series brings faculty together from across Canada with 3M Teaching Excellence award winners to share teaching and learning best practices in a collaborative and stimulating environment. Preconference workshops on general topics, such as teaching large classes and technology integration, will also be offered. We will also work with you at your own institution to customize workshops that best suit the needs of your faculty.

About the Authors

To my students, who make teaching a joy.

Robert S. Feldman is a Fellow of both the American Psychological Association and the American Psychological Society. He is a winner of a Fulbright Senior Research Scholar and Lecturer award and has written some 100 scientific articles, book chapters, and books. His books, some of which have been translated into Spanish, French, Portuguese, and Chinese, include *Fundamentals of Nonverbal Behavior, Development of Nonverbal Behavior in Children, Understanding Psychology, 6/e,* and *Development Across the Life Span, 3/e.* His research interests encompass the study of honesty and truthfulness in everyday life, development of nonverbal behaviour in children, and the social psychology of education. His research has been supported by grants from the National Institute of Mental Health and the National Institute on Disabilities and Rehabilitation Research. With the last of his three children starting college last fall—and facing the proverbial empty nest— Professor Feldman occupies his spare time with serious cooking and earnest, but admittedly unpolished, piano playing. He also loves to travel with his wife, who is also a college professor. He lives with her in a home that looks out on the Holyoke mountain range in Amherst, Massachusetts.

To my fellow teachers who go above and beyond to help others succeed.

Carlos Frewin is a learning and development specialist with extensive experience in business and education. He has followed a lifetime interest in helping people learn and succeed in different learning environments. He is the designer of many training programs in the private and public sector, and led the development of one of the first distance learning systems in Ontario at Confederation College in Thunder Bay, Ontario.

At present, Carlos is a professor at Humber Institute of Technology and Advanced Learning in Toronto, Ontario, and a Managing Partner of inLearn Inc., a human resources development consulting firm. At Humber, Carlos is a Program Coordinator who, with a group of dedicated instructors, teaches college success skills in the School of Applied Technology.

Carlos has a Doctorate in Adult Education from the University of Toronto and lives just north of Toronto in the Caledon Hills with his wife, Jan, and Golden Retriever, Emma. When not working at his desk, Carlos enjoys sailing, and is currently renovating the house.

Acknowledgments

I am grateful that Bob Moulton, the now retired Dean of the School of Applied Technology at Humber, decided to invest in the future of our students by creating college success and job search courses for all students. This decision led me to an intensive four-year involvement in the development and delivery of college student success courses. That, along with other experience, created the opportunity to be involved in this, the Third Canadian Edition of *P.O.W.E.R. Learning*.

I would like to thank the many coworkers and students who have helped me learn over the years. In particular, the contributions of Susan Krausz, Kerry Johnston, Connie Eggins, and David Temple have helped with this book because of their interest in discussing ideas and finding ways to add to student success.

Thanks to the reviewers of the Third Canadian Edition for their insightful feedback and their recommended changes. I appreciate the time they took to carefully identify areas of improvement and recognize areas that met their needs:

Joanne Bakker, *Niagara College*

Hedy Chase-Rattner, *Seneca College*

Cindy Chisvin, *Seneca College*

Dana Copeland, *Fanshawe College*

Gayle Cross, *St. Clair College*

Angela Devoe-Coleman, *Mount Saint Vincent University*

Jean Flynn, *Mount Saint Vincent University*

Gail Foy, *Georgian College*

Thomas Groulx, *St. Clair College*

Jane Guzar, *Mohawk College*

Jillian Hull, *Douglas College*

Ian McKergow, *Mount Saint Vincent University*

Patricia Mongeon, *Durham College*

Peter B. Moran, *Seneca College*

Hyacinth C. Randall, *Seneca College*

Allen Richert, *Confederation College*

Kerri Shields, *Centennial College*

Carol M. Shirley, *Mount Saint Vincent University*

Lazaros Simeon, *George Brown College*

Sue Slessor, *Georgian College*

Maureen Simpkins, *University College of the North Atlantic*

Debby Vollbrecht, *Capilano College*

I also appreciate the willingness of the special people who agreed to be profiled in the "Speaking of Success" features. Their real life stories add impact to the text.

Farzana Jamal

Todd Currie

Emm Gryner

Jenny Zhang

Kofi Boateng

Elaine Hudson

Rachel Trail

Asta Kovanen

Shawn Thomson

John Lu

Jeff Goplin

Dr. Anthony Brissett

Krista Bailey

Murray Baker

My gratitude is extended to the McGraw-Hill Ryerson editorial and production team including the Media Technology team who look after the Online Learning Centre. The project started with Karen Ritcey, the signing Sponsoring Editor, and then was steered along by Lisa Rahn, Sponsoring Editor, Christine Gilbert, Developmental Editor, and Maria Chu, Senior Developmental Editor. They were a group of professionals who were a pleasure to work with.

Finally, thanks to a long list of people I have learned from over the many years. Special thanks to my son, Gregg, who helped me understand more about his generation, but especially to my dear wife, Jan, for her insightful, practical feedback and her encouragement and understanding throughout this process.

Carlos Frewin
carlos.frewin@rogers.com

P.O.W.E.R. Learning: Becoming a Successful Student

1

The first day of school started with a bang—literally. Miriam Motumba was easing out of bed, trying not to waken the baby, when *bang!*—she heard the door slam. Her 7- and 8-year-old sons were up and arguing already. Miriam had hoped to have a quick shower before making lunches and getting breakfast ready, but that hope was now dashed. She quickly separated the boys, sitting them at opposite ends of the room, and went to wake up her daughter. Miriam wondered whether she was doing the right thing. She had been out of school for 10 years and had four kids—two in school and two in daycare. Could she succeed in getting a decent education and providing a better life for herself and her kids?

As Kendra Jackson sat in her car, waiting for a parking space on her first day of classes, the car behind her suddenly bumped into her—bang! Already tense, afraid she would be late, and not even knowing where her classrooms were, Kendra burst into tears. The accident was minor, but Kendra took it as a bad omen. She didn't know whether she was doing the right thing by moving to the city and studying environmental technology. She knew her parents were counting on her, but right then Kendra wanted to go home and forget about college.

Jamie Stuart glanced up at the clock, wondering how much time was left in his night shift, as—bang!—the stamping machine came down on another sheet of metal. Jamie was on automatic pilot, having performed the same manoeuvre all night, and he stifled a huge yawn. He needed the extra shifts, because his student loan hadn't arrived yet, and he had to buy his paramedic textbooks, equipment, and uniform this week. Jamie had taken extra science courses to be accepted into the paramedic program, and he was excited about saving lives, but Jamie didn't know whether he could afford to stay in school.

As Jing Zhou struggled to find her bus pass on the crowded bus, she lost her grip on her coffee and—bang!—it fell to the floor, splattering everyone. Mortified, Jing tried to apologize, but she couldn't; all her English words had deserted her. Although she had been in Canada for a few weeks, her confidence when speaking was low. As she glanced at the strangers on the bus, she worried about how she was ever going to succeed in a school with English-speaking students. How was she going to make friends and feel included?

Looking ▶▶
Ahead

If you are reading this book, it likely means that you have decided to take the big step of going to college or university. And, because less than half of high-school students end up attending college or university, you have also succeeded in getting there. Now, how are you going to succeed in this new environment? What kind of plan do you have to make the most of your investment of time and money? What is your strategy to achieve your goals?

Going to school is a job with its own set of knowledge and skills required for success. You may find the courses are harder, there may be much more homework than you are used to, and classes are often larger, with less opportunity for help from the professor. It is up to you to attend classes and complete your assignments. You have the opportunity to pass or fail based on what you decide to do. You can use P.O.W.E.R. Learning to help you enjoy the learning process more and help you learn the skills you need to succeed.

Some students say they don't need a student success course, at least in the beginning. But do you know how you learn and study best? Can you describe your strengths and how they fit your career choice? How can you get more value from your reading time, take better notes, and get the best possible marks on your exams?

Give the P.O.W.E.R. Learning process a chance to work for you because there are two things we know for sure: (1) Students who have clear goals, a plan for success, and basic academic skills have higher rates of success in college or university, and (2) By far, most students who say they don't need a college success course in the beginning say they are glad they took one in the end.

When you have completed this chapter you will be able to answer these questions:

- **What are your reasons for going to college or university?**

- **How does using P.O.W.E.R. Learning as a tool increase your personal effectiveness?**

- **What are your learning goals for this course?**

- **What are your key employment goals?**

- **How would you define the meaning of success?**

Why Go to College or University?

Mike had a job at one stage in his life that serves as a perfect example of why it is important go to school. Mike made mixing bowls in a manufacturing plant. The job involved placing a piece of metal in a stamping machine that formed the metal into a bowl. Mike made about $10/hour and while the company brochure talked a lot about workplace safety and job satisfaction, no one seemed to really care if he was happy or sad or fulfilled in his job; only if he could make 180 parts per hour. He was not offered any training or involved in any projects or problem-solving groups. For all he knew there was no future beyond his current job. There are a lot of these kinds of jobs.

There are also other kinds of jobs. People in these jobs might earn twice the pay that Mike earned because these people have "the complete package" that employers want. They have technical skills, but they also have the ability to problem solve, learn new things, work in groups, be members of teams, and get along with others in diverse workplaces. These jobs often require a college diploma or a university degree just to get a job interview.

There are many reasons to go to college or university. For the people mentioned at the beginning of the chapter, attending school meant different things. For Miriam Motumba it meant getting a better job and proving she can succeed in school. Kendra Jackson's parents wanted her to be the first in her family to get a college diploma but Kendra is not sure of her own reasons. Jamie Stuart wanted to become qualified for a better job with more action, variety, and excitement. Jing Zhou wants to learn English and begin to build a future in her new country.

Over time, people with a diploma or a degree usually earn about 30 to 50 percent more than people with a high-school education. At that rate, it doesn't take long to earn back your financial investment. (For some example salaries, go to the Salary Centre at monster.ca and compare.) Higher education also provides access to jobs with more interest, variety, and advancement, with a longer-term future. Complete Try It! 1—"Why Am I Going to College or University?"—to describe your own reasons for why are you attending college or university.

As for Mike, he went back to college and completed his diploma. He now has a job that is helping him gain a foothold in the competitive field of photography. Even more important to him, his prospects for the future are better and he is working to establish a lifestyle that meets his needs. He feels he has more choice in his life.

The value of postsecondary education extends beyond the ability to earn more money and enjoy more job satisfaction. The following are also reasons for pursuing a higher education:

- You will know how to learn
- You will learn to think and communicate better
- You will be more able to deal with changes in knowledge and technology
- You will be able to work more effectively in diverse workplaces

P.O.W.E.R. Learning

A system designed to help people achieve their goals, based on five steps: prepare, organize, work, evaluate, and rethink

Why Am I Going to College or University?

Place a 1, 2, and 3 by the three most important reasons that you have for attending college or university:

_____ I want to get a good job when I graduate.
_____ My parents want me to go.
_____ I couldn't find a job.
_____ I want to get away from home.
_____ I want to get a better job.
_____ I want to gain a general education and appreciation of ideas.
_____ I want to improve my reading and study skills.
_____ I want to become a more cultured person.
_____ I want to make more money.
_____ I want to learn more about things that interest me.
_____ A mentor or role model encouraged me to go.
_____ I want to prove to others that I can succeed.
_____ I want to feel better about myself.
_____ I want to improve life for my family and me.
_____ I want to prove to myself that I can do it.
_____ I want to grow up.

_____ _____
_____ _____

What do your answers tell you about yourself? Did you think about these reasons when you filled out your application form? How do your reasons compare with those of your classmates? Go to the website at www.mcgrawhill.ca/olc/power to see what other students have to say.

www.mcgrawhill.ca/olc/power

P.O.W.E.R. Learning: The Five Key Steps to Achieving Success

Do you want to be freer to manage yourself and to make your own decisions and choices? Most students who go to college or university want to be free to make more decisions and choices than they did in high school. They sometimes complain when they feel they are being treated like "high-school students." Learning the skill of self-management is part of the process of becoming more independent.

Self-management means using your personal resources and the resources in your environment to achieve your goals and objectives. These resources might be financial, physical, psychological, social, spiritual, or emotional. For example, on the personal resource level, you may be a very reliable person who works well as part of a team. On the external level, you may know how to use databases in the library to complete a research assignment.

P.O.W.E.R. Learning is one resource that will help you achieve your goal of obtaining a college or university education. It is a process you can use to develop

Journal REFLECTIONS

My School Experiences

Throughout this book, you will be given opportunities to write down your thoughts. These opportunities—called Journal Reflections—will permit you to record your reactions to what you have read, your ideas, notes, questions, and concerns. Above all, be honest in your reactions. If you save these entries and return to them later, you may be surprised at the changes they record over the course of the term. Go to the text website to see an example of a journal: www.mcgrawhill.ca/olc/power.

1. Overall, how would you describe your experiences at school so far? Has your school career been positive? Negative? Pleasant? Unpleasant? Why?

2. Describe one successful experience you've had in school.

3. What made the experience successful? Think of the teacher's methods, the subjects you were studying, how you did your work, interactions you had with others, and other elements of the experience.

4. What did you learn from it?

5. Did you ever have a "light bulb" experience—one in which you suddenly "saw the light" about something that had seemed beyond understanding before? If so, how did it happen?

6. Describe an unsuccessful experience or failure you've had in school.

7. Why did it occur? What choices did you make that contributed to it?

8. What did you learn from it?

9. What other comments do you have?

strategies and make decisions in school and in life beyond school. It's a simple but effective framework that will increase your chances of success at any task from choosing a career to completing an assignment.

There are five steps in the P.O.W.E.R. Learning process:

Prepare	Develop a purpose or goals for the task or activity
Organize	Plan for the resources—equipment and skills—that you need
Work	Manage your motivation to do the work
Evaluate	Compare your results to your goals
Rethink	Reanalyze, question, and challenge your assumptions

The P.O.W.E.R. Learning framework can be used to organize your approach to major actions or decisions, or to help you complete smaller tasks. It is used both of these ways in the text. Sections of most chapters have been organized around the P.O.W.E.R. framework, and this framework has also been used to help you organize your approach to the "Try It!" activities in each chapter.

 repare

Self-management means utilizing resources to achieve your purpose and your goals. The first step in managing for success is to establish a purpose and set re-lated goals.

P.O.W.E.R. Plan

Long-term goals
Aims relating to major accomplishments that take some time to achieve

Short-term goals
Relatively limited steps toward the accomplishment of long-term goals

Everything begins with a purpose. You may want to work to improve the lives of others, get enough money to buy an iPod, or end a relationship with a friend that is no longer working for you. Even if your purpose is doing nothing, it is still a purpose and that purpose guides your actions and behaviour.

Sometimes we respond to another person's purpose by doing what we are asked to do, sometimes we respond to our own pur-pose and do what we think is best. Sometimes our response is a mixture of both. Most people respond more to a purpose that comes from them, especially if it is personally compelling or mo-tivating. Most of us have had the thrill of working on something that was really important and meaningful to us.

Occasionally, we all go about our lives as if we were on autopi-lot. We don't think consciously about our purpose and don't put together a plan to achieve a purpose. It's like being on a journey without a destination in mind and wondering why we didn't get there. Student success is clearly linked to having a purpose and a plan to achieve that purpose. Complete Try It! 2—"How I Can Benefit from My Student Success Course?"—to describe how you can benefit from this course.

Having a purpose can help you in three major ways:

1. A purpose can provide a reason to get up in the morning and go about your life.

2. A purpose provides a basis for choosing your actions and behaviour. Does the behaviour you choose help you achieve your purpose?

3. Achieving all or part of your purpose can provide a feeling of success and give you something to feel good about and celebrate.

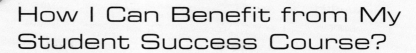

How I Can Benefit from My Student Success Course?

Academic journeys are similar to other major trips and they require the same sort of preparation. Think of the student success course as "The Lonely Planet Guide to Higher Education." Just as if you were planning to go to Nepal or Ecuador, some things you know; some things you think you know; some things you have heard about; and some things are totally foreign to you. Your student success course will help orient you to the new culture and expectations of postsecondary education.

Prepare: The purpose of this task is to identify potential benefits from this student success course.

Organize: To complete this task you will need the Table of Contents for the book and one or more study partners to compare notes.

Work: Go through the Table of Contents and put the topics in one of the four columns in the chart below. Now check your attitude. Are you open to learning?

Evaluate: Have you been able to identify some benefits that you can use to help your motivation?

Rethink: This course will also help you decide if you could first benefit from an attitude change, or if going to school is the right thing to do at this time.

What I Know	What I Think I Know	What I've Heard About	What's Totally New to Me

Attitude Check!

Just as your attitude can make the difference between a great trip and a disaster, the same is true at college or university. Is your attitude going to ensure your student success course is a positive experience? If so ... cool! If not ... adjust it!

Working in a Group: Compare your lists with others in your group. Discuss what you have learned, where you have learned it, how you used the learning, and your goals for this course.

Setting Goals

Goals represent the steps required to achieve your purpose. Goals can be **long-term** or **short-term** and are usually specific and measurable. For example, suppose you choose to get some form of physical exercise for the purpose of improving

"After working a couple of years after high school, I realized that with no education, my growth in the company and as a person would be very limited. After completing my first year at another college, I had a better understanding of what I wanted out of a school, so I investigated the school I am currently at. I realized that it held the best options for me to learn and be involved with the sorts of things that I wanted to do."

Paul Miles, Student, Sir Sanford Fleming College

your health and fitness. You know walking can help achieve your purpose of improving your health and fitness. This becomes a goal when you choose to do something specific. For instance, you might choose to walk three kilometres, five days a week, in under one hour. The best goals are specific, measurable, achievable, realistic, and time based.

The idea to start walking has very little power to change your behaviour until it is linked to a purpose and broken down into specific measurable targets you can achieve.

Sometimes it seems easier to focus on long-term goals. They may point to a bright future but because they are so far off it is tempting to say "I'll start tomorrow." Most successful people follow a pattern of translating longer-term goals into short-term goals so they can work toward something specific each day. These smaller achievements go together to build a foundation for success. For example, say you set a goal to complete one of your high-priority assignments *before* you watch TV. You may think it's not much of a goal, but it is one step toward passing the course and achieving your larger goal of graduating. You will likely enjoy the break more and you'll have a reason to feel better about your choices. Imagine doing this for 30 school days in a row to see how small actions can build bigger things. Complete Try It! 3, "Course Goals," to assist you with this exercise.

What's the best way to set appropriate goals? Here are some guidelines:

- **Make goals realistic and attainable.** Someone once said, "A goal without a plan is but a dream." We'd all like to win gold medals at the Olympics or star in rock videos or write best-selling novels; few of us are likely to achieve such goals.

  Be honest with yourself. There is nothing wrong with having big dreams, but it is important to be realistically aware of what it takes to achieve them. If our long-term goals are unrealistic and we don't achieve them, the big danger is that we may wrongly believe that we are inept and lack ability and use this belief as an excuse for giving up. Instead, we should realize that the problem has less to do with our abilities than with poor goal-setting strategies. If goals are realistic, we can develop a plan to attain them, spurring us on to attain more.

- **State goals in terms of behaviour that can be measured against current accomplishments.** Goals should represent some *measurable* change from a current set of circumstances. We want our behaviour to change in some way that can usually be expressed in terms of numbers—to show an increase ("raise my grade point average 10 percent") or a decrease ("reduce wasted time by two hours each week"), or to be maintained ("keep in touch with my out-of-town friends by writing four e-mail messages each month"), developed ("participate in one workshop on critical thinking"), or restricted ("reduce my phone expenses 10 percent").

- **Ensure your goals involve behaviour over which you have control.** We all want world peace and an end to poverty. Few of us have the resources or

TRY IT!

www.mcgrawhill.ca/olc/power

Course Goals

Prepare: The purpose of this task is to learn to assign different priorities to course goals and determine short-term and long-term goals.

Organize: To complete this task you will need a course outline or a calendar description of one of your core courses and one or more study partners to compare notes.

Work: Consider the core course and brainstorm a list of as many goals as you can think of for taking the class. Review the list and assign a rating of the importance of the goal to you: 1—not important to you; 2—somewhat important to you; 3—important to you. Next, assign a rating of the time frame for each goal; short-term—this semester; long-term—this school year and beyond. Select the goals that are most likely to motivate you.

Evaluate: Were you able to assign different priorities and time frames to your goals?

Rethink: What kind of goal is most likely to motivate you?

_____
_____
_____
_____
_____
_____
_____
_____
_____
_____

The goals you've listed most likely range from the specific ("passing the class with a good grade") to the more general and vague ("becoming educated in the subject matter of the class").

What is the difference between those goals that are most important to you and those least important to you? Are your goals mostly short-term or long-term? How specific are your goals? What implications might your different goals have for your future success in the course?

 Working in a Group: Compare *your* goals for the course with those of other students and consider the similarities and differences.

---

capabilities to bring either about. However, it is realistic to want to work in small ways to help others, such as by becoming a Big Brother or Big Sister or by volunteering at a local food bank.

- **Take ownership of your goals.** Make sure that the goals you choose are *your* goals and not the goals of your parents, teachers, brothers, sisters, or friends. Trying to accomplish goals that "belong" to others is a recipe for disaster. If you're attending school only because others have told you to, and you have no commitment of your own, you'll find it hard to maintain the enthusiasm—not to mention the hard work—required to succeed.

- **Identify how your short-term goals fit with your long-term goals.** Your goals should not be independent of one another. Instead, they should fit together into a larger vision of who you want to be. Periodically, step back and consider how what you're doing today relates to the kind of person you would ultimately like to be. Complete the activity in Try It! 4, "Course Goals, Revisited."

Organize

Once you have set a purpose and goals for your success, a self-manager then looks at the resources required to achieve the purpose and the goals. Some of the resources will come from within yourself, such as personal qualities, academic skills, and life experience, and some will be physical resources, such as computers, printers, and lab equipment, and will come from your environment.

Success will depend on qualities such as academic skills, being able to work in teams, time management, honesty, reliability, and persistence. But you will also need access to a computer, a printer, textbooks, transportation to school, and maybe a locker. You may also require financial assistance to complete your studies.

Students are often capable of getting the physical resources they need to achieve their purpose but are limited by their lack of academic skills. These academic skills vary from self-knowledge to math or English skills along with reading, studying, notetaking, and exam skills. Most of this book was created to help students get the academic skills they require to be successful in school.

Students who are in a hurry to meet a deadline often think it is better to dive in and figure out how to get it done as they go along. This often results in students spending more time to achieve less on assignments. They lose the benefits of effectiveness and efficiency that come from good planning. They end up redoing work and making poor use of their time and resources. The most common example is students who are missing basic computer skills often spend more time figuring out the computer skills to do an assignment than they do working on the assignment itself.

Of course this does not mean there are no surprises along the way. Good luck and timing are factors in many successes, but we often make our own luck through careful preparation and organization.

What kind of resources will you need to achieve your purpose? How will you get the resources you need?

If you are attending a college or university you are in one of the most resource-rich environments you will ever find. There are resources to help with almost any problem common to students such as health clinics, remedial math and English classes, counselling, peer tutors, financial assistance, gym facilities, and personal training assistance. Students are often unaware of these services, so part of being a self-manager is learning about the resources in your environment and building your skills to be a better self-manager.

Some suggestions for using resources on campus are:

- Attend information sessions that help you learn about what is available

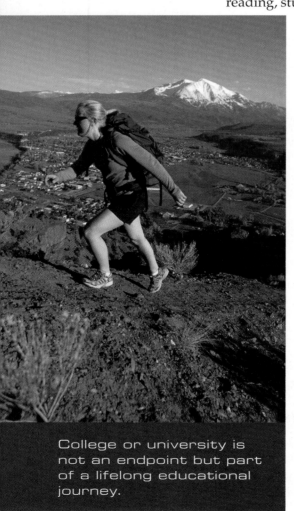

College or university is not an endpoint but part of a lifelong educational journey.

TRY IT!

www.mcgrawhill.ca/olc/power

Course Goals, Revisited

Prepare: Identify the resources you need to achieve your goals for this semester and how you access them.

Organize: You will need a list of the resources available at your college or university.

Work: Use the Student Handbook and the school website to make a list of the resources available to students. Include help with academic skills such as English, math, or computer skills. Also include sources of financial assistance. What kind of resources would have helped you in the past? Why are some students hesitant to go for help? In the space below, list the resources you plan to use this semester to achieve your goals.

Evaluate: Were you able to identify the resources you will need to succeed and how you access them?

Rethink: Were you able to identify a few resources that, had you used them, would have helped you to overcome problems you have had in the past?

_____

_____

_____

_____

_____

_____

_____

_____

_____

_____

_____

Working in a Group: Work with other students in your class to identify the resources you might need this semester. Include academic skills and physical resources. Discuss why students are often reluctant to use resources that can help. How can students work together to help each other succeed?

- Look at the college or university website to get information
- Find out whom you can ask about assistance for a variety of issues

While investigating these resources, find answers to questions such as:

- What is the room number for the counselling department and what services do they provide?
- What is the room number for medical services?
- What does the student council provide?
- How do I get a school locker?
- What is the URL for online financial assistance applications?
- Who is the Department Head of my program?
- What is the URL for Academic Regulations?

ork

Once you have prepared by setting a purpose and goals for your success, and have organized your approach by acquiring the skills and resources you need to complete your assignments, a self-manager then begins to apply those resources toward completing the work required to achieve the purpose and the goals.

There are times when professors and school staff have to tell students it's late and to leave and go home. Very often the students are involved in a project that has caught their interest and they are enjoying the work. Time seems to disappear and motivation is not an issue. Has this ever happened to you?

> "Education is not merely a means for earning a living or an instrument for the acquisition of wealth. It is an initiation into a life of spirit, a training of the human soul in the pursuit of truth and the practice of virtue."
>
> Vijaya Lakshmi Pandit

Motivation

The decision to invest our physical and intellectual resources in getting something done

On the other hand, we have all experienced times when it is difficult to get down to work even when we know we are procrastinating. In seems to be true that we sometimes spend more creative energy thinking up reasons or excuses for not working than we spend actually doing the work. How can we become motivated and stay motivated?

Motivation is a decision, the choice to invest our physical and intellectual resources in getting something done. Inherent in this definition is the element of choice. It means that you can choose whether you feel motivated or not. What can you do to maintain your motivation even in difficult times?

1. Create purposes and goals that are personally compelling and key to your success.
2. Focus on that purpose or goal and what it will mean if you achieve success.
3. Manage self-talk. Give yourself positive messages even if you have to talk over negative messages that you have learned to give yourself. You can't control what comes in to your mind but you can control what stays there.
4. Take responsibility for both your successes and your failures. Don't blame others or circumstances for your actions or your behaviour. It is not what happens to you in life that makes the big difference. It is how you respond and what you do about what happens to you.
5. Accept that some things are out of your control. Understand what you can change and what you cannot. Work on the things you can change. Let go of what you cannot change.

Complete Try It! 5—"Managing Your Motivation"—to learn about and use the conditions that are likely to be motivating for you.

E valuate

At this stage in the P.O.W.E.R. Learning process you have Prepared by developing a purpose and setting goals, Organized the resources you need to achieve your goals, and performed the Work. The next step is to Evaluate how well you accomplished your goals.

5 Managing Your Motivation

Do you know what motivates you? Think about a time when you were really motivated to do something. Why were you motivated? What helped or hindered your desire to achieve something? Make a list of things that help you feel motivated and things that don't. Use these lists to manage your own motivation. Try to emphasize conditions that motivate you and deal with conditions that you find demotivating.

Motivators	Demotivators

An **evaluation** of your work will tell you if there is a good match between the work you did or what you accomplished and the goals the work was intended to meet. Is there more work to be done? Did you meet the expectations for your assignment? How would you evaluate the work you are handing in? Would a little more work make a big difference in the results?

If you evaluate your own work and then compare your evaluation to the instructor's, you will build your performance on a solid base of information about what is required to succeed. You won't end up spending a lot of time on an assignment when it is not needed, or spending too little time on a major assignment worth a higher mark.

When you have completed your evaluation, you are ready to Rethink your approach and change it if required to achieve your purpose.

Evaluation

An assessment of the match between a product or activity and the goals it was intended to meet

R ethink

Alex was 22 years old. He did fairly well at school and wanted to become a lawyer, but he was also a very capable guitar player and vocalist. He faced the choice of continuing in school to become a lawyer or following his musical interests and being part of a band. His father, a successful businessman, naturally wanted him to follow the plan to become a lawyer and play his music as a hobby. But he also understood that following your dreams is part of build-

TRY IT!

www.mcgrawhill.ca/olc/power

POWER

The Good and The Bad

Prepare: Consider the importance of the Rethink stage in P.O.W.E.R. Learning.

Organize: Take the time to do some reflection.

Work: Think back and make a list of a time in your life when you wished you had taken the time to rethink a decision or an action in your life. This would be a time when your first choice may not have been the best and you knew it, but you didn't look for other solutions or plan to change the result the next time. This might be how you completed an assignment, answered a job ad, cheated on an exam, or attended classes.

Evaluate: Were you able to identify an outcome you wished had been different? Would using the Rethink stage of decision making have produced a different result?

Rethink: Would you now consider using Rethink to improve the outcome of more your actions and decisions in the future?

_____
_____
_____
_____
_____
_____
_____
_____
_____
_____
_____

Working in a Group: Discuss your answers with other group members. Does the group agree that rethinking is an essential part of growing in knowledge and experience?

ing success so he was ready when Alex explained that he wanted to quit school and start a band.

After much discussion, Alex and his dad agreed that it was the right time in life for Alex to follow his band dreams, but it was equally important that he set a target for rethinking the decision. In pursuing any dream there are going to be low spots and part of the learning process is overcoming the obstacles and continuing on. Instead of leaving it open, Alex and his dad decided to rethink the decision in three years.

Life for Alex and the band was just about what you can imagine. Along with the fun of living the lifestyle came long hours, seemingly endless travel, smoky bars, customers who heckled, living from one gig to the next, and never quite getting to record their own CD.

When the time came to rethink the decision after three years, Alex found it easy to return to school because the band was not going to be the way for Alex to achieve his purpose or his goals. He went on to become a leading human rights lawyer and still plays in a local band when his time permits.

Rethinking means learning from what you have done and deciding what you need to do differently the next time to achieve your purpose. When rethinking, use **critical thinking**—thinking that involves reanalyzing, questioning, and challenging—to reconsider not just the outcome of your efforts, but the ideas and the process you've used to get there. Take some time to reflect by completing Try it! 6, The Good and the Bad.

The P.O.W.E.R. process is not only for big decisions. It will help you make smaller decisions as well. It might even help you decide whether to get up in the morning and go to class.

Most people learn much more from their failures than they do from their successes, but whether you are rethinking a decision because it didn't work or because you want to make sure you are still on the best track for you, the following guidelines will help you ask the right questions:

The daring mission to repair the Hubble space telescope was the culmination of months of rethinking how to fix the flaw in the telescope. It worked: A new time-lapse movie of images taken by the telescope showed the seasonal changes on Uranus, as well as other celestial wonders.

1. **Reanalyze by reviewing how you accomplished the task.** Consider the approach and strategies you used. What worked best? Are there any alternatives that might work better the next time?

2. **Question the outcome.** Take a "big picture" look at what you have accomplished. Are you pleased and satisfied? Is there anything you missed?

3. **Identify your underlying assumptions and challenge them.** Consider the assumptions you made in approaching the task. Are these underlying assumptions reasonable? If you had used different assumptions, would the result have been similar or different?

4. **Consider alternatives rejected earlier.** You likely discarded possible strategies and approaches before completing your task. Now's the time to think about those approaches once more and determine whether they might have been more appropriate than the road you followed. It's still not too late to change course.

Critical thinking

A process involving reanalyzing, questioning, and challenging underlying assumptions

Completing the Process The rethinking step of P.O.W.E.R. Learning is meant to help you understand your process of work and to improve the final product if necessary. But mostly it is meant to help you grow, to become better at whatever it is you've been doing.

- **Know that there's always another day.** Your future success does not depend on any single assignment, paper, or test. Don't fall victim to self-defeating thoughts such as "If I don't do well, I'll never graduate" or "Everything is riding on this one assignment." You almost always have an opportunity to recover from a failure.

- **Realize that deciding when to stop work is often as hard as getting started.** For some students, knowing when enough is enough is as hard as taking the first step on an assignment. Knowing when you have put in enough time studying for a test or have revised a paper sufficiently is as much a key to success as preparing properly. If you've carefully evaluated what you've done and have seen that there's a close fit between your goals and your work, it's time to stop work and move on.

P.O.W.E.R. Learning Meets the World of Work

What skills do you think employers look for? What skills do employers say have a direct bearing on success in the workplace? The Conference Board of Canada asked employers to identify key skills required in Canadian workplaces and published their findings in *Employability Skills Profile 2000+*.[1] You might be surprised to learn that the skills that make a difference are fundamental skills such as communication and problem solving, personal management skills, and teamwork skills. Look at the list that follows for more information, then complete Try It! 7—"Employability Skills Profile"—for a self-assessment of these important skills.

Fundamental Skills

You will be better prepared to progress in the world of work when you can

Communicate

- read and understand information presented in a variety of forms (e.g., words, graphs, charts, diagrams)
- write and speak so others pay attention and understand
- listen and ask questions to understand and appreciate the points of view of others
- share information using a range of information and communications technologies (e.g., voice, e-mail, computers)
- use relevant scientific, technological, and mathematical knowledge and skills to explain or clarify ideas

Manage Information

- locate, gather, and organize information using appropriate technology and information systems
- access, analyze and apply knowledge and skills from various disciplines (e.g., the arts, languages, science, technology, mathematics, social sciences, and the humanities)

Use Numbers

- decide what needs to be measured or calculated
- observe and record data using appropriate methods, tools, and technology
- make estimates and verify calculations

Personal Management Skills

You will be able to offer yourself greater possibilities for achievement when you can

Demonstrate Positive Attitudes & Behaviours

- feel good about yourself and be confident
- deal with people, problems, and situations with honesty, integrity, and personal ethics
- recognize your own and other people's good efforts
- take care of your personal health
- show interest, initiative, and effort

Be Responsible

- set goals and priorities balancing work and personal life
- plan and manage time, money, and other resources to achieve goals
- assess, weigh, and manage risk
- be accountable for your actions and the actions of your group
- be socially responsible and contribute to your community

Be Adaptable

- work independently or as a part of a team
- carry out multiple tasks or projects
- be innovative and resourceful: identify and suggest alternative ways to achieve goals and get the job done
- be open and respond constructively to change

Teamwork Skills

You will be better prepared to add value to the outcomes of a task, project, or team when you can

Work with Others

- understand and work within the dynamics of a group
- ensure that a team's purpose and objectives are clear
- be flexible: respect, be open to and supportive of the thoughts, opinions, and contributions of others in a group
- recognize and respect people's diversity, individual differences, and perspectives
- accept and provide feedback in a constructive and considerate manner
- contribute to a team by sharing information and expertise
- lead or support when appropriate, motivating a group for high performance
- understand the role of conflict in a group to reach solutions
- manage and resolve conflict when appropriate

Participate in Projects & Tasks

- plan, design or carry out a project or task from start to finish with well-defined objectives and outcomes
- develop a plan, seek feedback, test, revise, and implement
- work to agreed quality standards and specifications

Fundamental Skills

Think & Solve Problems

- assess situations and identify problems
- seek different points of view and evaluate them based on facts
- recognize the human, interpersonal, technical, scientific, and mathematical dimensions of a problem
- identify the root cause of a problem
- be creative and innovative in exploring possible solutions
- readily use science, technology and mathematics as ways to think, gain and share knowledge, solve problems and make decisions
- evaluate solutions to make recommendations or decisions
- implement solutions
- check to see if a solution works, and act on opportunities for improvement

Personal Management Skills

- learn from your mistakes and accept feedback
- cope with uncertainty

Learn Continuously

- be willing to continuously learn and grow
- assess personal strengths and areas for development
- set your own learning goals
- identify and access learning sources and opportunities
- plan for and achieve your learning goals

Work Safely

- be aware of personal and group health and safety practices and procedures, and act in accordance with these

Teamwork Skills

- select and use appropriate tools and technology for a task or project
- adapt to changing requirements and information
- continuously monitor the success of a project or task and identify ways to improve

The Conference Board of Canada
Insights You Can Count On

7

Employability Skills Profile

1. Go to the P.O.W.E.R. Learning website at www.mcgrawhill.ca/olc/power and rate yourself on the key skills required for success in the Canadian workplace.

2. Look at the ads in the Career section of the newspaper or on Internet job sites such as monster.ca and see how many jobs list soft skills in the job requirements.

3. Ask someone that you know who has a job as a manager or a supervisor what skills they find the hardest to get or wish more employees had in their workplace.

4. List five skills that you want to learn more about that also add to your success at school and at work.

Building Success

This book is all about helping you achieve success in your academic program. But what does success mean to you? Does it mean you passed or does success mean you got honours? Will you consider yourself to be successful only if you drive a Lexus or earn $75,000 a year? Is your success connected to pleasing your parents or friends, or do you decide?

Success is both a journey and a destination. Success comes from accomplishing your long- and short-term goals. Hopefully, you will consider yourself a success when you graduate from college or university, but that is only one stop or milestone on your way to achieving your next goal. You will enjoy success when you accomplish that goal and then move on to the next destination. Success is an ongoing, lifelong journey with many accomplishments along the way to savour and enjoy before moving on.

Sometimes things don't work out as they were planned. What happens if you fail to achieve a short-term goal? Does that mean you are no longer a success? It all depends on what you do about it. If you are critical of yourself or blame yourself every time things go wrong you may see yourself as a failure. However, if you use failure as a way to learn and grow for the next challenge then you can be successful every time. It's all up to you.

Are you able to enjoy success? Successful people learn how to enjoy the smaller successes along the way. They learn to celebrate their achievements and those of others. They learn to build success through a series of smaller accomplishments. They can accept and give recognition for a job well done and keep going through the tough times to get where they want to go. Perseverance is one of the biggest contributors to success.

By now, you should be able to see that success comes from putting the right things in place. These things include compelling goals, personal and physical resources, working to achieve your goals, celebrating your successes, and evaluating and rethinking your approach to the next destination. It also includes learning from failures and giving yourself positive and encouraging messages. If this seems like a long list, please remember that the more you do something the more it becomes a habit and part of your everyday life.

A Word About Ethics

Ethics…academic honesty…character. Should I lie to my professor when my assignment is late? Should I take the easy way out and copy a section of a website to include as my own in an assignment? Should I blow off a team meeting for a class project when I know everyone will get the same mark anyway? The choices you make are part of building your success and your reputation. Building character by making the right choices is an essential part of genuine, lasting success.

Looking Back

At this point you have taken the following steps toward the achievement of your goals:

1. Described your reasons for going to college or university
2. Used P.O.W.E.R. Learning as a tool to increase your personal effectiveness

Speaking of Success

Farzana Jamal

Bachelor of Commerce (Entrepreneurship)
Ryerson University

Passionate, dedicated, driven, creative, and ambitious are just a few of Farzana's many traits. Goal setting was something instilled in Farzana by her family from a very young age. Her academic goal when she entered Seneca College was to provide herself with a solid foundation for a successful future.

Farzana, like other students, found it difficult to manage her time with school, work, and the other obstacles that all students face in everyday life. Fortunately, she was surrounded by an excellent support network at home and at school to help her overcome these challenges. Her family constantly supported her and told her that in order to survive any of life's tests she needed to be resilient and committed. So Farzana decided to speak to her Student Advisor, Sheilagh Stephenson, who she had never previously met. Sheilagh took the time to listen to Farzana's story and helped her design a customized solution just for her.

That was the first step to the beginning of the rest of Farzana's life. That was the day she decided to live life fully and courageously no matter what life threw at her. She surrounded herself with a network of people who wanted her to succeed, which was also taught to her by her family at a very young age and reinforced in the student success course. This was ultimately the key to her success.

From that point on, the sky was the limit for Farzana. Her drive and determination enabled her to graduate from Seneca with her Advanced Accounting & Finance Diploma. Farzana didn't feel that a full-time job would be personally fulfilling at this stage in her life, so she, along with a friend, began their own door-to-door dry cleaning service. Although the concept was fantastic, (one day service at unbeatable prices) business began at a very slow pace. However, with Farzana's motivation and confidence in her teams' abilities she didn't allow them to give up. Sure enough the business took off and began to grow. With this achievement and her newly found entrepreneurial interest, Farzana decided to apply to Ryerson University for the Direct Entry Entrepreneurship program she had recently read about. Within eight months of graduating with her diploma, she found herself back in school aiming to achieve more. This she feels is probably due to her family's (networks) belief in lifelong learning.

While at Ryerson University, Farzana's motivation continued to build as she found that her college education thoroughly prepared her for the Degree Program, allowing her to excel in all her courses. She went on to apply to the Ryerson Internship Program where she was granted acceptance based on her academic average.

Farzana is currently in her final year of the program and will be graduating with her 4-year BComm, majoring in Entrepreneurship. She is consistently setting and achieving high goals for herself. She states that luck has had no part in her success. She believes that the strong network she has from her family and her academic leaders, along with her personal willingness and dedication to achieve anything "we desire" are what have enabled her to come as far as she has and as far as she hopes to go.

Quotes and Phrases Farzana lives by:

"Failing to plan, is planning to fail."
"Struggle is the meaning of life."
"Always aim for the top."
"You are what you make it."

3. Begun to record your thoughts in a journal
4. Described your learning goals for this course
5. Identified your key employment skills
6. Defined what success means to you

The next step in the journey is to learn to describe your learning style, preferences, and values to use as a foundation for your plan for success.

P.O.W.E.R. Portfolio

Employability Skills

Using your information from Try It! 7, "Employability Skills Profile," begin developing an employability skills section for your portfolio. List the five skills you identified as part of your learning goals. Using the goal-setting suggestions from this chapter, identify short-term goals for yourself in these areas, and create specific plans of action to accomplish these learning goals. Repeat this process to learn as many skills as you can over the length of your program. You will have a lot of evidence to support your skill level, and you will have developed the vital habit of lifelong learning.

Resources

On Campus

If you are commuting to school, your first "official" encounters on campus are likely to be with representatives of the Student Affairs Office or its equivalent. The Student Affairs Office has the goal of maintaining the quality of student life, helping to ensure that students receive the help they need.

If you are living on campus, your first encounter will more likely be with representatives of the student residence. Their job is to help you settle in and orient you to the campus. Your residence also probably has student residential advisers living on every floor; they can give you an insider's view of life on campus.

During your first days of college or university, don't feel shy about asking whatever school representative you encounter questions regarding what you may expect, how to find things, and what you should be doing.

In future chapters you'll find specific information about which college officials you should turn to. Seek them out if you are experiencing difficulties. They are there to help you get the most out of your higher education.

In Print

Virginia N. Gordon and T.L. Minnick's helpful book, *Foundations: A Reader for New College Students* (Wadsworth Publishing; 2nd edition, 2001) includes articles and essays on the most important topics that a college or university student faces. A number of different perspectives are presented, fostering critical thinking.

Navigating Your Freshman Year (Students Helping Students Series), by Allison Lombardo (Natavi Guides; 1st edition, 2003) is a compilation of student advice to incoming college or university students on such diverse topics as budgeting, developing university-employee contacts, roommate ground rules, and writing your first college or university essay.

On the Web

The following sites on the World Wide Web provide the opportunity to extend your learning about the material in this chapter. Although the Web addresses were accurate at the time the book was printed, check the P.O.W.E.R. Learning website, <www.mcgrawhill.ca/olc/power>, for any changes that may have occurred.

www.campusaccess.com

This site provides links to all the colleges and universities in Canada and contains many useful articles of interest for postsecondary students.

www.topachievement.com/articles.html

On this page, you'll find several articles on motivation and goal setting.

www.careerintern.ca/Career_Center/employability_portfolio.htm

This site houses a wealth of information on employability portfolios, including a dozen links to other employability portfolio sites.

The Case Of...

No Clue

It was during the second week of classes that the questioning started. Until then, Roger hadn't thought much about his decision to attend a large community college in a Vancouver suburb. It had seemed like a good idea, and he was excited when he was accepted, but he couldn't really pinpoint why he was there.

That was becoming a problem. As he was walking to class, he began to think about all that had happened to him in the last few weeks. First-year orientation . . . meeting his roommate and trying to deal with his odd neatness . . . enrolling for classes . . . finding his way around campus . . . meeting a huge number of new people and trying to figure out where he fit in. Everyone else seemed to know what they were doing. Why didn't he?

It was overwhelming. He wanted to run that minute and call his parents and tell them to come pick him up. He needed to lie on his bed in his room where it was familiar and comfortable and try to figure out what he should do. Nothing seemed to make sense. He began to question his decision to attend college. What was he going to do with his life? The question made him feel even more overwhelmed. Did he really need a college diploma? With his computer skills, he could probably get a job right away. Hadn't his father's friend told him that he had a job waiting for him whenever he wanted it? At least then he'd be making money.

"Why bother?" he thought to himself. "What an expense, and what a hassle. For what?" He realized, to his surprise, he had no real clue as to why he was in college.

1. What arguments could you provide Roger as to the value of a college education?

2. Do you think that Roger's doubts are common? Why? Do people often attend college or university without thinking about it very much?

3. What might you suggest that Roger do to help deal with his doubts about the value of higher education? How can he manage his motivation more effectively?

4. Why might a student's doubts about the value of postsecondary education be especially strong during the beginning weeks of school?

5. Do you share any of Roger's concerns about the value of higher education? Do you have additional ones? Did you think carefully about the reasons for attending school before you enrolled?

Recognizing How You Learn, Who You Are, and What You Value

2

he transformation began when Shawn Ahermaa got his first Java project back from his Introductory Software professor. It wasn't so much the grade—which was good—but what the instructor said, almost as an afterthought, as she handed the project back to Shawn: "Nice job. Your design was very creative. Keep it up."

Shawn was pleased. He had always known that he was good at software engineering, and he could write code without making mistakes, but he had never felt very confident in his ability as a designer.

But now something clicked; Shawn's perspective on who he was started to change. Maybe he did have the ability to succeed in a career involving software design. It was a gradual transformation, but after his professor praised his work, Shawn's view of himself began to change.

Looking ▶▶
Ahead

Through the experiences we have in life, we build a sense of our strengths and weaknesses, what we like and dislike about ourselves. In the process, the sense of who we are also affects the choices we make and the things that we do. So it's not surprising that the accuracy of our understanding of ourselves has an important effect on our success.

Picture yourself in a square room sitting in the only chair in the centre of the room. Each wall has a window, and you have the unique opportunity to step outside of yourself and look at yourself through the windows. Would you just look through one window? You would probably try to get the best view of yourself you could by looking through all of the windows. What would you see? In this chapter you have the same type of opportunity to learn more about yourself and how you learn by looking through several different windows.

You will also have the opportunity to explore how you prefer to make decisions and take action, along with identifying your personal values and your overall purpose. This is designed to help you increase your knowledge of who you are and where you are likely to be happiest and most successful in the future.

When you complete this chapter you will be able to answer these questions:

- **What are my learning styles and how have they affected my academic success?**

- **How do I describe self-concept and how does it affect my success?**

Discovering Your Learning Styles

Differences in learning styles have the potential to reshape our lives and our definition of success. Learn about how the lives of two brothers were shaped by their learning styles.

One of the brothers was very good with words. He could read easily, remember what he read, and he did well on written assignments and exams. He was also skilled at working with numbers. He generally did very well at school when he invested some time and energy and as a result received praise from teachers and parents and was seen as an outstanding student. He was encouraged to go to university and without question, graduated.

The other brother was more skilled at mechanical things. He seemed to have a knack for design and could easily view things in three dimensions. He could see the relationship between moving parts and make things from sketches with limited detail. But in those days these skills were not recognized in high school. In subjects like history, his marks were borderline, and he faced criticism for not trying hard enough and not paying attention. He was not encouraged to go on to higher education although he did graduate from technical school. For years he questioned his ability to succeed.

This is a familiar story for many people whose learning styles did not fit into the education system and who did not learn best in traditional ways.

In this section, you'll get a glimpse through the window of five different learning styles. You will learn that each of us has preferred ways of learning that work best for us, and that our success is not only dependent on how well we learn but also on knowing how we learn well.

Learning styles reflect our preferred manner of acquiring and using knowledge. These styles are not abilities, but methods of learning.

We don't have just one learning style but a profile of styles. Even though our ability may be equal to someone else's, our learning styles might be quite different.

You probably already know quite a lot about your learning styles. Maybe you do particularly well in your Biology class while struggling with English. Or it may be the other way around. Because biology tends to be about natural processes, teachers present the subject as a series of related facts. English, however, requires you to think more abstractly, analyzing and synthesizing ideas presented in a variety of ways. Whichever subject you prefer, it is almost certain you prefer it because of your learning style.

Though we may have general preferences for fact-based learning or learning that requires more abstract thinking, we all use a variety of learning styles. Some involve our preferences regarding the way information is presented to us, some relate to how we think and learn most readily, and some relate to how our personality traits affect our performance. Different approaches to learning overlap one another, and these can be revealed by looking through the different learning style windows. Depending on your instructor and your interest, it may not be necessary to review each of the five windows, but we'll start by considering the preferences we have for how we initially perceive information.

Learning style
A person's preferred manner of acquiring, using, and thinking about knowledge

Are You a Primarily Visual, Auditory, or Tactile Learner?

Receptive learning style

How the initial receipt of information relates to learning preferences

The first window reveals the way in which we initially receive information from our sense organs—our **receptive learning style.** Some of us have primarily **visual learning styles,** recalling the spelling of a word, for example, or the structure of a chemical compound by reviewing a picture in our head. Or maybe you learn best when you have the opportunity to read about a concept rather than listening to a teacher explain it. Students with visual learning styles find it easier to see things in their "mind's eye"—to visualize a task or concept—than to be lectured about them.

Visual learning style

A style that involves visualizing information in the mind's eye, favouring reading and watching over touching and hearing

Have you ever asked a friend to help you put something together by having her read the directions to you while you worked? If you did, you may have an **auditory learning style.** People with auditory learning styles prefer listening to explanations rather than reading about them. They love class lectures and discussions, because they can easily take in the information that is being talked about.

Auditory learning style

A style that favours listening as the best approach to learning

Students with a **tactile** or **kinesthetic learning style** prefer to learn by doing—touching, manipulating objects, and doing things. For instance, some people enjoy the act of writing because of the feel of a pencil or a computer keyboard—the tactile equivalent of "thinking out loud" (which would be preferred by someone with an auditory learning style). Or they may find that it helps them to make a three-dimensional model to understand a new idea.

Having a particular receptive learning style simply means that it will be easier to learn material that is presented in that style. It does not mean you cannot learn any other way!

Tactile or kinesthetic learning style

A style that involves learning by touching, manipulating objects, and doing things

You may have a good idea about which learning style suits you best, but Try It! 1, "Learning Style Inventory," will help you further understand your style.

Handling Information: Do You Focus First on Pieces or the Whole?

Analytic learning style

A style that starts with small pieces of information and uses them to build the big picture

The second window for looking at your learning style shows how you start the learning process. When you are assembling something new that you bought, do you focus more on the individual pieces and how each one fits together with the one next to it, or is your strategy to concentrate on the whole picture, keeping the finished product in mind?

The way you approach assembling something new that you bought provides a clue to the process by which you fit together bits of information. Specifically, the strategy you use suggests which of the following two learning styles you are more comfortable with:

- People with **analytic learning styles** learn most easily if first exposed to the individual components and principles behind a phenomenon or situation. Once they have identified the underlying components involved, they find it easier to figure out and grasp the broad picture and determine whether particular cases exemplify the principle.

Relational learning styles

A style that starts with the big picture and breaks it down into its individual components

- Those with **relational learning styles** learn most readily if exposed to the full range of material that they are aiming to learn. Rather than focusing on the individual components of a problem, as those with analytic styles prefer to do, people with relational learning styles do best when they are first given the full picture. They can then take this broad view and break it down into its individual components.

TRY IT!

www.mcgrawhill.ca/olc/power

Learning Style Inventory: Are You a Visual, an Auditory, or a Kinesthetic Learner?

Prepare: Discover your preferred receptive learning style.

Organize: Review the clues and tips to identify your learning style and highlight how you learn best.

Work: Complete the questionnaire and obtain your score.

Evaluate: Were you able to discover a style that seems to fit you?

Rethink: Does this information cause you to rethink how you approach learning and study?

Read each statement and select the appropriate number response as it applies to you.[1]

Often (3)   Sometimes (2)   Never (1)

Visual (See)

_____ I remember information better if I write it down.

_____ Looking at the person helps keep me focused.

_____ I need a quiet place to get my work done.

_____ When I take a test, I can see the textbook page in my head.

_____ I need to write down directions, not just take them verbally.

_____ Music or background noise distracts my attention from the task at hand.

_____ I don't always get the meaning of a joke.

_____ I doodle and draw pictures on the margins of my notebook pages.

_____ I have trouble following lectures.

_____ I react very strongly to colours.

_____ **Total**

Auditory (Hear)

_____ My papers and notebooks always seem messy.

_____ When I read, I need to use my index finger to track my place on the line.

_____ I do not follow written directions well.

_____ If I hear something, I will remember it.

_____ Writing has always been difficult for me.

_____ I often misread words from the text (i.e., "them" for "then").

_____ I would rather listen and learn than read and learn.

_____ I'm not very good at interpreting an individual's body language.

_____ Pages with small print or poor quality copies are difficult for me to read.

_____ My eyes tire quickly, even though my vision checkup is always fine.

_____ **Total**

Kinesthetic/Tactile (Do)

_____ I start a project before reading the directions.

_____ I hate to sit at a desk for long periods.

_____ I prefer first to see something done and then to do it myself.

_____ I use the trial and error approach to problem solving.

_____ I like to read my textbook while riding an exercise bike.

(continued on next page)

27

Learning Style Inventory— Continued

_____ I take frequent study breaks.

_____ I have a difficult time giving step-by-step instructions.

_____ I enjoy sports and do well at several different types of sports.

_____ I use my hands when describing things.

_____ I have to rewrite or type my class notes to reinforce the material.

_____ **Total**

Total the score for each section. A score of 21 points or more in receptive style indicates strength in that area. The highest of the three scores indicates the most efficient method of information intake. The second highest score indicates the style that boosts the primary strength. For example, a score of 23 for visual indicates a strong visual learner. Such a learner benefits from reading a text, from filmstrips, charts, graphs, and so on. If the second highest score is auditory, then the individual would benefit from audiotapes, lectures, and the like. If you are strong kinesthetically, then taking notes and rewriting class notes will reinforce information.

Learning Styles— Clues and Learning Tips

Identify 3 or 4 points that illustrate your style for learning more effectively.

CLUES

Visual learners usually

- Need to see it to know it.
- Have strong sense of colour.
- May have artistic ability.
- Often have difficulty with spoken directions.
- May overreact to sounds.
- May have trouble following lectures.
- Often misinterprets words.

Auditory learners usually

- Prefer to get information by listening; they need to hear it to know it.
- May have difficulty following written directions.
- Have difficulty with reading.
- Have problems with writing.
- Are unable to read body language and facial expressions.

TIPS

Visual learners should

- Use graphics to reinforce learning: films, slides, illustrations, diagrams, and doodles.
- Colour code to organize notes and possessions.
- Ask for written directions.
- Use flow charts and diagrams for notetaking.
- Visualize spelling of words or facts to memorize them.

Auditory learners should

- Use tapes for reading and for class and lecture notes.
- Learn by interviewing or by participating in discussions.
- Have test questions or directions read aloud or put on tape.

Continued

Kinesthetic learners usually

- Prefer hands-on learning.
- Can assemble parts without reading directions.
- Have difficulty sitting still.
- Learn better when physical activity is involved.
- May be very well coordinated and have athletic ability.

Kinesthetic learners should

- Engage in experiential learning (making models, doing lab work, and role-playing).
- Take frequent breaks in study periods.
- Trace letters and words to learn spelling and remember facts.
- Use a computer to reinforce learning through the sense of touch.
- Memorize or drill while walking or exercising.
- Express abilities through dance, drama, or gymnastics.

Analytic learners usually

- Focus on facts and specific principles.
- Excel at organizing information.
- Tend to work best on their own.
- Experience few problems with science and math.

Analytic learners should

- Ask the instructor for a week-by-week plan or a critical path for the course.
- Use tools to organize information and material.
- May be more effective working on a problem alone before participating in group activities.

Relational learners usually

- Perceive things globally.
- Like to think in terms of the big picture.
- Like subjects that require a broad overview of material such as English and history.
- Go from the big picture to individual components.

Relational learners should

- Ask the instructor to describe the purpose and the end goal of the course.
- Understand how each part fits into the overall purpose or goal.
- Use group discussion to generate concepts and ideas before working on details.

Ask people to provide information in the way that suits you best. For example a Relational learner might say: "Show me the big picture first before we get into the details." An Analytical learner might say: "Start with one part and go through each part in detail and then put the parts together."

How I Learn

1. Suppose a friend is teaching you a new and complex procedure (such as a complicated card game or the way to use a piece of computer software). Do you prefer to get the big picture first or the details?

2. Do you think you would ask your friend to slow down while you get the details, or would you be impatient to get started? Would you rather try doing it while your friend talks you through it?

3. Do you tend to picture things while you're learning?

4. When you're in class, what do you do during lectures—try to write down the instructor's exact words, draw pictures, jot down a few big ideas, doodle, tune out?

5. When someone gives you directions to a new place, what do you do?

6. What is your preference when you want information? Would you rather search the Internet, call another student, or watch it on TV?

7. When you get a new piece of electronic equipment, do you like to read the instructions or just play with it until you get the hang of it?

Multiple Intelligences

The third window for looking at your learning style exposes you to information about multiple intelligences. The theory of multiple intelligences, developed by Dr. Howard Gardner, proposes that the conventional view of intelligence, based on I.Q. testing, is too narrow. Dr. Gardner asserts that there are eight different approaches to interpreting intelligence, significantly expanding our traditional understanding of the word.

These intelligences are:

- Verbal/Linguistic ("word smart")
- Logical/Mathematical ("number/reasoning smart")
- Visual/Spatial ("picture smart")
- Bodily/Kinesthetic ("body smart")
- Musical/Rythmic ("music smart")
- Interpersonal ("people smart")
- Intrapersonal ("self smart")
- Naturalist ("nature smart")

By tradition, academic and cultural environments have esteemed linguistic and logical/mathematical intelligence, resulting in our valuing articulate or logical people. However, using multiple intelligence theory, individuals displaying capacity in other intelligences, such as artists, architects, musicians, naturalists, designers, dancers, therapists, entrepreneurs, and others who enrich the world in which we live are also acknowledged, recognized, and esteemed for their gifts.

Research shows that all human beings have elements of these different types of intelligence. Depending on your background and age, some intelligences are more developed than others. Try It! 2, "You and Your Multiple Intelligences," will help you discover what your strengths are. Knowing this, you can work to strengthen the other intelligences that you do not use as often or focus on the intelligences that are well developed.

Personality Styles

Our learning styles are also influenced by our personality, and the fourth window for looking at your learning style reveals your personality type. Are you a person who is likely to try out for school productions? Or is the idea of getting on a stage something that is totally lacking in appeal (if not completely terrifying)? Do you relate to the world around you primarily through careful planning or by spontaneously reacting?

According to the rationale of the *Myers-Briggs Type Indicator,* a questionnaire frequently used in business and other organizations, our personality type plays a key role in determining how we react to different kinds of situations. Specifically, the idea is that we work best in situations in which others—both students and instructors—share our preferences and in which our personality preferences are most suited to the particular task on which we are working.

According to studies done on personality, four major dimensions are critical. Although we'll describe the extremes of each dimension, keep in mind that most of us fall somewhere in between each of the endpoints of each dimension.

- **Introverts versus extroverts.** A key difference between introverts and extroverts is whether they enjoy working with others. Independence is a key characteristic of introverted learners. They enjoy working alone and they are less affected by how others think and behave. In contrast, extroverts are outgoing and more affected by the behaviour and thinking of others. They enjoy working with others, and they are energized by having other people around.

> "To be fond of learning is to be near to knowledge."
>
> Tze-Sze

- **Intuitors versus sensors.** Intuitors enjoy solving problems and being creative. They get impatient with details, preferring to make leaps of judgment, and they enjoy the challenge of solving problems and taking a big-picture approach. People categorized as sensors prefer a concrete, logical approach in which they can carefully analyze the facts of the situation. Although they are good with details, they sometimes miss the big picture.

- **Thinkers versus feelers.** Thinkers prefer logic over emotion. They reach decisions and solve problems by systematically analyzing a situation. In

You and Your Multiple Intelligences

Prepare: Determine your multiple intelligence type or types and your preferred learning style.

Organize: To complete this task you will need the questionnaire below.

Work: Complete the questionnaire and total your scores. Use the results to choose one or more styles of learning that seem to fit you. Circle the characteristics of the learning styles that represent you best. Use the summary chart provided.

Evaluation: Were you able to determine your intelligence type and your preferred learning style? Do the results reflect your own self-knowledge?

Rethink: Do the results suggest a change in how you learn and the learning environments that are most productive for you?

Read the following statements and check any sentence that accurately describes you. Total your checkmarks and determine if your highest scores are an accurate reflection of you and your multiple intelligences.

TRY IT!

www.mcgrawhill.ca/olc/power

Verbal/Linguistic Intelligence

____ I enjoy telling stories and jokes

____ I have a good memory for trivia

____ I enjoy word games (e.g., Scrabble and crossword puzzles)

____ I read books just for fun

____ I am a good speller usually

____ In an argument I tend to use put-downs or sarcasm

____ I like talking and writing about my ideas

____ If I have to memorize something I create a rhyme or saying to help me remember

____ If something breaks and won't work, I read the instruction book first

____ For a group presentation, I prefer to do the writing and library research

____ Total

Visual/Spatial Intelligence

____ I prefer a map to written directions

____ I daydream a lot

____ I enjoy hobbies such as photography

____ I like to draw and create

____ If I have to memorize something I draw a diagram to help me remember

____ I like to doodle on paper whenever I can

____ In a magazine, I prefer looking at the pictures rather than reading the text

Logical/Mathematical Intelligence

____ I really enjoy math class

____ I like logical math puzzles or brain teasers

____ I find solving math problems to be fun

____ If I have to memorize something I tend to place events in a logical order

____ I like to find out how things work

____ I enjoy computer and any math games

____ I love playing chess, checkers, or Monopoly

____ In an argument, I try to find a fair and logical solution

____ If something breaks and won't work, I look at the pieces and try to figure out how it works

____ For a group presentation, I prefer to create the charts and graphs

____ Total

Bodily/Kinesthetic Intelligence

____ My favourite class is gym since I like sports

____ I enjoy activities such as woodworking, sewing, and building models

____ When looking at things, I like touching them

____ I have trouble sitting still for any length of time

____ I use a lot of body movements when talking

____ In an argument I try to keep my distance, keep silent, or visualize some solution

____ If something breaks and won't work I tend to study the diagram of how it works

____ For a group presentation, I prefer to draw all the pictures

____ **Total**

Musical/Rhythmic Intelligence

____ I enjoy listening to CDs and the radio

____ I tend to hum to myself when working

____ I like to sing

____ I play a musical instrument quite well

____ I like to have music playing when doing homework or studying

____ If I have to memorize something I try to create a rhyme about the event

____ In an argument I tend to shout or punch or move in some sort of rhythm

____ I can remember the melodies of many songs

____ If something breaks and won't work I tend to tap my fingers to a beat while I figure it out

____ For a group presentation, I prefer to put new words to a popular tune or use music

____ **Total**

Intrapersonal Intelligence

____ I like to work alone without anyone bothering me

____ I like to keep a diary

____ I like myself (most of the time)

____ I don't like crowds

____ I know what I am good at and what I am weak at

____ I find that I am strong-willed, independent, and don't follow the crowd

____ If I have to memorize something I tend to close my eyes and feel the situation

____ If I have to memorize something I write it out a number of times until I know it

____ I tend to tap my fingers or play with my pencil during class

____ In an argument I tend to strike out and hit or run away

____ If something breaks and won't work I tend to play with the pieces to try to fit them together

____ For a group presentation, I prefer to move the props around, hold things up or build a model

____ **Total**

Interpersonal Intelligence

____ I get along well with others

____ I like to belong to clubs and organizations

____ I have several very close friends

____ I like helping teach other students

____ I like working with others in groups

____ Friends ask my advice because I seem to be a natural leader

____ If I have to memorize something I ask someone to quiz me to see if I know it

____ In an argument I tend ask a friend or some person in authority for help

____ If something breaks and won't work I try to find someone who can help me

____ For a group presentation, I like to help organize the group's efforts

____ **Total**

Naturalist Intelligence

____ I am keenly aware of my surroundings and of what goes on around me

____ I love to go walking in the woods and looking at the trees and flowers

____ I enjoy gardening

____ I like to collect things (e.g., rocks, sports cards, stamps, etc)

____ As an adult, I think I would like to get away from the city and enjoy nature

____ If I have to memorize something, I tend to organize it into categories

(continued on next page)

You and Your Multiple Intelligences—Continued

Intrapersonal Intelligence—con't.

___ In an argument I will usually walk away until I calm down

___ If something breaks and won't work, I wonder if it's worth fixing

___ For a group presentation I like to contribute something that is uniquely mine, often based on how I feel

___ Total

Naturalist Intelligence—con't.

___ I enjoy learning the names of living things in our environment, such as flowers and trees

___ In an argument I tend to compare my opponent to someone or something I have read or heard about and react accordingly

___ If something breaks down, I look around me to try and see what I can find to fix the problem

___ For a group presentation, I prefer to organize and classify the information into categories so it makes sense

___ Total

TOTAL SCORE

_____	Verbal/Linguistic	_____	Musical/Rhythmic
_____	Logical/Mathematical	_____	Interpersonal
_____	Visual/Spatial	_____	Intrapersonal
_____	Bodily/Kinesthetic	_____	Naturalist

Eight Styles of Learning

Read the following descriptors and comment on the information; you can utilize the information to power-up your postsecondary learning experience. Circle your top 2 or 3 multiple intelligences and words that represent your learning style the best.

Verbal/Linguistic Learner

likes to: read, write, and tell stories.

is good at   memorizing names, places, dates, and trivia.

learns best by: saying, hearing, and seeing words; teaching others.

Comments: _____

Logical/Mathematical Learner

likes to: do experiments; figure things out; work with numbers; ask questions and explore patterns and relationships.

is good at: math, reasoning, logic, and problem solving.

learns best by: categorizing; classifying and working with abstract patterns/relationships; organizing information sequentially.

Comments: _____

Visual/Spatial Learner

likes to: draw, build, design, and create things; daydream; look at pictures/slides; watch movies and play with machines.

is good at: imagining things; sensing changes; mazes/puzzles and reading maps and charts.

Continued

www.mcgrawhill.ca/olc/power

TRY IT!

learns best by: visualizing; dreaming; using the mind's eye and working with colours/pictures.
Comments: _____

Musical/Rhythmic Learner
likes to: sing; hum tunes; listen to music; play an instrument and respond to music.
is good at: picking up sounds; remembering melodies; noticing pitches/rhythms and keeping time.
learns best by: rhythm, melody, and music.
Comments: _____

Bodily/Kinesthetic Learner
likes to: move around; touch and talk and use body language.
is good at: physical activities (sports/dance/acting) and crafts.
learns best by: touching; moving; interacting with space and processing knowledge through bodily sensations.
Comments: _____

Interpersonal Learner
likes to: have lots of friends; talk to people and join groups.
is good at: understanding people; leading others; organizing; communicating; manipulating and mediating conflicts.
learns best by: sharing, comparing, relating, cooperating, and interviewing.
Comments: _____

Intrapersonal Learner
likes to: work alone and pursue own interests.
is good at: understanding self, focusing inward on feelings/dreams; following instincts; pursuing interests/goals and being original.
learns best by: working alone; individualized projects; self-paced instruction and having own space.
Comments: _____

Naturalistic Learner
likes to: be outside, with animals, geography, and weather; interacting with the surroundings.
is good at: categorizing; organizing a living area; planning a trip; preservation, and conservation.
learns best by: studying natural phenomenon, in a natural setting; learning about how things work.
Comments: _____

Summary of Multiple Intelligences
Use the chart below to summarize your preferred multiple intelligences.

Intelligence Type	Likes to	Is good at	Learns best by

contrast, feeling types rely more on their personal values when responding. They are aware of others and their feelings, and they are influenced by their emotional responses and attachments to others.

- **Perceivers and judgers.** Before drawing a conclusion, perceivers attempt to gather as much information as they can. Because they are open to multiple perspectives and appreciate all sides of an issue, they sometimes have difficulty completing a task. Judgers, in comparison, are quick and decisive, sometimes making decisions before they have all the available information. They like to set goals, accomplish them, and then move on to the next task.

Each personality type has specific likes and dislikes when it comes to learning preferences. For example, introverts usually enjoy working alone, while extroverts usually enjoy cooperative learning and projects involving many people. Intuitors most enjoy creative problem solving, while sensors flourish with assignments that are concrete and logical. Thinkers prefer to systematically use logic to analyze a problem, and feelers enjoy assignments that involve others and their emotional reactions. Finally, perceivers favour work on which there are multiple sides to an issue, while judgers' preferences are to be decisive, determining goals and sticking to them.

A short, free adaptation of the *Myers-Briggs Type Indicator*, "Personality Pathways: What Is Your Myers-Briggs Personality Type?" can be found at <www.personalitypathways.com/type_inventory.html>. This site has an online Myers-Briggs test as well as descriptors of all 16 types, along with information about careers and personal relationships. To determine how your personality affects your learning style, complete Try It! 3, "Personality Type and Learning Style."

Experiential Learning

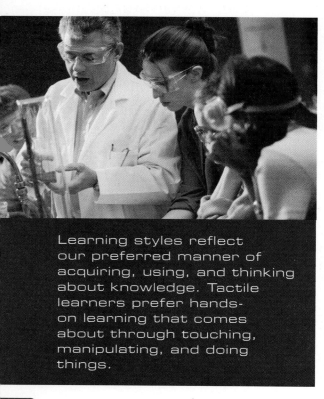

Learning styles reflect our preferred manner of acquiring, using, and thinking about knowledge. Tactile learners prefer hands-on learning that comes about through touching, manipulating, and doing things.

The fifth window for looking at your learning style is Kolb's Learning Style Inventory, which is based on the idea that learning should be active and grounded in experience. The model has four stages: *watching, thinking, feeling, doing*. Kolb's theory is that learners prefer to start the learning cycle in one of the stages but that we learn from all four stages. The model is often shown in two dimensions, with the horizontal grid focusing on the task, moving from *doing* on the left and *watching* on the right. The vertical dimension focuses on our thought and feeling processes, moving from *feeling* on the top to *thinking* on the bottom. See Figure 2.1.

- *Watching:* Learners who prefer *watching* (RO: reflective observation) use observation to make judgments, preferring lectures, learning logs, or journals to process their learning.

- *Doing:* Learners who prefer *doing* (AE: active experimentation) learn best when they can actively engage in projects, homework, or class discussions.

- *Feeling:* Learners who prefer *feeling* or *sensing* (CE: concrete experience) learn best when they can make feeling-based judgments using specific examples (such as exercises and simulations) in which they can be involved.

3

Personality Type and Learning Style

Prepare: Use the *Myers-Briggs Type Indicator* to determine your preferred learning style.

Organize: You will need the questionnaire at www.personalitypathways.com/type_inventory.html and the style descriptions below.

Work: Complete the personality type questionnaire and use the results to describe your preferred learning style. The result of the assessment of your personality style is a four-letter symbol such as ENFP or ISTJ. Take the middle 2 letters of your personality type and use the following chart to see the common learning style preferences for people with your personality type. Highlight the items that are most like you.

Evaluate: Were you able to use the MBTI to expand your understanding of your preferred learning style?

Rethink: Does this information about your learning style mean that you would be more effective learning or studying a different way?

The **SF** learner:
- Tends to be action oriented
- Needs the freedom to act
- Needs physical involvement and hands-on activity; likes to manipulate objects
- Enjoys competition and risks
- Dislikes routine and repetition; prefers frequent change of pace
- Tends to dislike instructor-dominated classrooms; prefers shared control
- Tends to be verbal and visual
- Is not stimulated by workbook exercises
- Is unlikely to complete homework assignments

The **ST** learner:
- Wants to belong
- Likes responsibility, dependability, duty, and service
- Fits into the traditional classroom
- Requires clear directions to proceed with a task
- Prefers instructor-led activities
- Participates most effectively in a safe environment with time to prepare for activities
- Will do homework exercises
- Completes assignments on time

The **NT** learner:
- Tends to be motivated by the desire to be competent
- Wants to understand ideas
- Is intellectually curious
- Prefers independent learning
- Is interested in sharing ideas but overall prefers to work alone
- May appear aloof and reserved
- Considers fun a waste of time
- Needs to understand the reason for an activity before he/she will respond

The **NF** learner:
- Tends to be motivated by recognition, dialogue, and caring
- Thrives on personal recognition and interaction
- Prefers cooperation; intensely dislikes conflict
- Wants to focus on and contribute to the social environment in a classroom
- Prefers small-group interaction

TRY IT!

www.mcgrawhill.ca/olc/power

Figure 2.1

Kolb's Experiential Learning Styles

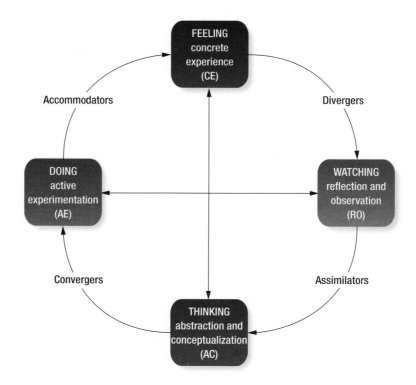

- *Thinking:* Learners who prefer *thinking* (AC: abstract conceptualization) learn best when they can apply thinking and analysis to their learning by using case studies or theoretical readings.

Within the quadrants formed by the grids are the learning styles of each person: *theorists* (assimilators), *pragmatists* (convergers), *activists* (accommodators), and *reflectors* (divergers).

- *Assimilators* use abstract conceptualization and reflective observation in their learning process. They ask, "How does this relate to that?" They prefer case studies, reading, and thinking. Their strength is in their ability to create theoretical models. Instructors who lecture and assign papers are effective for learners with this learning style.

- *Convergers* use abstract conceptualization and active experimentation to learn effectively. They ask, "How can I apply this in practice?" They prefer peer feedback and activities that apply skills. Their strength is in their ability to apply skills and ideas. A coach or helper is an ideal instructor for this type of learner.

- *Accommodators* use concrete experience and active experimentation to learn best. They say, "I'm game for anything." They prefer practising the skills, problem solving, small-group discussions, and peer feedback. Experts who model professional practices are effective instructors for these learners.

- *Divergers* like to use reflective observation and concrete experience to learn well. They ask, "What does that mean?" They prefer lectures, with time to think or write about their subject. Their strength lies in their imaginative ability. They like instructors who can provide expert interpretation and set external criteria for evaluation.

To discover where you fit into Kolb's Learning Style Inventory, complete Try It! 4, "Experiential Learning Styles."

Chapter 2   Recognizing How You Learn, Who You Are, and What You Value

Experiential Learning Styles

Prepare: Determine your experiential learning style.

Organize: You will need the questionnaire included here along with a description of the four different styles. (See page 38.)

Work: Complete the questionnaire and review the description of the style associated with your score. Highlight words or phrases that seem like you.

Evaluate: Were you able to determine your experiential learning style and words or phrases associated with that style?

Rethink: Does this information suggest you should rethink how you learn and study for maximum effectiveness?

What kind of learner are you? Read each statement carefully. To the left of each statement, write the code that best describes how each statement applies to you.[2]

SECTION 1

Place either an AE or RO next to each statement below, depending on which part of the statement most closely describes you:

_____ (AE): I often produce off-the-cuff ideas that at first might seem silly or half-baked. (RO): I am thorough and methodical.

_____ (AE): I am normally the one who initiates conversations. (RO): I enjoy watching people.

_____ (AE): I am flexible and open-minded. (RO): I am careful and cautious.

_____ (AE): I like to try new and different things without too much preparation. (RO): I investigate a new topic or process in depth before trying it.

_____ (AE): I am happy to have a go at new things. (RO): I draw up lists of possible courses of actions when starting a new project.

_____ (AE): I like to get involved and to participate. (RO): I like to read and observe.

_____ (AE): I am loud and outgoing. (RO): I am quiet and somewhat shy.

_____ (AE): I make quick and bold decisions. (RO): I make cautious and logical decisions.

_____ (AE): I speak slowly, after thinking. (RO): I speak fast, while thinking.

Total of AEs: _____. Total of ROs: _____. The one that has the larger number is your task preference.

SECTION 2

Place either an AC or a CE next to each statement below, depending on which part of the statement most closely describes you:

_____ (AC): I ask probing questions when learning a new subject. (CE): I am good at picking up hints and techniques from other people.

_____ (AC): I am rational and logical. (CE): I am practical and down to earth.

_____ (AC): I plan events down to the last detail. (CE): I like realistic but flexible plans.

_____ (AC): I like to know the right answers before trying something new. (CE): I try things out by practising to see whether they work.

_____ (AC): I analyze reports to find the basic assumptions and inconsistencies. (CE): I rely on others to give me the basic gist of reports.

(continued on next page)

TRY IT!

Experiential Learning Style— Continued

_____ (AC): I prefer working alone. (CE): I enjoy working with others.

_____ (AC): Others would describe me as serious, reserved, and formal. (CE): Others would describe me as verbal, expressive, and informal.

_____ (AC): I use facts to make decisions. (CE): I use feelings to make decisions.

_____ (AC): I am difficult to get to know. (CE): I am easy to get to know.

Total of ACs: _____. Total of CEs: _____. The one that has the larger number is your thought or emotional preference.

SCORING PROCEDURES

Each preference (high score) from the two above sections is used to determine your learning style. Note that you learn in *all* four styles, but you normally learn best by starting in and using one style the most.

- If you are an AE and a CE then you are a Doer/Accommodator.
- If you are an RO and a CE then you are a Watcher/Diverger.
- If you are an RO and an AC then you are a Thinker/Assimilator.
- If you are an AE and an AC then you are a Feeler/Converger.

Facts to Remember about Learning, Personality, Experiential, and Processing Styles

- **You have a variety of styles.** As you can see in Table 2.1 (on page 41) and Try It! 5, "What I Know About My Learning Styles" (on page 42), there are several types of styles. For any given task or challenge, some types of styles may be more relevant than others. Furthermore, success is possible even when there is a mismatch between what you need to accomplish and your own pattern of preferred styles. It may take more work, but learning to deal with situations that require you to use less-preferred styles is important practice for life after college or university.

- **Your style reflects your preferences regarding which abilities you like to use—*not* the abilities themselves.** Styles are related to our preferences and the mental approaches we like to use. You may prefer to learn tactilely, but that in itself doesn't guarantee that the products that you create tactilely will be good—you still have to work!

- **Your style will change over the course of your life.** You can learn new styles and expand the range of learning experiences in which you feel comfortable. In fact, you can conceive of this book as one long lesson in learning styles because it provides you with strategies for learning more effectively in a variety of ways.

Table 2.1

Learning, Processing, Personality, and Experiential Styles

Category	Description
Receptive Learning Styles	
Visual	A style that involves visualizing information in the mind, favouring reading and watching over touching and listening.
Auditory	A style in which the learner favours listening as the best approach.
Tactile	A style that involves learning by touching, manipulating objects, and doing things.
Information Processing Styles	
Analytic	A style in which the learner starts with small pieces of information and uses them to build the big picture.
Relational	A style in which the learner starts with the big picture and breaks it down into its individual components.
Personality Styles	
Introvert versus Extrovert	Independence is a key characteristic of introverted learners, who enjoy working alone and are less affected by how others think and behave. In contrast, extroverts are outgoing and more affected by the behaviour and thinking of others. They enjoy working with others.
Intuitor versus Sensor	Intuitors enjoy solving problems and being creative, often taking a big-picture approach to solving problems. Sensors prefer a concrete, logical approach in which they can carefully analyze the facts of the situation.
Thinker versus Feeler	Thinkers prefer logic over emotion, reaching decisions and solving problems by systematically analyzing a situation. In contrast, feelers rely more on their emotional responses and are influenced by their personal values and attachments to others.
Perceiver versus Judger	Before drawing a conclusion, perceivers attempt to gather as much information as they can and are open to multiple perspectives. Judgers, in comparison, are quick and decisive, sometimes making decisions before they have all the available information; they enjoy setting goals and accomplishing them.
Experiential Styles	
Divergers	They prefer to observe or watch others, think, and record thoughts about learning.
Assimilators	They prefer to read or listen to instructions, understand theories, and create theoretical models.
Convergers	They prefer to be coached, learn from an expert, and go step-by-step through a learning process.
Accommodators	They prefer hands-on learning, practising, and working with others.

- **You should work on improving your less-preferred styles.** Although it may be tempting, don't always make choices that increase your exposure to preferred styles and decrease your practice with less-preferred styles. The more you use approaches for which you have less of a preference, the better you'll be at developing the skills associated with those styles.

- **Work cooperatively with others who have different styles.** If your instructor asks you to work cooperatively in groups, seek out classmates who have styles that are different from yours. Not only will your classmates' differing styles help you to achieve collective success, but you can learn from observing others' approaches to tackling the assignment.

What I Know About My Learning Styles

Prepare: Create a summary of your learning styles. How do you learn best? What strengths do you have that can lead to success at school? What is the best way for you to prepare for exams?

Organize: To do this task you will need the results of your learning style investigation using the five windows in this chapter and a chart similar to the example shown in the text. Go to the OLC at www.mcgrawhill.ca/olc/power to get a sample of the chart and see an example.

Work: Complete a chart similar to the one shown in the text. Create a summary statement of your learning style. Be prepared to describe your style to others in the class.

Evaluate: Were you able to create a summary statement of your learning style?

Rethink: Do the results of your investigation suggest changes you should make to the way you learn and study? Would this information have helped you in the past?

LEARNING STYLE	I AM BEST DESCRIBED AS:	MY STRENGTHS ARE:	I LEARN BEST BY:
Visual, Auditory, Kinesthetic			
Multiple Intelligences			
Analytic, Relational			
Myers-Briggs Type Indicator			
Kolb's Learning Style Inventory			
Statement of Learning Style			

Self-Concept: "Who Am I?"

Of course you know who you are: You know your first and last name, you know where and when you were born, and you have no trouble identifying your ethnic background. You may even be able to recite your social insurance number with ease.

But if this information is all that comes to mind when you think about who you are, you're missing a lot of the picture. What makes you unique and special are your thoughts, your beliefs, your dreams. You have a unique past history, and this set of experiences together with your genetic makeup—the combination of genes you inherited from your parents—is unlike anyone else's.

> "When I discover who I am, I'll be free."
>
> Ralph Ellison, U.S. author

Our view of ourselves—our **self-concept**—has three parts:

1. Our *physical self* is both who we are physically—the colour of our eyes or the curliness of our hair—and how we feel about our physical form. We all have our blemishes, protruding stomachs, long noses, or other physical quirks, but we don't all feel the same way about them.

2. Our *social self* is made up of the roles we play in our social interactions with others. As you're reading these words, you're not only a student; you're also a son or daughter, a friend, a citizen, and possibly an employee, a spouse, a lover, or a parent. Each of these roles plays an important part in defining your self-concept.

3. Finally, our self-concept also contains a *personal self*—our inner core, which is that private part of ourselves that no one knows about except us. It consists of the innermost thoughts and experiences that we may or may not choose to share with others.

Self-concept

Your view of yourself that forms over time, comprising three components: the physical self, the social self, and the personal self

Self-Concept and Self-Fulfilling Prophecies

The way we view ourselves determines how we interact with others, what challenges we feel ready to take on, and our expectations for future success. If you see yourself as a successful student, you are likely to expect that you'll continue to be a successful student; if you see yourself as an incapable, inept student, your chances for future success are diminished.

In short, our self-concept can act as a self-fulfilling prophecy. A **self-fulfilling prophecy** is the tendency to act in accordance with our expectations and beliefs, thereby increasing the likelihood that events or behaviours consistent with those expectations and beliefs will occur. In other words, believing that something will happen can lead to actions that make it more likely that it actually will happen.

For instance, a person who views herself as a poor student may find herself thinking: "Why bother working hard? I'm no good as a student; that's just the way I am." It's easy to see how such a view could lead to a self-fulfilling prophecy: By not working hard, the student guarantees that the prophecy of poor performance comes true.

On the other hand, self-fulfilling prophecies can have positive effects. A person who sees herself as a good student will probably be motivated to study and will

Self-fulfilling prophecy

The tendency to act in accordance with our expectations and beliefs, thereby increasing the likelihood that events or behaviours consistent with those expectations and beliefs will occur complete assignments enthusiastically. Her view of herself can bring about the expected behaviour—in this case, success.

To get a clearer picture of your own self-concept:

- **Examine the roles you play.** To understand who we are, we need to understand the different roles that we play in life. Consider which of these roles are central to who you are—and who you want to be. Think about the time you spend each day and how much of it is devoted to each of these roles.

- **Identify your strengths and weaknesses.** Look at yourself with a clear and objective eye, and consider what you do particularly well and what you don't do particularly well. If you're honest, you'll come up with several areas in which you need work—and many other areas in which you're already quite strong. Use Table 2.2 to help you organize your thoughts and build an initial inventory of your strengths and weaknesses.

As you consider your strengths and weaknesses, don't place a value on them. The fact that you procrastinate and put off tasks doesn't make you a bad person, just as the fact that you're a good student doesn't necessarily make you a good person. The point in seeking to identify who you are is to determine your self-concept with accuracy, not to determine how good (or bad) a human being you are.

Furthermore, be sure you construct your own definition of who you are. Don't let what you believe others think about you determine what *you* know you're good at and bad at. See yourself through your own eyes, not somebody else's.

"Know Thyself."

- **Pull your selves together.** Try to form a coherent view of your self-concept. Seek to understand how the various parts of your self-concept—physical, social, and personal—fit together.

If you consider your self-concept this way, you'll find that the whole is greater than the sum of the parts. We're not just the bodies we inhabit, the roles we play, and the experiences we have, but something bigger and better.

- **Accept your entire self-concept.** If you're being honest with yourself, you'll find that there are parts of yourself that you like more than others. That's okay. Don't disown the parts you don't like; they're also part of who you are. Instead, accept that some parts of yourself need work, while others are the source of justifiable pride.

Not everything we do belongs in our self-concept. If you once shop-lifted when you were a child, that doesn't mean you were a juvenile delinquent then or are a criminal now. Failing a course in high school doesn't make you a failing student.

Make Sure Your Self-Concept Is Yours

Our own perceptions are not the only source of self-fulfilling prophecies. We sometimes permit *others'* views of who we are and their expectations about us to determine our behaviour.

For example, if we think an instructor views us as a particularly hard worker, we may not want to disappoint him by slacking off. If we believe that our boss admires our persistence, we may be motivated to show her our persistence when we're working on a difficult problem.

Table 2.2

Inventory Your Strengths and Weaknesses

Aspects of Self	Strengths	Weaknesses
Physical Self		
Health and fitness		
Sports		
Nutrition and diet		
Appearance		
Other		
Social Self		
Friend		
Son/daughter		
Lover/spouse		
Citizen/community member		
Employee		
Student		
Roommate		
Classmate		
Team or group member (e.g., sports, band, club)		
Other		
Personal Self		
Personal experiences		
Unique traits		
Personality		
Spiritual self		
Habits		
Attitudes/opinions		
Ideas/thoughts		
Other		

Responding to others' positive perceptions can be fine, for the results are good. But what happens if someone holds a negative view of who we are? What if we're constantly told that we're not working hard enough, or that we're not as smart as our older brother, or that we are the hard worker but not the creative one?

The results can be devastating. If we consistently hear such messages about who we are, we can come to believe them. Even worse, our behaviour can begin

> "A lot of my fellow classmates are younger than me, and therefore concerned with different things."
>
> Kim Ritchie, Student, Lambton College

to reflect the negative messages. If we're constantly told that we don't work hard enough, we may in fact *not* work very hard. If we're told we're not as smart as someone else, we may begin to think of ourselves as not very bright. Or if someone tells us we're not creative, we may not try very hard to be creative.

In short, the negative messages that we hear from others can come to act as a prison of others' negative beliefs about who we are and what our capabilities are. It's crucial, then, not to buy into others' negative views of who we are. Instead, we need to create our own self-concept, independent of what we believe others think about us. Our biggest help, and sometimes hinderance, in this effort is self-esteem.

Breaking the Cycle of Failure "Okay," you may be saying to yourself, "I understand that self-esteem is important. But how am I supposed to ignore a lifetime of learning and improve my self-esteem, especially when I have low self-esteem to begin with?"

It's not a simple matter to shed a less-than-ideal view of ourselves and adopt a more positive one. You certainly won't be able to change your basic conception of yourself in the course of a few days.

Figure 2.2

The Cycle of Failure

Low self-esteem can lead to low performance expectations. In turn, low performance expectations can produce reduced effort and high anxiety, both of which can lead to failure—and ultimately reinforce the low self-esteem that started the cycle.

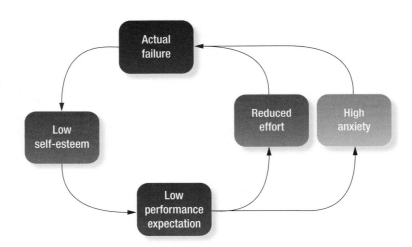

Calvin and Hobbes — by Bill Watterson

But you can take some steps to bring yourself closer to an ideal level of self-esteem:

- **Accept yourself, warts and all.** No one is perfect, and becoming a perfect person should not be your goal in life. If it is, you are doomed to failure, because you will never measure up.

  Accept the fact that you're not pleased with certain aspects of yourself and your life. If you didn't realize that some things about yourself need improvement, you are out of touch with who you are.

- **Understand that everyone has value and self-worth.** Every individual has value and self-worth, some unique spark that sets him or her apart from everyone else. Examine yourself and your life, and get a picture of the particulars that make you *you*.

- **Distinguish the different parts of who you are.** No one is all bad, just as no one is all good. Maybe a person who never reached the level of success she wanted to in school turns out to be an excellent employee, the person who always seems to be asked to solve problems or take on challenges no one else can deal with. Another person may not be the kind of husband he wants to be but turns out to be a terrific parent.

  Understanding that you have failings in one area of life doesn't mean that you can't be successful in others. It makes no sense to base your self-esteem on what you do worst in life, so don't focus solely on your failings and minimize your successes.

- **Don't just rely on—or wait for—others' praise.** Your self-esteem should not be solely dependent on the praise you get from others. Use your own judgment to evaluate the level of success you've achieved on a given task.

  For instance, you know when you've done your best in writing a paper. If you feel proud of it, celebrate your accomplishment and take pride in it. Instead of waiting for your instructor's feedback, permit yourself to feel good about what you've done. Your self-esteem should be based on your own assessment of your accomplishments, not only on others' assessments.

- **Understand that building self-esteem is a lifelong undertaking.** It's taken a lifetime to develop whatever level of self-esteem you currently have. Your self-esteem is not going to change overnight.

  Rebuilding self-esteem isn't easy. It's particularly hard to do at a time when you face a major life transition, such as the beginning of your postsecondary experience. Your oldest friends and your family may not be nearby, and the level of academic work you encounter presents new challenges. But starting college or university presents a special opportunity to grow and develop. It's a new environment, giving you the opportunity to unlearn old patterns of behaviour that have held you back and master new ones that will permit you to have a more positive view of yourself. Don't let low self-esteem keep you from becoming what you can be.

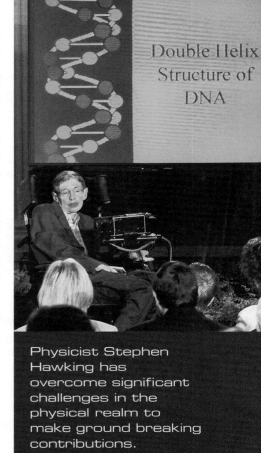

Physicist Stephen Hawking has overcome significant challenges in the physical realm to make ground breaking contributions.

Preparing a Personal Mission Statement

One way to get a clearer picture of your life is to create a formal statement of what you hope to achieve during your lifetime. The P.O.W.E.R. framework provides a series of steps that can help you look inward and determine how you want to carry out this period in your life.

Prepare: Identify Your Values

The first step toward understanding yourself is to assess your underlying values. Do this by determining what you hold most dear. Here are some examples: world peace, beauty, equality, security, freedom, happiness, love, self-respect, knowledge, hard work.

"Authentic values are those by which a life can be lived."

Allan Bloom

Go to the OLC at www.mcgrawhill.ca/olc/power for more information about personal values.

To gain more insight, choose five values and for each one, answer the following questions: *Why* is it important you? *Who* taught it to you? *How* has it affected your behaviour in the past? *In what ways* can you affirm it through your future behaviour?

Organize: What Do You Want To Be Remembered For? What Kind of Person Would You Like to Be?

Most of us have things that we want people to say about us, or things we want to be remembered for. Some of these things might be close to your values, but express things from a different point of view such as: *he wanted to help people; he tried to be a good friend, he was a hard worker; he kept his word*; What would you like your family and friends to say about you?

Think about adjectives you would like to use to describe yourself in the future. Consider words such as: *kind, friendly, helpful, powerful, wealthy, fit, good-looking, generous, energetic, caring,* and *sensitive.* Try to choose five adjectives to describe yourself.

Work: Write Your Personal Mission Statement

Use the information you have gathered so far to write your own personal mission statement. Take a piece of paper and draw a line across about halfway down. In the upper half, write values, key adjectives, goals, and hopes. In the lower half, write sentences that use the words or phrases in the upper half. Then, put the sentences together in some kind of order so that you know the meaning.

You might state how you plan to achieve your emotional needs and personal values through out your career. Describe the person you want to be and what you can contribute to your surroundings. Describe your intended lifestyle and the type of community you want to live in and the nature of your ideal family. To gain further insight, complete Try It! 6, "Your Personal Mission Statement."

Evaluate: Assessing Your Personal Mission Statement

After you've written a personal mission statement, consider whether it accurately captures what you are looking for in life. Would a friend who knows you well see it as a valid reflection of who you are? Does the mission statement take

6 Your Personal Mission Statement

Prepare: The goal for this task is to develop a personal mission statement that reflects your personal values, needs, and priorities for the next five or more years.

Organize: Use the information in the text and on the website as you prepare to develop your mission statement. Discuss your findings with one or more study partners to compare notes.

Work: To create your own personal mission statement, complete the following steps:

Step 1—Summarize your most important values.
Step 2—Consider what you want to be known and remembered for.
Step 3—Reflect on the kind of person you want to be.
Step 4—Write your personal mission statement.

Evaluate: Does your mission statement capture what you are looking for in life? Would a friend who knows you well see it as a valid reflection of who you are? Does the mission statement reflect not just where you are now, but where you want to be in the future? Does it suggest what makes you special?

Rethink: A mission statement doesn't change every week or every month, but it should change as you change and grow. At least once a year take out your statement and ask if it still reflects your values, needs, and priorities or whether it should it be changed.

www.mcgrawhill.ca/olc/power

a long-term view, reflecting not just where you are now, but where you want to be in the future? Is it general enough to fit the many different circumstances in which you will find yourself?

Only you can determine the ability of your personal mission statement to capture what is important to you. If you feel it doesn't, rewrite it. Eventually you'll come up with a statement that illustrates what you feel makes you special.

R ethink: Reconsidering Your Options

Personal mission statements are not set in stone; they should be considered living documents that you can change as you become clearer about what you want for yourself.

That's why it's important to periodically revisit your personal mission statement. When you do, ask yourself whether it still represents your values and motivational needs. Consider whether it should be amended to reflect changes that have occurred in your life.

Even if you don't modify it, periodically reading your personal mission statement is important. It will remind you of who you are and what you are trying to get from the one life you have. (For a summary of the steps involved in creating a personal mission statement, see the P.O.W.E.R. Plan to the right.)

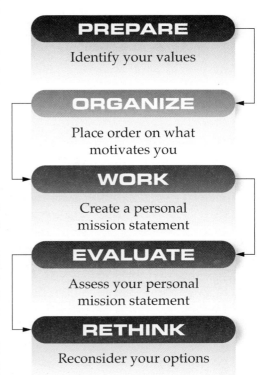

PREPARE
Identify your values

ORGANIZE
Place order on what motivates you

WORK
Create a personal mission statement

EVALUATE
Assess your personal mission statement

RETHINK
Reconsider your options

P.O.W.E.R. Plan

For many reasons, such as improving workplace communication, increasing productivity and efficiency, creating well-balanced teams, or even ensuring corporate security, Canadian workplaces increasingly use personality testing as part of their hiring or orientation process. Employers sometimes use certain tests to help judge an applicant's suitability for a particular kind of job or level of responsibility; in other words, to match people to the jobs for which they are best suited. Tests may also measure specific aptitudes such as mechanical skills or sales abilities, or characteristics such as trustworthiness.

In an ideal situation, a person would do the job that best matches her personality, but that is not always possible. However, mismatching a personality to a job can frequently lead to poor performance and employee dissatisfaction. Employers want to know about employees' personalities to reduce conflict and maximize and coordinate staff abilities. Once an individual is on the job, personality testing can be used to identify a person's management or executive abilities in order to promote from within the organization or to do succession planning.

After completing the assessments in this book and at the Online Learning Centre, you should have a good idea of yourself, your strengths, weaknesses, interests, values, and motivations—strategic preparation for the world of work!

> Enterprise Rent-A-Car suggests interested applicants consider their emotional intelligence (or EQ) when considering a career with E-Car. EQ describes a set of characteristics that influence a person's ability to be successful in everything from relationships to the workplace, that is, persistence, optimism, self-awareness, and social skills. Enterprise Rent-A-Car is particularly interested in hiring entrepreneurial individuals, feeling that entrepreneurs are happiest when running a business. Take the EQ test at Enterprise Rent-a-Car's website: <www.erac.com/recruit/EQ.htm>.

To Thine Own Self Be True: No One Is Responsible for Your Life But You

"Don't take too many English courses; they're a waste of time because they won't help you get a decent job." "How about going to med school? You'd make a great doctor." "You owe it to your family to be a business major so you can join the family business when you graduate."

Sound familiar? Many of us have heard suggestions like these proposed by parents or others close to us. Such comments are almost always well-intentioned, and often they sound quite reasonable.

Why, then, should suggestions like these be taken with great caution? The reason is they relate to decisions that you, and only you, should make. You are the one who must live with their consequences. You are the one who must live with yourself.

One of the worst reasons to follow a particular path in life is that other people want you to. Decisions that affect your life should be your decisions—decisions you make after you've considered various alternatives and chosen the path that suits you best.

Speaking of Success

Todd Currie

*Golf Course Technician Diploma
Seneca College*

Todd Currie's job at West Haven Golf and Country Club means 12-hour workdays during peak season and zero chance of a summer vacation, but he loves his work. Todd is Superintendent of Maintenance at West Haven, a private facility in Hyde Park, Ontario. His responsibilities are many; he supervises a staff that fluctuates from six during the winter to over 20 during the summer. He and his staff do everything from looking after the golf course and gardens to maintaining and repairing all the equipment to investigating and ordering materials.

Todd was attending university, studying to be a physical education teacher, when he realized it was taking education graduates years to get teaching jobs. As someone who loved golf and had worked at golf courses in the summer to earn tuition, he enrolled in Seneca College's Golf Course Technician Program and hasn't looked back since. Todd, who

loves to work outdoors, was very happy with the Golf Course Technician Program, as the learning was very hands-on and focused on getting a job in the golf industry.

Todd continues to take courses in subjects such as pesticide and herbicide use, business administration, communication skills, resource management, and environmental awareness so he can

Seneca

provide the best product possible for the members of the golf and country club. He attends industry conferences as well to keep up with the latest innovations and practices in his field.

Todd says there are many false impressions about careers in the golf industry. Two key misconceptions are

that golf courses are major polluters and irrigate constantly in order to keep grass green. Todd says golf courses use the minimum amount of herbicide and pesticide possible, as it is important to keep costs down, but also the health and safety of wildlife, staff, and patrons is paramount. Todd, who is a member of the Oxbow Creek Watershed Project, a committee affiliated with the Upper Thames River Conservation Authority, is also concerned with water use. He states that new varieties of grass make irrigating less necessary and in fact, the drier the greens are the better, as far as golf is concerned.

Todd reiterates that anyone considering a career as a golf course technician must be flexible, as the job entails long hours and lots of variety, but that for people who want to work outdoors, it is a wonderful career.

Making your own decisions does not mean that you should ignore the suggestions of others. For instance, your parents do have their own unique experiences that may make their advice helpful, and they sometimes may know you better, in certain respects, than you know yourself: Having participated in a great deal of your personal history, they may have a clear view of your strengths and weaknesses. Still, their views are not necessarily accurate. They may still see you as a child, in need of care and protection. Or they may see only your strengths. Or, in some unfortunate cases, they may focus on only your flaws and shortcomings.

The bottom line is that you need to make your own decisions. People will always be giving you advice. It's up to you, though, to decide whether or not to heed the advice. You need to determine the course of your life and the way you want it to unfold.

It's important to realize that making your own decisions may have costs. For instance, in some cultures loyalty to family and family wishes is a dominant value. If you don't follow your family's suggestions, you may be seen as rebellious and uncaring. Ultimately, though, you have to make your own judgments about what's right for you, following your head—and your heart.

Looking ◀◀
Back ◀—

What are my learning styles, and how have they affected my academic success?

- People have diverse patterns of learning styles—characteristic ways of acquiring and using knowledge.
- Learning styles include visual, auditory, and tactile styles (the receptive learning styles), and analytic and relational styles (information processing styles).
- Personality styles that influence learning are classified along dimensions of introversion/extroversion, intuition/sensing, thinking/feeling, and perceiving/judging.
- Experiential learning styles are reflected in Kolb's Inventory of divergers, assimilators, convergers, and accommodators.

What is self-concept and how does it affect me?

- Self-concept is the understanding of the self that a person forms over time. Its major components are the physical, social, and personal self.
- Self-concept is important because of the effects it has on people's attitudes and behaviour. Self-concept can act as a self-fulfilling prophecy, in that people act in accordance with their self-concepts.

How does my level of self-esteem affect my behaviour?

- Self-esteem is the overall evaluation we give ourselves as individuals.
- High self-esteem can lead to greater happiness, an enhanced ability to cope with adversity, a sense of security and confidence, and self-efficacy.
- Low self-esteem can lead to insecurity, low self-efficacy, and a cycle of failure.

P.O.W.E.R. Portfolio

Self-Improvement

Look back at Table 2.2. Choose several of your major strengths and consider how you can demonstrate these qualities. Identify two or three of your weaknesses and turn them into challenges or goals. For example, "My preference is to work independently, but this semester I will improve my teamwork skills by participating in a study group and volunteering for the foot patrol squad at school." Once you have elaborated on your strengths and weaknesses, put the final copy in your portfolio.

Resources

On Campus

If you are interested in learning more about your pattern of learning styles, visit your campus counselling centre or career centre, where you may be able to take special assessment tests that can pinpoint your learning preferences and offer study strategies based on those preferences.

When dealing with the uncertainties of life and establishing your own sense of direction, it may help to speak to someone who has perspective and experience with college or university students. Here, too, a good place to start on campus is either a general counselling centre or one that is designed to help students choose career paths. Mental health offices can also be helpful in putting you in touch with a therapist with whom you can explore issues revolving around your self-concept and self-esteem. Don't hesitate to get help; you are doing it for yourself.

In Print

Please Understand Me II: Temperament, Character, Intelligence by David Keirsey (Prometheus Nemesis Book Co. Inc., 1998) is a helpful book that states that differing styles and temperaments are to be expected and embraced.

Don't Sweat the Small Stuff . . . and It's All Small Stuff (Hyperion, 1997), written by Richard Carlson, is a down-to-earth guide that is meant to help you sort out what is—and is not—important in your life.

On the Web

The following sites on the World Wide Web provide the opportunity to extend your learning about the material in this chapter. Although the Web addresses were accurate at the time the book was printed, check the P.O.W.E.R. Learning website <www.mcgrawhill.ca/olc/power>, for any changes that may have occurred.

http://career.missouri.edu

This site has an online version of the *Career Interests Game,* designed to help you match your interests and skills with careers. It can help you begin thinking about how your personality will fit in with specific work environments and careers.

www.keirsey.com
www.keirsey.com/matrix.html

The Keirsey site provides two online personality questionnaires. The inventories are based on Myers-Briggs, but Keirsey groups personality types according to temperaments.

www.cdm.uwaterloo.ca/step1_3.asp

This site offers an online values exercise that might be helpful in writing your personal mission statement.

http://www.lifecolorsonline.com/lifecolorslite.html
http://www.similarminds.com
http://www.coloruiz.com
http://assessment.monster.ca/

All these sites include self-assessment quizzes that allow you to get feedback on who you are.

http://www.matthewbarr.co.uk/simpsons/

Take the Simpsons Personality Test and find out which character you resemble.

http://www.ullazang.com/personality.html

This is interesting and fast…just one question.

The Case Of...

The Instructor who Spoke Too Much

Lana Carlson, a 26-year-old woman living in Calgary, Alberta, was at her wits' end. The instructor in her Diagnostic Procedures class spent each 50-minute lecture talking nonstop. He barely paused to acknowledge students' questions, and his only goal seemed to be to present as much material as possible. He even gave assignments in the same fast, nasal tone that he used throughout class.

If it weren't for her friend Darren Rubbell, who was in the same class and patiently explained material after class was over, Lana would never have managed to figure out how to complete the homework assignments. The strange thing was that Darren didn't seem to have much trouble with the professor's endless talking. In fact, he claimed to enjoy the class a lot. He had no trouble following the lectures and understanding the assignments, seeming to absorb like a sponge the information the instructor was spouting.

1. Based on what you know about learning styles, what might be the source of Lana's difficulties?
2. What learning style does the instructor apparently assume all students have? Do you think this is one of Lana's learning styles? Why or why not?
3. How might the instructor change his presentation to accommodate diverse learning styles?
4. Why does Lana's friend Darren have so little trouble with the instructor's lectures?
5. Why do you think Lana has less trouble understanding Darren after class than she has understanding her instructor?
6. If you were Lana, what might you do to improve your situation?

Making the Most of Your Time

3

Scott had slept in again, and now he was going to miss class and the weekly quiz. He wondered what excuse he could use this time. The teacher was starting to apply penalties to late assignments, and Scott's marks were getting worse. If things didn't change very soon, all the money and time he'd spent taking the course would be wasted because he would fail.

Scott would say that school was a priority, but his behaviour said something else. He behaved like school requirements were getting in the way of his social life. The most common excuse Scott gave for not handing in assignments or for missing classes was that he was so busy he couldn't get them done. Most of his friends were also having problems juggling all of the demands—there was just never enough time.

Underneath it all, Scott knew he was blowing his chance to succeed in school. Success would mean that sooner or later Scott would have to start making better use of his time.

Looking ▶▶
▶Ahead

Are your days like Scott's? Are you constantly trying to cram more activities into less time? Do you feel as if you never have enough time? Or do you feel overwhelmed and paralyzed by all you know you have to do?

You're not alone: Most of us wish we had more time to accomplish the things we need to do. However, some people are a lot better at juggling their time than others. What's their secret?

No one has more than 168 hours a week, no matter how industrious. Instead, it comes down to figuring out priorities and using time more efficiently.

This chapter will give you strategies for improving your time management skills. After helping you learn to account for the ways you currently use—and misuse—time, you'll learn strategies for

planning your time, including some ways to deal with the inevitable interruptions and counterproductive personal habits that can sabotage your best intentions.

We also consider techniques for dealing with competing goals. Special challenges are involved in juggling the priorities of college work with other aspects of life, especially when they include childrearing or holding a job.

After reading this chapter, you'll be able to answer these questions:

- **How can I manage my time most effectively?**
- **How can I better deal with surprises and distractions?**
- **How can I balance competing priorities?**

Time for Success

Without looking up from the page, answer this question: What time is it?

You've probably got some idea of the current time. In fact, most people are pretty accurate in their answer. If you don't know for sure, it's very likely that you can find out quickly. You may have a watch on your wrist; there may be a clock on the wall, desk, or computer screen.

Time is something from which we can't escape. Even if we ignore it, it's still going by, ticking away. Our lives are moving forward in time whether we choose to pay attention to it or not. So the main issue in using your time well is, "Who's in charge?" We can allow time to slip by and let it be our enemy, or we can take control of it and make it our ally.

By taking control of how you spend your time, you'll increase your ability to do the things you must do to be successful as a student. More than that, the better you are at managing the time you devote to your studies, the more time you will have to spend pursuing your interests.

We all know people who seem to be able to find time to do everything. Successful time managers make conscious choices about how they spend their time. Being in control of their time enables them to shape their future in the way *they* want, rather than feeling as if they are running around trying to keep up with a timetable set by others or by circumstance.

"Hello and welcome to the game that'll be put off until tomorrow, but should've been played today."

How do you handle this much detail if attention to detail is not one of your strengths? All tasks require some attention to detail so challenge yourself to use detail to accomplish your goals.

The goal of time management is not to schedule every waking moment of the day. Instead, the goal is to make informed choices as to how we use our time. Rather than letting the day slip by, largely without our awareness, the time management procedures we'll discuss can make us more aware of time's passage and better able to harness time for our own ends.

Prepare: Learning Where Time Is Going

Before you get somewhere, you need to know where you're starting from and where you want to go. So the first step in improving your time management skills is figuring out how you're managing your time now.

What follows are some ways to figure out how you are now spending your time.

Create a Time Log "Where did the day go?" If you've ever said this to yourself, one way of figuring out where you've spent your time is to create a **time log.** A time log is the most essential tool for improving your use of time.

Time log

A record of how time is spent

Create a Time Log

Prepare: The goal of this task is to keep track of how you spend your time over seven days and identify changes you can make to use your time more effectively.

Organize: Go to the text's Online Learning Centre at www.mcgrawhill.ca/olc/power to get a blank, seven-day time log to fill in and to see a completed example. Your day planner or time planner may also help you with this task.

Work: Keep track of how you spend your time on an hour-by-hour basis. In some cases you can use half-hour increments by dividing the cell using a diagonal line. The easiest way is to keep a copy of the log with you and fill it in as you go through the day. In some cases keep notes in your time planner and then complete your log at the end of the day.

After you complete your log, add up the amount of time you spend in each category. You may wish to add a category if it requires a significant amount of time. Look at your results and answer the following questions:

1. What requires the most time?

2. What was the biggest surprise?

3. Does how you spend your time reflect your goals? (This is the big question.)

4. What would you change to manage your time more effectively?

5. Is there any such thing as free time without a schedule?

Evaluate: Were you able to document how you spend your time and identify changes you can make that reflect your goals?

Rethink: Sometimes people find time wasters that they know are not helping them accomplish their goals. Is it time to let go of some of these? This is a great exercise to do once a year to make sure you are using time as a precious resource.

A time log is simply a record of how you actually have spent your time—including interruptions. It doesn't have to be a second-by-second record of every waking moment. But it should account for blocks of time in increments as short as 30 minutes.

Look at the blank time log in Try It! 1, "Create a Time Log." As you fill out the log, be specific, indicating not only what you were doing at a given time (for example, "reading history assignment") but also the interruptions

	hygiene	food	classes	studies	work	TV	recreation	personal	sleep	social
12:00 A.M. (MIDNIGHT) to 1:00 A.M.										
1:00 A.M. to 2:00 A.M.										
2:00 A.M. to 3:00 A.M.										
3:00 A.M. to 4:00 A.M.										
4:00 A.M. to 5:00 A.M.										
5:00 A.M. to 6:00 A.M.										
6:00 A.M. to 7:00 A.M.										
7:00 A.M. to 8:00 A.M.										
8:00 A.M. to 9:00 A.M.										
9:00 A.M. to 10:00 A.M.										
10:00 A.M. to 11:00 A.M.										
11:00 A.M. to 12:00 P.M. (NOON)										
12:00 P.M. (NOON) to 1:00 P.M.										
1:00 P.M. to 2:00 P.M.										
2:00 P.M. to 3:00 P.M.										
3:00 P.M. to 4:00 P.M.										
4:00 P.M. to 5:00 P.M.										
5:00 P.M. to 6:00 P.M.										
6:00 P.M. to 7:00 P.M.										
7:00 P.M. to 8:00 P.M.										
8:00 P.M. to 9:00 P.M.										
9:00 P.M. to 10:00 P.M.										
10:00 P.M. to 11:00 P.M.										
11:00 P.M. to 12:00 A.M. (MIDNIGHT)										
Total Hours										

Analyze your log

Working in a group: Compare *your* use of time during an average week with that of your classmates. What are the major differences and similarities in the use of time?

that occurred (such as "answered phone twice" or "switched to Internet for 10 minutes").

Keep your time log for at least seven days, using a typical week. Obviously, no week will be completely typical, but if it's near normal, it will provide you with enough information to give you a good sense of where your time goes. You may want to use the notes you make in your time planner to fill in your time log.

By looking at how much time you spend doing various activities, you now know where your time goes. How does it match with your perceptions of how you spend your time? Be prepared to be surprised, because most people find that they're spending time on a lot of activities that just don't matter very much.

Identify the Black Holes That Consume Your Time Do you feel as if your time often is sucked into a black hole, disappearing without a trace?

We all waste time, spending it on unimportant activities that keep us from doing the things that we should be doing or really want to do. For example, suppose that when you're studying you get a phone call from a friend, and you end up speaking with her for an hour. You could have (1) let the phone ring and not answered it; (2) answered, but told your friend you were studying and promised to call her back; or (3) spoken to her, but only for a short while. If you had done any of these things, you would have taken control of the interruption and kept time from sinking into a black hole.

To get a sense of how your time is sucked into black holes, complete Try It! 2, "Identify the Black Holes of Time Management."

Priorities

The tasks and activities that you need and want to do in a period of time rank-ordered from most important to least important

Set Your Priorities By this point you should have a good idea of what's taking up your time. But you may not know what you should be doing instead.

Assign priorities to tasks and activities to figure out the best use of your time. **Priorities** are tasks or activities that you need and want to do to be able to accomplish your goals and are rank-ordered in terms of importance or urgency. If you have a major assignment due in two weeks time, working on the assignment is

Where Does My Time Go?

1. On the typical weekday morning, what time do you wake up? When would you prefer to wake up if you had the choice?

2. On the typical weekday evening, when do you go to bed? What time would you prefer to go to bed?

3. Would you characterize yourself as a "morning person," who accomplishes the most in the early morning, or do you see yourself more as a "night person," who is most comfortable doing work in the evenings? What implications does this have for your scheduling of classes and when you do the most work?

4. Do you generally get to classes early, late, or on time? Why? How does this pattern affect your experience and performance in class?

5. If a day suddenly contained more than 24 hours, how would it change your life? What would you do with the extra time? Do you think you would accomplish more?

6. Generally speaking, how would you characterize your time management skills? What would be the benefit to you personally if you could manage time more effectively?

Identify the Black Holes of Time Management

Prepare: Identify the black holes in how you spend your time and describe the degree you have control over your time wasters. Identify the need for change.

Organize: To complete this task you will need your completed time log and the list of common problems from the chart below.[1]

Work: Review your time log and then look at the list of common problems. Identify the degree to which any of these common distractions is a problem for you. Be prepared to share your insights in a working group. Look for ways people can support each other to make changes in their time management.

Evaluate: Were you able to identify any of the common problems as an issue for you? Did you develop a solution and gain support from another person to make the changes?

Rethink: Do the results of this exercise give you some things to think about? Remember you can't get to a new place in your life by doing the same things you did to get to where you are now.

TRY IT!

www.mcgrawhill.ca/olc/power

	Big Problem for Me	Often a Problem	Seldom a Problem	Controllable (C) or Uncontrollable (U)?
1. Telephone				
2. Drop-in visitors				
3. E-mail interruptions				
4. Hobbies				
5. Mistakes				
6. Inability to say "no"				
7. Socializing				
8. Snacking				
9. Errands and shopping				
10. Meals				
11. Children's interruptions				
12. Perfectionism				
13. Family appointments				
14. Looking for lost items				
15. Redoing mistakes				
16. Jumping from task to task				
17. Surfing the World Wide Web				
18. Reading newspapers, magazines, recreational books				
19. TV				
20. Computer games				
21. Alcohol/recreational drugs				
22. Listening to music				
23. Romantic/family problems				
24. Illness/fatigue				
25. Other				

Working in a group: Examine the problems that affect each group member, and then discuss these questions: Do time management problems fall into any patterns? What strategies for dealing with such problems have you used in the past? Are there problems that at first seem uncontrollable that can actually be controlled? How have you dealt with time management challenges in the past?

Figure 3.1
List of Priorities

Priority	Priority Index
Study for each class at least 30 minutes/day	1
Start each major paper 1 week in advance of due date	2
Hand in each paper on time	1
Review for test starting a week before test date	2
Be on time for job	2
Check in with Mom once a week	3
Work out 3 x/week	3

Each of us has an internal body clock that helps govern when we feel most alert. Becoming aware of your own body clock can help you to schedule study sessions at times when you're able to work at peak efficiency.

important but likely not urgent. If you have a major assignment that is due tomorrow morning you have a very important task that is also very urgent. And then, there are all the other things you need to or want to do.

Write your priorities on the chart in Try It! 3, "Set Priorities." After you've filled out the chart, organize it by giving each priority a "priority index" number from 1 to 3. A "1" represents a priority that absolutely must be done. For instance, a paper with a fixed due date should receive a "1" for a priority ranking; carving out time to take those guitar lessons you always wanted to take might be ranked a "3" in terms of priority. The important point is to rank order your priorities to reveal what is and is not important to accomplish during the term to achieve your goals.

Setting priorities will help you to determine how to make the best use of your time. No one has enough time to complete everything; prioritizing will help you make informed decisions.

Identify Your Prime Time Take a look inward. Do you enthusiastically bound out of bed in the morning, ready to start the day and take on the world? Or is the alarm clock a hated and unwelcome sound that jars you out of a pleasant slumber? Are you the kind of person who is zombie-like by 10 at night, or a person who is just beginning to rev up at midnight?

Each of us has our own style based on some inborn body clock. Being aware of the time or times of day when you can accomplish your best work will help you plan and schedule your time most effectively. If you're at your worst in the morning, try to schedule easier, less-involving activities for those earlier hours. If morning is the best time for you, schedule activities that require the greatest concentration at that time.

"Time moves slowly, but passes quickly."

Alice Walker, *The Color Purple*

But don't be a slave to your internal time clock. Even night people can function effectively in the morning, just as morning people can accomplish quite a bit in the evening. Don't let your concerns become a self-fulfilling prophecy.

Set Priorities

Prepare: Identify priorities for this term to serve as a base for planning your time.

Organize: To complete this task you will need your Time Management information from Try It! 1 and Try It! 2, a list of key dates for this term, and a List of Priorities form like the one below.

Work: You may have to make up a list of key dates for the term by getting some information from the college or university website and the course descriptions for the classes you are taking this term. Please ensure you have the due dates for major assignments, mid term tests, and final exams.

Complete the List of Priorities form by listing priorities in areas such as schoolwork, other work, family, other relationships, spiritual needs, and health. Don't worry about the order. Once you have listed your potential priorities assign a rating to each item. Give a "1" to the highest priority, a "2" to the medium priority and a "3" to the items with the lowest priority. Review your ratings to make sure your priorities match you goals. Do your highest priorities reflect your goals?

Redo the list using the "Final List of Priorities" form to record your priorities from the most important to the least important. Look at your highest priorities and decide if you have time to accomplish these tasks or activities. Continue to make adjustments until you have a practical, realistic plan for using your time. Make sure you plan for time for yourself to relax, have fun, and renew your energy.

Evaluate: Do you feel you were able to identify your priorities, and can you use these as a base for planning your time?

Rethink: Planning your life around your priorities is a new thing for many people. Do you need to recommit to your priorities?

List of Priorities

Priority	Priority Index

Now redo your list, putting your number 1's first, followed by as many of your number 2's and 3's to which you feel you can reasonably commit.

(continued on next page)

Set Priorities—Continued

Final List of Priorities

Priority
1.
2.
3.
4.
5.
6.
7.
8.
9.
10.
11.
12.

What does this list tell you about your greatest priorities? Are they centred around school, friends and family, jobs, or some other aspect of your life? Do you have so many "1" priorities that they will be difficult or impossible to accomplish successfully? How could you go back to your list and trim it down even more? What does this listing of priorities suggest about how successful you'll be during the term? Do your priorities reflect your goals?

Master calendar

A schedule showing the weeks of a longer time period, such as a college or university term, with all assignments and important activities noted on it

Weekly timetable

A schedule showing all regular, prescheduled activities due to occur in the week, together with one-time events and commitments

Daily to-do list

A schedule showing the tasks, activities, and appointments due to occur during the day

Organize: Mastering the Moment

Your time management preparation has brought you to a point where you now know where you've lost time in the past, and your priority list is telling you where you need to be headed in the future.

Now for the present. You've reached the point where you can organize yourself to take control of your time. Here's what you'll need:

- A **master calendar** that shows all the weeks of the term, seven days per week on one page. (See the example of a master calendar on page 67.)
- A **weekly timetable.** The weekly timetable is a master grid with the days of the week across the top and the hours, from 6 A.M. to midnight, along the side.
- A **daily to-do list.** Finally, you'll need a daily to-do list. The to-do list can be written on a small, portable calendar that includes a separate page for each day of the week. Or it can simply be a small notebook, with a separate sheet of paper for every day of the week.
- **Coloured pens or markers** so you can colour-code your schedules. Consider using different colours for classes, assignments, tests, study times, flex time, and so on, so it is immediately obvious how much time you have allotted to each activity.

Master Calender Sample

M	T	W	TH	F	SA	S
Sept. 1	8	9 Classes start	10	11	12 Camping →	13
14	15 Add/drop ends	16	17 English short paper due	18	19	20
21	22	23	24 English short paper due	25 Sociology quiz	26	27
28	29 Psych exam	30	OCT 1 Music quiz, English short paper due	2 1st Psych paper due	3	4
5	6 Music paper due	7	8 English short paper due	9 Sociology quiz	10	11
12 Holiday! Thanksgiving	13	14	15 Music quiz, English short paper due	16	17	18
19 First yr seminar journal due	20	21 Psych exam	22 English short paper due, Dad's bd-call	23 Theatre Midterm	24 Bartending job	25
26 Sociology midterm exam	27 English midterm exam	28	29 Eng short paper due, Music quiz	30	31	NOV 1
2	3	4	5 English short paper due	6 Sociology short paper due	7	8 Darcey's Wedding!
9	10	11	12 Eng short paper due, Music quiz	13 Sociology quiz, Psych exam	14	15
16 First yr seminar group project due	17	18 Preregistration for next semester	19 English short paper due	20	21	22
23	24	25	26	27	28	29
30	DEC 1 Music paper due	2	3 English short paper due	4 Sociology quiz	5	6
7 First yr seminar final journal due	8	9	10 Music quiz	11 Theatre project due, Psych exam, Last day of class!!	12	13
14 English final exam	15 Theatre final exam, Sociology final exam	16	17 Psych final exam	18 Music exam, My birthday!	19	20

The basic organizational task you face is filling in these three schedules. You'll need at least an hour to do this, so set the time aside. In addition, there will be some repetition across the three schedules, and the task may seem a bit tedious. But *every minute you invest now in organizing your time will pay off in hours that you will save later.*

Follow these steps in completing your schedule:

1. **Start with the *master calendar*, which shows all the weeks of the term on one page.** In most classes, you'll receive a syllabus, a course outline that explains what the course is all about. Traditionally, a syllabus includes course assignments and their due dates, and the schedule for tests that will be given during the term. Write on the master calendar

every assignment you have, noting it on the date that it is due. If the instructors haven't included due dates, ask; they probably already know, or at least have a general idea of, the week that various assignments will be due. Pencil in tentative assignments on the appropriate date.

Don't only put assignments on the master calendar. Also include important activities from your personal life, drawn from your list of priorities. For instance, if you're involved in a club that is bringing a guest speaker to campus, mark down the date of the event. Finally, schedule some free time—time when you will do something that is just plain fun. Consider these days to be written in stone—promise yourself that you won't use them for anything else except for something enjoyable.

You now have a good idea of what the term has in store for you. In most cases, the first few weeks have few assignments or tests. But as the term rolls on—particularly around the middle and end of the term—things will get more demanding. The message you should take from this: *Use the off-peak periods to get a head start on future assignments.*

Completing a master schedule also may help you head off disaster before it occurs. Suppose, for instance, you find that six weeks in the future you have two papers due and three tests—all in the same week!

After cursing your bad luck, it's time to take action. Begin to think of strategies for managing the situation, such as working on the papers or studying in advance. You might also try to change some due dates. Instructors are far more receptive to requests for extensions on papers if the requests are made well in advance. Similarly, it might be possible to take a test later—or earlier—if you make prior arrangements.

2. **Now move to the *weekly timetable* provided in Figure 3.2.** Fill in the times of all your fixed, prescheduled activities—the times that your classes meet, when you have to be at work, the times you have to pick up your child at daycare, and any other recurring appointments.

Once you've filled in the weekly timetable, as in the one on page 69, you get a bare-bones picture of the average week. You will still need to take into account the specific activities that are required to complete the assignments on the master calendar.

To move from your average week to specific weeks, make photocopies of the weekly timetable that now contains your fixed appointments. Make enough copies for every week of the term. On each copy write the week number of the term and the specific dates it covers.

Using your master calendar, add assignment due dates, tests, and any other activities on the appropriate days of the week. Then pencil in blocks of time necessary to prepare for those events.

How much time should you allocate for schoolwork? One rough guideline holds that every one hour that you spend in class requires, on average, two hours of study outside class to earn a B and three hours of study outside class to earn an A. Do the arithmetic: If you are taking 15 credits (with each credit equivalent to an hour of class per week), you'll need to plan for 30 hours of studying each week to earn a B average—an intimidating amount of time. Of course, the amount of time you must allocate to a specific class will vary from week to week, depending on what is happening in the class.

For example, if you estimate that you'll need five hours of study for a midterm exam in a certain class, pencil in those hours. Don't set up a single block of five hours. People remember best when their studying is

Weekly Timetable

Week of: _____   Week # _____

	Mon	Tues	Wed	Thurs	Fri	Sat	Sun
6–7 A.M.							
7–8 A.M.							
8–9 A.M.							
9–10 A.M.							
10–11 A.M.							
11–12 A.M.							
12 (noon)–1 P.M.							
1–2 P.M.							
2–3 P.M.							
3–4 P.M.							
4–5 P.M.							
5–6 P.M.							
6–7 P.M.							
7–8 P.M.							
8–9 P.M.							
9–10 P.M.							
10–11 P.M.							
11 P.M.–12 (midnight)							

Figure 3.2

A Weekly Timetable

Make a single copy of this blank timetable. Then fill in your *regular, predictable* time commitments. Next, make as many copies as you need to cover each week of the term. Then, for each week, fill in the date on the left and the number of the week in the term on the right, and add in your *irregular* commitments.

spread out over shorter periods rather than attempted in one long block of time. Besides, it will probably be hard to find a block of five straight hours on your weekly calendar.

Similarly, if you need to write a paper that's due on a certain date, you can block out the different stages of the writing process that we'll describe in Chapter 9. You'll need to estimate how much time each stage will take, but you probably have a good idea from previous papers you've written.

Keep in mind that estimates are just that: estimates. Don't think of them as set in stone. Mark them on your weekly calendar in pencil, not pen, so you can adjust them if necessary.

But remember: It's also crucial not to overschedule yourself. You'll still need time to eat, to talk with your friends, to spend time with your family, and to enjoy yourself in general. If you find that your life is completely filled with things that you feel you must do and there is no room for fun,

Weekly Timetable

Week of: 9/28   **Week #** 3

	Mon	Tues	Wed	Thurs	Fri	Sat	Sun
6–7 A.M.							
7–8 A.M.							
8–9 A.M.							
9–10 A.M.	9.05 Psych	9.05 Music	9.05 Psych	9.05 Music	9.05 Psych		
10–11 A.M.		↓		↓			
11–12 A.M.		11.15 English		11.15 English			
12 (noon)–1 P.M.	12.20 Theatre	↓	12.20 Theatre	↓	12.20 Theatre		
1–2 P.M.	↓		↓				
2–3 P.M.							
3–4 P.M.	3:00 Sociology		3:00 Sociology		3:00 Sociology		
4–5 P.M.	First-year seminar	Work		Work			
5–6 P.M.	↓						
6–7 P.M.							
7–8 P.M.		↓		↓			
8–9 P.M.							
9–10 P.M.							
10–11 P.M.							
11 P.M.–12 (midnight)							

then step back and cut out something. Make some time for yourself in your daily schedule. Finding time for yourself is as important as carving out time for what others want you to do.

3. **If you've taken each of the previous steps, you're now in a position to work on the final step of organization for successful time management: completing your *daily to-do list*.** Unlike the master calendar and weekly timetable—both of which you develop at the beginning of the term—you shouldn't work on your daily to-do list far in advance. In fact, the best approach is to complete it just one day ahead of time, preferably at the end of the day.

List all the things that you intend to do during the next day. Start with the things you know you must do that have fixed

To-Do List for _9/28_ (date)	
Item	**✓**
Call Chris & get English notes	✓
Meet with Prof. Hernandez	✓
Do laundry	
Work on outline for psych paper	
Return books to library	✓
Call Nettie	
Set up meeting with music group	
Meet Deena	
Review Sociology	✓

times, such as classes, work schedules, and appointments. Then add in the other things that you need to accomplish, such as an hour of study for an upcoming test; working on research for an upcoming paper; or finishing up a lab report. Finally, list things that are enjoyable—set aside time for a run or a walk, for example.

The idea is not to schedule every single minute of the day. That would be counterproductive, and you'd end up feeling as if you'd failed if you deviated from your schedule. Instead, think of your daily to-do list as a path through a forest. If you were hiking, you would allow yourself to deviate from the path, occasionally venturing onto side tracks when they looked interesting. But you'd also be keeping tabs on your direction so you would end up where you needed to be at the end and not kilometres away from your car or home.

As in the sample daily to-do list that follows, include a column to check or cross off after you've completed an activity. There's something very satisfying in acknowledging what you have accomplished. As you look at your to-do list with its checkmarks you will also feel a surge of energy, knowing you can get things done.

W ork: Controlling Time

Time management is largely about preparation and organization; the work itself involves completing the activities that you need and want to complete. If you've prepared and organized carefully, you'll be ready to complete your work (see Try It! 4, "Build a Daily To-Do List").

In short, the work of time management is to follow the schedules that you've put together. But that doesn't mean it will be easy. *Our lives are filled with surprises:* Things take longer than we've planned. A friend we haven't spoken to in a while calls to chat, and it seems rude to say that we don't have time to talk. A crisis occurs; buses are late; computers break down; kids get sick.

The difference between effective time management and time management that doesn't work lies in how well you deal with the inevitable surprises.

4 Build a Daily To-Do List

Prepare: Based on your priorities, create a to-do list for the day or the week.

Organize: To do this task, you will need your day planner or the to-do list form provided on the website at www.mcgrawhill.ca/olc/power.

Work: Review your priorities and other commitments and create a to-do list for the day. Place a checkmark beside items you completed, an "O" for outstanding beside items to be carried over to the next day, and an "X" beside items to be dropped off the list. Create a series of to-do lists as you progress through the semester. This may seem a little difficult at first but your skill will increase quickly and this process will enable you to achieve your time management goals.

Evaluate: Were you able to create a useable to-do list? As a guideline, most college students begin to fall behind at school when they work at a job for more than 20 hours per week. How many hours are you planning on working?

Rethink: Do you have priorities that don't seem to get done? What do think the problem is? How can you redirect your time and effort?

To-Do List

for_____
(date)

Item	✓

There are several ways to take control of your days and permit yourself to follow your intended schedule:

- **Just say no.** You don't have to agree to every request and every favour that others ask of you. You're not a bad person if you refuse to do something that will eat up your time and prevent you from accomplishing your goals.

- **Get away from it all.** Go to the library. Lock yourself into your bedroom.

  Either place can serve to isolate you from everyday distractions and thereby permit you to work on the tasks that you want to complete. Try to adopt a particular spot as your own, such as a corner desk in a secluded nook in the library. If you use it enough, your body and mind will automatically get into study mode as soon as you seat yourself at it.

- **Enjoy the sounds of silence.** Although many students insist they accomplish most while a television, radio, or CD is playing, scientific studies suggest otherwise: We are able to concentrate most when our environment is silent. So even if you're sure you work best with a soundtrack playing, experiment and work in silence for a few days. You may find that you get more done in less time than you would in a more distracting environment.

- **Take control of your communications.** The telephone, e-mail, text-messaging, or instant messenger—who doesn't love to receive messages from others?

  We may not be able to control when communications arrive, but we can control communications until we are ready to receive them. Telephone calls can be stored on answering machines or voice-mail systems, cell phones can be turned off, and e-mail can be read later. If you wait until you have the time to take a message, you'll be able to follow your time management plans far better.

- **Use technology to help.** As the old advertisement for the Yellow Pages said, "Let your fingers do the walking." Use the variety of technology-based tools available to help save time. Using e-commerce technology to bank online, employing the automated prompt feature on e-calendars as a reminder, and managing your communication by e-mail or voice mail are just a few ways technology can help save you time.

- **Expect the unexpected.** Interruptions and crises, minor and major, can't be eliminated. However, they can be prepared for. By making sure your schedule has some slack in it, you'll have the opportunity to regain time lost to unexpected events.

  Even more important, try to anticipate the unanticipated. How is it possible to plan for surprises? Keep an eye out for patterns. Perhaps one instructor routinely gives surprise assignments that aren't listed on the syllabus. Maybe you're asked to work extra hours on the weekends because someone doesn't show up.

  You'll never be able to escape from unexpected interruptions and surprises that require your attention. But by trying to anticipate them, and thinking about how you'll react to them, you'll be positioning yourself to react more effectively when they do occur.

  > "Procrastination has no place if one is trying to reach a goal."
  >
  > Doug Tettman, Student, Langara College

- **Don't procrastinate.** Procrastination is like a microscopic parasite on your day, invisible to the naked eye, but eating up your time nonetheless.

  It's 10 A.M. You've just come out of your Statistics class. You know that there's going to be a test next week, and you've planned to go over the study notes you made last night. It's right there in your schedule: "10 A.M.—study Statistics." But you're thirsty after sitting in class, so you decide to go and buy yourself something to drink.

  As you head into the snack bar, you pass by the campus store, and you think about how you need to buy a couple of pens. After finding the kind of pen you like, you go to the checkout line. You pass by a rack of magazines, and, after leafing through a few, decide to purchase one. You can read it while you have your drink. You make your way to the cafeteria, buy a coffee, and sip it as you read the magazine.

  Suddenly, half an hour has gone by. Because so much time has passed, you decide that it won't be worth it to start studying your Statistics notes. So you spend a little more time reading the magazine and then head off to your next class, which is at 11 A.M.

  You can't control interruptions and crises that are foisted upon you by others, but even when no one else is throwing interruptions at us, we make up our own. **Procrastination** is the habit of putting off work that needs to be

Procrastination

The habit of putting off tasks that are to be accomplished

done. As these tasks tend to be important, putting them off quickly becomes a problem. Sometimes taking a break helps you to be more productive when you return to work; sometimes it's just a way to avoid doing what you have to do. Most people know the difference. Almost everyone procrastinates some of the time. To identify if it is a problem for you, use Try It! 5, "Find Your Procrastination Quotient." Examine the steps you can use to help yourself procrastinate less.

If you use the time management techniques that we've been discussing, procrastination should be minimized. But if you find yourself procrastinating, several steps can help you:

Break large tasks into small ones. People often procrastinate because a task they're seeking to accomplish appears overwhelming. If writing a 15-page paper seems nearly impossible, think about writing five three-page papers. If reading a 750-page book seems impossible, think of it as reading several 250-page books.

Start with the easiest and simplest part of a task, and then do the harder parts. Succeeding initially on the easy parts can make the harder parts of a task less daunting—and make you less apt to procrastinate in completing the task.

Work with others. Working with others who must accomplish the same task can help prevent procrastination. Just being in the same physical location with others can motivate you sufficiently to accomplish tasks that you consider unpleasant and on which you might be tempted to procrastinate. For instance, studying vocabulary words can be made easier if you plan a session with a study group. Beware, though—if you spend too much time socializing, you lower the likelihood of success.

One antidote to procrastination is working with a study group. You'll be motivated by the presence of others who face the same challenges and assignments that you do.

Keep the costs of procrastination in mind. Procrastination doesn't just result in delay; it may also make the task harder than it would have been if you hadn't procrastinated. Not only will you ultimately have less time to complete the task, but you may have to do it so quickly that its quality is diminished. In the worst scenario, you won't even be able to finish it.

Balance school and family demands. If you are a full-time student and full-time caregiver for children, time management is especially challenging. Not only do children demand—and deserve—substantial quantities of time, but juggling school and family obligations can prove to be more than a full-time job. Some specific strategies can help, however:

–*Provide activities for your children.* Kids enjoy doing things on their own for part of the day. Plan activities that will keep them happily occupied while you're doing schoolwork.

–*Make spending time with your children a priority.* Carve out "free play" time for your kids. Even 20 minutes of good time devoted to your children will give you and them a lift. No matter how busy you are, you owe it to your children—and yourself—to spend time as a family.

Find Your Procrastination Quotient

Prepare: Determine how much procrastination affects the achievement of your goals.

Organize: You will require the procrastination questionnaire provided here.

Work: Complete the questionnaire[2] by circling the number that best applies for each question, and totalling your score out of 40. What is your score? If your total is below 20, you might be a procrastinator on occasion; between 20 and 30 procrastination affects your results to a limited degree; above 30 procrastination is likely to be a significant factor in your success.

Evaluate: Were you able to determine if procrastination is a problem worth paying attention to? You probably knew if you were a procrastinator already, but have these results suggested this habit affects the achievement of your goals?

Rethink: The same message is repeated here as before. If you want to get to a new place you will have to do something different than what you did to get to where you are now.

1. I often invent reasons and look for excuses for not acting on a problem.

    Strongly agree   4   3   2   1   **Strongly disagree**

2. It takes a lot of pressure to get me to work on difficult assignments.

    Strongly agree   4   3   2   1   **Strongly disagree**

3. I take half measures that will avoid or delay unpleasant or difficult tasks.

    Strongly agree   4   3   2   1   **Strongly disagree**

4. I allow too many interruptions and crises to interfere with accomplishing my major goals.

    Strongly agree   4   3   2   1   **Strongly disagree**

5. I always neglect to carry out important tasks.

    Strongly agree   4   3   2   1   **Strongly disagree**

6. I schedule work on big assignments too late to get them done as well as I know I could.

    Strongly agree   4   3   2   1   **Strongly disagree**

7. I'm sometimes too tired to do the work I need to do.

    Strongly agree   4   3   2   1   **Strongly disagree**

8. I often start new tasks before I finish old ones.

    Strongly agree   4   3   2   1   **Strongly disagree**

9. When I work in groups, I try to get other people to finish what I don't.

    Strongly agree   4   3   2   1   **Strongly disagree**

10. I put off tasks that I really don't want to do but know that I must do.

    Strongly agree   4   3   2   1   **Strongly disagree**

If you do procrastinate often, why do you think you do it? Are there particular subjects or classes or kinds of assignments on which you are more likely to procrastinate?

Working in a Group: Think about the last time you procrastinated. Describe it as completely as you can. What was the task? What did you do rather than doing what needed to be done? What could you have done to avoid procrastinating in this situation? Ask others what strategy they might suggest for avoiding procrastination.

- *Enlist your child's help.* Children love to play "grown up" and, if they're old enough, ask them to help you study. Maybe they can help you clear a space to study. Perhaps you can give them "assignments" that they can work on while you're working on your assignments.

- *Encourage your child to invite friends over to play.* Some children can remain occupied for hours if they have a playmate.

- *Use television appropriately.* Television viewing is not all bad, and some shows and videos can be not just engaging but educational. The trick is to pick and choose what your children watch and not use TV as an all-purpose babysitter. *The Magic Schoolbus, Sesame Street,* and videos of children's classics, for example, can, for an hour or so, be a worthwhile way for children to spend their time while you study.

- *Find the best childcare or babysitters that you can.* The better the care your children are getting, the better you'll be able to concentrate on your schoolwork. You may still feel guilty that you're not with your children as much as you'd like, but accept that guilt. Remember, your attendance of college or university builds a better future for your children.

- *Accept that studying will be harder with kids around.* It may take you longer to study, and your concentration may suffer from the noise that kids make. But remind yourself what that noise represents: the growth and development of someone whom you love. One day your children will be grown, and without a doubt there will be times that you'll miss their high level of energy and activity.

- **Balancing school and work demands.** Juggling school and a job can be exhausting. Not only must you manage your time to complete your schoolwork, but in many cases you'll also face time management demands while you are on the job. Here are some tips to help you keep everything in balance:

  - *Make to-do lists for work, just as you would for your schoolwork.* In fact, all the time management strategies that we've discussed can be applied to on-the-job tasks.

  - *If you have slack time on the job, get some studying done.* Of course, you should never do schoolwork without your employer's permission. If you don't get permission, you may jeopardize your job.

  - *Ask your employer about flextime.* If your job allows it, you may be able to set your own hours, within reason, as long as the work gets done. If this is an option for you, use it. Although it may create more time management challenges for you than would a job with set hours, it also provides you with more flexibility.

  - *Accept new responsibilities carefully.* If you've barely been keeping up with the demands of work and school, don't automatically accept new job responsibilities without carefully evaluating how they fit with your long-term priorities. If your job is temporary, you might want to respectfully decline substantial new duties or an increase in the number of hours you work. If you do plan to continue in the job once you're finished school, then accepting new responsibilities may be more reasonable.

  - *Always keep in mind why you're working.* If you're working because it's your sole means of support, you're in a very different position from

Time Management at Work

Mira, a manager at a Canadian property management company, recently complained that she often receives between 50 and 60 e-mails and 20 to 30 voice mails each day, in addition to her full schedule of appointments and meetings. Her work requires travel as well. This type of workday is very common in many business environments.

How do people deal effectively with these demands? When you ask Mira how she deals with this workload she says effective time management is an essential skill. She sets priorities, knows where her time goes, aligns her time with her mission and goals, and finds a balance between being available to people and controlling her time. She still works a lot of hours, but says she always knows what her priorities are for the day—what has to be done and what can wait. In this way, she spends time on the most urgent items for at least part of the day.

Mira also makes use of equipment to make the most of her time. Beyond e-mail and voice mail, she also uses a Blackberry to link to her computer from wherever she is. If she has to wait in line for something she uses that time to connect to others or read and send e-mail. She regularly reviews her use of time to make sure it matches career and personal goals.

Mira also plans time for learning and as she calls it "goofing off." She understands there is no free time unless you plan it and often says she has time to do what is important and no time at all to waste. She sometimes complains that life is moving too fast and that there are too many demands. She wonders if it is all worthwhile, but for the moment, what she is doing matches her goals and definition of success. A large part of her success is dependent on using effective time management skills.

There is a strong connection between time management skills and student success as well. Completing work on time, studying for exams, keeping a part-time job, and having a social life, demand effective use of your time. The skills you learn now will serve you throughout your career.

someone who is working to earn a bit of extra money for luxuries. Remember what your priorities are. In some cases, school should always come first; in others, your job may have to come first, at least some of the time. Whatever you decide, make sure it's a thoughtful decision, based on an evaluation of your long-term priorities.

 E valuate: Checking Your Time

Evaluating how you use your time is pretty straightforward: You either accomplished what you intended to do in a given period, or you didn't. Did you check off all the items on your daily to-do list? If you go over your list at the end of every day, not only will you know how successful your time management efforts have been, but you will be able to incorporate any activities you missed into the next day's to-do list.

The check-off is important because it provides an objective record of what you have accomplished on a given day. Just as important, it provides you with concrete reinforcement for completing the task. As we have noted, there are few things more satisfying than gazing at a to-do list with a significant number of checkmarks.

Of course, you won't always accomplish every item on your to-do list. That's not surprising, nor even particularly bad, especially if you've included some second-level and third-level priorities that you don't absolutely have to accomplish and that you may not really have expected you'd have time for anyway.

R ethink: Reflecting on Your Personal Style of Time Management

At the end of the day, after you've evaluated how well you've followed your time management plan and how much you've accomplished, it's time to rethink where you are. Maybe you've accomplished everything you set out to do, every task for the day is completed, and every item on your to-do list has a checkmark next to it.

Or maybe you have the opposite result. Your day has been a shambles, and you feel as if nothing has been accomplished. Because of a constant series of interruptions and chance events, you've been unable to make headway on your list.

Or—most likely—you find yourself somewhere in between these two extremes. Some tasks got done, while others are still hanging over you. Now is the time to rethink in a broad sense how you manage your time. Visit the Online Learning Centre at www.mcgrawhill.ca/olc/power to view an example of building a career time line.

PREPARE

Learn where time is going

ORGANIZE

Use a master calendar, weekly timetable, and daily to-do list

WORK

Follow the schedules you've put together

EVALUATE

Keep track of your short-term and long-term accomplishments

RETHINK

Reflect on your personal style of time management

P.O.W.E.R. Plan

Reconsider Your Personal Style of Time Management We've outlined one method of time management (summarized in the P.O.W.E.R. Plan to the left). Although it works well for most people, it isn't for everyone. Some people just can't bring themselves to be so structured and scheduled. They feel confined by to-do lists.

If you're one of the those people, you don't need to follow the suggestions presented in this chapter exactly. In fact, if you go to any office supply store or your campus bookstore, you'll find lots of other aids to time management. Many publishing companies produce elaborate planners, such as Day-Timer. Similarly, software companies produce computerized time management software, such as Microsoft's Outlook and the Lotus Organizer, and some time management systems are on the World Wide Web (see the Resources section at the end of this chapter or the Online Learning Centre).

Whatever system you choose, the important thing is that you need to pay attention to how you use your time and follow *some* time management strategy. It might consist of jotting down due dates, and then each day looking at them and figuring out what to do that day. It might consist of visualizing yourself completing the tasks you need to and using that visualization to guide your behaviour each day. Or perhaps it might mean working on assignments as soon as you get them. Rather than waiting until the last minute, try to accomplish your work as soon as you know it needs to be done.

Whatever approach to time management you choose, it will work best if it is compatible with your own personal values and strengths. Keep experimenting until you find an approach that works for you.

Consider Doing Less If you keep falling behind, do less. Sometimes we just have so much to do that, even with the best time management skills in the world, we could never accomplish everything. A day has only 24 hours, and we need to sleep for about a third of the time. In the remaining

Managing your time effectively will allow you to spend more of it doing the things that are important to you.

hours, it is simply impossible to carry a full load of classes *and* work full-time *and* care for a child *and* still have some time left to have a normal life.

Consequently, if you consistently fall behind in your work, it may be that you are just doing too much. Reassess your goals and your priorities, and make choices. Determine what is most important to you. It's better to accomplish less, if it is accomplished well, than to accomplish more, but poorly.

Do More If you consistently accomplish everything you want to do and still have time on your hands, do more. Although it is a problem that many of us would envy, some people have too much time on their hands. Their classes may not be demanding, or work commitments may suddenly lessen. Or perhaps a child for whom they are caring begins to attend school full time. In such situations, they may suddenly feel as if their life is proceeding at a more leisurely pace than before.

If this happens to you, there are several responses you might consider. One is to simply relax and enjoy your more unhurried existence. There is much to be said for having time to let your thoughts wander. We need to take time out to enjoy our friends, exercise, or consider the spiritual side of our lives.

> "Our costliest expenditure is time."
>
> Theophrastus, quoted in Diogenes Laertius, *Lives and Opinions of Eminent Philosophers*

If you consistently have more time than you know what to do with, rethink how to make use of your time. Reflect on what you want to accomplish with your life, and add some activities that will help you reach your goals. For example, consider becoming involved in an extra-curricular activity. Think about volunteering your time to needy individuals and organizations. Consider taking an extra course next term.

But whatever you decide to do, make it a decision. Don't let the time slip away. Once it's gone, it's gone forever. Think of time as a valuable natural resource that should be conserved.

Speaking of Success

Emm Gryner

Music Industry Arts Diploma,
Fanshawe College, London, Ontario

Passionate. Creative. Talented. Artistic. Independent. Business-woman. All these words describe Emm Gryner who writes, records, and performs music, as well as runs her own independent label, *Dead Daisy Records.* Emm has released six albums to date and been nominated twice for a Juno award. She was part of the women's music festival, Lilith Fair, and has toured with big-name artists like David Bowie, Jann Arden, Ron Sexsmith, and the Cardigans. However, she has also established a reputation as a musician who is fiercely independent and maintains a strong connection with her fans through an online journal she has written for several years as well as performing in living room shows and smaller venue concerts.

To keep up with the demands of work, Emm uses her time well. She must balance competing demands and find time for personal priorities. Schedules and work planning are required for success.

Emm states that being in charge of the business side of the music business is challenging and requires a lot of dedication and responsibility. However, Emm thrives on work, and as president of her own label, she appreciates having artistic control and knows that when something is done, it is done to her liking.

Emm's solid work ethic and do-it-yourself attitude were instilled at an early age by her parents, who run an independent newspaper in Forest, Ontario. A love of music also developed while she lived in Forest. Emm took piano lessons from the age of 5, and by the

time she was a teenager she was also playing the bass, writing songs, and recording her own music. After high school, Emm was accepted into Fanshawe College's renowned Music Industry Arts program where she learned more about the production side of the music industry as well as the business side, focusing on topics such as contracts, royalties, copyright, and record marketing and promotion. It was a good background for Emm, who recorded with Mercury Records from 1997–1999, until a corporate takeover ended her deal with the big record company. Since then, with Dead Daisy Records, Emm has been self-directed and self-reliant in her career, saying that she is happy she can create the music she wants without interference from others and so far it's working out well.

How can I manage my time most effectively?

- Decide to take control of your time.
- Become aware of the way you currently use your time.
- Set clear priorities.
- Use such time management tools as a master calendar, a weekly timetable, and a daily to-do list.

How can I better deal with surprises and distractions?

- Deal with surprises by saying no, getting away from it all, working in silence, taking control of communications, using the telephone or computer to conduct transactions, and leaving slack in your schedule to accommodate the unexpected.

- Avoid procrastination by breaking large tasks into smaller ones, starting with the easiest parts of a task first, working with other people, and calculating the true costs of procrastination.

How can I balance competing priorities?

- You *can* balance competing priorities if you begin to see how they coexist. Manage work time carefully, use slack time on the job to perform school assignments (if permitted), use flextime, accept new responsibilities thoughtfully, and assign the proper priority to work.

P.O.W.E.R. Portfolio

Goal-Setting Models

Time is a non-renewable resource. Once it is gone, you can't get it back. This chapter has focused on helping you to learn more about how you spend your time and how you can make the best use of your time. Part of the information dealt with techniques and strategies to achieve your goals. List the specific actions and tools you will use to manage your time.

What are your goals?

How much time each day or each week do you have to pursue your goals?

How will you record your priorities and match your time to these priorities?

How will you adjust or change how you spend your time as your goals and priorities change?

Resources

On Campus

The official that schedules classes on campus is known as the *registrar*. If you are having difficulty scheduling your classes, the registrar's office can help. In addition, your academic advisor or program coordinator can help you work out problems in enrolling in the classes you want.

If you are having difficulty in managing your time, you can turn to several places. The campus counselling centre will help, as will campus learning centres. Your academic adviser can also be a source of aid.

In Print

Julie Morgenstern's helpful book, *Time Management from the Inside Out* (Owl Books, 2000), emphasizes deciding upon a time management system that fits one's own personal style—whether it be spur-of-the-moment and easily side-tracked or well-organized and efficient.

The Procrastinator's Handbook by Rita Emmett (Walker & Company, 2000) is a great book full of very helpful suggestions and important common sense about human nature, and our collective tendency to be procrastinators.

A helpful resource that offers sound advice on setting and achieving goals is *Goal Setting 101: How to Set and Achieve a Goal* by Gary Ryan Blair (Goalsguy Learning Systems Inc., 2000).

On the Web

The following sites on the World Wide Web provide the opportunity to extend your learning about the material in this chapter. Although the Web addresses were accurate at the time the book was printed, check the P.O.W.E.R. Learning website, <www.mcgrawhill.ca/olc/power>, for any changes that may have occurred.

http://csd.mcmaster.ca/student_achievement_series.htm
This is the website of a helpful booklet (one of several on study skills) entitled "Organizing Your Studies and Time," published by McMaster University. The booklet has effective techniques and rationales for attending to time management issues.

www.mindtools.com/page5.html
The focus of this site is how to get the most out of your time. Topics covered include analyzing what time is really worth, prioritizing goals, and planning effective use of the time you actually have.

The Case Of...

Where Does the Time Go?

As Carl Petersen walked into his apartment, he didn't really have to look at the time—he knew it was too late. He cringed. How could he have spent the entire night with the guys? At first, he had just wanted to play a little basketball with some buddies to burn off some energy. Then they had gone to the Outback Shack for some wings and a couple of games of pool. The next thing he knew, it was after 11 P.M. He and his friends had ended up sharing a few pitchers while watching the game on the big screen TV, and he had nothing to show for the evening.

It was not as if the afternoon had been any better! When he had gotten home from school at 4, he had been dead tired. After eating a bowl of cereal, Carl had taken a nap. When he woke up at 5:30, he checked his e-mail and that had taken an hour. Then, what was supposed to be an hour of hoops had turned into a whole evening shot!

Thinking about his medical terminology test the next day, Carl started to panic. He had to write the test and he had to pass this one. Luckily he had done the chapter exercises and review and was pretty sure he had brought his textbook home. What else was coming up? He clenched his fist as he remembered his logs for last weekend's ride-along shifts with the ambulance crew were now overdue. What else? He was way behind on his reading for anatomy and physiology and he hadn't started reading the book he needed to summarize and critique for next Monday. But he had the weekend to get caught up on everything.

Carl was resolving to change his ways when he suddenly remembered that it was his grandparents' 50th wedding anniversary this weekend and he had promised—promised—his mom he'd be home for the weekend. Carl mentally ran through the labs, assignments, projects, and tests due in the next week. He hadn't started any of them. His heart sank.

As he yawned and wandered into the kitchen to pour some orange juice for himself and begin what he hoped would be a few productive hours before going to bed, he stopped in his tracks. Where was his backpack? After a quick search, he realized it wasn't in his apartment. How was he supposed to study for his test tomorrow? Carl closed his eyes and put his head in his hands—how had he gotten so far behind on everything? He kicked at a pile of dirty clothes in the middle of the floor. His life was coming apart completely. How was he ever going to get it together?

1. What might you tell Carl to help solve his predicament?

2. What could Carl have done to avoid the situation he now faces?

3. What specific time management techniques might Carl have used to prevent these problems from arising?

4. What strategies might Carl use now to take control of his limited time during the coming week?

5. What advice could you give Carl in order to prevent time management problems during the next term?

Getting Along with Others

4

Despite her excellent technical skills, Cindy was feeling really frustrated. While her co-op work term had started well, it was beginning to fall apart. She'd been having difficulty forming positive working relationships in the office. Although she treated her colleagues the same way she treated her friends, it didn't seem to be working.

She couldn't understand why people wouldn't listen to her ideas. She thought her suggestions for improvements were great and often wondered why the other people didn't seem interested. She felt that her colleagues were being disrespectful, and her philosophy had always been to respect those who respected her. So, when her boss had asked her to help with some photocopying the other day, she'd told him that such a menial task wasn't in her job description.

One of the staff in her work area had tried to talk to her, but the only advice she'd offered Cindy was to listen more and try to find out why things were done the way they were. Cindy said to herself: "What a waste of time! Why didn't she just mind her own business?"

Cindy made it to the end of her co-op work term, but only just. She left with bad feelings and she missed opportunities to learn about building relationships with others. Chances are high that she will repeat the same mistakes in her next job until she builds her skills to get along with people.

Looking ▶▶ *Ahead*

Why does a chapter on getting along with others appear in the first part of this textbook? To answer this question, go back to Chapter 1 and review the skills that employers want most (page xx). As you review the list, remind yourself about how many of these skills are so called "people skills" or soft skills. Over and over employers report that people with technical skills are available, but people with the ability to get along with others, work in teams, and resolve conflicts are much harder to find. Because these skills are also essential in courses such as this one that involve groups or teamwork, our discussion of this topic is presented early to teach you how to develop and use this skill.

The Teamwork Skills highlighted by the Conference Board of Canada under "Work with Others" include understanding group dynamics, using active listening skills, showing respect for individual opinions and ideas, able to accept and provide constructive feedback, and managing and resolving conflict. Building and maintaining effective relationships is a critical success skill in college or university and in the workplace.

Up to this point in your life you have been able to build and maintain relationships at some level. The focus in the first part of this chapter is to add to your relationship-building skills and your ability to resolve conflict. In the second part of this chapter we focus on how social diversity and relationships affect your postsecondary experience. We look at practical strategies for acknowledging—and shedding—prejudice and stereotypes, and for being receptive to others on their own merits.

When you complete this chapter you will be able to answer the following questions:

- **What skills can I use to build lasting relationships and resolve conflicts?**

- How can I work more effectively with people of different cultures, skills, and backgrounds?

Building Lasting Relationships

No person prospers as an island. The reason for saying this is because relationships with others are critical to our sense of well-being. The support of friends and relatives helps us to discover and feel good about ourselves. Some studies suggest that our physical and psychological health may suffer without friendships. The social support of others can act as a guard against stress and provide healing.

We compare ourselves with others to understand our own abilities and achievements. Our attitudes, beliefs, and values are influenced and shaped by others. We are who we are in large part because of others who have influenced our lives.

To have a good friend, be a good friend.

Although some of us get to know others with ease, some find building relationships more difficult. But building relationships is not a mystery. Here are several ways to go about it:

- **Invest time in others.** There's no better way to demonstrate that you are interested in being friends than investing time. Relationships need to be nourished by the commitment of time. You can't expect friendships to flourish unless you spend time with people.

- **Reveal yourself.** Good friends understand each other. The best way to make that happen is to let others get to know you. Be open and honest about the things you like and dislike. Talk about where you come from, what your family is like. Find out about the other person. Having a deeper understanding of where someone comes from not only helps build bridges between people of different racial and ethnic backgrounds, it also helps build friendships. By honestly communicating your beliefs and attitudes, you give others the chance to learn those things you have in common—which, despite surface differences, may be substantial when it comes to basic values and approaches to the world.

- **Let others know you like them.** It may seem scary, but don't be coy and try to pretend you are uninterested in the friendships of others. Take the risk of being rebuffed. You don't have to announce outright that you like someone. Instead, reveal your interest in a friendship by inviting the person to do something with you or simply by engaging in conversation, sharing something about your life. Your actions will speak louder than words.

- **Accept others as they are, not as you would like them to be.** One mark of friendship is accepting of people the way they are, warts and all, and not the way you would like them to be. Do not impose conditions on accepting others. Keep in mind that no one is perfect and that everyone has both good and bad qualities.

- **Show concern and caring.** This is really the substance of friendship and the basis for the trust that develops between friends. Don't be afraid to show your interest in the fortunes of others and to share the sadness when they suffer some setback or loss.

- **Not everyone makes a good friend.** People who belittle you, consistently make you feel bad or unhappy, or behave in ways that violate your own personal standards are not friends, no matter what they may tell you. Choose your friends based on the good feelings you have when you are with them and the concern and caring they show for you. Friendship is a two-way street.

Complete Try It! 1 "Building Relationships" to examine your relationship–building skills.

TRY IT! 1

www.mcgrawhill.ca/olc/power

Building Relationships

Learning to build relationships is an ongoing process throughout your life and just when you think you know it all, life often shows us we have more to learn.

Prepare: Analyze how often you use key relationship-building behaviours and identify areas of improvement.

Organize: Complete the following task by using the questionnaire below to focus your review. You may want to compare your answers with others.

Work: Complete the questionnaire. Highlight the behaviours you would like to improve.

Evaluate: Were you able to identify areas of improvement?

Rethink: Is it time to change your approach to building relationships?

1. I am willing to invest the time needed to build relationships.	Almost Never	Sometimes	Almost Always
2. I give others the chance to get to know me.	Almost Never	Sometimes	Almost Always
3. I let people know if I like them.	Almost Never	Sometimes	Almost Always
4. I accept others as they are without trying to change them.	Almost Never	Sometimes	Almost Always
5. I listen to and show interest in others.	Almost Never	Sometimes	Almost Always
6. I am willing to let go of some relationships that are not working for me.	Almost Never	Sometimes	Almost Always
7. I have all the friends I need.	Almost Never	Sometimes	Almost Always

Beyond Friendship

Some relationships move beyond a casual friendship. This occurs when two people feel emotionally attached, fulfill each other's needs, and generally feel interdependent. When a true relationship exists, several components are present:

- **Trust.** Relationships must be built on a foundation of trust. We need to be able to count on others and feel that they will be open with us.

- **Honesty.** No relationship can survive if the partners are not honest with one another. Each partner must share a commitment to the truth. Your life does not have to be a completely open book—it's the rare individual who has no secrets whatsoever—but it is important to be honest about your fundamental beliefs, values, and attitudes. Those in good relationships accept one another, blemishes and all, and a relationship based on untruths or even half-truths lacks depth and meaning.

- **Mutual support.** Healthy relationships are characterized by mutual support. A partner's well-being should have an impact on you, and your well-being should affect your partner. In good relationships, the partners seek out what is best for each other, and they act as advocates for and defend each other.

- **Loyalty.** The mark of a good relationship is loyalty. Loyalty implies that relationship partners are supportive of each other, even in times of adversity and difficulty.

- **Acceptance.** Your best friend watches every reality show going, and is incredibly caught up by the action and personalities on each episode. You can't stand to watch this type of TV show. Do you decide that you can no longer be friends? Of course not.

  In good relationships small annoyances don't get in the way of the deeper connection between you and another person. We don't have to like everything others do to maintain relationships with them. We don't even have to appreciate or approve of every aspect of their personalities. What is crucial is the willingness to accept others as they are, without constantly yearning for changes. All of us want to be accepted by others as we are, not as they'd like us to be; we should offer the same approval to those with whom we maintain relationships.

- **Willingness to embrace change.** Change is part of everyone's life. As people grow and develop, they change. So do relationships.

  We need to accept change as a fundamental part of relationships and build on that change. In fact, we need to welcome change. Although change brings challenges with it, it also helps us to understand ourselves and our own place in the world more accurately.

  It is only natural that some relationships will fade over time. People do outgrow one another. That's inevitable. What's important is not to live in fear that your relationship is so fragile that you have to avoid or ignore changes in who you and your partner are. Instead, both partners in a relationship should do their best to accept changes and development in the relationship as a part of life.

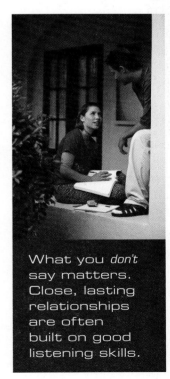

What you *don't* say matters. Close, lasting relationships are often built on good listening skills.

Communicating in Relationships

Communicating well in personal relationships is a blend of talking and listening. Not only does it help to do both well, it is also important to know when it's time to listen and when it's time to speak up. Listening is an often overlooked skill in personal relationships. We may be so busy trying to communicate our feelings and interests that we overlook the need of the other person to be heard. As friendships develop into personal relationships, simply talking isn't enough. How you express yourself, especially in moments of difficulty, can be very important to getting your message across.

Being a Good Listener: The Power of Supportive Silence

When it comes to building relationships, how you listen is often much more important than what you say. The silence involved in listening is a powerful force, one that can bind us more closely to others.

Later in Chapter 7, we will discuss the art and science of listening as it applies to academic success. The same principles that promote learning about lecture topics also promote learning about our friends. You can't call yourself a good friend without knowing what others are like and what they are thinking. Good listening is one of the ways to enhance your understanding of others.

> "Maybe the single most important thing I have learned is that I don't need to become friends with every one out there."
>
> Alicia Fuchs, Student, Trinity Western University

When we are heard, we appreciate it because we get the message that our listeners care about us, not just about themselves. Similarly, when we listen, we show that we have respect for those who are speaking, are interested in their ideas and beliefs, and are willing to take the time to pay attention to them.

You can improve your ability to listen in five ways:

1. **Stop talking!** Are you the kind of person who revels in telling stories about what happened to you? Do you wait eagerly for others to finish what they are saying so that you can jump in with a response? Do you even accidentally cut other people off or finish their sentences while they are speaking?

   No one likes to be interrupted, even in casual conversation. In more personal relationships, it really is a sign of not respecting what the other person has to say and, thus, is disrespectful of *them*.

   One way to break the habit of overtalking is to consciously slow the conversation down. Wait several seconds (mentally count to three) before making a response.

2. **Demonstrate that you are listening.** Linguists call them "conversational markers"—those nonverbal indications that we're listening. They consist of head nods, uh-huh's, okay's, and other signs that we're keeping up with the conversation. Eye contact is important too. Listening this way shows that we're paying attention and are interested in what the other person is saying.

3. **Use reflective feedback.** Carl Rogers,[1] a respected therapist, developed a very useful way to lend support to someone and draw him or her out. In **reflective feedback,** a listener rephrases what a speaker has said, trying to echo the speaker's meaning. For example, a listener might say, "as I

Reflective feedback

A technique of verbal listening in which a listener rephrases what a speaker has said, trying to echo the speaker's meaning understand what you're saying . . . ," or "you seem to feel that . . . ," or "in other words, you believe that . . . ."

In each case, the summary statement doesn't just "play back" the speaker's statements literally. Instead, it is a rephrasing that captures the essence of the message in different words.

Reflective feedback has two big benefits. First, it provides speakers with a clear indication that you are listening and taking what they're saying seriously. Second, and equally important, it helps ensure that you have an accurate understanding of what the speaker is saying. If your reflective feedback is inaccurate, you can be certain that the speaker will attempt to correct your erroneous impression.

4. **Ask questions.** Asking questions shows that you are paying attention to a speaker's comments. Questions permit you to clarify what the speaker has said, and they can move the conversation forward. Further, people feel valued when others ask them about themselves.

5. **Admit when you're distracted.** We've all had those moments: Something is bothering you and you can't get it out of your mind, or you've simply got to finish something and don't really have time to chat. If at the same time someone wants to engage you in conversation, your distraction will undoubtedly show, making the other person feel you are not interested in her or him.

The way to deal with this situation is to admit that you're distracted. Simply saying, "I'd love to talk, but I've got to finish reading a chapter" is enough to explain the situation to a classmate who wants to talk about his date. If you don't say anything, you will probably feel resentment, anger, or some other negative emotion, which will surely be conveyed to your friend.

Loneliness

Loneliness is a subjective state. We can be totally alone and not feel lonely, or we can be in the midst of a crowd and feel lonely. Loneliness occurs when we don't experience the level of connection with others that we desire. There are also different types of loneliness. Some of us feel lonely because we lack a deep emotional attachment to a single person, which can occur even if we have many friends. Others feel loneliness because they believe they don't have enough friends or relatives.

Although people may feel lonely because they have an insufficient number of relationships, the reality is that no standard indicates the "right" number of relationships. Is it enough to have one or two close friends? Does having many acquaintances replace having a single, enduring, close relationship? Obviously, there are no hard-and-fast rules, and you shouldn't think that there's a single standard against which to measure yourself and the number, and kind, of relationships that you have. It's something you need to decide.

What is clear is that certain situations produce loneliness. First-year college and university students almost always report higher degrees of loneliness than students in subsequent years of study. Feeling socially connected at school is important for student success.

Loneliness

A subjective state in which people do not experience a desired level of connection with others

Loneliness is not inevitable. Several strategies for dealing with loneliness follow:

- **Become involved in campus activities.** Join a club. Volunteer to help some social organization. Try out for a play. You'll soon get to know others who have similar interests.

- **Find a study partner.** Ask one of your classmates to study with you. You can review your class notes, work together on a project, or study for tests together. Working together will not only help you to master the class material, it will also help you make what can become an important social connection.

Participating in campus activities is a good way to meet people with similar interests and to avoid the loneliness that is sometimes a part of college or university life.

- **Understand how certain circumstances lend themselves to feeling lonely.** Why are first-year students lonely? It's because they haven't had time to meet people and become well-enough acquainted with anyone to develop a true friendship. Furthermore, many of the people whom they may have relied on previously are no longer present. The combination of no new friends and unavailable old friends can easily lead to loneliness. Simply knowing the reasons for your loneliness can help you deal with it.

- **Know that you're not alone in your loneliness.** If you're feeling lonely, you may find yourself looking at your classmates and noticing groups of people engaged in social activities. This can make you feel even more isolated. Don't be fooled by such social illusions into believing that you are the only one experiencing loneliness. Remember that for every person you notice who is socializing, there are others who are not doing so.

- **Take advantage of orientation and first-year student social events.** Even if you don't consider yourself particularly good at socializing, it's important to make the effort. If you're shy—and even if you're not—consider it a social success if you meet just one new person at such an event.

- **Take a job on campus.** Campus jobs not only provide income, but social connections as well. Through work you can meet members of the college or university staff and make connections with other students.

- **Remember that loneliness is a subjective—and typically temporary—state.** Whether you experience isolation depends on how you interpret your current state. If you interpret your feelings of isolation as due to your personal failings ("I'm alone because I'm not a very likable or interesting person"), you'll experience loneliness. If you view your isolation as a consequence of temporary, short-term factors ("Everyone has a lot of work this semester and few opportunities to socialize"), you're less likely to feel loneliness. In short, try to pinpoint why you're feeling lonely, and don't blame yourself for your sense of loneliness.

What if your feelings of loneliness are extreme and you experience a sense of complete isolation and alienation from your classmates? If the feeling persists, it's wise to talk to someone at your campus counselling centre, a health service provider, or your advisor. Although everyone feels isolated at times, such feelings shouldn't be extreme. Counsellors can help you deal with them.

It's Not Just Talk: Avoiding and Handling Conflicts in Relationships

Listening communicates a great deal in personal relationships, but, as discussed previously, it is also important to put yourself forward. Generally, close relationships are built on good communication, so day-to-day there may be no problem in this regard. But when misunderstandings or conflicts occur—as they definitely will from time to time—communication can fall apart. In these situations your ability to communicate in words is tested, and more-sensitive listening and more-careful ways of saying what you think and feel are needed.

The Subject Is "I," and Not "You" Suppose a close friend says something with which you disagree: "All you guys are the same—you expect to get everything your way!" You might respond by directing anger at the other person, directly or indirectly accusing them of some imperfection. "You never have any ideas! You're just looking for something to complain about!" Such responses (and, as you will notice, the initial statement) typically include the word *you*. Consider these possible responses to indicate disagreement: *"You* really don't understand"; *"You're* being stubborn"; and "How can *you* say that?"

The problem with such statements is that each includes the word you, putting the speaker on the defensive. These types of statements cast blame, make accusations, express criticism, and make assumptions about what's inside the other person's head. And they lead to defensive replies that will probably do little to move the conversation forward: "I do so understand"; "I'm not being stubborn"; and "I can say that because that's the way I feel."

A far more reasonable tactic is to use "I" statements. **"I" statements** cast responses in terms of yourself and your individual interpretation. Instead of saying, for example, "You really don't understand," a more appropriate response would be, "I feel we have a misunderstanding." "You're being stubborn" could be rephrased as "I feel as though you're acting in a stubborn way." And "how can you say that" becomes "I don't understand why you're saying that." In each case, "I" statements permit you to state your reaction in terms of your perception or understanding, rather than as a critical judgment about the other person. (Practise using "I" statements in Try It! 2, "Switch 'You' to 'I'.")

"I" statements
Statements that cast responses in terms of yourself and your individual interpretation

Resolving Conflict: A Win–Win Proposition Even with careful attention to putting our own feelings forward instead of making accusations, whenever two people share their thoughts, concerns, fears, and honest reactions with each other, the chances are that sooner or later some sort of conflict will arise.

Conflict is not necessarily bad.

Often, people are upset simply by the fact that they are having a conflict. It is as though they believe conflicts don't occur in "good" relationships. In fact, conflict is helpful in some very important ways. It can force us to say what is really on our minds. It can allow us to clear up misconceptions and miscommunications before they begin to undermine the relationship. It can even give us practice at resolving conflicts with others with whom we might not share such good relations.

Like anything else, though, there are good ways to resolve conflict, and there are bad ways. Good ways move people forward, defining the problem and promoting creative problem solving. Bad ways make the situation

⚐ Working in a Group
Switch "You" to "I"

Prepare: Learn how to turn "you" statements into "I" statements.

Organize: Use the list of statements provided, but add your own examples if you wish.

Work: Work in pairs to convert each statement into a less aggressive "I" statement. Say the statement out loud to hear how it sounds.

Evaluate: Were you able to complete the task?

Rethink: How often do you use "you" statements that tend to promote conflict?

You Statements

1. You just don't get it, do you?

2. You never listen to what I say.

3. You don't really believe that, do you?

4. You never try to see my point of view.

6. Please stop interrupting me and listen to what I'm saying for a change.

7. Stop changing the subject!

8. You're not making sense.

9. You keep distorting what I say until I don't even know what point I'm trying to make.

10. You use too many "you" statements. Use more "I" statements when you're talking to others.

worse, driving people apart rather than bringing them together. The following are some fundamental principles of conflict resolution that you can use when conflict occurs in personal and professional relationships:

- **Stop, look, and listen.** In the heat of an argument, all sorts of things that otherwise would go unsaid get said. If you find yourself making rash or hurtful statements, stop, look at yourself, and listen to what you and the other person are saying.

  Stopping works like a circuit breaker that prevents a short circuit from causing a deadly fire. You've probably heard about counting to 10 when you are angry. Do it. Take a break and count to 10 . . . or 20 . . . or more. Whether you count to 10 or 100, stopping the action gives you time to think and not to just react.

- **Defuse the argument.** Anger is not an emotion that encourages rational discourse. When you're angry and annoyed with someone, you're not in the best position to evaluate logically the merits of various arguments or excuses others may offer. It may feel exhilarating to get our fury off our chests in the heat of an argument, but you can bet it isn't taking anyone any closer to resolving the problem.

Don't assume that you are 100 percent right and the other person is 100 percent wrong. Make your goal *solving the problem* rather than winning the argument.

- **Share responsibility.** Perhaps you've heard others suggest that you should avoid getting personal in an argument. In one sense that's true: You don't want to accuse people you're arguing with of having character flaws that make some aspect of their behaviour unacceptable.

  At the same time, you should be willing to admit personal responsibility for at least part of the conflict. The conflict would not exist without you, so you need to accept that the argument has two sides and that you are not automatically blameless.

- **Listen to the real message.** When people argue, what they say is often not the real message. There's typically an underlying communication—a meta-message—that is the source of the conflict.

  It's important, then, to dig beneath what you're hearing. If someone accuses you of being selfish, the real meaning hidden in the accusation may be that you don't give anyone else a chance to make decisions. Remember, arguments are usually about behaviour, not underlying character and personality. What people *do* is not necessarily synonymous with what they *are*.

  If you rephrase the person's statement in your own mind, it moves from an insult ("You're a bad person") to a request for a change of behaviour ("Let me participate in decision making"). You're much more likely to respond reasonably when you don't feel that your personal essence is under attack.

- **Show that you're listening.** It's not enough only to listen to the underlying message that someone is conveying. You also need to acknowledge the message. For example, saying something like "Okay, I can tell you are concerned about sharing the work/the responsibility on our group project, and I think we should talk about it" acknowledges that you see the issue and admit that it is worthy of discussion. This is a far more successful strategy than firing back a countercharge each time your partner makes a complaint.

- **If you are angry, acknowledge it.** Don't pretend that everything is fine if it isn't. Ultimately, relationships in which the partners bottle up their anger suffer more than those in which the partners express their true feelings. If you're angry, say so.

- **Ask for clarification.** As you're listening to another person's arguments, check your understanding of what is being said. Don't assume that you know what's intended. Saying something like "Are you saying . . ." or "Do you mean that . . ." is a way of verifying that what you *think* someone means is really what is meant.

- **Make your requests explicit.** If you're upset that your roommate leaves clothes lying around your apartment or dorm room, remarking that he or she is a "pig" shows more than that you are angry. It also shows that your intent is to hurt rather than to solve the problem.

  It's far better to be explicit in your concerns. Say something like "It would make me feel better if you would pick up your clothes from the floor." Couching your concern in this way changes the focus of the message from your roommate's personality to a specific behaviour that potentially can be changed.

• **Always remember that life is not a zero-sum game.** Many of us act as if life were a **zero-sum game,** a situation in which when one person wins, the other person automatically loses. It's what happens when you make a bet: If one person wins the bet, the other person loses.

Life is not like that. If one person wins an argument, it doesn't mean that others automatically have to lose it. And if someone loses an argument, it doesn't mean that others have automatically won. In fact, all too often conflict escalates so much that the argument turns into a lose–lose situation.

However, life can be a win–win situation. The best resolution of conflict occurs when both parties walk away with something they want. Each may not have achieved *every* goal they had, but they at least have enough to feel satisfied. (For practice in resolving conflict, do Try It! 3, "Resolve That Conflict.")

Getting Along With Difficult People

Do you have people in your life who seem difficult to get along with or even just talk to? Everyone can identify someone who it is difficult to deal with on a daily basis whether it is someone they work with, someone they share an apartment with, a family member, or even their boss at work.

A difficult person is someone who makes it hard for you to accomplish your purpose or your goals. What can you do to make these relationships more effective?

1. Follow the guidelines in this chapter for building and maintaining relationships. The goal is to make sure you are part of the solution not part of the problem.
2. Try hard not to take things that happen personally. They are seldom meant that way. More often you just happen to be there.
3. Seek understanding of the other person. Try to put yourself in their shoes. What upsets them? What do they expect? How do they communicate?
4. If you can't shrug it off, talk about how the problem behaviour affects you and what might work better for you.
5. Be willing to meet the other person halfway.
6. Understand when you have done what you can for now. Be polite. Leave the door open.

Changing Relationships: Surviving Endings

Not all relationships last a lifetime. Sometimes they just wind down, as the two people involved slowly lose interest in maintaining their partnership. At other times, they break apart, as disagreements build and there is not a strong enough bond to hold the two parties together. Or there may be an abrupt rupture if some event occurs that destroys one partner's feeling of trust.

Caring for others is rewarding, but risky. When relationships don't work out, their endings can be painful, even devastating, for a time. Even when relationships evolve naturally, and change is expected, the transformation in a relationship may not be easy. Couples break up. Best friends grow apart. Parents die. Children grow up and move away from home. Siblings get new jobs on the other side of the country.

Resolve That Conflict

Prepare: Identify words and phrases that lead to conflict and suggest changes that would be less confrontational.

Organize: Use the common sources of conflict and the principles of conflict resolution described in the previous pages.

Work: As an individual or as a group complete the task.

Evaluate: Were you able to achieve the task objective? If not, what would be required?

Rethink: Can you think of ways you could change some of your words and your behaviour to be less confrontational?

Shira: I'd like to run the women's basketball conference finals article as the lead story on this week's sports page.

Todd: Wait a minute. Women's basketball doesn't precede men's basketball. We always lead with the men's team.

Sara: Yeah, and the NBA and even the NHL are mentioned before women's sports. The Lions are in the conference finals, and the men's game this week is meaningless.

Dushan: Meaningless? There'll be 200 more fans at the men's game than at the girls' game.

Shira: That's *women's game*! Well, that's partly the problem. With the women's sports columns stuck after NASCAR racing and the World Wrestling Entertainment (WWE), who can find out about how well our teams are doing?

Sara: I agree! And you know men's teams are funded like, 10 times more than women's—they can't afford to advertise like the guys can. With such little publicity, the women's team hasn't drawn as many supporters, but now we're in the finals ... I think the school paper should lead the way in raising the profile of women's sports.

Dushan: You never pass up a chance to complain about the WWE. Why don't you get it? Guys *like* the WWE and they *like* to read columns about racing. Kevin Bidwell is gonna croak if I give him the ladies' game as his assignment this weekend.

Shira: Why don't *you* get it? The last I heard, female students' tuitions paid for this paper too! More than 50 percent of the students here are female, but 85 percent of the writers and editorial staff are male. That's why the coverage is so biased! Why not let one of us write the article? Why does Kevin always get the big story? What Sara and I say has no weight when you male editors wield all the power here!

Todd: How about reason A: your familiarity with sports jargon is severely limited, and B: Kevin is the sports editor, and his stories always lead. That's the way it works around here. If you don't like it, you can always go to student council.

Shira: Oh, right. As if Kyle Douglas is going to listen to us. Student council is no better than here. Only the VP for internal affairs is female; everyone else is male. This place is a bastion for male, hierarchical thinking.

Dushan: Whoa, Nellie McClung. Haven't you heard that feminism is dead? Expired. Deceased. Finito. Next item on the agenda?

Can you think of several approaches for resolving each of the various conflicts? Which of the resolution possibilities you've devised do you think would work best? Are there any approaches that should be avoided?

One sure cure exists for the heartache of a lost relationship: time. You can do some other things, however, as you wait for time to pass and for the pain to ease:

1. **Do something—anything.** Mow the lawn, clean out the closets, go for a run, or see a movie. It won't completely get your mind off your loss, but it beats languishing on your bed, thinking about what you might have done differently or what could have been.

2. **Accept that you feel bad.** If you're not experiencing unhappiness over the end of a relationship, it means that the relationship wasn't terribly meaningful in the first place. Understand that unhappiness normally accompanies the end of a relationship, and allow yourself some satisfaction over the fact that you were able to maintain a relationship that, at least at one point, was meaningful.

3. **Talk to a friend or relative.** Talking about your sadness will help you to deal with it better. Other people can help you feel better about yourself, offer different perspectives, and simply support you by listening. Make use of your network of existing relationships to get you through a difficult period.

4. **Write about the relationship.** If you have a journal, writing about the relationship and its aftermath can be therapeutic. You can say whatever you want without fear of being contradicted.

5. **Talk to a professional.** If your sadness over a relationship feels totally overwhelming or continues for what you perceive to be too long a time, talk to a counsellor or other professional. He or she can help you gain a better understanding of the situation and perhaps help you understand why you are taking it so hard. And remember that, ultimately, the pain *will* disappear: Time does heal most wounds.

Becoming Comfortable in a Multicultural, Diverse World

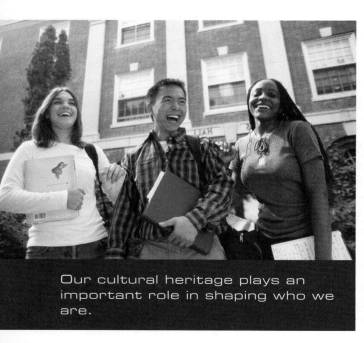

Our cultural heritage plays an important role in shaping who we are.

No matter where we live, our contacts with others who are racially, ethnically, religiously, and physically different from us are increasing. The Internet and World Wide Web are bringing people from across the globe into our homes, as close to us as the computer sitting on our desk. Businesses now operate globally, so coworkers are likely to come from many different countries and cultures. Being comfortable with people whose backgrounds and beliefs differ from our own is not only a social necessity, but it is also virtually a requirement for career success.

Canada has the most culturally diverse population in the world. Noted author and commentator Gwynne Dyer declares, "Canada is becoming the world in one country."[2] He states that Canada's current immigration patterns mirror the distribution of the global population, with 25 percent of immigrants coming from East Asia, 25 percent from South and Southeast Asia, 10 percent from the Middle East, 10 percent from Africa and the Caribbean,

10 percent from Latin America, and about 20 percent from Europe and the United States. University and college enrollments reflect these changes, especially in large cities like Toronto, Montreal, and Vancouver. For example, visible minorities have grown from 3 percent of the population of Toronto to more than 50 percent in the past 30 years.

Race, Ethnicity, and Culture

Are you black or African-Canadian? Caucasian or white or Euro-Canadian? Salvadoran-Canadian or Latino? Native Canadian or Aboriginal? or are you like Tiger Woods?

Cablinasian. That's the word coined by star golfer Tiger Woods to describe his racial heritage. "Cablinasian" means a mix of Caucasian, Black, Indian, and Asian, and it was a label he didn't find on forms asking for his racial identity when he began college.

But Woods did not want to fit himself into some arbitrary racial category. His mother is from Thailand and his father was African-American, and none of the standard racial categories were appropriate to describe him.

But to Woods, it didn't matter. His background is less important than who he is now and where he is going in the future. "I'm just who I am," he told one interviewer, "whoever you see in front of you."[3]

Whether you have skin that is black or white or brown, are Jewish or Muslim or Greek Orthodox, were born in Calgary or Vietnam or Bosnia, are able-bodied or have a disability, higher education presents new opportunities with regard to diversity and your relationships with others. Because almost every postsecondary institution draws students from a wider sphere than the average high school, college or university permits you to encounter people with very different backgrounds from your own. If you take the opportunity to form relationships with a wide variety of individuals, you will stretch your understanding of the human experience and enrich your life.

One of the difficulties in understanding diversity is that many of the terms we use are ill defined and often are overlapping. The term **race** is generally used to refer to obvious physical differences that set one group apart from others. According to such a definition, whites, blacks, and Asian-Canadians are typically thought of as different races, determined largely by biological factors.

Ethnicity refers to shared national origins or cultural patterns. In Canada, for example, Ukrainian-, Irish-, and Italian-Canadians are categorized as ethnic groups. However, ethnicity—like race—is very much in the eye of the beholder. For instance, an Indo-Canadian who is a third-generation citizen of Canada may feel few ties or associations to India. Yet whites may view her as "South Asian."

Finally, **culture** comprises the learned behaviours, beliefs, and attitudes that are characteristic of an individual society or population. Culture also encompasses the products that people create, such as architecture, music, art, and literature. Culture is created and shaped by people, but at the same time it creates and shapes people's behaviour.

Race, ethnicity, and culture shape each of us to an enormous degree. They profoundly influence our view of others, as well as who we are. They affect how others treat us, and how we treat them in turn. They determine whether we look people in the eye when we meet them, how early we arrive when we're invited to dinner at a friend's house, and even, sometimes, how well we do in school.

Race

Biologically determined physical characteristics that distinguish one group from another

Ethnicity

Shared national origins or cultural patterns

Culture

The learned behaviours, beliefs, and attitudes—as well as the products people create—that are characteristic of an individual society or population

Building Cultural Competence

Cultural competence
Knowledge and understanding about other races, ethnic groups, cultures, and minority groups

We're not born knowing how to drive a car or cook. We have to learn how to do these things. The same is true of developing a basic understanding of other races, ethnic groups, cultures, and minority groups. Called **cultural competence,** this knowledge of others' customs, perspectives, background, and history can also teach us a great deal about ourselves.

The building of cultural competence proceeds in several steps, as outlined in the P.O.W.E.R. Plan to the left.

Prepare: Accepting Multiculturalism and Diversity as a Valued Part of Your Life

PREPARE
Accept diversity as a valued part of your life

ORGANIZE
Explore your own prejudices and stereotypes

WORK
Develop cultural competence

EVALUATE
Check your progress in attaining cultural competence

RETHINK
Understand how your own racial, ethnic, and cultural background affects others

P.O.W.E.R. Plan

In the title of her book on social diversity, psychologist Beverly Tatum asks, *Why Are All the Black Kids Sitting Together in the Cafeteria?*[4] She might just as well have asked a similar question about the white kids, the Chinese-Canadian kids, and so forth. It often appears as if the world comes already divided into separate racial, ethnic, and cultural groups.

It's more than appearances. We form relationships more easily with others who are similar to us than with those who are different. It's easier to interact with others who look the same as we do, who come from similar backgrounds, and who share our race, ethnicity, and culture because we can take for granted certain shared cultural assumptions and views of the world.

But this doesn't mean that easy and comfortable are good. We can learn a great deal more, and grow and be challenged, if we seek out people who are different from us. If you look beyond surface differences and find out what motivates other people, you can become aware of ways of thinking about family, relationships, earning a living, and the value of education that are very different from your own. It can be liberating to realize that others may hold very different perspectives from your own and that there are many ways to lead your life.

Letting diversity into your own life may not be simple or easy, but it's incredibly helpful in and important to achieving your own growth and understanding. Understanding diversity also has very practical implications: As we discuss in Career Connections, "Cultural Competence in the Workplace," learning to accept and work with people who are different from you is a crucial skill that will help you in whatever job you hold.

Organize: Exploring Your Own Prejudices and Stereotypes

Arab, lesbian, African-Canadian, tattooed, female—quick: What comes into your mind when you think about each of these labels? If you're like most people, you

Career Connections

Cultural Competence in the Workplace

Cross-cultural issues are a part of Canada's workplaces.[5] Employers must deal with issues ranging from arranging a private space for Muslim employees to pray to deciding whether the partner of a gay or lesbian worker should be covered by the worker's benefit insurance.

The gulf in the workplace between people with different cultural backgrounds may be wide. For instance, in Japan, the cultural expectation is that people should stress their incompetence; for a new immigrant, having to outline his or her accomplishments in a job interview would be considered highly immodest.

Canada requires immigration for its population to grow since our birth rate is very low. In addition, Canada needs more skilled workers to have enough replacements for retiring baby boomers.

The increasingly diverse and multicultural Canadian workplace means that increasing your cultural competence is necessary. It will help you perform on work-group teams that comprise people of different races and ethnic backgrounds; it will help you supervise people whose native language and customs may be different from yours; and it will help you to work for a boss from another country and cultural background.

Photonics is the science of harnessing light at a microscopic level to make communication networks more efficient. It is an emerging trillion-dollar industry, and it has a critical shortage of trained personnel. Photonics Research Ontario says Canada does not have the capacity to produce enough skilled workers to meet demands. Currently Eastern European universities produce the most capable graduates, but since it takes two years or more for skilled workers to immigrate to Canada independently, shortages still exist. Therefore, Canadian businesses are urging the government to speed up the process, allowing more skilled workers into Canada to fill job vacancies.

don't draw a blank. Instead, a collection of images and feelings comes into your mind, based on what you know, have been told, or assume about the group.

The fact that we don't draw a blank when thinking about each of these terms means that we already have a set of attitudes and beliefs about them and the groups they represent. Acknowledging and then examining these preexisting assumptions is a first step toward developing cultural competence. We need to explore our own prejudices and stereotypes to know where we're starting from.

Prejudice refers to evaluations or judgments of members of a group that are based primarily on membership in the group, rather than on an individual's particular characteristics. For example, the auto mechanic who doesn't expect a woman to understand the repair he is undertaking or the supervisor who finds it unthinkable that a father might want to take childcare leave are engaging in gender prejudice, evaluating individuals based on their being male or female and not on their own specific characteristics or abilities. Similarly, prejudice can be directed toward individuals because of their race, ethnic origin, sexual orientation, age, physical disability, or even degree of physical attractiveness.

Prejudice is maintained by **stereotypes,** beliefs and expectations about members of a group that are held simply because of their membership in the group. For example, do you think that women don't drive as well as men? Do you agree that "white men can't jump"? Do you believe that people raised in the jungles of South America are less intelligent than those raised in a Western society? Do you think

Prejudice

Evaluations or judgments of members of a group that are based primarily on membership in the group, and not on the particular characteristics of individuals

Stereotypes

Beliefs and expectations about members of a group that are held simply because of their membership in the group that people on welfare are lazy? If you answered yes to any of these questions, you hold stereotypes about the group being referred to. It is the degree of generalization involved that makes stereotypes inaccurate. Some white men *can't* jump. But the fact is, many can—and do—and the stereotypes ignore this diversity.

To develop cultural competence, it's important to identify our prejudices and stereotypes and to fight them. Sometimes they are quite subtle and difficult to detect. For instance, a wealth of data taken from observation of elementary school classrooms shows that teachers often are more responsive to boys than to girls. The teachers don't know they're doing it; it's a subtle, but very real, bias.

Why does this happen? In part it's because we're exposed to stereotypes from a very young age. Parents and relatives teach them to us, sometimes unwittingly, sometimes on purpose. The media illustrate them constantly, and often in very subtle ways. For instance, African-Canadians and Aboriginal people are often portrayed as unemployed or as criminals, and women are less likely than men to be shown as employed.

But it's not only stereotypes that lead us to view members of other groups differently from those of our own. For most people, their own membership in a cultural or racial or ethnic group is a source of pride and self-worth. There's nothing wrong with this. However, these feelings can lead to a less desirable outcome: the belief that their own group is superior to others. As a result, people inflate the positive aspects of their own group and belittle groups to which they do not belong. The bottom line is continuing prejudice.

To overcome stereotypes and to develop cultural competence, we must first explore and identify our prejudices. To begin that process, complete Try It! 4, "Check Your Stereotype Quotient."

Journal REFLECTIONS

Thinking about Race, Ethnicity, and Culture

1. How do you feel about living in a diverse culture?

2. Was diversity discussed in your family? In what ways?

3. How has race or ethnicity affected your schooling?

4. How has race or ethnicity affected your friendships and social life?

5. If you are a member of a majority group, imagine yourself as a member of a minority group. In what ways would your childhood and adolescence have been different? If you are a member of a minority group, perform this exercise in reverse.

6. Are you proud of your ethnicity? Why? What traces of ethnicity do you show?

7. What are some cultural differences between you and members of *other* races or ethnicities?

8. How many "cultures" can you identify among your fellow students? Among your friends?

9. Have you taken steps to learn more about persons of another race, ethnicity, or culture? What steps might you take in the future?

Check Your Stereotype Quotient

Prepare: Identify your tendency to use stereotyping.

Organize: Use the nine questions provided here and your own experience.

Work: As an individual or as a group answer the questions provided.

Evaluate: Were you able to identify circumstances where you are likely to use stereotyping?

Rethink: Can you think of ways you could reduce or eliminate your tendency to use stereotyping?

1. When you see five African-Canadian students sitting together in the cafeteria, do you think that they are exhibiting racism? How is your reaction similar or different when you see five white students sitting together in the cafeteria?

2. When you are speaking with a person who has a speech-related disorder such as stuttering, are you likely to conclude that the person is less intelligent than a fluent speaker?

3. When an elderly woman can't remember something, do you assume her forgetfulness is because she is old or perhaps has Alzheimer's disease?

4. When an attractive blonde female student states an opinion in class, are you surprised if the opinion is intelligent and well expressed?

5. If a person with a mobility disorder turns down your offer for assistance, would you be offended and resentful?

6. When you meet a student with a Vietnamese or Chinese last name, are you surprised if he or she speaks fluent, unaccented Canadian English?

7. When an African-Canadian student whom you don't know joins an athletic team you're on, are you happy because you believe he or she will be a good athlete?

8. If you see a group of three large males walking toward you in the distance at night, are you more nervous if they're members of a different race from yours than if they're members of your own race?

9. If a male student and a female student each ask you the same question about a technical topic you understand thoroughly, do you respond differently or in the exact same way?

Do you think you would have answered any of these questions differently five years ago? Do you think you will answer any of them differently five years from now? What experiences would make you change your responses?

Working in a group, compare your responses with those of your classmates. What similarities and differences do you see? Do you have the sense, not just from this exercise but from your general experience, that stereotypes are still prevalent?

Work: Developing Cultural Competence

Although it's neither easy nor simple to increase your understanding of and sensitivity to other cultures, it can be done. Several strategies are effective:

- **Study other cultures and customs.** Take an anthropology course, study religion, or learn history. If you understand the purposes behind different cultural customs, attitudes, and beliefs, you will be able to understand the richness and meaning of other people's cultural heritage.

  Many colleges and universities offer workshops on multiculturalism, diversity, and prejudice reduction. Student religious groups and ethnic associations and clubs often hold open houses, discussions, and celebrations and invite all interested people to attend. These can help too. The important point is that understanding comes from knowledge, and you won't be able to fully appreciate others without learning about their background.

> "We also know that racial discrimination is perhaps the epitome of human indignity and that if we tolerate it even privately—in our own hearts—then we have diminished our own stature."
>
> Pierre Trudeau

- **Travel.** There is no better way to learn about people from other cultures than to see those cultures firsthand. College and university vacations offer you the time to travel, and relatively inexpensive charter flights can take you to Europe, Asia, and other places around the globe. Sometimes, in fact, it's cheaper to take a transoceanic flight than to travel to closer locations within Canada.

  If you can't afford airfare, take a car or bus ride to the United States or Mexico. Travel need not be international, however. If you are from the Atlantic provinces, head west. If you are from British Columbia or Alberta, consider heading east. A visit to Quebec can be an eye-opening and culturally enriching experience, whether you choose to visit the bright lights of Montreal or the relative quiet of Trois-Pistoles. No matter where you go, simply finding yourself away from home can aid your efforts to learn about other cultures by putting you in a new context.

- **Don't ignore people's backgrounds.** None of us is blind to a person's colour, or blind to ethnicity, or to culture. It's impossible to be completely unaffected by people's racial, ethnic, religious, and cultural backgrounds. So why pretend to be? Cultural heritage is an important part of other people's identity, and to pretend that their background doesn't exist and has no impact on them is unrealistic at best, and insulting at worst. It's important, though, to distinguish between accepting the fact that other people's backgrounds affect them and pigeonholing people and expecting them to behave in particular ways.

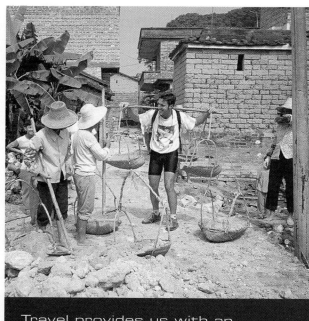

Travel provides us with an opportunity to become immersed in very different cultures and to see the world—and ourselves—through different eyes.

- **Don't treat people as representatives of the groups to which they belong.** If you're a member of a minority group, you've probably been asked how members of your group think, feel, or behave with respect to a particular issue. Somehow, as a member of the group, you're expected to know how every other member feels about a topic.

"...all individuals should have an equal opportunity to make for themselves the lives that they are able and wish to have, consistent with their duties and obligations as members of society..."

Canadian Human Rights Act

Of course, that's impossible; no single individual can speak for an entire group. Furthermore, group members are likely to display little uniformity on most issues and in most behaviours, and so this type of question is ultimately impossible to answer. In short, it makes little sense to treat others as if they were representatives of the racial, ethnic, religious, or cultural group to which they belong.

- **Accept differences.** Different does not mean better. Different does not mean worse. Different just means not looking, acting, or believing exactly the same as you. We shouldn't attach any kind of value to being different; it's neither better nor worse than being similar.

Even people who seem obviously different on the surface probably share many similarities with you. Like you, they are students; they have fears and anxieties like yours; and they have aspirations and dreams, just as you do.

The important point about differences is that we need to accept them. All people want to be accepted for who they are—their abilities and talents, their attitudes and beliefs, their interests and accomplishments—not just because they are similar to you. In Canada, individuals are protected by federal and provincial legislation against discrimination. The idea behind human rights legislation is that people should not be placed at a disadvantage because of their age, sex, race, religion, or other grounds covered by federal and provincial Acts.

E valuate: Checking Your Progress in Attaining Cultural Competence

Because cultural groups are constantly changing, developing cultural competence is an ongoing process. To evaluate where you stand, ask yourself the following questions:

- Do I make judgments about others based on external features, such as skin colour, ethnic background, religious attire, cultural customs, gender, weight, or physical appearance?
- Who are my friends? Do they represent diversity or are they generally similar to me?
- Do I openly express positive values relating to diversity? Do I sit back passively when others express stereotypes and prejudices, or do I actively question their remarks?
- Am I educating myself about the history and varying experiences of different racial, ethnic, religious, and cultural groups?
- Do I give special treatment to members of particular groups, or am I evenhanded in my relationships?

- Do I recognize that, despite surface differences, all people have the same basic needs?
- Do I feel so much pride in my own racial, ethnic, religious, and cultural heritage that it leads me to look less favourably on members of other groups?
- Do I seek to understand events and situations through the perspectives of others and not just my own?

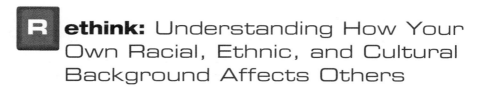

Rethink: Understanding How Your Own Racial, Ethnic, and Cultural Background Affects Others

If you are a member of a minority group, you probably don't need to be told that your race, ethnicity, religious, and cultural background affects the way that others treat you. But even if you are a member of a majority group, the way in which others respond to you is, in part, a result of others' assumptions about the groups of which you are a part.

In short, both how we view others and how we ourselves are viewed are affected by the groups to which we—and others—belong. But keep this in mind. No matter how different other students are from you in terms of their race, ethnicity, religious, and cultural background, they undoubtedly share many of the same concerns you do. Like all of us, they question themselves, wonder whether they will be successful, and fret about what they will do for the rest of their lives. Bridging the surface difference between you and others can result in the development of close, lasting social ties—a topic we consider next.

Working in Groups

Almost all jobs require the ability to work in teams or groups. Employers want people from a variety of technical backgrounds who are able to work together to solve problems and develop new products in groups or teams.

Have you ever had a bad experience working in a group? If so, you are definitely not alone. Most people can talk about wasted time, interpersonal conflicts, people who didn't meet commitments, and feeing that their ideas and suggestions were ignored. It doesn't have to be that way. The following information is designed to help you work in teams more effectively.

Team Dynamics

Teams that work together effectively on an ongoing basis are joined by a common purpose, trust each other, know each other's strengths, learn to deal with each other's personalities, and look beyond the occasional conflict. Most of all, they know how to share and build on each others' ideas. But it takes a while to build an effective team.

According to R.W. Tuckman, there are four stages of team development:[6]

Forming: Team is excited about the task but anxious about the work and the other people on the team. Team is looking for direction and ground rules.

Storming: Work on the task has started and the reality of the work sets in. Members may not understand some work assignments, expectations seem too high, and there is frustration over the challenges of working together.

Members are likely to feel that they would be better off working on their own. It is critical to deal with issues in a positive, constructive way.

Norming: Team members understand they have to work together to get the job done. They begin to develop ground rules as a group and begin using more effective ways of working together. Members are more comfortable expressing and critiquing each other's ideas. Team members begin to share responsibilities for team leadership and effectiveness.

Performing: Team begins really working together to achieve the objective. Members begin to rely on each other to complete tasks. Communication is open and constructive. Members learn and grow together. There is a strong sense of interdependence and camaraderie.

These stages are particularly true of teams where the members don't know each other and the pressure to achieve project expectations is high. There are some teams that never quite get to the Performing stage generally due to a lack of leadership and purpose. Teams may cycle back through a stage or two if there is a new member.

Do these stages seem similar to your own experience? Think of some examples that strengthen your opinion.

The suggestions for building lasting relationships in the next section of this chapter apply to work groups, teams, and individual relationships.

Working in Teams

There are five conditions required for team effectiveness:

1. A clear purpose or objective that is understood and shared by the members. Remember the old saying: "You never have to worry about teamwork in a fire because the purpose is clear."
2. Members need to know their role and responsibility for achieving the team's purpose.
3. Create an atmosphere of trust and collaboration where people expect to be treated with dignity and respect.
4. Ideas are listened to and discussed without penalty for the contribution.
5. The team has the resources required for a reasonable chance of achieving the goal.

What would you add to this list? Is there something that makes a difference in your ability to work effectively in a group?

Conducting Effective Meetings

Students are often required to work together in small groups to complete course assignments. What are some of the things you can do to make your group meetings more effective? The following suggestions will help:

1. Choose a coordinator who can help keep the meeting on track and make sure everyone can contribute.
2. Set a target for the length of the meeting and try to stick to it.
3. Make sure everyone understands the reason for the meeting.
4. Encourage input from all members. Don't let one person dominate the group.

Speaking of Success

Jenny Zhang

International Business, Centennial Community College, Toronto, Ontario

Jenny Zhang is currently studying international business at Centennial College in Toronto. Her long-term goal is to become involved in the growing trade between Canada and China. A recent immigrant from Jiangsu, China, Jenny took one semester of English as a Second Language before passing Centennial College's English test and beginning the International Business program where she studies with English-speaking Canadians as well as with other immigrants and international students. Jenny is enjoying her program and achieving an A average in subjects such as finance, marketing, mathematics of finance, computers, introduction to Canadian business, operations management, and international business.

The biggest challenge in higher education in Canada for Jenny is language,

especially spoken English. She feels her listening has improved since beginning classes in her postsecondary program, but as with many second-language learners, Jenny finds it difficult to practise speaking. Because there are so many group projects and presentations in community college business courses, Jenny is confident that with increased practise, she will achieve more progress. Jenny sometimes gets nervous when making presentations, but has found her professors to be very helpful. She knows that her classmates are a supportive audience and want her and her team members to succeed. In addition, she is very familiar with using presentation software, such as PowerPoint, to enhance her presentations.

Although adjusting to a new country and new culture takes time, Jenny and

her husband are enjoying their new life in Canada. Jenny says her International Business courses are much more practical and useful for her career. And she says she is confident about overcoming adjustment difficulties in her schooling and life in Canada. Her advice for other new Canadian postsecondary students is to have a career goal. She recommends that students know why they are studying and what they will do in the future; in that way education is more meaningful. In addition, she encourages students whose first language is not English to get active and to enjoy their new lives in Canada. Jenny says if people are enjoying themselves, their learning will be better.

5. Make notes about any decisions and assignments including due dates.

6. Summarize conclusions, decisions, or key points.

7. Debrief the meeting to look for improvements.

8. Thank people for their participation.

Looking ◀◀ Back

How can you build working relationships, listen effectively, and resolve conflicts?

- The ability to build and maintain relationships is an essential skill according to many employers and is a vital component of college success.

- The central components of good relationships are trust, honesty, mutual support, loyalty, acceptance, and a willingness to embrace change.

- Listening is an important skill for relationship building, demonstrating that the listener really cares about the other person.

- Conflict is inevitable in relationships, and sometimes it is useful because it permits us to clear up misconceptions and miscommunications before they escalate.

- Although the end of a relationship can be very painful, the pain does subside over time.

Why is the increasing racial, ethnic, and multicultural diversity of society important to you?

- The multiculturalism and diversity of Canada—and of Canadian campuses—is increasing rapidly, and the world is becoming closer as television, radio, the Internet, the World Wide Web, and international commerce bring other peoples and cultures into our lives, and vice versa.

- Being aware of diversity can allow you to accept the challenge and opportunity of living and working with others who are very different.

How can you become more at ease with differences and diversity?

- Learn to accept even embrace diversity and deal with your own prejudices and stereotypes to work effectively in our diverse society.

P.O.W.E.R. Portfolio

Getting Along with Others

1. Consider including any evidence of skill or training in conflict resolution, multicultural education, peer mediation, justice circle involvement, or diversity awareness workshops. Evidence could include certificates, photographs, brochures, letters, or notes taken during courses. Include a reflective passage to indicate your understanding and learning.

2. Do in-depth research on a Canadian who has succeeded despite physical or social barriers, for example, Rick Hansen, Susan Aglukark, Tomson

Highway, Milton Acorn, or Jeff Healey. In doing so, try to focus on what qualities that individual has that have contributed to his or her success. What have you learned about yourself because of this research?

3. Reflect on the multicultural diversity at your school and do an "environmental scan." Is there room for improvement? What ideas do you have to create change for the better? Are there groups or individuals deserving of credit or praise? Write a proposal to a committee or group (or your student newspaper) with your suggestions. Include your proposal and rationale in your portfolio.

Resources

On Campus

One of the most frequent sources of difficulties for first-year students involves roommate problems. If you and your roommate are having problems getting along, begin by speaking with your resident advisor or residence director. If the problem persists, talk with a member of the residential life office. You can also speak with a counsellor at the counselling office.

Anyone who feels he or she is facing discrimination based on race, gender, ethnic status, or national origin should contact a university official *immediately.* Often there is a specific office that handles such complaints. If you don't know which campus official to contact, speak to your academic adviser or someone in the dean's office and you'll be directed to the appropriate person. The important thing is to act and not to suffer in silence. Discrimination is not only immoral, but it's also against the law.

In Print

Beverly Daniel Tatum's *Why Are All the Black Kids Sitting Together in the Cafeteria?* (Basic Books, 5th edition, 2003) explores race, racism, and the everyday effect of prejudice.

In *Emotional Intelligence* (Bantam, 1997), Daniel Goleman discusses how we can learn to become more sensitive and emotionally aware of others.

Finally, Stewart Levine's *Getting to Resolution: Turning Conflict into Collaboration* (Berrett-Koehler, 2000) suggests a variety of practical approaches to resolving conflict.

On the Web

The following sites on the World Wide Web provide the opportunity to extend your learning about the material in this chapter. Although the Web addresses were accurate at the time the book was printed, check the P.O.W.E.R. Learning website, <www.mcgrawhill.ca/olc/power>, for any changes that may have occurred.

www.islandnet.com/~wwlia/ca-hr.htm
This site, from the Canadian Human Rights Law Centre, has links to the Canadian Human Rights Commission, as well as provincial commissions and other interesting and informative human rights resources.

www.couns.msu.edu/self-help/pamphlets.htm#relationship
This site has a great selection of pamphlets, some of which deal with conflict resolution, relationship issues, and diversity.

http://mentalhelp.net/psyhelp/chap13/
As a portion of Mental Health Net's Psychological Self-Help site, this is a good starting point for developing skills in conflict resolution.

The Case Of...

Answering for All

Kenisha Kinkaid stood out in any crowd. Being six-feet tall, she towered above most of her classmates. Even when she was seated at a desk, she looked tall. And since she was an African-Canadian, her skin colour set her apart from her classmates, almost all of whom were white.

Although most people were polite and nice to her, Kenisha felt isolated from most of her peers and instructors. While she had one or two good friends from high school with whom she kept in touch, she was not close to many people on campus. Her isolation came to a head, however, in the most public of places: her Canadian Literature class. It happened when her instructor, a white man, was leading a discussion on *Land to Light On,* a novel by noted black writer Dionne Brand. The instructor turned to Kenisha and asked her to comment on a passage from the novel.

"Does it ring true to you, Kenisha, as an African-Canadian?" asked her instructor, who then went on to inquire, "What do African-Canadians think about the perspective that Brand is taking?"

Kenisha was taken aback. What was she supposed to say? She hardly felt like a representative of all black people. She barely knew how she felt, let alone everyone else who was African-Canadian. Furthermore, her roots were in Nova Scotia, not the Caribbean. What an absurd situation to be placed in—her instructor asking her to answer for thousands of other people. She felt awful—embarrassed, upset, and angry with her instructor for putting her on the spot.

1. Why was the instructor's question so troubling to Kenisha? If the instructor really wanted Kenisha's opinion about the passage, what should he have said?

2. Would the question have had a different effect if the instructor had also been African-Canadian? Why or why not?

3. What are some cultural assumptions that the instructor is making about Kenisha? about African-Canadians? about white people?

4. What response might Kenisha make in this situation to make her feelings clear without causing excessive conflict?

Taking Notes

5

For Michael Wong, the realization that something fundamental had changed came when he went to his first class in the second term of university. Instead of taking a seat in the back row of class—as he had done in high school and at the start of his first university term—he sat down in the first row.

The change had come as a result of a workshop on notetaking he had attended last semester after getting Cs on three midterms. He had done every assignment and even reviewed extensively, but it turned out that what he had reviewed—his notes—was the problem. In the workshop, he'd learned ways of making sure he got the important information down as he listened to lectures or read assignments. He tried them out, and—a bit to his surprise—found they helped. By the end of the semester, he'd pulled his grades up.

At the same time, Michael's improved notetaking skills led him to pay more attention in class, something he found easier to do sitting closer to the front. As a result, he had become considerably more engaged and interested in what his instructors were saying and ended up with some of the best grades of his scholastic career so far.

Looking ▶▶
Ahead

Michael Wong's move from the back to the front of the classroom was both a source and a symbol of his academic success. Michael's ability to take good notes is also likely to pay future dividends, because notetaking skills not only help produce academic success in university but also contribute to career success.

Think for a moment about the number of times in your career you will have to write down or summarize something you have read or heard. These situations might include taking meeting notes, compiling and distributing accurate directions for completing a task, or even summarizing the content of an important telephone call. You will have to take notes for yourself and for others many times in your career.

In this chapter we discuss effective strategies for taking notes during class lectures, during other kinds of oral presentations, and from written sources such as textbooks. There's a lot more to good notetaking than you probably think—and a lot less if you view notetaking as essentially "getting everything down on paper." As we consider notetaking, we'll pause along the way to discuss the tools of the notetaking trade, how to think your way to good notes, and how to deal with disorganized instructors.

After reading this chapter, you'll be able to answer these questions:

- **What is effective notetaking?**

- **How can I take good notes in class?**

- **What techniques apply to taking notes from written materials?**

Taking Notes in Class

In Canadian colleges and universities, good notetaking is not just a matter of trying to write down everything your instructor says. Students may be enrolled in a class of 30 with an interactive format. Or a large lecture hall with 80 or 800 students trying to make sense of their professor while following a PowerPoint slide show on a big screen. Or a seminar of 12 students having an in-depth discussion. Or a lab where problem-based learning is the norm. Or an online course where students must post response papers to an instructor's query.

All of these learning environments require notetaking but one style of notetaking—writing down everything that the teacher says—is no longer always appropriate. What is important is knowing how to develop an effective approach, adapt it depending on your situation and learning style, and apply it consistently. The P.O.W.E.R. Plan for notetaking can help.

P repare: Considering Your Goals

As with other academic activities, preparation is a critical component of notetaking. The following steps will prepare you for action:

- **Identify the instructor's—and your—goals for the course.**
  On the first day of class, most instructors discuss what they'll be covering that term. They talk about their objectives, what they hope you'll get out of the class, and what you'll know when it's over. Most restate the information on the class syllabus, the written document that explains the assignments for the semester. For example, they may say that they want you to "develop an appreciation for the ways that statistics are used in everyday life."

  The information you get during that first session and through the syllabus is critical, because it allows you to calculate the basic direction the instructor plans to take during the course. And even if the instructor's goals aren't stated explicitly, you should attempt to figure them out.

  But don't just stop with the instructor's goals for the course. In addition to those "external" goals, you should have your own goals. What is it you want to learn from the course? What is it you hope to accomplish? How will the information from the course help you to enhance your knowledge, achieve your dreams, improve yourself as a person?

- **Complete assignments before coming to class.** Your instructor enthusiastically describes the structure of the neuron, recounting excitedly how neurons don't physically touch one another and how electrons flow across neurons, changing their electrical charge. One problem: You have only the vaguest idea what a neuron is. And the reason you don't know is that you haven't read the assignment.

  Chances are you have found yourself in this situation at least a few times, so you know firsthand that sinking feeling

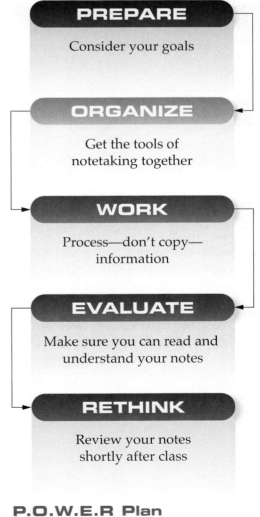

PREPARE

Consider your goals

ORGANIZE

Get the tools of notetaking together

WORK

Process—don't copy—information

EVALUATE

Make sure you can read and understand your notes

RETHINK

Review your notes shortly after class

P.O.W.E.R Plan

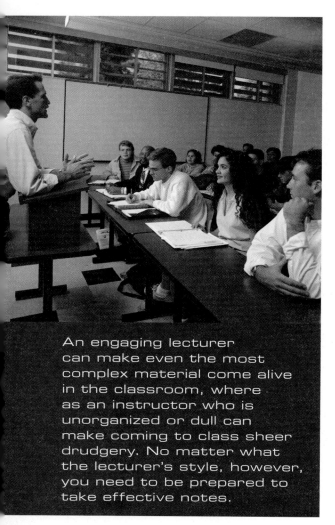

An engaging lecturer can make even the most complex material come alive in the classroom, where as an instructor who is unorganized or dull can make coming to class sheer drudgery. No matter what the lecturer's style, however, you need to be prepared to take effective notes.

as you become increasingly confused. Because you can't follow the discussion, you can't get interested either, so the class seems boring. But really it is you who are lost. Not only have you begun to fall behind in your course work, you have now wasted an entire class session, simply because you didn't complete the reading you were supposed to before class.

Always go to class prepared: Do all your assignments beforehand. Instructors assume that their students have done what they've assigned, and their lectures are based on that assumption. It's virtually impossible to get the gist of a lecture if you haven't completed the assignments.

- **Accept the instructor, warts and all.** Not every instructor is a brilliant lecturer. Accept the fact that, just as there are differences in skills among students, some instructors are more adept at lecturing than others.

  Don't let a lousy lecture style—or the fact that the instructor has a bad haircut or badly wrinkled clothing—get in the way of your education. You're going to notice these things, but don't let them interfere with your goals. Good notetaking requires being prepared to listen to the material.

- **Perform a preclass warm-up.** No, this doesn't mean doing jumping jacks just before each class. As you head to class or settle into your seat, review your notes from the previous lecture, looking over what the instructor said and where that lecture left off. You should also briefly review any reading you've been assigned.

  Just read the main headings or summary section. The warm-up doesn't have to be long. The goal is simply to refresh yourself, to get yourself into the right frame of mind for the class. In the same way that a five-minute warm-up before a run can prevent muscle spasms in your legs, a five-minute mental warm-up can prevent cramped and strained brain muscles.

"We have to keep putting education as a priority; use your opportunity to instill a love of learning."

Roberta Bondar

- **Sit as close to the teacher as possible.** Be sure that you can clearly see the chalkboard or screen if there are overheads, a Power-Point presentation, or a computer screen. If you are easily distracted, sit away from your friends and try and maintain eye contact with your teacher.

rganize: Getting Your Notetaking Tools Together

Start by getting the tools and equipment you need to take notes:

- Taking notes with pens makes it easier to use several different colours. You might use red to write or emphasize material your instructor says will be on the exam, blue for material that is copied from the board, and black for additional information your instructor provides.

- For notebooks, loose-leaf is the best. You can reorganize and insert or remove pages to create a set of notes. Always write on one side only so you can spread out your notes and see the flow.

- Get a notebook with sections so you can divide your notes into lecture notes, assignments, project outlines, and key dates. Date everything that goes in the notebook.
- If you miss a class, borrow or copy notes from a classmate and then review them in detail to make sure you understand the material.

In this chapter, three different ways to take notes are presented—the Cornell system, the Outline, and the Concept Map. Each of these methods present a strategy for organizing your notes on the page but they all depend on effective listening, effective approaches to notetaking, and review shortly after the lecture. Try each of these to see what best fits your learning style and the material you are summarizing.

The Cornell Method

According to educator Walter Pauk[1] from Cornell University there is a better way to configure or layout your notetaking pages. The best way to do this is to draw a line down the left side of your notebook page, about 6.5 cm from the left margin and another line 4 cm from the bottom of the page (illustrated in Figure 5.1). Keep the notes you write in class to the right of the line. Indent major supporting details beneath each main idea, trying to use no more than one line for each item, and leave space between topics to add information. When it comes time to review your notes later, you'll be able to jot down a key word, phrase, or major idea on the left side of the page. Or, you could write test questions related to your notes in this margin. Use the bottom section to summarize main ideas.

Cornell Notetaking

A notetaking technique that involves splitting the page to include notes, main points, and summary sections

Journal REFLECTIONS REFLECTIONS

How Do I Take Notes?

1. Overall, how effective are your notetaking techniques?

2. Describe your typical notetaking techniques in a few sentences. Do you try to write down as much of what the instructor says as possible? Do you tend to take only a few notes? Do you often find you need more time to get things down?

3. In which classes do your techniques work best? Worst? Why?

4. Do your notes ever have gaps in them, due to lapses of attention or times when you couldn't get down everything you wanted to? When do you usually discover them? What do you do about them?

5. Do you ever ask to borrow someone else's notes, even when you've been to class and taken your own notes?

6. Does anyone ever ask to borrow your notes? Would others want to use your notes?

7. How often—and when—do you consult your notes (after each class, before the next class, while doing homework assignments, when writing papers, when preparing for exams, etc.)?

Figure 5.1

Cornell Notetaking In this example of a student's notes on a lecture about memory, she has written the material in the larger right column during class. Later, when reviewing her notes, she wrote down key pieces of information in the left column.

EDCN 180	Memory October 15/08
	3 ways to store information
	sensory memory—everything sensed
aka working memory (like	short term memory—15-25 sec.
computer RAM)	stored as meaning
	5-9 chunks
(like hard disk)	long-term memory—unlimited
Rehearsal: STM to LTM	rehearsal
	visualization
Chunking	Organize information into chunks:
	birds, instruments, body parts, etc.
	Mnemonics
Roy G. Biv	acronyms
Every good boy deserves fun	acrostics
30 days hath September	rhyming
Unfinished Symphony	jingles
pato, caballo	keyword technique
room and furniture	loci technique
sun, zoo, me, store . . .	peg method
	using senses
	moving
	draw, diagram
	visualize
	Overlearning

Summary: Try various memory techniques to discover which ones work best for short-term and long-term memory!

Some disciplines, such as nursing or paramedicine, may require a different kind of notetaking. Any new style will require some getting used to, but noting and organizing reported information is most effective when you have a systematic approach.

Figure 5.2
A Sample Outline

I. Difficulties faced by students seeking affordable housing
   A. Students are subjected to high rents for housing close to campus
      1. Forced to share apartments
      2. Sometimes must live far from campus
   B. Made to sign leases with strict provisions
II. Possible solutions
   A. School offers subsidized housing
      1. Advantage is that housing costs can be lowered
      2. Potential problems
         a. School becomes students' landlord
         b. School uses funds for housing that could be otherwise invested in education
   B. Rent control
      1. Advantage: Rent control can provide reasonably priced rents
      2. Disadvantages
         a. Creates a permanent, expensive rent-control bureaucracy
         b. Landlords may neglect rent-control property
         c. The present shortage of apartments would worsen, because little incentive for owners to increase the number of rental units
         d. Competition for units would dramatically increase
III. Summary
   A. There are advantages and disadvantages to both solutions
   B. May need new, creative solutions

The Outline Form

It is often useful to take notes in the form of an outline. An *outline* summarizes ideas in short phrases or headline form and indicates the relationship among concepts through the use of indents and numbers or letters. You start with a title and then group the material connected to the title by using one or more indents. See Figure 5.2 for an example. Start a new title when the topic changes and group information about the new topic under that topic.

When outlining, it's best to be formal about it, using roman numerals, regular numbers, and capital and small letters. Or, if you prefer, you can also simply use outlining indentations without assigning numbers and letters.

Outlining serves several functions. It forces you to try constantly to determine the structure of the lecture to which you're listening. Organizing the key points and noting the connections among them helps you to remember the material better because you have processed it more. Outlining also keeps your mind from drifting away from the lecture. The effort involved in seeking out the structure of the lecture will help keep you focused on the material being discussed. Use Try It! 1, "Outline a Lecture," on page 120 to practice your outlining skills.

The Concept Map

A Concept Map is a visual representation of key information and how the parts are connected. It is a method of graphically grouping and connecting key ideas and themes.

Concept mapping is a method of structuring written material by graphically grouping and connecting key ideas and themes. In contrast to an outline,

Concept mapping

A method of structuring written material by graphically grouping and connecting key ideas and themes

🏃 Working in a Group:
Outline a Lecture

Prepare: The purpose of this activity is to learn to pick out the main points in a lecture.

Organize: You will need a pencil or pen, a blank piece of paper, and a copy of the passage below.

Work: Working as a group, have members take turns reading one or two of the paragraphs in the passage.[2] Write the down the main points. Then compare your notes with other group members. As a group produce an outline of the important points in the article.

Evaluate: Were you able to write down most of the main points? Were your notes different than the other group members? Did you try to write everything down or were you able to listen for the main purpose of the passage and take notes that reflected this purpose?

Rethink: What would you do differently if you had to do this again? How could you improve your notetaking ability?

Nunavut became Canada's newest province in 1999. This eastern Arctic territory is home to 24 000 people, mostly Inuit. Though Nunavut lacks heavy industries, it receives a lot of their toxic fallout. The Inuit people of Canada live 1 000 kilometres from any significant source of pollution, yet studies have shown that somehow they carry in their bodies twice the amount of *dioxin* as Canadians living near areas where it is produced. The breast milk of Inuit women in Nunavut, for example, contains twice the average concentration of dioxin found in the milk of women in southern Quebec.

Dioxin is the name for closely related chemicals produced in burning, chiefly the incineration of waste. In high doses, it is very toxic, causing skin diseases in humans and cancer in animals.

According to a study initiated by the Commission for Environmental Cooperation (CEC) to test the feasibility of tracking dioxins from source to receptor, of 44 000 different cement kilns, incinerators, and other dioxin producers, most of Nunavut's dioxin comes from industrial combustion in United States. Some even originates as far away as Mexico. The major polluters had the most favourable weather patterns for quickly transporting pollution north and included sources in Iowa, Pennsylvania, and California.

Dioxin released from a smokestack moves with the weather, depositing a light dusting as it travels. Humans take in dioxin by eating. Sometimes, it is deposited on grass, where cows take it up during grazing and their bodies absorb it into the fat cells, where it gradually accumulates. The dioxin then makes its way into meat and milk. At other times, when the dioxin falls on water, it is picked up by algae, which in turn are consumed by crustaceans and fish, and then by the marine mammals that eat them.

In Nunavut, it is the caribou that eat lichens and the seals that eat fish that are the bridge from airborne dioxin to the Inuit table. The Inuit eat both caribou and seal, and because their traditional diet is heavy with animal fats—the repositories of dioxin—they find themselves with unusually high amounts of dioxin in their bodies.

Only 19 of 44 000 sources accounted for more than a third of the dioxin in Nunavut. And only about 600 sources accounted for more than 75 percent of the dioxin. Because the study releases the names of polluters, the Inuit in Nunavut have a way to take their concerns to the source of their problems. The data the people of Nunavut now have offers policy makers and communities a tool for understanding the global impacts of persistent organic chemicals. Many, such as dioxin, are slated for elimination. Environmentalists and scientists, as well as residents of Nunavut hope the data prompt efforts to reduce toxic chemicals at their sources.

a concept map visually illustrates how related ideas fit together. The pictorial summary gives you another handle to store the information in memory, and it focuses your thinking on the key ideas from the lecture.

In a concept map, each key idea is placed in a different part of the map, and related ideas are placed near it—above, below, or beside it. What emerges does not have the rigid structure of an outline. Instead, a "finished" concept map looks something like a map of the solar system, with the largest and most central idea in the centre (the "sun" position), and related ideas surrounding it at various distances. It has also been compared to a large tree, with numerous branches and sub-branches radiating out from a central trunk. (Figure 5.3 presents a sample concept map.)

Figure 5.3

A Concept Map of Margaret Laurence's *The Stone Angel*

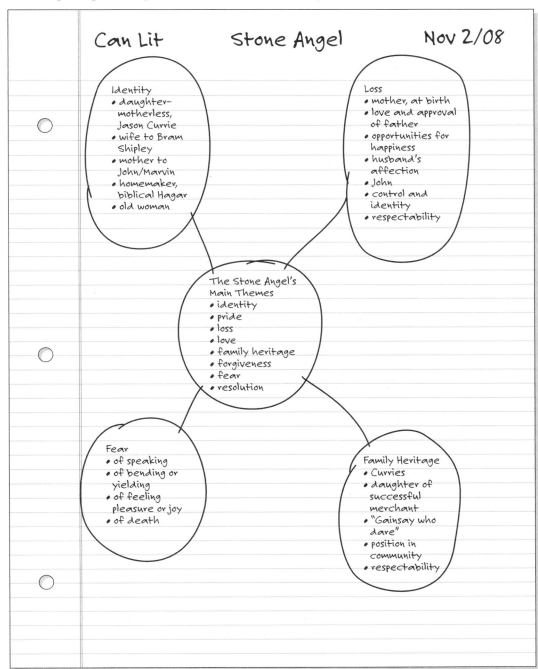

Building a concept map has several advantages. It forces you to rethink the material in your notes in a new style—particularly important if you used traditional outlining while taking the notes. In addition, it helps you to tie together the material for a given class session. Finally, it will help you to build a master concept map later, when you're studying the material for a final exam.

Using Notebook Computers to Take Notes If you're quite comfortable with computers and have a laptop or notebook computer, you might want to consider using it to take notes. There are several advantages: Legibility problems are avoided, and it's easy to go back and revise after you've taken the notes. It's also simple to add material later. Some students with disabilities depend on notebook computers if writing is difficult for them. Printing or e-mailing notes to a classmate absent from class is both helpful and efficient.

Despite their pluses, laptops also have minuses. For one thing, it's hard to make notes in the margins, copy graphical material that the instructor may present in class, reproduce formulas, or circle key ideas. Furthermore, the clattering of the keyboard may be annoying to your fellow students.

A Word of Caution Using notebook computers in the classroom can be distracting in other ways, as well. Students need self-discipline, focus, and commitment to their goals and the goals of the course while using laptops in the classroom in order to avoid temptations such as playing computer games, working on other assignments, surfing the Web, checking e-mail, or instant messaging. Despite a growing tendency to multi-task while on computers, students need to remember that notebook computers are tools to assist in notetaking and should be used responsibly.

Despite concerns, notebook computers in the classroom are becoming more commonplace. Laptop programs are being instituted in several campuses across Canada. Every student in these programs has a notebook computer and brings it to all classes, where lectures and notetaking are being radically changed. For further information about laptop programs, read about Acadia University's program at <www.acadiau.ca/advantage/> or Sheridan College's program at <www.sheridanc.on.ca/academic/mobile/>.

Work: Processing—Not Copying—Information

With pen poised, you're ready to begin the work of notetaking. The instructor begins to speak, and you start to write as quickly as you can, taking down as many of the instructor's words as possible.

> "My notes have become briefer, more succinct. I try to pay attention to what is going on rather than try to get every little word down."
>
> Markian Hlynka, Student, University of Alberta

Stop! You've made your first mistake. The central act in taking notes is not writing. Notetaking involves *listening* and *thinking* far more than writing. The key to effective notetaking is to write down the right amount of information—not too much, and not too little. To see how this is true, consider the following recommendations for taking notes:

- **Listen for the key ideas.** Not every sentence in a lecture is equally important, and one of the most useful skills you can develop is separating the key ideas from supporting information. Good lecturers strive to make just a few main points. The rest of what they say consists of explanation, examples, and other supportive material that expands on the key ideas.

  Your job, then, is to distinguish the key ideas from those that are of less importance. To do this, you need to be alert and always searching for the meta-message of your instructor's words. The **meta-message** consists of the underlying main ideas that a speaker is seeking to convey—the meaning behind the overt message you hear.

  How can you discern the meta-message? One way is to *listen for key words.*

  For instance, listen for clues about the importance of material. All phrases like "don't forget . . . ," "be sure to remember that . . . ," "you need to know . . . ," "the most important thing to consider . . . ," "there are four problems with this approach . . . ," and—a big one—"this will be on the test . . . " should cause you to sit up and take notice. Another good sign of importance is repetition. If an instructor says the same thing in several ways, it's a clear sign that the material being discussed is important.

  Be on the lookout for nonverbal signals too. When instructors pause, raise their eyes, glance at their notes, or otherwise change their demeanour, these behaviours are a signal that what they're about to say is important.

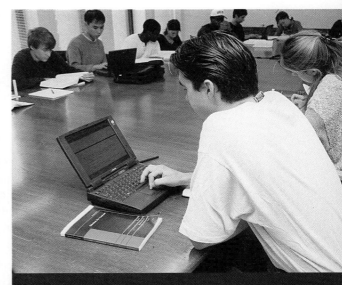

Using a laptop computer to take class notes ensures that they will be legible and that it will be easy to revise them after class. However, it's difficult to input graphical material, such as complex formulas, and there's also a danger that you'll be tempted to take too many notes.

Meta-message

The underlying main ideas that a speaker wants to convey; the meaning behind the overt message

- **Use short, abbreviated phrases—not full sentences.** Forget everything you've ever heard about always writing in full sentences. If you try to write notes in complete sentences, you'll soon become bogged down, paying more attention to your notes than to your instructor. In fact, if you use full sentences, you'll be tempted to try transcribing every word the instructor utters, which, as you now know, is not a good idea at all.

  Instead, write in phrases, using only key words or terms. Save full sentences for definitions or quotes that your instructor clearly wants you to know word for word. For example, consider the following excerpt from a lecture:

  > There are two kinds of job analyses: job- or task-oriented analyses, and worker- or employee-oriented analyses. Job analyses just describe the tasks that need to be accomplished by a worker. Employee-oriented job descriptions need to describe knowledge, skills, and abilities the employee must have in order to get the job done. Most job analyses include elements of both job-oriented and employee-oriented types.

  If you were taking notes, you might produce the following:

  > 2 kinds job analyses:
  > (1) job-oriented (= task-oriented): what worker must do to get job done
  > (2) worker-oriented (= employee-oriented): describe knowledge, skills, abilities needed
  > most analyses include both

  Note that the lecturer used 67 words, while the notes used only 29 words—fewer than half.

Take Notes During Discussions

Prepare: The purpose of this activity is to learn to recognize cues that will help you to pick out the main points in a discussion.

Organize: You will need a pencil or pen, a blank piece of paper, and a copy of the passage below.

Work: Working as a group, assign members one of the roles in the discussion. Read the parts and use cues from the instructor to identify major points. Each member will write down the main points. Then compare your notes with other group members. As a group produce an outline of the important points in the discussion.

Evaluate: Were you able to write down most of the main points? Were your notes different than the other group members? Did you try to write everything down or were you able to listen for the main purpose of the passage and take notes that reflected this purpose?

Rethink: What would you do differently if you had to do this again? How could you improve your ability to take notes during a discussion?

Instructor:	According to a recent survey, 90 percent of Canadians have a positive overall attitude to their jobs. Why might the interpretation of these results be inaccurate? Alicia?
Alicia:	Um …well, I think a lot of people lie on surveys—you know, they might be afraid what they say will get back to their employers.
Instructor:	Hmmm, well we can question the validity of survey statistics in general, but there is more to it than just not telling the truth. Anyone else? Kamal?
Kamal:	Yeah, I read an article that said that workers are reluctant to admit they made a mistake and so they put an optimistic spin on the situation. I can't remember where I read it.
Instructor:	Good point, Kamal. A 1996 Angus Reid poll indicated that although 90 percent of workers reported overall job satisfaction, other factors such as employee recognition, pay, job security, and career advancement had much lower rates. What else?
Emily:	Well, job satisfaction is also expressed in work behaviour—last year it seemed as though every time you opened a newspaper or watched the news on TV, people in every part of the country were going on strike or holding protests. I think that indicates that many employees in Canada aren't too happy.

- **Use abbreviations.** One way to speed up the notetaking process is through the use of abbreviations. Among the most common are the following:

and	*& or +*	with	*w/*	without	*w/o*
care of	*c/o*	leads to; resulting in	*↗*	as a result of	*↙*
percent	*%*	change	*△*	number	*#*
that is	*i.e.*	for example	*e.g.*	and so forth	*etc.*
no good	*n.g.*	question	*?*	compared with	*c/w*
page	*p.*	important!	*!!*	less than	*<*
more than	*>*	equals, same as	*=*	versus	*vs. or v.*

- **Copy information written on the board or projected from overheads.** If your instructor takes the time to write something out to be displayed in

Instructor:	Right. These behaviours are indicative of dissatisfaction—particularly related to pay. How else do workers express dissatisfaction?
Mark:	What about things like violence in the workplace or industrial sabotage? We keep hearing those stories about disgruntled employees going postal and killing their bosses and coworkers.
Nalani:	Get real, Mark. That only happens in the States.
Instructor:	Okay, you've hit on some extreme examples, but unfortunately some of them have occurred in Canada, like the Fabrikant murders at Concordia University. Other more common behaviours you might want to consider are employee theft, absentee rates, employee retention, and mental or physical health claims, particularly related to stress or workplace injury. Any other comments?
Patty:	What about performance? Isn't job performance correlated to satisfaction?
Ron:	Not necessarily, Patty. When I was researching my project on job performance, I found out there wasn't a link.
Instructor:	Yes and no, Ron. While studies haven't found a strong correlation, there is research that indicates that employees with high job satisfaction provide better customer service and engage in more organizational citizenship activities, such as extending beyond normal duties when necessary, avoiding conflict, or occasionally tolerating minor impositions.

Good discussion, folks. Just to bring this to a end, although Canadians may not be quite as satisfied with their jobs as some surveys suggest, 76 percent would recommend their place of employment to a friend, compared with 66 percent of Americans. In addition, in a recent *Globe and Mail* article, Canadians reported the highest job satisfaction rate of 13 countries—so it may be true that Canadians have a better working life than people in many other countries.

Write your notes here:

class, you should take the time to copy it. Definitions, quotes, phrases, and formulas—if you see them in writing, they're quite likely important enough to include in your notes. In fact, material displayed prominently has "test item" written all over it. You might want to highlight such material in some way in your notes.

- **Use different notetaking techniques for class discussions.** Not every course is structured as a lecture. Classes that are based less on lectures and more on class discussion pose greater challenges for notetaking. (Use Try It! 2, "Take Notes During Discussions," on page 126.)

For example, a discussion of the use of tax support of private schools in a sociology class may raise a variety of issues. As students in the class provide their ideas about the meaning of the work, how much—and what—should you place in your notes?

Figure 5.4
Notes on a Lecture

Here is an instructor's introductory lecture on Margaret Laurence's *The Stone Angel*. At the bottom of the page are two students' notes. Which student—A or B—did a better job of capturing the important points in the lecture?

In today's class, we'll discuss Margaret Laurence's *The Stone Angel*. As I'm sure you all know, Laurence is one of the most important and beloved literary figures in Canada. Born Jean Margaret Wemyss, in Neepawa, Manitoba, in 1926, Laurence wrote some of the most insightful works of Canadian fiction. She received two Governor General's Awards for Fiction and numerous honorary degrees, and she was named Companion of the Order of Canada. Laurence died in 1987.

The Stone Angel was a seminal work for Laurence and for Canadian literature. The first of five "Manawaka" novels, it is a narrative of the memories of Hagar Currie Shipley, who relives her long life as she battles to come to terms with herself and her life before she dies.

Hagar is a unique and complex character whose stubbornness and fierce pride deprive her of knowing love or joy and render her rigid, critical, and unyielding. Despite raging against her impending death, Hagar views her choices and failures unsentimentally, although in the end she does recognize her great losses.

The narrative structure, the weaving of past and present, and themes of motherhood, family heritage, and women's empowerment will be the primary focus of our discussion. I am particularly interested in your views on the roles of identity and loss in this book. Is Hagar's life, in the end, a failure? What resolution and self-understanding, if any, does Hagar achieve?

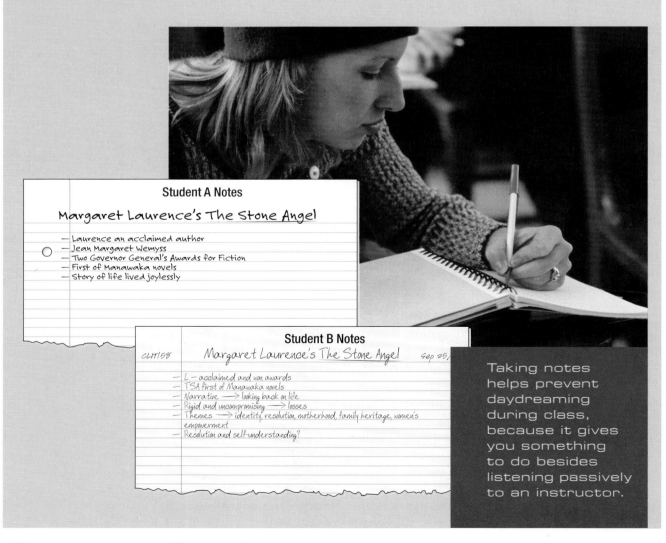

Student A Notes

Margaret Laurence's The Stone Angel

— Laurence an acclaimed author
○ — Jean Margaret Wemyss
— Two Governor General's Awards for Fiction
— First of Manawaka novels
— Story of life lived joylessly

Student B Notes

CLIT158   Margaret Laurence's The Stone Angel   Sep 25/

— L — acclaimed and won awards
— TSA first of Manawaka novels
— Narrative ⟶ looking back on life
— Rigid and uncompromising ⟶ losses
— Themes ⟶ identity, resolution, motherhood, family heritage, women's empowerment
— Resolution and self-understanding?

Taking notes helps prevent daydreaming during class, because it gives you something to do besides listening passively to an instructor.

In such situations, the best approach is to take your cue from the course instructor. Often the instructor will pose some questions to get the discussion rolling. Note those questions—they're an important indicator of what the instructor is interested in. The instructor's reaction to particular comments is another clue. Listen to his responses. If he responds enthusiastically to a particular point, highlight it in your notes.

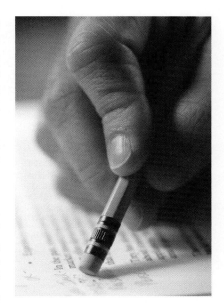

- **Pay particular attention to the points raised by instructors at the end of discussion and lecture classes.** Instructors often provide a summary of the discussion, which is worthy of inclusion in your notes.

Use Special Techniques for "Problem Instructors" As we all know from painful experience, some instructors' lectures are impossible to outline. How do you take notes when the instructor starts talking about one topic and then rambles off onto another one without warning and never seems to get back to the original point? Or if the instructor speaks very quickly and covers too much material too fast for you to follow?

The fact is that all you can do is make the best of a bad situation and adapt your notetaking strategy to it. If no clear message or logical sequence is present in the lecture material, you may be unable to take notes in outline form. In such cases, focus more on creating a summary of what is being said, rather than trying to tease out its underlying structure. Write short "paragraphs" that focus on the major ideas being presented. Although the paragraphs certainly shouldn't consist of full sentences, they should provide a reasonable condensation of what the instructor said. Use a concept map to relate what the instructor said to a central theme or concept.

When you're writing in paragraph form, be sure to leave space after each paragraph. By leaving space, you'll make it easier to go back later and restructure the material at a point when its underlying meaning is clearer.

You might be able to get a better sense of what the instructor is trying to convey by using your textbook to clarify obscure points. It also may be helpful to pool your notes with those of other students in the class. When the instructor's train of thought is all over the place, two—or more—heads are better than one!

Finally, don't hesitate to ask instructors to clarify what they are saying. In some cases, they simply may not realize how far off track they have gotten. You'll be doing them—and certainly your fellow classmates—a favour by asking for clarification.

Keep a Balance between Too Many Notes and Too Few Notes The key to effective notetaking is to keep a balance between too many and too few notes.

The best way to achieve this balance is by paying close attention in class. By being alert, engaged, and involved in class, you'll be able to make the most of the techniques we've discussed. The result: notes that capture the most important points raised in class and that will optimize your recall and mastery of the course subject matter. (See a sample of two students' notes in Figure 5.4.)

Evaluate: Thinking Critically about Your Notes

Toward the end of class, look over your notes. Now's the time—before the class has ended—to evaluate what you've written.

After being sure you can answer "yes" to the most basic question—can I read what I've written?—ask yourself these questions:

- Do my notes do a good job of representing what was covered in class?
- Do they reflect the emphases of the instructor?
- Are there any key points that are not entirely clear?
- Do I need help clarifying any of the points my instructor made?

Evaluating your notes is a critical part of the notetaking process. You can get a sense of how effective your notetaking has been while you still have a chance to ask your instructor to clarify anything that is still not clear.

Perhaps, for example, you've left out a key word in a definition. Maybe you don't understand a concept fully, even though you've written about it in your notes. Possibly you've left out the third step in a list of six steps necessary to accomplish something.

If you look over your notes while you're still in class, you have time to ask your instructor for clarification. Or you can wait till the end of class and then go up and raise your question. Most instructors will be happy to answer questions from students who have obviously been actively listening. Just make sure that you add what they tell you to your notes so you'll be able to refer to them later. (To practise evaluating your notes, complete Try It! 3, "Evaluate Your Class Notes," on page 129.)

R ethink: Activating Your Memory

The lecture has ended and class is over. You put the top on your pen, close your notebook, stash everything in your backpack, and head out for a cup of coffee before your next class.

Wait! Before you close up your notebook, finish the P.O.W.E.R. process. Rethink what you've heard. Spending 5 or 10 minutes reconsidering what you've written right now can save you *hours* of work later. The reason: Rethinking promotes the transfer of information into long-term memory (something discussed more in Chapter 6). As you link the new information you've taken down to what you already know and then integrate it, you essentially plug this information into your memory in a much more meaningful way, which means you can remember it better and more easily.

If you looked over your notes to clarify and evaluate the information in them in class, you've already begun the process. Once class is over, you need to review the material more formally. Here's how to do it:

- **Rethink as soon as possible.** Time is of the essence! The rethinking phase of notetaking doesn't have to take long; 5 to 10 minutes is usually sufficient. The more critical issue is *when* you do it. The longer you wait before reviewing your notes, the less effective the process will be.

> "It is not enough to have a good mind; the main thing is to use it well."
>
> René Descartes

There's no doubt that the best approach is to review the material just after the class has ended. As everyone else is leaving, just stay seated and go over your notes. This works fine for classes late in the day, when no other class is scheduled in the room. But what if you must vacate the room immediately after class? The next best thing is to find a quiet space somewhere nearby and do your rethinking there.

Evaluate Your Class Notes

Prepare: The purpose of this activity is to assess your notetaking skills and identify improvements.

Organize: You will need a pencil or pen, and the chart below or the one on the website.

Work: Take the notes you made recently during one of your classes and use the chart criteria to evaluate them.

Evaluate: Were you able to use the criteria to evaluate your notes? How well did you do?

Rethink: What would you do differently to improve your notetaking ability?

Statement	Not Even Slightly	Slightly	Moder- ately	Pretty Well	Very Well
1. I can read my notes (i.e., they are legible).					
2. Someone else can read my notes.					
3. My notes are complete; I missed nothing important.					
4. My notes represent the key points that were covered in class.					
5. My notes reflect the instructor's emphases.					
6. The instructor's key points are clear and understandable.					
7. The notes contain only important points, with no extraneous material.					
8. I understand not only the notes but the class content they reflect.					
9. Using only the notes, I will be able to reconstruct the essential content of the class in three months.					

Even if you have another class immediately afterwards, you can do your rethinking before that class if you get there early enough. However you do it, the same rule holds: Sooner is better.

In any case, don't let the day end without examining your notes. In fact, reconsidering material just before sleep is thought to be particularly effective. After rethinking, it may be a good idea to rewrite or copy your notes on a computer. Rewriting notes and adding additional material is a good way to transfer information to your long-term memory.

- **Make rethinking an active process.** Some people feel the notes they take in class are akin to historical documents in a museum, with Do Not Touch! signs hanging on them. You should think of your notes as a construction project and yourself as the person in charge of the project.

When you review your notes, do so with an eye to improving them. If any information is not entirely clear, change the wording in your notes, adding to or amending what's there. If certain words are hard to read, fix them; it won't be any easier to read them the night before a test—in fact, chances are you'll have even more trouble.

If, on rethinking the material, you just don't understand something, ask your instructor or a friend to clarify it. And when you receive an explanation, add it to your notes so you won't forget it. (You might want to use a different-coloured pen for additions to your notes, so you'll know they came later.)

- **Take the broad view.** When you rethink your notes, don't think of them only in terms of a single lecture or a single class. Instead, take a longer view. Ask yourself how they fit into the broader themes of the class and the goals that you and the instructor have for the semester. How will the information be useful to you? Why did the instructor emphasize a particular point?

If you've configured your notes by leaving a 6.5-cm column on the left-hand side of the page, now is the time to make use of that blank column. Write down key words, significant points, major concepts, controversies, and questions. The process of adding this information will not only help you to rethink the material now, it will also provide guideposts when you study before a test.

Taking Notes: Multimedia Technology

Many instructors use multimedia technology, such as PowerPoint and video or audio clips, to improve their lectures. Multimedia technology can deepen your understanding of a lecture, but it also makes notetaking more challenging. Often the classroom's lights are dimmed and it may be difficult to take legible notes. It may be more difficult to follow the message of multimedia presentations than a "chalk and talk" lecture. A PowerPoint slideshow likely includes just the main points in a lecture so don't be content with copying points from the slides . . . listen carefully to the content presented by your instructor and expand upon it in your notes.

Some professors post PowerPoint lectures on a course website before the start of class. If this is a feature of your course, consider printing out a copy of the lecture, and bring it to class to take notes on. However, this may be a very expensive way to take notes, as most computer labs in schools charge for printing and even printing off material at home adds up, compared with the cost of loose-leaf paper or notebooks. It may be more beneficial, as well as cheaper, to copy the notes manually. You will be more actively involved in the notetaking process, rather than just printing the notes off. Or save paper and download the notes and expand upon them on your notebook or desk computer.

In addition to using a printout, there is a way to take notes on a computer when you are following a PowerPoint presentation. Access the PowerPoint on your computer. Then select <File> <Send To> <Microsoft Word>. You will have a page split with the slide on the left side and space for notes on the right side.

If you are using the Cornell System, a Concept Map, or the Outline method to take notes on your computer, have templates made in Microsoft Word or another word processor so that all you have to do is enter key points from the lecture. It is difficult to create the page layout at the same time as you are taking notes. Make sure the instructor has agreed to your use of the laptop during class.

Some students may wish to make audio recordings of the lecture and play it back as they make notes. Others may wish to take a picture of the board used by the instructor. Please make sure you have the permission of your instructor before you do this.

Taking Notes as You Study

Weighing as much as 2.5 kg, bulky and awkward, and filled with tonnes of information, it's the meat-and-potatoes of postsecondary life: your course textbook. You might feel intimidated by its size; you might be annoyed at its cost; you might think you'll never be able to read it, let alone understand, learn, and recall the material in it. How will you manage?

The answer involves taking **study notes,** notes taken for the purpose of reviewing material. They are the kind of notes that you take now to study from later. (We'll consider *research notes,* notes that you take to write a paper or prepare a report, in Chapter 9 when we discuss writing papers.)

Several strategies are useful for taking study notes from material such as magazines, books, journals, and Web pages. Which approach works best depends on whether you can write on the material you want to take notes on.

Study notes

Notes taken for the purpose of reviewing material

Career Connections

Notetaking on the Job: Taking Minutes

Meetings are becoming increasingly important, especially in industries where product development and marketing programs rely heavily on teamwork across departments. Survey results show that executives on average spend 40 to 50 percent of their working hours in meetings.

The most important reason to create a record of meetings is to create a shared group memory. Individuals selectively perceive, retain, and recall their own experiences. Therefore, meeting participants will each remember a meeting quite differently. It is important that minutes accurately reflect what occurred in the meeting, the decisions that were made, and the things that individuals are committed to doing because of the meeting.

If you are assigned to take the minutes of a meeting, your notetaking skills will come in handy. Even if you are just an attendee, it is a good idea to take notes, to keep track of what you need to follow-up.

3M has a template of three basic steps that can simplify minute-taking:[3]

1. *Action items.* Action items are to-dos assigned to attendees at the meeting. Record the task, the person responsible, and the date agreed on to complete the task.

2. *Decisions.* All decisions that may affect future choices of the group should be recorded.

3. *Open issues.* New issues raised at the meeting but not resolved there should be recorded so they can be carried over to a future meeting.

Using a digital whiteboard allows meeting participants to see the minutes as they are compiled and have input into their creation. In addition, the digital whiteboard allows virtual meetings to occur, with attendees from various centres participating in the meeting and seeing the minutes produced in real-time. Rather than having the minutes reproduced on paper, they can be e-mailed to participants or placed on an Intranet.

Speaking of Success

Kofi Boateng

Law and Security Diploma, Niagara College

A graduate of the Law and Security Program at Niagara College, Kofi Boateng works as a child and youth worker. He works with teenagers who cannot live at home for a variety of reasons. As a member of a shift team that must work together in a very supportive and collegial manner, Kofi learned and refined many of these teamwork skills while at college.

Kofi was a member of the varsity basketball team at Niagara. Playing basketball required a huge time commitment, due to practices, games, and out-of-town tournaments, and at times Kofi worried about keeping up with his schoolwork. He found that professors would postpone assignments, or tests due to his athletic obligations, but generally Monday was the day teachers wanted him to catch up, which was difficult after an exhausting weekend playing away-games. Kofi and other teammates used their time on the bus heading to and from matches to read and study so they didn't fall behind in

their work. This was a good use of travelling time, and it also allowed the basketball players to remain in good academic standing, which ensured they could keep on playing for the team.

In addition, Kofi and several other classmates from Law and Security would informally gather to study course material

in preparation for tests and assignments. Kofi, an associative learner, listens to lectures and links new points with ideas or concepts already discussed. As a result, his notes were not always complete, so working with others was a

great way to fill in any blanks. Kofi could then use his recall of the group discussion and relate it to class lectures, discussion, and reading when studying.

Kofi's favourite class was psychology, but he found it difficult to listen to detailed lectures, full of new concepts, theories, and specialized vocabulary and take notes as well. Kofi noticed other classmates taping their professor's lectures and he also started to tape the lectures and write his notes after class. Not only did this strategy allow him to pay full attention to class discussions, it also allowed him to review course material as he worked on his notes.

At Niagara, working in teams—athletic or academic—helped Kofi prepare for employment in the group home; it also helped him realize the value of everyone's contribution to a common effort, a crucial skill he passes on to the at-risk youth he counsels.

Taking Study Notes on Material You Can Write On

Here are some suggestions for creating study notes for material on which you can annotate the text directly by underlining, highlighting, or writing in the margins:

- **Integrate your text notes into your study notes.** If you want to create study notes from written material on which you can write, start by annotating the pages as you normally would. Use the techniques that work best for you: highlighting, underlining, circling, making marginal notes—whatever you generally use. These techniques are discussed in detail in Chapter 7; you may want to look ahead to that discussion.

  After you've finished reading and annotating the material, it's time to create study notes. While it's still fresh in your mind, go back over the material and your text annotations, and create your study notes.

  The study notes should provide a summary of the key points. They might be in outline form or in the form of concept maps. They should supplement and summarize the annotations you've made on the text.

  Furthermore, any notes you take should stand on their own. For instance, they should include enough information to be useful whether or not you have the book or article on hand.

- **Use flash cards.** If you feel confident that the annotations you've written in the book are sufficiently comprehensive, you might consider taking notes on flash cards. **Flash cards** are simply index cards that contain key pieces of information that you need to remember.

Flash cards are particularly useful in subjects that present many small bits of information to remember, such as foreign language vocabulary words or scientific formulas. When you need to learn a list of foreign words, for instance, you can write a foreign word on one side of a card and its English meaning on the other side.

One of the greatest virtues of flash cards is their portability. Because they are small, they can fit into your pocket or handbag, and you can look at them at odd times when you have a spare moment.

Flash cards
Note cards that contain key pieces of information to be remembered

Taking Study Notes on Material You Can't Write On

Taking notes on material that can't be written on is a different story. Library books, magazines, journal articles, and materials on library reserve that are shared with others require a different approach.

- **Approach the written material as you would a class lecture.** The techniques we discussed earlier for taking notes in class can all be adapted for taking notes from written material. In fact, the task is often easier, because you'll be able to refer back to what was said earlier—it's in black and white in front of you.

- **Laptop computers can be especially helpful in creating study notes.** Because it's often easier and quicker to take notes using a word-processing program (if you're a good typist), computers can help you take more-detailed notes from written material on which you can't write. If your typing skills are below par, consider taking a word-processing course or use a typing tutorial software program to increase your speed and accuracy. Keyboard skills are now essential in the classroom and in the workplace.

- **Use all the tricks of the trade we discussed earlier for taking notes from a class lecture.** Look for the key ideas, definitions, quotes, and formulas, and include them in your notes. Use the headings that are included in the text, such as chapter and section titles. Bold or italic type is also a clue that an important point is being made. Graphs and charts often provide critical information.

- **Use the same form of notetaking that you use in class lectures.** If you take notes in class using the two-column method (in which you reserve a 6.5-cm column on the left side of your paper for adding comments during later review of the notes), use that technique here as well. If you write your notes in outline form, create an outline based on the written material. If you often create graphics such as concept maps, create them now. The point is to produce notes that are consistent with those you take during class lectures.

What is effective notetaking?

- The central feature of good notetaking is listening and distilling important information—not writing down everything that is said.

How can I take good notes in class?

- Prepare for taking notes by identifying the instructor's and your own goals for the course, completing all assignments before arriving in class, and warming up for class by reviewing the notes and assignments from the previous class.

- Sit as close to the teacher as possible. Be sure that you can clearly see the chalkboard or screen if there are overheads, a PowerPoint presentation, or a computer screen. If you are easily distracted, sit away from your friends and try and maintain eye contact with your teacher.

- Before writing notes, listen and think, processing the information that the instructor is attempting to deliver.

- Notes should be brief phrases rather than full sentences and, if possible, be in outline form to reveal the structure of the lecture. Material written on the board should usually be copied word for word.

- Before leaving class, evaluate your notes, verifying that they are complete and understandable while there is still time to correct them. As soon as possible after class, actively rethink your notes.

What techniques apply to taking notes from written materials?

- Taking good study notes from written materials involves many of the principles that apply to taking good notes from oral presentations, although the source material can be consulted repeatedly, making it easier to get the information down accurately.

- Concept maps and flash cards can be helpful tools for notetaking from textbooks.

P.O.W.E.R. Portfolio

Take Note

Consider including a set or example of study notes in your section on knowledge management. Or perhaps you could include notes you took at a meeting you attended, or an interview you did for your school's paper. Reflect on what skills or abilities are demonstrated in your submissions, as well as their importance to you as a learner.

Resources

On Campus

If you are having difficulty taking class notes effectively, talk with your course instructor. Bring your notes with you soon after a class has ended, and let the instructor assess what you are doing correctly and what could stand improvement.

If your problems persist, and you have great difficulty translating the spoken word into notes, then there's a small possibility that you suffer from an auditory learning disability. Be tested by your school's learning disabilities office or counselling office to address this or rule it out.

In Print

Take Notes (Career Press, 1994), by Ron Fry, provides an overall view of how to take good notes in classes.

Another approach can be found in James Roberts's *Bud's Easy Note Taking System* (Lawrence House, 1995), which offers many useful suggestions.

Finally, *Noteworthy: Listening and Notetaking Skills* (2nd ed.), by Phyllis Lim and William Smalzer (William S. Hein & Co., 1995) provides a fine overview of strategies for increasing your listening and notetaking expertise.

On the Web

The following sites on the World Wide Web provide the opportunity to extend your learning about the material in this chapter. Although the Web addresses were accurate at the time the book was printed, check the P.O.W.E.R. Learning website, <www.mcgrawhill.ca/olc/power>, for any changes that may have occurred.

www.yorku.ca/cdc/lsp/notesonline/note4.htm
York University's Counselling and Development Centre has an example of the Cornell system. One advantage of this system is that it allows you to make use of your existing strengths as a notetaker.

www.coun.uvic.ca/learn/program/hndouts/class1.html
An effective method for organizing complicated information is through concept mapping. This site has a tutorial that presents information in passage form and then asks you to create a concept map. The concept map created by the authors is only a click away.

The Case Of...

A Clean Sweep

Sunhee Park came home from school feeling pretty good about her semester. She attended all her classes, kept up with her assignments, and had gotten decent marks on two quizzes. Despite living on her own and working 12 to 15 hours a week at a local video store, Sunhee was confident that everything was under control.

However, mid-terms were two weeks away and it was time to get organized. Two hours later and her room was a total disaster . . . handouts, PowerPoint printouts, and folded pieces of paper with notes on them were all over her desk, bed, and chair. Her notebook was a jumble of all her course notes, and her textbooks were filled with notations, highlighted sections, folded-over pages, and scraps of paper. As she dumped her backpack out on the floor, pens, highlighters, two USB keys, and two illegible Post-It notes fell out.

Sunhee looked at the piles of stuff that represented her semester so far and wished she could have a "Clean Sweep" crew come and organize her life.

1. On a scale of 1 to 10, with 1 being terrible and 10 being wonderful, how would you rank Sunhee's dilemma? Why? Can she turn her situation around?

2. What stage of the P.O.W.E.R. process is Sunhee stuck in? What does she need to do to get back on track?

3. Why do you think Sunhee has managed to do so well up to this point in the semester?

4. What advice would you give to Sunhee on notetaking?

5. If a "Clean Sweep" crew took a look at your notes (from classes, online studies, and reading) what would its verdict be? Why? What kind of action will you take regarding your notetaking?

Improving Your Memory

6

The stack of note cards kept getting higher and higher.

And as it grew, so did Jamila Hassan's sense of panic. She had used online flash cards before but they were not available for this course so she'd decided to use index cards. Jamila had methodically written each new accounting vocabulary word she had encountered over the term onto an index card, just as her instructor had recommended. But as the term wore on and the stack grew higher, Jamila felt she'd never be able to memorize all the words in time for the final exam. There were already so many words, and there were still a few weeks left in the term. How could she ever manage to recall them all?

Jamila decided that desperate measures were called for. She began to take her stack of cards with her everywhere she went. Whenever she had a spare moment, she would shuffle through the cards, trying to memorize the words, one by one. She sometimes felt a little silly, sitting in the laundromat, eating meals, and riding on the bus with her thick stack of cards, but as she spent more time going over the words, she became more confident, and she began to recall more of them each time she reviewed them.

It worked! By the time of the final exam, half of which consisted of defining key terms, Jamila was thrilled to realize that she had succeeded in memorizing most of the words. The exam was easy for her, and she ended the semester with an A in the course.

Looking ▶▶
→ *Ahead*

Most of us have experienced the challenge of memorizing a seemingly insurmountable amount of information, and we tend to focus on our memory failures far more than our successes. But the truth is that our memory capabilities are truly astounding. If you are like the average college or university student, your vocabulary contains some 50 000 words. You know hundreds of mathematical facts, and you can recall detailed images from scenes you saw years ago. In fact, simply cataloguing the memories you already have might well take a lifetime.

In this chapter, you'll learn how you can improve the memory skills you already have. We'll examine what memory is, why it sometimes fails

us, and how this can be prevented. You will also become acquainted with specific ways you can learn information that will help you recall it when you need to.

After reading this chapter, you'll be able to answer these questions:

- **What is memory and how does it function?**

- **Why might I have problems with memory, and how can I deal with those problems?**

- **What are some techniques I can use for memorizing information?**

The Secret of Memory

There's one well-kept secret about memory, and you should never forget it: You remember everything.

Sure, sometimes you have trouble recalling information that you know you've learned. Or maybe you don't recall that you learned it, even though you did. But this is not because information has disappeared from your head; the problem is one of *retrieval*. **Retrieval** entails finding information stored in memory and returning it to consciousness for further use. Every piece of information that you've ever learned—if you really learned it at some point in the past—is buried somewhere in your brain. The problem is that you can't always find it.

The proof of this assertion comes from the biology of memory. Consider what happens when you're exposed to some new material. Say your geometry instructor spends a class talking about the Pythagorean formula in geometry, which maintains that the square of the length of the hypotenuse of a right triangle is equal to the sum of the squares of the lengths of the two other sides. (You may recall this formula as $a^2 + b^2 = c^2$.)

When you first learn the formula, the wiring connecting a handful of the 70 trillion or so brain cells in your head is changed—forever. The information on the Pythagorean formula is etched into some tiny part of your brain, and unless that part of the brain is damaged in some way through injury or disease, it will stay there for the remainder of your life. This doesn't mean that you will easily find the information when you need it. But it does mean that that particular piece of information remains patiently in place, potentially retrievable the next time you encounter a geometry problem.

The practical outgrowth of this biological process is straightforward: You already remember everything you need to know, and a lot more. With some effort, you could remember the names of everyone in your third-grade class. You know what you ate when you went to the eighth-grade dance. You remember the name of the body of water that borders Iraq. And you even could have remembered where you left your keys the last time you misplaced them.

> "A retentive memory may be a good thing, but the ability to forget is the true token of greatness."
>
> Elbert Hubbard, *The Note Book*

The key to successful recall is to learn the material initially in a way that will allow you to recall it easily later. If you have trouble remembering material that you've already learned, then the trick is figuring out a way to retrieve that material from memory. In short, we need to devise ways to free the memories that reside within our brains.

As important as memory is, however, forgetting is helpful at times, too.

The Value of Forgetting

Legend has it that the actress Ingrid Bergman once said, "Happiness lies in good health and a bad memory."[1]

Although it's tempting to think of forgetting as the enemy of memory, in fact it's just the opposite. If we never forgot anything, think how cluttered our minds would be. Forgetting permits us to disregard inconsequential details about people, experiences, and other sources of information that otherwise would burden us.

For example, would it really be useful to know that we dropped our fork in the middle of dinner six weeks ago? Would it be helpful to remember that a professor wore the same stained sweater six classes earlier? Would our lives be any richer if we knew that the subway car we took a day ago had a defaced advertisement for sunscreen? One man—whose memory was so good that he could repeat passages that he'd read 15 years earlier (in a foreign language he didn't even speak!)—was dull and disorganized. He couldn't even read with ease, because virtually every word he came across evoked a tidal wave of memories from his past.

In short, think of forgetting as a friend that permits your memory to operate at peak efficiency. Of course, forgetting shouldn't be your *best* friend. The focus of this chapter will be to figure out how to hold onto memories that we want to keep, using the strategies summarized in the P.O.W.E.R. Plan below.

repare: Determining What You Need to Remember

PREPARE

Determine what you need to remember

ORGANIZE

Relate new material to what you already know

WORK

Use proven strategies to memorize new material

EVALUATE

Test your recall of new information

RETHINK

Consolidate memories through repeated review

P.O.W.E.R Plan

Memorize what you need to memorize. Forget about the rest.

The average textbook chapter has something like 20 000 words. If you had to recall every word of the chapter, it would be nearly impossible. Furthermore, it would be a waste of time. Being able to spew out paragraphs of material is quite different from the more important ability to recall and deeply understand academic material in meaningful ways.

It helps to approach learning the material in a different way. You are not going to learn or memorize the 20 000 words in the chapter. So, try setting a goal to learn 20 concepts. You may find that within those 20 there are 10 that you already know something about. That leaves 10 new concepts to learn. Now add some detail to each those concepts. Because you have a purpose and framework, the details are easier to learn and remember. It is much harder to remember new information that is isolated without connections to what you already know or want to know.

In short, the first step in building a better memory is to determine just what it is that you want to recall. By extracting what is important from what is less crucial, you'll be able to limit the amount and extent of the material that you need to recall and you'll be able to focus on what you need to remember. See Try It! 1, "Remember Details," on the next page.

To determine what is important, look at the overall, big picture. Don't get lost in minute details. Instead, prepare yourself by taking a broad overview of the material you need to know and decide what your goal is going to be. Always set a goal or ask a question to help you focus.

rganize: Relating New Material to What You Already Know

Don't think of memorization as pumping gasoline (new information) into an almost-empty gas tank (your brain). You're not filling something that is empty. On the contrary, you are filling a container that already has a lot of things in it, that is infinitely expandable, and that never empties out.

Remember Details

Prepare: The goal of this activity is to learn to read to remember details.

Organize: Use the paragraph below.

Work: Read the story. Pay attention to details, but don't take any notes or make lists.

Evaluate: How well you remembered details in the story will be evaluated later on.

Rethink: Return to this exercise later. Do the techniques make a difference?

Demain entered the marketplace slowly, feeling his way. He had never seen such confusion.

Hundreds of wagons, caravans, booths, and carts were drawn up in a broad U-shape, occupying three sides of the enormous town square, their awnings and curtains open and inviting. The colours and odours were a sensual assault; he perceived them not just through his eyes and nose, but as if they were pressing forcibly against his skin. And the sounds! He could scarcely keep himself from bolting back the way he had come, to the safety of the countryside.

A sense of wonder pushed him forward. He walked past gold merchants, with their grey cloaks and watchful eyes, and a potter, her shop filled three shelves high with vases, bottles, and jars of deep blues, reds, and yellows that Demain—accustomed to the brown clay that adorned his mother's kitchen—had never even imagined possible. Cloths were on sale in the booth next to the potter's—shamelessly long bolts of impossibly patterned prints, depicting herons, bulls, schools of fish, a field of wheat, great bowls of fruit, and men and women engaged in the pursuits he knew from stories: They danced in bold colours and graceful postures, harvested vast fields of bounty, fought battles of intricate strategy, and drank and courted in riotous taverns.

Past the dealers in rugs, chairs, hats, shoes, and wagons; past the blacksmith's huge muddy arms beating out rugged tools and fine weapons; past the fortune tellers and musicians, Demain at last came to the vendors of food and drink. Never had he felt so hungry. He was lifted off his feet—he swore he was floating—by the aroma of long lines of sausages, sides of beef, whole lambs, chickens on spits the length of spears, bacon and hams, fried potatoes, great vats of boiling vegetables, stewing tomatoes, and breads—all shapes and sizes of loaves, twisted into braids, curled into circles, flattened, puffed, elongated, pocketed, and glazed.

Demain felt the two coppers in his pocket—his holiday bounty—and hoped they would be enough.

Note: We'll return to the story of Demain later. For now, read on . . .

If you approach each new memorization task as something entirely new and unrelated to your previous knowledge, you'll have enormous difficulty recalling it. However, if you connect it to what you already know, you'll be able to learn it more easily and recall it far better than if you just dump it into your head. The way to get your brain to do

> "Human memory works its own wheel, and stops where it will."
>
> William Saroyan, *Chance Meetings* (1978)

www.mcgrawhill.ca/olc/power

TRY IT!

this organizational work for you is by thinking about the associations the new material has with the old.

Say, for example, you need to remember information about the consequences of global warming, such as the fact that the level of the oceans is predicted to rise. One way to think about the new material you want to remember is to relate it to information that you already possess.

What would help you remember a person's name after you were introduced for the first time?

For example, you might think about the rising level of the ocean as it relates to your personal memories of visits to the beach. You might think what a visit to the beach would be like with dramatically higher water levels, visualizing a severely reduced shoreline with no room for sitting on the beach. Then, whenever you think about global warming in the future, your mind is likely to associate this fairly abstract concept with its concrete consequences for beaches. The association you made while rehearsing the information makes it personal, long-lasting, and useful.

Memories can also be organized by place. *Where* you learn something makes a difference in how well you can recall it. Memory researchers have found that people actually remember things better in the place where they first studied and learned them. Consequently, one of the ways to jog your memory is to try to recreate the situation in which you first learned what you're trying to remember. If you memorized the colours that litmus paper turns when it is placed in acids and bases while you were lying in bed, it might be helpful during a test to recall the correct colours by imagining yourself lying on your bed thinking about the colours. By mentally recreating your previous study session in bed, you can jog your memory.

Another effective place-related strategy is to introduce new data into your mind in the place that you know you're going to need to recall it at some future moment. For instance, suppose you know that you're going to be tested on certain material in the room in which your class is held. Try to do at least some of your studying in that same room. (The reviewing techniques we covered when discussing notetaking in Chapter 5 will be very helpful in this way as well.) Then, when you take the test, the associations you've formed between the material and the physical location of your studying may aid recall.

Work: Using Proven Strategies to Memorize New Material

One of the good things about the work of memorization is that you have your choice of literally dozens of techniques. Depending on the kind of material you need to recall and how much you already know about the subject, you can turn to any number of methods. Do the exercise in Try It! 2, "Organize Your Memory," on page 144.

As we sort through the various options, keep in mind that no one strategy works by itself. Choose a combination of strategies that works best for you, and feel free to devise your own strategies or add those that have worked for you in the past.

Review Your Notes After Class Research shows you forget up to 70 to 80 percent of material within 48 hours of class. You can change this simply by taking 10 to 15 minutes within one hour after class to review what you have learned. (Students who review in this manner tend to remember 70 to 80 percent of material two days later.)[2]

Rehearsal Think it again: rehearsal. Say it aloud: rehearsal. Think of it in terms of the three syllables that make up the word: re—hear—sal. Okay, one more time—say the word "rehearsal."

If you're scratching your head over the last paragraph, it's to illustrate the point of **rehearsal:** to transfer material that you encounter into memory. If you don't rehearse information in some way, it will end up like most of the information to which we're exposed: on the garbage heap of lost memory.

To test whether you've succeeded in transferring the word "rehearsal" into your memory, put down this book and go away for a few minutes. Do something entirely unrelated to reading this book. Have a snack, catch up on the latest sports scores on TSN, or read the front page of the newspaper.

Are you back? If the word "rehearsal" popped into your head when you picked up this book again, you've passed your first memory test. You can be assured that the word "rehearsal" has been transferred into your memory.

Rehearsal is the key strategy in remembering information. If you don't rehearse material, it will never make it into memory. Repeating the information, summa-

Rehearsal

The process of practising and learning material to transfer it into memory

---

Journal REFLECTIONS

What Sort of Memory Do I Have?

1. Overall, what kind of memory would you say you have: excellent, good, average, poor? Why?

2. What kinds of information do you remember best: faces, shapes, colours, smells, names, dates, or facts? Why?

3. What kinds of information do you have the greatest difficulty remembering? Why do you think this type of information is hard for you to remember?

4. Is there any particular source of information about which you can remember exceptional amounts, such as hockey records or movie trivia? Why do you think you remember this information so readily?

5. Think about some of the information from your early school years that you can still easily recall. What factors contributed to this information becoming firmly embedded in your memory?

6. What kinds of memorization techniques do you now use? Have you ever tried any in the past that didn't work? What do you think you can do to improve your memory?

7. Do you ever find yourself recognizing someone's face but being unable to recall the name that goes with it? What do you do? When you're introduced to new people, do you do anything special to remember their names? If so, what?

8. Do you ever feel that information is "on the tip of your tongue" but you just can't seem to retrieve it? Have you ever recalled the information you were seeking just a few minutes too late? What do you do if this happens?

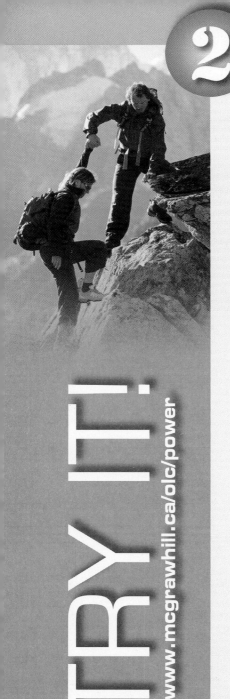

2

Organize Your Memory

As critical thinking expert Diane Halpern points out, having an organized memory is like having a neat bedroom: Its value is that you know you'll be able to find something when you need it. To prove the point, try this exercise she devised.[3]

Prepare: Does having an organized memory help you remember?

Organize: Use the two exercises below.

Work: Complete the first exercise. Record your results. Complete the second exercise. Record your results.

Evaluate: Were you able to determine if organizing material helps you remember?

Rethink: Can you apply this technique to your notes and study materials?

Read the following 15 words at a rate of approximately one per second:

girl

heart

robin

purple

finger

flute

blue

organ

man

hawk

green

lung

eagle

child

piano

Now, cover the list, and write down as many of the words as you can on a separate sheet of paper. How many words are on your list? _____

rizing it, associating it with other memories, and above all *thinking about it* when you first come across it will ensure that rehearsal will be effective in pushing the material into memory.

Mnemonics

Formal techniques used to make material more readily remembered

Mnemonics This odd word (pronounced in an equally odd fashion, with the "m" silent—"neh MON ix") describes formal organization techniques used to make material more readily remembered. **Mnemonics** are in fact the tricks-of-the-trade that professional memory experts use, and you too can use them to recall the sort of list items you will often need to recall for tests. See Try It! 3, "Do It Yourself Acronyms and Acrostics," on page 146.

After you've done that, read the following list:

green

blue

purple

man

girl

child

piano

flute

organ

heart

lung

finger

eagle

hawk

robin

Now cover this second list and write down as many of the words as you can on the other side of the separate sheet of paper.

How many words did you remember this time? Did you notice that the words on both lists are identical? Did you remember more the second time? (Most people do.) Why do you think most people remember more when the words are arranged as they are in the second list? Does it seem plausible that the organization of the second list makes it easier to remember the words?

Working in a group: Discuss with your classmates ways in which you can organize material from one of your current classes to make it easier to remember.

Among the most common mnemonics are the following:

- **Acronyms**

  FACE

  Roy G. Biv

  P.O.W.E.R.

  You're already well acquainted with **acronyms,** words or phrases formed by the first letters of a series of terms. For instance, FACE spells out the names of the notes that appear in the spaces on the treble clef music staff ("F," "A," "C," and "E," starting at the bottom of the staff.) Roy G. Biv is a favourite

Acronym

A word or phrase formed by the first letters of a series of terms

Working in a Group: Do It Yourself Acronyms and Acrostics

Prepare: Learn to create acronyms and acrostics.

Organize: Use the two assignments below.

Work: Complete the assignments individually and as a group. Compare the different answers to see if some are more useful than others.

Evaluate: Were you able to create an acronym and an acrostic?

Rethink: Would these techniques for remembering help you? Do you plan to add them to your memory aids?

In the first part of this exercise, work individually to create an acronym and an acrostic.

1. Figure out a Great Lakes acronym using the first letters of their names (which are Erie, Huron, Michigan, Ontario, and Superior).

2. Devise an acrostic to help remember the nine planets in order of their average distance from the sun. Their names, in order, are Mercury, Venus, Earth, Mars, Jupiter, Saturn, Uranus, and Neptune.

After you've tried to create the acronym and acrostic, meet in a group and discuss these questions: How successful were you in devising effective acronyms and acrostics? Do some of the group members' creations seem to be more effective than others? Why? Is the act of creating them an important component of helping to remember what they represent, or would having them created by someone else be as helpful in recalling them? For your information, a common acronym for the Great Lakes is **HOMES** (**H**uron **O**ntario **M**ichigan **E**rie **S**uperior), and a popular acrostic for the order of the planets is **M**y **V**ery **E**ducated **M**other **J**ust **S**erved **U**s **N**oodles.

of physics students who must remember the colours of the spectrum (**r**ed, **o**range, **y**ellow, **g**reen, **b**lue, **i**ndigo, and **v**iolet.) And P.O.W.E.R. stands for— well, by this point in the book, you probably remember.

The benefit of acronyms is that they help us to recall a complete list of steps or items. The drawback, though, is that the acronym itself has to be remembered, and sometimes we may not recall it when we need it. For instance, Roy G. Biv is not exactly the sort of name that readily comes to mind. And if we're unable to remember an acronym, it won't be of much use to us. Even if we do remember Roy G. Biv, we might get stuck trying to recall what a particular letter stands for. (For example, we'd probably prefer not to spend a lot of time during a test trying to remember if the "B" stands for brown, or beige, or blue.)

- **Acrostics.** After learning to use the acronym "FACE" to remember the notes on the spaces of the music staff, many beginning musicians learn that the names of the *lines* on the staff form the acrostic, "**E**very **G**ood **B**oy **D**eserves **F**udge." **Acrostics** are sentences in which the first letters spell out something that needs to be recalled. The benefits—as well as the drawbacks—of acrostics are similar to those of acronyms.

Acrostic

A sentence in which the first letters of the words correspond to material that is to be remembered

- **Rhymes and jingles.** "Thirty days hath September, April, June, and November . . . " If you know the rest of the rhyme, you're familiar with one of the most commonly used mnemonic jingles in the English language. Similarly, some of us learned the main theme of Schubert's *Unfinished Symphony* by singing the words "This is the symphony that Schubert wrote and never finished" when the theme first appears. For those who learned to recognize the symphony by using this mnemonic, it is virtually impossible to hear the symphony without recalling the words.

Although mnemonics are helpful, keep in mind that they have a number of significant shortcomings. First, they don't focus on the meaning of the items being remembered. Instead, mnemonic devices use characteristics such as the letters that make up the words being memorized. Consequently, the information is learned by rote, rather than by considering what it means and thinking critically about its relationship to other material. Because information that is learned in terms of its surface characteristics—such as first letters that form a word—is less likely to be retained than information that is learned in terms of its meaning, mnemonic devices are an imperfect route to memorization.

There's another problem with mnemonics: Sometimes it takes as much effort to create a mnemonic device as it would to memorize the material in the first place. And because the mnemonic itself has no meaning, it can be forgotten.

Despite their drawbacks, mnemonics can be useful. They are particularly helpful when the material being memorized includes a list of items or a series of steps.

The Keyword Technique Learning the vocabulary of a foreign language is often one of the toughest tasks for beginning students. The **keyword technique** can help ease the pain. In the keyword technique, a foreign word is paired with a common English word that has a similar sound. The English word is known as the keyword.

For example, suppose you needed to learn the Spanish word for duck, which is *pato*, pronounced "pot-o." The first thing you'd do would be to think of an English word that sounds like "pot-o" and to picture it in your mind. One obvious choice would be a pot, simmering on a stove. This is your keyword.

The next step is to form an image in your mind that relates the meaning of the Spanish word to the image of the keyword. Because *pato* means duck, the desired image will relate a duck and a pot. The clear choice: a duck simmering in a pot on a stove.

Here's another example. The Spanish word for horse is *caballo*, pronounced "cob-eye-yo." In this case, you might link a horse with a corncob and an eye, both of which would be keywords, and come up with an image of a horse with huge, bulging eyes munching on a corncob. Or perhaps you could incorporate all three syllables of *caballo* and form an image of a horse with bulging eyes eating a corn cob and playing with a yo-yo. It's fine that the result is an outlandish image. In fact, the more eccentric the image, the easier it will be to recall.

The Method of Loci and the Peg Method: Special Help for Recalling Sequences and Lists The ancient Greeks had a way with words. Their orators could deliver speeches that went on for hours, without notes. How did they remember what they wanted to say?

They used a procedure called the **method of loci.** *Loci* is the Latin word for "places," and it helps describe a procedure in which items in a sequence you want to remember—such as the sections of a speech or a series of events—are thought of as "located" in different places in a building.

Keyword technique

A memory technique in which a foreign word to be learned is linked by an image to an English word with a similar sound

Method of loci

A memory technique in which the elements in a list are visualized as occupying the parts of a familiar place

Consider, for example, a speech that has three major sections: an introduction, a main body, and a conclusion. Imagine further that each of the three sections has various subcomponents that you need to recall.

To use the method of loci, you first visualize the living room, kitchen, and bedroom of a house with which you are familiar. Next, you mentally "place" the introduction of the speech into the living room of the house. You then mentally place each of the *parts* of the introduction on a different piece of furniture, following the way in which the furniture is laid out in the room (for example, you might proceed clockwise from the door). The easy chair might contain the first point of the introduction, the sofa the next point, and an end table the last point. Then you'd move into the kitchen and do the same thing with the body of the paper, laying out your arguments on different pieces of kitchen furniture or appliances. Finally, you'd end up in the bedroom, where you'd "place" the conclusion.

A close cousin of the method of loci is the peg method. The **peg method** uses a series of key words tied to numbers to help in the recall of numeric information. For instance, a set of "pegs" that you could use would link numbers with these words:

One is a sun,

Two is a zoo,

Three is me,

Four is a store,

Five is a dive,

Six are sticks,

Seven is heaven,

Eight is a gate,

Nine is a pine,

Ten is a den.

By thinking of exotic images using the peg words tied to the numbers, you can recall specific numbers that you need to memorize. For instance, suppose you had trouble remembering the value of *pi*, used to calculate the circumference of a circle (3.14, in case you don't remember). Translate the number into the relevant peg words—me (three), sun (one), and store (four)—and imagine an image linking the three. One obvious possibility is an image of yourself wearing sunglasses, heading out to a store on a sunny day. A less obvious and more exotic possibility is an image of yourself bowling a large sun into the front of a store.

The peg system can also be used to memorize ordered lists of items, when the sequence in which they appear is important. In this use, the peg system is very similar to the method of loci. You simply link images of the ordered set of items to the 10 "numbers." The first item is linked with the sun, the second with a zoo, and so on. Refer to Try It! 4, "Peg the Memory."

Involve Multiple Senses The more senses you can involve when you're trying to learn new material, the better you'll be able to remember. Here's why: Every time we encounter new information, all our senses are potentially at work. For instance, if we witness a car crash, we receive sensory input from the sight of the two cars hitting each other, the sound of the impact, and perhaps the smell of burning rubber. Each piece of sensory information is stored in a separate location in the brain, and yet all the pieces are linked together in extraordinarily intricate ways.

Peg method

A memory technique in which a series of memorized words is linked by images to a list of items to be remembered

TRY IT!

www.mcgrawhill.ca/olc/power

Peg the Memory

Prepare: Use the "peg" poem to recall a list.

Organize: To complete this task you will need the "peg" poem guidelines on the previous page and the list in this exercise.

Work: Create a "peg" poem to make a phrase or saying connecting the number of the level of government to the description of that level.

Evaluate: Were you able to complete the task? Do you need more practice?

Rethink: Would you add this technique to your memory aids?

After you've learned the "peg" poem, it can come in handy in a variety of areas. Try it. Use the peg system to memorize the organization of the Canadian government in the list below. For instance, for the monarchy, think of an image that links the monarch with the sun (remember "one is the sun" from the poem). Do the same for the rest of the components of the government.

1. Monarchy: Monarch and Governor-General
2. Executive: Prime Minister, Cabinet, Privy Council, and federal departments
3. Legislature: Senate and House of Commons
4. Judiciary: Supreme Court, Federal Court, Tax Court

Now cover up the list. What is number two on the list? What is number four on the list?

How well did the peg method work for you? Do you see its value for other topical areas? If you are taking a foreign language class, can you apply the method? Could you apply it to other kinds of classes? Do you see any drawbacks to its use?

What this means is that when we seek to remember the details of the crash, recalling a memory of one of the sensory experiences—such as what we heard—can trigger recall of the other types of memories. For example, thinking about the *sound* the two cars made when they hit can bring back memories of the way the scene *looked*.

You can make use of the fact that memories are stored in multiple ways by applying the following techniques:

- **When you learn something, use your body.** Don't sit passively at your desk. Instead, move around. Stand up; sit down. Touch the page. Trace figures with your fingers. Talk to yourself. Think out loud. It may seem strange, but doing this increases the number of ways in which the information is stored. By involving every part of your body, you've increased the number of potential ways to trigger a relevant memory later, when you need to recall it. And when one memory is triggered, other related memories may come tumbling back.

- **Draw and diagram the material.** We've already considered (in Chapter 5) the power of concept maps, the method of structuring written material by graphically grouping and connecting key ideas and themes. When we create a concept map, one of the things we're doing is expanding the modalities in which information can be stored in our minds.

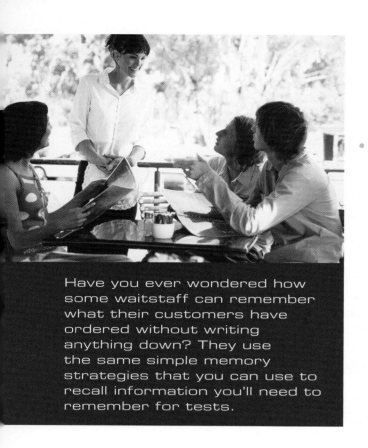

Have you ever wondered how some waitstaff can remember what their customers have ordered without writing anything down? They use the same simple memory strategies that you can use to recall information you'll need to remember for tests.

Other types of drawing can be useful in aiding later recall. Creating drawings, sketches, and even cartoons can help us remember better. Your creations don't have to be great art, or detailed, involved illustrations. Even rough sketches are effective, because creating them gets both the visual and tactile senses involved.

- **Visualize. Visualization** is a technique by which images are formed to ensure that material is recalled. For instance, suppose you're told that memory requires three basic steps: the initial recording of information, the storage of that information, and, ultimately, the retrieval of the stored information. As you read the three steps, you probably see them as logical and straightforward processes. But how do you remember them?

You might visualize a computer, with its keyboard, USB key, and monitor (as in Figure 6.1). The keyboard represents the initial recording of information. The USB key represents the storage of information. And the monitor represents the display of information that has been retrieved from memory. If you can put these images in your mind, it will help you to remember the three basic memory steps later.

Visualization serves several purposes: it helps make abstract ideas concrete, it engages multiple senses, it permits us to link different bits of information together, and it provides us with a context for storing information.

Visualization

A memory technique in which images are formed

What kind of visualization works best? There's a simple rule: Weird is good. The more extreme, outlandish, and eccentric the image you create, the more notable it will be and so the easier it will be to remember. And if you can remember the image, you'll probably remember the information that's attached to it. Refer to Try It! 5, "Visualize the Possibilities."

Figure 6.1
Visualizing Memory

Recording of information

Storage of information in memory

Display of information retrieved from memory

Visualize the Possibilities

Prepare: Test to confirm how important visualization is to memory by creating a concept map relating visualization to memory and mnemonic techniques.

Organize: Use a blank page or the space below to record your thoughts.

Work: Link all of the memory techniques you can think of to the central concept of memorization.

Evaluate: Does creating a concept map help your recall?

Rethink: For some types of learners in particular, the concept map is a high-impact visual technique requiring action on your part. If you haven't used it before would you add it to your memory techniques?

You may have noticed how important visualization is to memory. In fact, many of the techniques we've discussed in this chapter rely in some measure on visualization, especially your visualization of extreme or absurd images.

Test the truth of the role of visualization in memory techniques by drawing a chart showing the relationship of the concept of visualization to the memory techniques in this chapter. Review the memory techniques in this chapter if needed and place them on the chart around "visualization." Label the relationship to visualization. An example for the memory technique rehearsal is provided to help you get started.

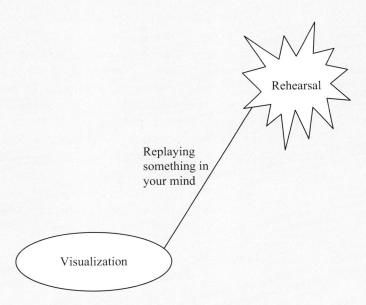

How well does this chart reflect what you know about visualization? Is it a useful tool for you? This type of chart is called a concept map and was discussed in more detail in Chapter 5, "Taking Notes."

Working in a group: Compare your concept map with those of your classmates. What are the major similarities and differences, and why do you think they occurred? Are some of the particular concept maps likely to help recall information about visualization more easily than others?

Go to the text's website at www.mcgrawhill/ca/olc/power for a sample of a concept map and blank form to complete.

Think Positively Emotions matter. If you're in a negative frame of mind when you try to memorize something, your negative feelings can become attached to the memory, making you less likely to recall it because you'll automatically tend to avoid those bad feelings. The opposite is also true: If you think positively about the process of memorization, those more-positive feelings will end up being etched into your memory.

Of course, feelings can't be turned off in the same way we're able to turn off a light. If you feel nervous and scared about memorizing all the formulas you need to for your chemistry midterm, you can't just tell yourself it's great fun. But if you recognize your feelings, they lose much of their power to influence you and to block memories.

Overlearning Think back to when you were learning your basic multiplication facts ($1 \times 1 = 1$; $1 \times 2 = 2$; and so forth). Let's suppose you had put each multiplication problem on a flash card, and you decided to go through your entire set of cards, trying to get every problem right.

> "A pessimist sees the difficulty in every opportunity; an optimist sees the opportunity in every difficulty."
>
> Sir Winston Churchill

The first time you went through the set of cards and answered all the problems correctly, would you stop there? Would you feel as if you'd actually learned and memorized them perfectly and that you'd never again make an error?

Probably not. The prudent assumption would be that you needed a few more instances of flawless performance before you'd be justified in concluding that you had adequately memorized the problems.

If this were your gut feeling—that you needed several instances of perfect performance to be sure you had learned the multiplication facts completely—you'd have stumbled on the principle of overlearning. **Overlearning** consists of studying and rehearsing material past the point of initial mastery. Through overlearning, recall becomes automatic. Rather than searching for a fact, going through mental contortions until perhaps the information surfaces, overlearning permits us to recall the information without even thinking about it.

Overlearning

Studying and rehearsing material past the point of initial mastery, to the point at which recall becomes automatic

To put the principle of overlearning to work, don't stop studying at the point when you can say to yourself, "Well, I'll probably pass this test." You may be right, but that's all you'll do—pass. Instead, spend extra time learning the material until it becomes as familiar as an old, comfortable shoe. At that point, overlearning has occurred, and you'll be able to recall the material with ease.

E valuate: Testing Your Recall of New Information

The memory strategies just described can bring you to a point where you probably feel comfortable in your ability to remember the material you've been learning. Once you've used one or more of them to help you process the material you are learning, it's time to test yourself—to evaluate whether you'll be able to recall the material when you need it. There are several ways to evaluate your memory:

- **Use in-text review questions and tests.** Many textbook chapters end with a quiz or a set of review questions about the material. Some have questions scattered throughout the chapter. Don't avoid them! Not only do such

Career Connections

Memory on the Job

Increasing your memory skills is not important only in college or university; having a good memory will also be important to your career success.

Not all professionals need the same kind of memory skills. TV camera operators must remember lighting combinations, while physicians have to keep track of a host of medical conditions and medicines. But in all professions, memory abilities are crucial.

A particularly important skill is remembering people's names. Remembering the names of coworkers, clients, and contacts is important professionally, and it is also a sign of good manners.

Shannon Smith, founder of Premiere Image International Inc., <www.premiereimageintl.com/>, coaches individuals on improving social skills, self-presentation, image, etiquette, and memory skills. Her clients include CBC, CIBC, Royal Bank, Digital, Upjohn, and the Bank of Montreal.

To remember names, Shannon Smith suggests you follow these six steps:

1. **Listen closely.** Did you hear the name correctly? Ask for the name to be repeated or for the spelling.

2. **Use the name** throughout the conversation.

3. **Anchor the name in your mind** by associating it with something that will come to mind when next you meet. Perhaps something with the same name—or make up a rhyme—Joe White can fight.

4. **Imprint the "image" of the person in** your mind—something always makes someone stand apart. It could be the walk, tilt of head, or the style in which the person is dressed.

5. **Write it down.** Take time after a meeting to jot down the names of the people you met.

6. **Pay attention to the smallest detail!** Be observant and you'll be successful in remembering those names.

The big secret is paying close attention, as if that person were the only one in the room who mattered.

questions indicate what the writer of the book thought was important for you to learn and memorize, but they can also provide an excellent opportunity for evaluating your memory.

Even if you've answered the review questions earlier—while you were first reading the material (which is always a good idea), answer them again later as you study for the test and then the final exam.

- **Test yourself.** Temporarily transform yourself into your instructor, and prioritize what you're most likely to be tested on. Then create your own test, writing out some questions.

  Later, after as little as a few hours, take the test, and then grade it. How have you done? If you've achieved a "grade" that you're satisfied with, fine. If you've missed some key pieces of information, then you'll want to return to work and spend more time on memorization.

- **Team up with a friend.** When it comes to evaluating your memory, two heads are often better than one. Working with a classmate can help you test the limits of your memory and assess areas in which you need work.

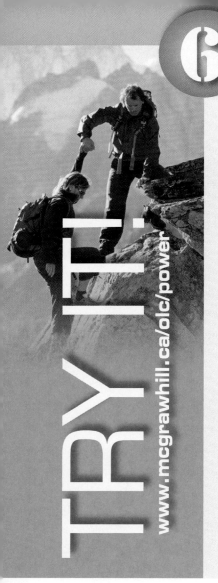

Remember Demain

Prepare: Use a memory aid to see if your results are different.

Organize: Use the paragraph you read in Try It! 1.

Work: Follow the directions below.

Evaluate: Were you able to see if memory aids make a difference?

Rethink: What memory aids would you add to your academic skills?

Remember the passage earlier in this chapter (Try It! 1) about Demain, who found himself in the midst of a colourful, aromatic bazaar of booths and shops? Without turning back to the passage, write down everything you can remember about what Demain experienced in the marketplace—the shops, sights, and foods.

_____

_____

_____

_____

_____

_____

_____

_____

_____

_____

_____

_____

For instance, you and a friend can take turns testing yourselves, switching back and forth between asking and answering questions. Turn it into a contest: One of you can be Alex Trebek of *Jeopardy!*, and the other, a contestant. You can even work in groups. The important thing is to switch who's asking and who's answering the questions. Even when you're directing questions to others—officially evaluating their memory—you're giving your own memory a workout.

Rethink: Consolidating Memories Through Repeated Review

Memory consolidation

The process by which the physical links between brain cells that represent memory become fixed and stable over time

Like fine wines, memories need time to age. Psychologists talk about this as the process of **memory consolidation.** What this means is that the physical links between brain cells that represent memory in the brain need time to become fixed and stable. This process explains why information is not suddenly and permanently established in memory the first time we're exposed to it. In fact, the process of consolidation may continue for days and even—in some cases—for years.[4]

Obviously you don't have years to wait. But it does pay to try to memorize material in advance of the time that you'll really need to use it. Then, when you go back to reconsider it, it will become even more well-established in your mind.

_____

_____

Now reread the passage, trying to remember its details by using one or more techniques from this chapter. You might use the method of loci, the peg method, the method of organizing ideas into chunks, or other techniques. Then answer these questions about the passage:

1. What scenes were depicted on the cloths? _____

_____

_____

2. What were the gold merchants wearing? _____

_____

3. After the cloth shop, what businesses did Demain pass to arrive at the vendors of food and drink? _____

_____

4. What foods did Demain see and smell at the fair? _____

_____

_____

How would you assess your performance on these questions? Do you think you would have remembered more initially if you had used some of the memory techniques in this chapter? Do you see how you could employ these techniques in your own studying? Did one seem to work better for you than others?

The phenomenon of memory consolidation explains why cramming is not a great idea. As we discussed in the chapter on taking tests, cramming is the process of spending the preceding evening or even the hours just before a test trying to memorize as much as possible. The memories that come from cramming simply don't last, because they aren't rehearsed and processed sufficiently. It's far more effective to distribute studying over many shorter sessions, rather than squeezing it into a single, long session just before a test. Fatigue and anxiety prevent long, last-minute practice sessions from being as effective as practice that is spread out.

The best way to ensure good memory is to return to the material even after your personal evaluation tells you that you can recall it easily. Wait several days, if possible, and then review it again. You'll be able to identify the aspects of the material that you know well, and the things that just haven't jelled yet in your memory. Rethinking the material not only permits you to take another look at what's in your memory, but it also helps you identify where you need more work. Refer to Try It! 6, "Remember Demain."

The Canadian inventors of *Trivial Pursuit* knew how much fun memory games could be. Players know the value of having a teammate to help remember obscure facts. In the same way, studying with others can help you test and expand your own memory and reveal areas that need more work.

Speaking of Success

Elaine Hudson

Computer Information Systems—Networking Diploma, Nova Scotia Community College (Truro)

Elaine Hudson, who graduated from Nova Scotia Community College's Computer Information Systems—Networking Diploma with an A+ average, says that returning to school "was the best thing I've ever done for myself." As an adult student with high personal expectations and a solid work ethic, Elaine started NSCC with a strong commitment to school and was not satisfied until she did as well as she knew she could. For her academic excellence, Elaine received the prestigious *Alan Murray Award*, *Xerox* Canada Aboriginal Scholarship's top award.

To reach her academic goals after 20 years of working, Elaine had to work hard and develop her learning skills. Elaine admits she struggled to remember course material at first. There was a lot of material to understand and remember as well as the fact that she was out of practice remembering this kind of information. Part of her success depended on using a variety of memory techniques to move information from short-term memory to long-term memory. It was only after graduating that Elaine was diagnosed with Arteriovenous Malformation, a rare disease characterized by both motor and sensory deficits. Elaine's memory was somewhat affected and she had to work all the harder to retain information. For Elaine, the memory skills in this chapter were an important part of her success.

NSCC
NOVA SCOTIA COMMUNITY COLLEGE
Education that **Works**

Giving back to the community and helping others are very important to Elaine. She contends that compassion helps to extend people's vision, stating, "Too often our vision is directed inward to our own little corner of the world. We don't look outward until something happens to impact that. It is important for all of us to look outside ourselves and have some responsibility for the world around us. Many little inputs make a big impact." Elaine is employed doing accounting and computer work at Ulnooweg Development, a corporation that serves the needs of aboriginal small businesses in the Maritimes. She has also been involved in the Davis Inlet Relocation project, where she built a computer program that tracks people, properties, and property maintenance. In addition, Elaine devotes time to environmental and animal rescue issues and serves on the board of the Society for the Prevention of Cruelty to Animals.

Elaine encourages students to persevere and find other avenues if they find roadblocks to achieving their goals, saying, "Just do it! You may feel overwhelmed at times, but it will definitely be worth it!"

What is memory and how does it function?

- Information we actively process is permanently etched into the brain, but it is not always readily available for retrieval. The challenge is to recall information when we need it, and the key to effective recall is learning material in a way that makes recall easy.

- Forgetting is essential to permit us to disregard unimportant details and focus on what is important.

Why might I have problems with memory, and how can I deal with those problems?

- The problems we have with memory are mostly related to the inability to recall or retrieve information when it is needed. However, if information is rehearsed carefully, you can usually recall it more easily.

- Memory can be improved through careful preparation, by selecting in advance the pieces of information that are worthy of memorization and rehearsal.

- Another key to effective memorization is linking new information to information that is already in memory.

What are some techniques I can use for memorizing information?

- Many memory techniques are available to improve memorization. Rehearsal is a primary one, as is the use of mnemonics such as acronyms, acrostics, and rhymes.

- Other memory techniques are the keyword technique, the method of loci, the peg method, visualization, and the use of multiple senses while learning new material.

- Overlearning is a basic principle of memorization.

- Memory takes some time—days or even longer—to reach the point of consolidation, at which the physical links between brain cells that represent memory become stable. The need for consolidation explains why cramming is ineffective for long-term recall.

P.O.W.E.R. Portfolio

Keep It in Mind

Consider your most effective techniques for improving your memory. What seems to work for you? Include examples of techniques you developed to remember information, along with an assessment of your use of these skills. For example, you may have created an acronym for the phases of a project, developed a concept map showing the critical steps in writing an essay, or created flash cards for learning the parts of a skeleton. These examples demonstrate your motivation to learn but can also show your creative problem-solving skills.

Resources

On Campus

If you have considerable difficulty in memorizing material compared with your classmates, it's possible that you might have a learning disability. If you suspect this, visit the campus learning disabilities office or counselling centre.

In Print

Harry Lorayne's and Jerry Lucas's *The Memory Book* (Ballantine, 1996) offers a simple system for improving memory.

Carol Turkington's *12 Steps to a Better Memory* (Pocket Books, 2003) is helpful if you want to have a better memory for lists and other difficult-to-remember material.

Your Memory: How It Works and How to Improve It, by Kenneth L. Higbee (Marlowe & Company, 2nd edition, 2001) deals with numerous memory techniques, such as the link and story, loci, peg, and phonetic mnemonic systems. Detailed and informative, students can learn to remember to-do lists, names and faces, speeches, concrete facts, dates, and numbers.

On the Web

The following sites on the World Wide Web provide the opportunity to extend your learning about the material in this chapter. Although the Web addresses were accurate at the time the book was printed, check the P.O.W.E.R. Learning website, <www.mcgrawhill.ca/olc/power>, for any changes that may have occurred.

www.coun.uvic.ca/learn/program/hndouts/map_ho.html
This site aids in concept mapping, an effective memory aid that improves recall by building meaning structures around key concepts.

www.mindtools.com/memory.html
This comprehensive site provides several methods for improving memory. It includes examples of how each technique can be applied to such topics as remembering lists and foreign languages.

The Case Of...

The Group of Seven

For Jason Marchuk, Canadian art history had always been a hard subject. Although he had no trouble with his studio art classes, he had difficulty keeping names, dates, and places straight.

Consequently, when his Art History instructor, Ms. Teeler, announced that a major exam was coming up, Jason panicked. He hadn't even finished all the assigned reading, and here he was expected to learn what seemed to be virtually everything there was to know about Canadian art history since 1665. Ms. Teeler had said that the test would focus in particular on Tom Thomson and the Group of Seven. When Jason couldn't even recall three members of the Group of Seven, he knew he'd better get started memorizing. But where should he begin?

1. How should Jason prepare for the exam? Should he simply get the art history textbook and start reading? Why or why not?

2. How can Jason prevent the facts of art history from appearing to be a jumble of random words and numbers? How should he use his existing knowledge to structure historical information? Why might this become easier the more often Jason does it?

3. Jason is expected to remember the names of the Group of Seven, names that seem unusual to him and very hard to remember. Which memory technique is likely to be most effective? How would it work?

4. To remember lists of events in the development of the Group of Seven, what technique would you recommend that Jason use? How would it work?

5. How could Jason use multiple senses while learning about Tom Thomson and the Group of Seven?

Building Your Reading and Listening Skills

7

"**R**ead the first two chapters in your accounting textbook by next Thursday." "I've put three marketing articles on reserve in the library, and you'll need to have them read by our next class." "Take a look at the first three problems in your economics book, and see if you can solve them."

For purchasing student Chris O'Hara, these reading assignments—handed down by different instructors on the same day in early October—felt like nails in his coffin. How was he supposed to finish all this reading in the next two days, in addition to studying for a computer test, writing a paper for communications, and putting in eight hours at his part-time job?

Although the papers and tests were hard enough to deal with, it was the constant reading that was proving the most difficult challenge for Chris during his first term of college. He was a conscientious student who attempted to get everything done, but no matter how hard he tried, he just couldn't get everything read on time. When he pushed himself to read more quickly and absorb more, he actually read and retained *less.* Thoughts about how he needed to read more quickly crowded out the meaning of whatever he was reading, and he had to go back over all the material again, slowing him down even more as the reading assignments kept piling up.

Looking ▶▶ *Ahead*

For many students like Chris O'Hara, reading assignments are the biggest challenge in college or university. The amount of required reading is often enormous. Even skilled readers are likely to find themselves wishing for a way to read more quickly and effectively.

Fortunately, you can improve your reading skills. In this chapter, we'll go over several strategies that will help you to read more effectively. You can assess your attention span, consider what you should do before you even start reading an assignment, and discover some ways of getting the most out of your reading.

Then we shift gears, moving from the written word to the spoken word. We'll look at ways of listening effectively and actively. We'll consider how you should listen and what you should be listening *for.* We'll also talk about "problem" instructors, whose lectures . . . well, let's just say they leave something to be desired.

After reading this chapter, you'll be able to answer the following questions:

- **How do my reading style and attention span affect my reading?**

- **How can I improve my concentration and read more effectively?**

- **What is active listening, and what is the difference between hearing and listening?**

- **How can I improve my listening skills?**

Sharpen Your Reading Skills

What kind of reader are you? Do you plod through reading assignments, novels, and magazines and, like Chris, end up feeling that you're taking far too long? Or, do you whip through chapters, devour books, and fly through the daily newspaper and then find you can't recall the information as precisely as you'd like, or remember where you saw the data on television violence that you need for your sociology paper?

Before going any further, think about your own *reading style*—your characteristic way of approaching reading tasks—by completing the Journal Reflections.

Read for Retention, Not Speed

You may have seen advertisements promoting reading systems that promise to teach you to read so quickly that you'll be reading entire books in an hour or so.

Forget it: It's not going to happen. For one thing, certain biological aspects relating to the eye movements involved in reading simply prevent people from reading (and ultimately comprehending) so rapidly.

The act of reading is designed to increase our knowledge and open up new ways of thinking. It can help us achieve new levels of understanding and get us thinking more broadly about the world and its peoples. In the end, then, it ultimately doesn't matter how fast we can read. The key to good reading is understanding—not speed.

Journal REFLECTIONS

How I Read

Think about how you read by answering these questions.

1. When you open a textbook you have never seen before, what do you tend to look at first? Do you read any of the materials in the front or back of the book? Do you check out the table of contents?

2. When you start a new textbook chapter, what do you do first?

3. Are your reading habits the same or different for pleasure reading versus assignment reading?

4. What is the most difficult book you are reading this semester? Why is it difficult?

5. What is the easiest book you are reading this semester? Why is it easy?

6. How do college or university reading assignments differ from high-school reading assignments?

7. What do you do when something you're reading makes absolutely no sense to you?

8. Do your reading habits differ depending on the subject you're reading about?

Common Reading Problems . . . or Are They? If you get headaches, become easily fatigued, or experience blurred vision when reading, your trouble might not be a reading problem . . . it could be related to your vision. Be sure to get an eye exam—if your difficulties are physiological in nature, you might need glasses or contact lenses.

On the other hand, if you get bored quickly while reading, procrastinate on your reading assignments, or are easily distracted, you may need to clarify your goals, work on time management, or organize your reading space so it is easier to concentrate.

In describing how the principles of P.O.W.E.R. Learning can be used to become a better reader, we'll focus on the type of reading that is typically called for in academic pursuits—text chapters, original texts, worksheets, and the like. However, the same principles will help you get more benefit and enjoyment out of your recreational reading as well.

P repare: Approaching the Written Word

Preparing before you start can help you read more effectively. Always begin reading for school with a purpose or a question. This helps focus your mind and decide what to pay attention to. If you weren't given a purpose or question for your reading, create one for yourself.

Survey the material you are about to read to see how the information can help you. Once you have a purpose or a question, begin to skim the material looking for keywords or phrases of interest to you. When you find the keywords or phrases you can slow down and read more carefully. Don't spend time reading material that won't help you answer your question or achieve your purpose. Use advance organizers to help focus your attention.

This approach can be summarized using the SQ3R technique for reading. SQ3R stands for **Survey Question Read Recite Review**.

Survey: Look over what you are going to read. Scan the material. Use introductory paragraphs, charts, pictures, and chapter summaries to get an idea of what the material provides. This text also has margin notes, boldface, and highlighted text to emphasize important material.

Question: Always have a purpose for reading or a question to answer when you begin to read. The questions may be from exercises in the text, an assignment, or notes from your class. Pay attention to what will answer your question and skim over the rest.

Read: This stage of the process requires active reading. Focus on your question. Look for highlighted material. Do your own highlighting. Go back over important sections.

Recite: Once you have completed the reading and found answers to your questions, test your understanding by saying the answers to yourself or to another person. You may want to use a concept map or develop a rhyme depending on your preferred learning style.

Review: Find a way to use memory techniques to help you remember. If you close the book and don't revisit the material you have learned, it will likely be forgotten. Use flash cards, take notes, say it out loud, make up an acronym, or any other technique that works for you.

Your aim in preparation is to become familiar with any advance organizers provided in your text or other reading material or to create a set of advance organizers regarding the material you're planning to read. **Advance organizers** are broad, general ideas related to new material that pave the way for subsequent learning. Ultimately they can help us recall material better after we've read it. (To prove the value of advance organizers, look at Try It! 1, "Discover How Advance Organizers Help.")

Advance organizers

Broad, general ideas related to material that is to be read or heard that pave the way for subsequent learning

What's the Point of the Reading Assignment? Before you begin an assignment, think about what your goal is. Will you be reading a basic textbook, on which you'll be thoroughly tested? Is your reading supposed to provide background information that will serve as a context for future learning but that isn't essential to your success in the course? Is the material going to be

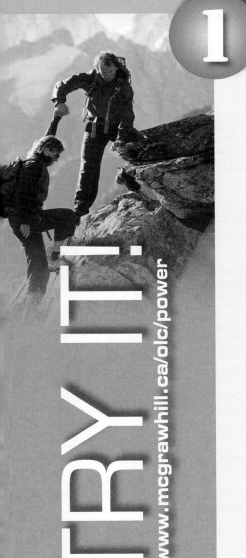

TRY IT!

www.mcgrawhill.ca/olc/power

POWER

1

Discover How Advance Organizers Help

Prepare: The goal of this exercise is to demonstrate the value of advance organizers in understanding and remembering what you read.

Organize: You will need the paragraph below.

Work: Read the passage beginning with: "The procedure is actually quite simple." When you are finished, read the concluding paragraph to find out the purpose of the passage. Now reread the first passage with that purpose in mind.

Evaluate: Did having the purpose as an advance organizer make a big difference?

Rethink: Does this exercise help you decide to use preparation and advance organizers as an aid to reading? Why or why not?

> The procedure is actually quite simple. First you arrange items into different groups. Of course, one pile may be sufficient, depending on how much there is to do. If you have to go somewhere else due to lack of facilities, that is the next step; otherwise, you are pretty well set. It is important not to overdo things. That is, it is better to do too few things at once than too many. In the short run this may not seem important but complications can easily arise. A mistake can be expensive as well. At first, the whole procedure will seem complicated. Soon, however, it will become just another facet of life. It is difficult to foresee any end to the necessity for this task in the immediate future, but then one can never tell. After the procedure is completed, one arranges the materials into different groups again. Then they can be put into their appropriate places. Eventually, they will be used once more and the whole cycle will then have to be repeated. However, this is a part of life.[1]

If you're like most people, you don't have a clue about what this all means. But suppose you had been given some context in advance and you knew before reading it that the description had to do with washing laundry. Now does it all fall into place? Read the passage once more, and see how having an advance organizer helps.

useful to you personally? Realistically, how much time can you devote to the reading assignment?

The way you answer questions about your goal for reading will help you determine the reading strategy to adopt. You aren't expected to read everything with the same degree of intensity. Some material you may feel comfortable skimming; for other material you'll want to put in the maximum effort.

Understand the Point of View of the Material Itself Is what you are reading a textbook or an essay or article? If it is an essay or article, why was it written? to prove a point? to give information? to express the author's personal feelings? Knowing the basic purpose behind what you are reading (even if its specific point and message aren't yet clear) can really help as you read because it gives you a sense of why the writer wrote the piece.

Frontmatter

The preface, introduction, and table of contents of a book

Start with the Frontmatter If you'll be using a text or other book extensively throughout the term, start by reading the preface and introduction and scanning the table of contents—what publishers call the **frontmatter.** Instructors often don't formally assign the frontmatter, but reading it can be a big help because it is there that the author has a chance to step forward and explain, often more personally than elsewhere in a scholarly book, what he or she considers important. Knowing this will give you a sense of what to expect as you read.

By reading the frontmatter, you can get inside the author's head, obtaining insight into the author's goals, values, and strategies in writing the book. You also might find information about the author's background, and perhaps even a photo. Use this material to "personalize" the author, to gain some insight into the kind of person he or she is. The information you obtain from the frontmatter will provide a mental hook on which you can hang the new ideas to which you'll be exposed. (For practice with frontmatter, do Try It! 2, "Read the Frontmatter.")

Create Advance Organizers To create advance organizers, skim through the table of contents, which provides the main headings of what you will be reading. Textbooks often have chapter outlines, listing the key topics to be covered, and these also can provide a way of previewing the chapter content. As you read the outline, thoughts about what you already know about the topic are likely to come to mind, and you can begin to consider how the new material in the book may relate both to what you know as well as to your goals for the reading assignment itself and your more long-term goals.

Texts also often have end-of-chapter summaries, and many articles include a final section in which the author states his conclusions. Take a look at these ending sections as well. Even though you haven't read the material yet and the summary probably won't make complete sense to you, by reading the summary, you'll get an idea of what the author covers and what he considers important in the chapter.

You can also get a sense of advance organizers from what your course instructor says about the chapter or its topic. Sometimes instructors will mention things to pay particular attention to or to look for, such as "When you read Will

Read the Frontmatter

Prepare: Use the front matter of this book as a framework for reading.

Organize: You will need the text. Turn to the Preface beginning on page 00.

Work: Survey the Preface to get an overview of why the book was written and the features contained in the text that can help you learn. Then read it in detail to answer the questions below.

Evaluate: Do you think having an overview of the text will help you read and remember the information? When you started to answer the questions, did it help you focus and use the information more effectively?

Rethink: Are you convinced yet that having an overview and a purpose or questions for your reading makes a big difference?

What are the goals of this book? _____

_____

_____

_____

_____

Who are the authors, and what qualifies them to write this book? _____

_____

_____

Do you think the authors have an understanding of students? _____

Do you think the authors have an understanding of what students should do to become successful in their studies? _____

Is there anything in the frontmatter that made you curious? Does anything seem particularly interesting? _____

_____

_____

After reading the frontmatter, do you feel confident that you can learn what the authors want to teach? Do you feel that you want to learn it? _____

Kymlicka's *Citizenship and Identity in Canada,* notice how he lays out his argument and what his key points are." Sometimes instructors will say why they assigned a reading. Such information provides clues that can help you develop a mental list of the key ideas relating to the chapter.

Whatever you use to construct them, the crucial feature of advance organizers is to provide a framework and context for what you'll be reading. And having a framework and context can spell the difference between fully comprehending what you read and misunderstanding it.

Try It! 3, "Create an Advance Organizer," illustrates how to put all this practice to good use.

Create an Advance Organizer

Prepare: Learn to prepare an advance organizer for a chapter.

Organize: Use the exercise outline below.

Work: Prepare a detailed advance organizer for this chapter. Use the information you have. Survey the section headings. Examine the "Looking Back" chapter summary on pages 185–186. Review your lecture notes. Think of questions you would ask about this information.

Evaluate: Does preparing this advance organizer help you to read more effectively?

Rethink: Do you agree that preparing advance organizers can increase your reading effectiveness? Why?

Complete the following statements to prepare your organizer:

The key topics that will be covered in the rest of this chapter are . . .

_____   _____
_____   _____
_____   _____
_____

I think I will be most interested in . . .

_____
_____
_____
_____

I think I will be least interested in . . .

_____
_____
_____
_____

I hope the chapter covers this topic: _____

Words, phrases, and ideas that are unfamiliar to me include . . .

_____
_____
_____

If the authors were here, I would ask . . .

_____
_____
_____

Note: You may want to use this Try It! as a starting point for advance organizers for each chapter in this book.

Organize: Gathering the Tools of the Trade

It's obvious that the primary item you'll need to complete a reading assignment is the material that you're reading. But there are other essential tools you should gather to organize yourself, potentially including the following:

- A pencil or pen to write notes in the margin.
- A highlighter to indicate key passages in the text.
- A copy of the assignment, so you'll be sure to read the right material.
- A pad of paper or index cards for notetaking if the material is particularly complex. If you routinely use a word processor to take notes, get it ready.
- A dictionary. You never know what new words you'll encounter while you're reading, and a dictionary is the reference tool of choice. If you don't have a dictionary handy, you'll be tempted to skip over unfamiliar words— a decision that may come back to haunt you. Avoid the temptation to say "I'll do it later" by keeping a dictionary close by.

Give Yourself Time There's one more thing you need to prepare successfully for a reading assignment: enough time to complete it. The length of reading assignments is almost never ambiguous. You will typically be given a specific page range, so you will know just how much material you will need to cover.

Now get a watch and time yourself as you read the first three pages of your assignment, being sure to pay attention to the material, not the time! Timing how long it takes to read a representative chunk of material gives you a rough measure of your reading speed for the material—although it will vary even within a single reading assignment depending on the complexity of the material.

You'll also need to consider your current reading **attention span**—the length of time that you usually sustain attention. You can get a general sense of this by using Try It! 4, "Discover Your Attention Span."

Use the three pieces of information you now have—the length of the assignment, your per-page reading speed at full attention, and your typical attention span—to estimate roughly how long it will take you to complete the reading assignment. In addition to distractions, you may need to interrupt your reading to look up words in the dictionary, get a drink, stretch, answer the phone, or do a number of other things. You may also decide to break your reading into several sessions, in which case your total reading time may be greater since you will have to get reacquainted with the reading assignment each time you sit down again. Finally, as you begin to use the techniques in this chapter regularly, your reading attention span should increase, which will change your calculation.

Attention span
The length of time that attention is typically sustained

Work: Getting the Most Out of Your Reading

Finally, it's time to get down to work and start reading.

Obviously—because it's what you're doing at this very moment—you know how to read. But what's important is what you do *while* you're reading. Here

Discover Your Attention Span

Prepare: Get an idea of the length of your attention span and what affects it.

Organize: Make a chart similar to the one below or get a facsimile from the website to use to record the time. Have copy of a textbook you are using.

Work: Complete five timed reading sessions.

1. Choose one of the textbooks you are using this semester.
2. Start reading a section without any preparation. Record in the chart the time when you start reading.
3. When your mind starts to wander and think of other things or it is difficult to remember what you just read, note the time in the chart.
4. Repeat this on five different occasions during the week. Choose times when you think you might be at your best and your worst.
5. Determine your average attention span.

Evaluate: Were you able to get a rough idea of your attention span? Answer the questions below.

Rethink: Do you think it is a good idea to plan on study intervals that take your attention span into account? Why or why not?

Trial #1:   Starting time: _____   Ending time: _____
     Number of minutes between start and end times: _____

Trial #2:   Starting time: _____   Ending time:
     Number of minutes between start and end times: _____

Trial #3:   Starting time: _____   Ending time: _____
     Number of minutes between start and end times: _____

Trial #4:   Starting time: _____   Ending time: _____
     Number of minutes between start and end times: _____

Trial #5:   Starting time: _____   Ending time:
     Number of minutes between start and end times: _____

Reading attention span (the average of the number of minutes in the last column, found by adding up the five numbers and dividing by five) = _____ minutes

---

Ask yourself these questions about your reading attention span.

1. Are you surprised by the length of your reading attention span? In what way?
2. Does any number in the set of trials stand out from the other numbers? For instance, is any number much higher or lower than the average? If so, can you account for this? For example, what time of day was it?
3. Do the numbers in your trials show any trend? For instance, did your attention span tend to increase slightly over the course of the trials, did it decrease, or did it stay about the same? Can you explain any trend you may have noted?
4. Do you think your attention span figures would be very different if you had chosen a different textbook? Why?

are several things that will help you get the most out of the process of reading.

Stay focused The TV show you watched last night, your boyfriend forgetting to meet you at the bus stop, your father's heart attack, your grumbling stomach—there are a million and one possible distractions that can invade your thoughts as you read. Your job is to keep distracting thoughts at bay and focus on the material you are supposed to be reading. It's not easy, but there are things you can do to help yourself stay focused:

If you are reading a long assignment, taking a break can be a reward and should reinvigorate you.

- **Read in small bites.** If you think it is going to take you four hours to read an entire chapter, break up the four hours into more manageable time periods. Promise yourself that you'll read for one hour in the afternoon, another hour in the evening, and the next two hours the following day. One hour of reading is far more manageable than a four-hour block.

- **Take a break.** Actually, plan to take several breaks to reward yourself while you're reading. During your break, do something enjoyable—eat a snack, watch a bit of a ball game on television, play a video game, or the like. Just try not to get drawn into your break activity to the point that it takes over your reading time.

- **Deal with distractions.** Sometimes problems have a way of popping into our minds and repeatedly distracting us. If a particular problem keeps interrupting your concentration—such as a difficulty you're having on the job—try to think of an action-oriented strategy to deal with it. You might even write your proposed solution down on a piece of paper. That can move the problem out of the mental realm of your head and put it into concrete form on paper, potentially making it less intrusive.

Write While You Read Writing is one of the most important aspects of reading. If you haven't underlined, jotted notes to yourself, placed checkmarks on the page, drawn arrows, constructed diagrams, and otherwise defaced and disfigured your book while you're reading, you're not doing your job as a reader.

"What is reading but silent conversation?"

Walter Savage Landor, *Imaginary Conversations*

Writing helps you engage with the material you are reading. You have to deal with the material in your mind in order to translate what you are reading into notes especially if you are using your own words. This is especially important for some learning styles. Learn to say what you are writing to yourself. Also, having to move your hands to write may help you stay focused.

The idea of writing on a book page may go against everything you've been taught in the past. (And of course you should never write on a library book or one that you've borrowed from a friend.) If your practice has been to "save" your textbooks, either because you want to keep them untarnished for your old age or because they will fetch a higher price if you sell them back to the bookstore, rethink your strategy. The greater success you'll experience by writing extensively in your book while you're reading is a far better tactic in the long run.

What should you be writing while you are reading? There are several things you should write down:

- **Rephrase key points.** Make notes to yourself, in your own words, about what the author is trying to get across. Don't just copy what's been said. Think about the material, and rewrite it in your own words.

  Writing notes to yourself in your own words has several consequences, all good. First, you make the material yours; it becomes something you now understand and part of your own personal knowledge base.

  Second, trying to summarize a key point in your own words will make it very clear whether you truly understand it. It's easy to be fooled into thinking we understand something as we're reading along. But the true test is whether we can explain it to ourselves (or someone else) on our own, without referring to the book or article.

  Third, the very act of writing engages an additional type of perception, involving the tactile sense of moving a pen or pressing a keyboard. Engagement of an additional perceptual system will help you learn the material in a more active way.

  Finally, writing notes and phrases will help you study the material later. Not only will the key points be highlighted, but your notes will also quickly bring you up to speed with your initial thoughts.

- **Highlight or underline key points.** Very often the first or last sentence in a paragraph, or the first or last paragraph in a section, will present a key point. (Remember those lessons about "topic sentences" you had in high-school English classes? Writers really use them.)

  Before you highlight anything, though, read the whole paragraph. Then you'll be sure that what you highlight is, in fact, the key information. Topic sentences do not always fall at the beginning of a paragraph.

  Be selective in your highlighting and underlining. A page covered in yellow highlighter may be artistically appealing, but it won't help you understand the material any better. Highlight only the key information. It may be that only one or two sentences or phrases are highlighted on a page. That's fine. What is important is that when you go back to study the material, your memory will be jogged. *In highlighting and underlining, less is more.* One rule of thumb is that no more than 10 percent of the material should be highlighted or underlined.

- **Use arrows, diagrams, outlines, tables, time lines, charts, and other visuals to help you understand and later recall what you are reading.** If there are three examples given for an assertion, number them. If a paragraph discusses a situation in which an earlier point does not hold, link the original point to the exception by an arrow. If a sequence of steps is presented, number each step.

  For example, after you have annotated *this* page, it might look something like what is shown on the next page:

the bookstore, rethink your strategy. The greater success you'll experience by writing extensively in your book while you're reading is a far better tactic in the long run.

What should you be writing while you are reading? There are several things you should write down:

Put key points into my own words. ①

- **Rephrase key points.** Make notes to yourself, in your own words, about what the author is trying to get across. Don't just copy what's been said. Think about the material, and rewrite it in your own words.

  Writing notes to yourself in your own words has several consequences, all good. First, you make the material yours; it becomes something you now understand and part of your own personal knowledge base. ✓✓

  Second, trying to summarize a key point in your own words will make it very clear whether you truly understand it. It's easy to be fooled into thinking we understand something as we're reading along. But the true test is whether we can explain it to ourselves (or someone else) on our own, without referring to the book or article.

  Third, the very act of writing engages an additional type of perception, involving the tactile sense of moving a pen or pressing a keyboard. Engagement of an additional perceptual system will help you learn the material in a more active way.

  Finally, writing notes and phrases will help you study the material later. Not only will the key points be highlighted, but your notes will also quickly bring you up to speed with your initial thoughts.

Use highlighter — but less is more. Not more than 10% highlighted. ②

- **Highlight or underline key points.** Very often the first or last sentence in a paragraph, or the first or last paragraph in a section, will present a key point. (Remember those lessons about "topic sentences" you had in high-school English classes? Writers really use them.) ← *topic sentence*

  Before you highlight anything, though, read the whole paragraph. Then you'll be sure that what you highlight is, in fact, the key information. Topic sentences do not always fall at the beginning of a paragraph.

  Be selective in your highlighting and underlining. A page covered in yellow highlighter may be artistically appealing, but it won't help you understand the material any better. Highlight only the key information. It may be that only one or two sentences or phrases are highlighted on a page. That's fine. What is important is that when you go back to study the material, your memory will be jogged. ✓ *In highlighting and underlining, less is more.* One rule of thumb is that no more than 10 percent of the material should be highlighted or underlined.

- **Use arrows, diagrams, outlines, tables, time lines, charts, and other visuals to help you understand and later recall what you are reading.** If there are three examples given for an assertion, number them. If a paragraph discusses a situation in which an earlier point does not hold, link the original point to the exception by an arrow. If a sequence of steps is presented, number each step. ③

  ← *use visuals*

  For example, after you have annotated *this* page, it might look something like what is shown on the next page:

Particularly if your learning style is a visual one, representing the material graphically will get you thinking about it—and the connections and points in it—in new and different ways. Rather than considering the material solely in verbal terms, you now add visual images. The act of creating visual annotations will not only help you to understand the material better but it will also ease its later recall as well. See Try It! 5, "Mark up a Book Page."

- **Look up unfamiliar words in a dictionary.** Even though you may be able to figure out the meaning of an unfamiliar word from its context, use a dictionary to ensure that what you think it means is correct. A dictionary

5

Working in a Group:
Mark Up a Book Page

Prepare: Practise the techniques for highlighting important information on a page.

Organize: Have a highlighter or a coloured pencil or pen. Refer to pages 171–173 on marking up a portion of text.

Work: Survey the material and develop a purpose or question for reading the information. Reread the section and highlight information that helps you achieve your purpose or answer your question. Complete the "working in a group" exercise below.

Evaluate: How confident are you in your skill to highlight important information in a section of text. Think about using the concept map described in Try It! 6 as a valuable aid.

Rethink: Is highlighting a reading technique you should use more often? Why?

TRY IT!

www.mcgrawhill.ca/olc/power

The more parents speak to their children, the better their children's language skills.

Understanding Language Acquisition: Identifying the Roots of Language

Anyone who spends even a little time with children will notice the enormous strides that they make in language development throughout childhood. However, the reasons for this rapid growth are far from obvious. Two major explanations have been offered: one based on learning theory and the other on innate processes.

The **learning-theory approach** suggests that language acquisition follows the principles of reinforcement and conditioning discussed in Chapter 6. For example, a child who utters the word "mama" is hugged and praised by her mother, which reinforces the behavior and makes its repetition more likely. This view suggests that children first learn to speak by being rewarded for making sounds that approximate speech. Ultimately, through a process of shaping, language becomes more and more like adult speech (Skinner, 1957).

The learning theory approach is supported by research that shows that the more parents speak to their young children, the more proficient the children become in language usage (see Figure 8-11). In addition, higher levels of linguistic sophistication in parents' speech to their young children are related to a greater rate of vocabulary growth, vocabulary usage, and even general intellectual achievement by the time the children are 3 years of age (Hart & Risley, 1997).

On the other hand, the learning theory approach is less successful when it comes to explaining the acquisition of language rules. Children are reinforced not only when they use proper language, but also when they respond incorrectly. For example, parents answer the child's "Why the dog won't eat?" as readily as they do the correctly phrased question "Why won't the dog eat?" Both sentences are understood equally well. Learning theory, then, has difficulty in providing the full explanation for language acquisition.

Pointing to such problems with learning theory approaches to language acquisition, Noam Chomsky (1968, 1978, 1991), a linguist, provided a ground-breaking alternative. Chomsky argued that humans are born with an innate linguistic capability that emerges primarily as a function of maturation. According to his analysis, all the world's languages share a similar underlying structure called a **universal grammar.** Chomsky suggests that the human brain has a neural system, the **language-acquisition device,** that both permits the understanding of the structure of language and provides strategies and techniques for learning the unique characteristics of a given native language.

learning-theory approach: The theory suggesting that language acquisition follows the principles of reinforcement and conditioning

universal grammar: Noam Chomsky's theory that all the world's languages share a similar underlying structure

language-acquisition device: A neural system of the brain hypothesized to permit understanding of language

---

Working in a group, compare and contrast your annotations with those of some classmates. How do their annotations differ from yours? Why did they use the annotations they did? Which annotation techniques worked best? Which were easiest to use? How might these annotations help you to remember what is important? If there were different sorts of material presented on the page, such as mathematical formulas, would you use different kinds of annotations?

will also tell you what the word sounds like, which may be important if your instructor uses the word in class.

E valuate: Considering What It Means and What You Know

Evaluation is a crucial step in reading. You need to be able to answer the seemingly simple question: "What does all this mean?"

But there's another aspect to evaluation. You need to evaluate, truthfully and honestly, your own level of understanding. What do you know as a result of your reading? Evaluation, then, consists of the following steps:

- **Identify the main ideas and themes and their value** *to you personally.* Try to determine the take-home message of the material you've read. For example, the take-home message of a chapter in a recreation management textbook might be, "Future challenges involve meeting the needs of diverse populations, marketing in a fiscally responsible and entrepreneurial manner, involving partners from all sectors, and using technology for efficiency and improved customer service."

  Sometimes the main ideas and themes are spelled out, and at other times you will have to deduce them for yourself. Evaluate the main ideas and themes in terms of their usefulness to your own understanding of the topic.

- **Prioritize the ideas.** Of all the information that is presented, which is the most crucial to the main message and which is the least crucial? Make a list of the main topics covered and try to rank them in order of importance.

- **Think critically about the arguments presented in the reading.** Do they seem to make sense? Are the author's assertions reasonable? Are there any flaws in the arguments? Would authors with a different point of view dispute what is being said? What other perspectives might the author have taken?

- **Talk out loud! Pretend you are explaining the material to a fellow classmate who missed the assignment.** This is one time when talking out loud when no one is around is not only normal but also beneficial. Summarize the material aloud, as if you were talking to another person.

  Talking out loud does two things. First, it helps you identify weak spots in your understanding. Talking to yourself will help you nail down concepts that are still not clear in your mind. Second, and equally important, because you are transforming the written word into the spoken word, you are thinking about the information in an additional way, which will help you remember it better.

- **Be honest with yourself.** Most of us are able to read with our minds on cruise control. But the net result is not much different from not reading the passage at all. If you have drifted off while you've been reading, go back and reread the passage.

- **Pat yourself on the back.** Just as you've done during each of your reading breaks, reward yourself for completing the reading passage. But keep in mind there's one more step before you can really relax, and it's a crucial one: rethinking what you've read.

R ethink: Getting It the Second Time

You're human, so—like the rest of us—when you finish a reading assignment you'd probably like nothing more than to heave a sigh of relief and put the book and what you've read away.

By now you know that there's a crucial step you should take that will assist you in cementing what you've learned into memory: rethinking what you've read. If you do it within 24 hours of first reading the assignment, it can save you hours of work later.

The best way to rethink an assignment is to reread it, along with any notes you've taken. "Yeah, right," you're probably thinking. "Like I have time for that." The benefits of rereading can't be overstated. Rereading transfers material from your short-term memory to your long-term memory. It solidifies information so that it will be remembered far better over time.

> "I can always stop reading a book or magazine if I am not enjoying it, but I have to plough through a dull textbook."
>
> Keely Robinson, Student, Niagara College

Rereading will take *far* less time than the first read-through did. In fact, it isn't necessary to read word for word. You already know what's important and what's not important, so you can skim some of the less important material. But it is wise to reread the more difficult and important material carefully, making sure that you fully understand what is being discussed and why.

Rethinking should be the central activity as you reread the passage and your notes. You need to be sure that your understanding is complete and that you're able to answer any questions that you had earlier about the material.

Concept mapping

A method of structuring written material by graphically grouping and connecting key ideas and themes

The Concept Map As a Rethinking Tool As we saw in Chapter 5, **concept mapping** is a method of structuring written material by graphically grouping and connecting key ideas and themes. Each key idea is placed in a different part of the map, and related ideas are placed near it—above, below, or beside it. A concept map looks similar to a graphic of the solar system, with the central idea in the middle, surrounded by related concepts.

Concept maps help you to rethink material you've read, especially if you used a more traditional outline earlier. Furthermore, once you have developed a concept map for a particular aspect of the material, you can create additional, expanded concept maps involving related information.

Concept maps are particularly useful for people with learning styles that have particular strengths involving spatial relationships. Furthermore, students with certain kinds of learning disabilities—a topic to which we turn in the next section—can also benefit from the use of concept maps.

An example of a concept map involving the material we've discussed so far is illustrated at the top of the next page. Note how it summarizes the material and shows how it is related to the central topic of "Reading with Understanding." Also, see Try It! 6, "Make a Concept Map," on page 178.

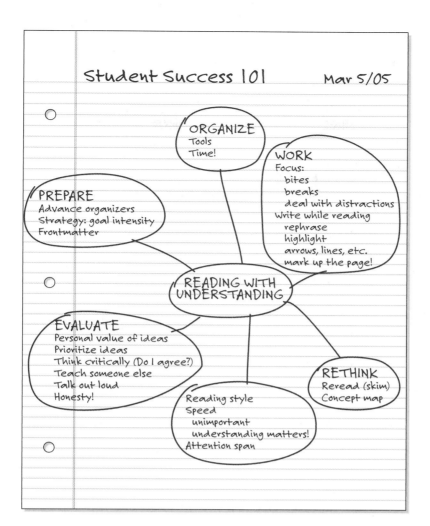

This concept map illustrates the key ideas of reading with understanding.

Student Success 101   Mar 5/05

ORGANIZE
Tools
Time!

WORK
Focus:
  bites
  breaks
  deal with distractions
Write while reading
  rephrase
  highlight
  arrows, lines, etc.
  mark up the page!

PREPARE
Advance organizers
Strategy: goal intensity
Frontmatter

READING WITH UNDERSTANDING

EVALUATE
Personal value of ideas
Prioritize ideas
Think critically (Do I agree?)
Teach someone else
Talk out loud
Honesty!

RETHINK
Reread (skim)
Concept map

Reading style
Speed
  unimportant
  understanding matters!
Attention span

Dealing with Learning Disabilities

Approximately 1 in every 10 Canadians, or about three million people across the country, are affected by a learning disability, and they come from all age, ethnic, and social groups.[2] **Learning disabilities** are characterized by difficulties in processing information when listening, speaking, reading, or writing, in which there is a discrepancy between learning potential and actual academic achievement.

One of the most common kinds of learning disabilities is dyslexia, a reading disability that produces the misperception of letters during reading and writing, unusual difficulty in sounding out letters, spelling difficulties, and confusion between right and left. Although its causes are not yet completely understood, one likely explanation is a problem in the part of the brain responsible for breaking words into the sound elements that make up language.

People with learning disabilities are sometimes viewed as unintelligent. Not so! There is no relationship between learning disabilities and IQ. For instance, dozens of well-known and highly accomplished individuals suffered from dyslexia, including physicist Albert Einstein, poet William Butler Yeats, Walt Disney, and Cher.

Learning disabilities

Difficulties in processing information when listening, speaking, reading, or writing, characterized by a discrepancy between learning potential and actual academic achievement

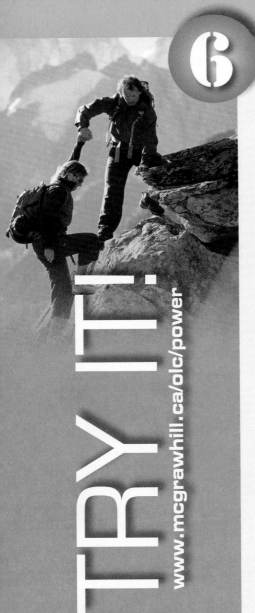

Make a Concept Map

Prepare: Practise the technique of using a concept map to record highlights and organize information in a section of text.

Organize: Use the concept map on the previous page and a blank piece of paper or the space below.

Work: Put the main topic "Tips for Active Listening" in a circle at the centre of the page. Read this section and as you encounter main points put them on the chart. Include notes on any point in the circle with that point. Link points with arrows to show relationships. Sketch what comes to mind as a memory aid. Put it away for a day or two and come back to it. Does it still make sense?

Evaluate: How confident are you in your skill to use the concept map as a way to summarize your reading?

Rethink: Is using a concept map a reading technique you should use more often? Why?

By the time they reach a postsecondary school, most people with learning disabilities have already been diagnosed. If you do have a diagnosed learning disability, it is important to disclose your situation to your instructors and other school officials if you need special services.

In some cases, students with learning disabilities have not been appropriately evaluated before college or university. If you have difficulties such as mixing up and reversing letters frequently and suspect that you have a learning disability, someplace on campus can provide you with guidance. One place to start: your school's counselling or student services centre.

However, just because you are having trouble with reading assignments doesn't automatically mean that you have a learning disability. Not only is the kind of reading you do in college or university more difficult than what you did in high school, there's more of it. It's only when reading represents a persistent, long-term problem—one that won't go away no matter how much work you do—that a learning disability becomes a possible explanation.

Building Listening Skills

Consider these basic two facts: Most of us talk at a rate of around 125 words a minute, but the average listener can comprehend close to 700 words per minute.

Then why is it so hard to listen closely to what someone is saying? Why do our minds wander, and why do we often recall so little about a class when it is over?

The answer rests on the difference between *hearing* and *listening*. Although our sensory capabilities permit us to *hear* far more words than are produced in a given minute by the average speaker, that doesn't mean we actively *listen* to speech. **Hearing** is the involuntary act of sensing sounds. The annoying drip of a faucet or the grating sound of a roommate's voice speaking on the phone in the next room are two examples of how hearing is both involuntary and often meaningless.

In contrast, **listening** is the voluntary act of focusing on what is being said, making sense of it, and thinking about it in a way that permits it to be recalled accurately. Listening involves concentration, and it requires shutting out competing thoughts, such as what we need to pick up at the grocery store or why our date last night was so terrific.

Active listening is an essential component of success, not only in school but also in the broader world. For animals, recognizing the warning cry of another member of the same species can literally mean the difference between life and death. For people, effective listening permits us to know that even though our friend says it's fine if we postpone our hiking trip, she is really disappointed; it enables us to hear the sound of a horn warning us not to walk into a car's path, allows us to respond emotionally to the lyrics of a song, and helps us decide whether a defendant in a trial is telling the truth.

Hearing
The involuntary act of sensing sounds

Listening
The voluntary act of focusing on sounds and making sense of them

> "I'm glad I understand that while language is a gift, listening is a responsibility."
>
> Nikki Giovanni, *Racism 101*

When you are in class, it's essential that you listen and understand. Active listening will help you understand class presentations better. It will aid you in mastering material, permit you to participate more in class, and help you work with your classmates more effectively.

Tips for Active Listening: Listen Up!

You already know many of the techniques of effective listening from the chapter on notetaking. In fact, if you are taking good notes, chances are you are an active listener already. Before you continue, complete Try It! 7, "Determine Your Listening Style."

What follows is a list of the most important techniques of active listening and some tips for listening even when the speaker is making it difficult to stay interested.

- **Choose a seat that will promote active listening.** You should certainly choose a seat that will permit you to see and hear clearly, but there's more to your choice than that. Picking the right seat in a classroom can make a big difference.

Determine Your Listening Style

Prepare: Use this exercise to determine your listening style.

Organize: Use the questionnaire below.

Work: Select the question in each of the pairs below that best describes your listening style.

Evaluate: Can you identify actions you can take to be a more active listener?

Rethink: Would becoming a more active listener improve your study skills and perhaps your relationships?

Consider the following pairs of statements. Place a check next to the statement in each pair that more closely describes your style.

- ☐ 1a. When I'm listening in class, I lean back and get as comfortable as possible.
- ☐ 1b. When I'm listening in class, I sit upright and even lean forward a little.
- ☐ 2a. I let the instructor's words wash over me, generally going with the flow of the lecture.
- ☐ 2b. I try to guess in advance what the instructor is going to say and what direction the lecture is taking.
- ☐ 3a. I regard each lecture as a separate event, not necessarily related to what the instructor has said before or will say the next time.
- ☐ 3b. As I listen, I regularly ask myself how this relates to what was said in previous classes.
- ☐ 4a. When I take notes, I try to reproduce the instructor's words as closely as possible.
- ☐ 4b. When I take notes, I try to interpret and summarize the ideas behind the instructor's words.
- ☐ 5a. I don't usually question the importance of what the instructor is saying or why it's the topic of a lecture or discussion.
- ☐ 5b. I often ask why the content of the lecture is important enough for the instructor to be speaking about it.
- ☐ 6a. I rarely question the accuracy or logic of a presentation, assuming that the instructor knows the topic better than I do.
- ☐ 6b. I often ask myself how the instructor knows something and find myself wondering how it could be proved.
- ☐ 7a. I just about never make eye contact with the instructor.
- ☐ 7b. I often make eye contact with the instructor.

If you tended to prefer the "a" statements in most pairs, you have a more passive listening style. If you preferred the "b" statements, you have a more active listening style. Based on your responses, consider ways that you can become a more active listener.

TRY IT!

www.mcgrawhill.ca/olc/power

Where is the best place to sit? Usually it's near the front centre of the classroom. Instructors make more eye contact with the people near them, and they sometimes believe that the best, most-engaged students sit closest. Conversely, they may assume that students who sit as far toward the back of the room as they can get are less involved. (There's a certain reality to that assumption: Research shows that more questions are asked by students sitting close to instructors than by those farther back.)

Furthermore, sitting in the back of the class may make you feel disengaged and out of touch with what is happening at the front of the room. In turn, this may make it easier for your mind to wander.

Everyone needs to make a personal choice about what works best. If you feel as if you're on display in the front of the class and sitting there inhibits your asking questions, then choose a different seat.

- **Focus on what is being said.** Active listening involves listening not just to a speaker's individual sentences, but also to the overall message. Ask yourself what the speaker's overall theme is. As you saw in the chapter on taking notes, compared with the written word, which provides thematic clues such as titles, headings, and paragraphs, the spoken word is less concrete. Consequently, you have to work to figure out the structure of the speaker's message. Good lecturers have a series of broad ideas that they want to convey. It's your job, as an active listener, to unearth them while not losing track of the details of the message.

In essence, successful listening involves paying attention to two kinds of messages: the actual message and what's called the meta-message. The actual message consists of the verbatim transcript; it is what the speaker actually says, on a surface level. But all speakers also have a **meta-message,** the underlying main ideas that they want to convey through the spoken message.

Sometimes a speaker will explicitly state the meta-message. For example, an instructor might say at the start of a class, "Today I'll be trying to give you

Meta-message

The underlying main ideas that a speaker wants to convey through a spoken message

Career Connections

Active Listening in the Workplace: A Matter of Life and Death

Effective listening is required across all sectors and all types of jobs. Many organizations specifically train call centre staff or customer service reps in effective listening skills; similarly, managers also frequently receive training to improve communication, including listening skills. So, honing your listening skills now will pay big dividends when you enter the world of work. All jobs involve listening, to some extent, but for employees in careers like law enforcement, emergency services, medicine, social work, air traffic control, or crisis intervention, the quality of their listening skills could be a matter of life and death.

Situations that involve people who are ill, injured, distressed, difficult to deal with, or in danger usually require clarification and sometimes negotiation, both of which require advanced listening skills.

The RCMP considers effective listening a functional competency and trains and tests cadets on their listening skills. See <www. rcmp-learning.org/fr-welc.htm> for the RCMP Online University information on listening. Numerous other police departments across Canada train officers to use active listening to defuse potentially dangerous situations, such as domestic disputes. In some situations, such as are often found in community policing, negotiating or mediating alternative resolutions to disputes can reduce the trauma and long-term effects that traditional policing can sometimes produce.

a feel for the ways that social protest informed the national consciousness in the 1960s." In other cases, though, the meta-message may not be so obviously stated, and listeners will have to figure out the underlying themes. Some strategies for doing so follow.

- **Pay attention to the nonverbal messages that accompany the verbal message.** Does an instructor get excited about a particular topic? Does she get agitated? Does the speaker seem unenthusiastic when talking about something? Use nonverbal cues to gauge the importance of a particular part of a message relative to other things being said. Being able to "hear" nonverbal messages can also help you pick up the unspoken messages people give. (See *Career Connections* on the previous page for a discussion of the importance of listening in a professional context.)

- **Listen for what is *not* being said.** Sometimes silence is not just golden, but informative as well. By noting what topics are *not* being covered in class, or are presented only minimally, you can gauge the relative importance of ideas in comparison with one another.

  This is where preparation comes in. The only way to know what's not being discussed is to have done the assigned readings in advance. This information is important. It will help you get a good sense of an instructor's priorities and help you later when the time comes to study for exams.

- **Take notes.** As you no doubt know from experience, no one's memory is infallible. Unless you take careful and accurate notes, you're likely to end up with little or even no recollection of the details of a speaker's message, as we discussed in Chapter 5. Furthermore, taking notes will aid active listening by helping you to focus on the speaker's message.

- **Adopt a questioning attitude, in which your goal is not passive acceptance of the instructor's message but active evaluation.** Do you agree with the speaker? Do you understand the reasoning behind the speaker's arguments? Are the arguments logical? Is this information consistent with other material that's been presented earlier?

- **Ask questions.** One of the most important things you can do during a class is to ask questions. Raising questions will help you evaluate, clarify, and ultimately better understand what your instructor is saying. Even beyond these critical goals, questions serve several other purposes.

  For one thing, raising questions will help you to personalize the material being covered, permitting you to draw it more closely into your own framework and perspective. Furthermore, when you ask a question and it is answered satisfactorily, you become personally engaged in what the instructor is saying.

  Questioning also increases your involvement in the class as a whole. If you sit back and never raise questions in class, you are much less likely to feel a real part of the class. Becoming an active questioner will rightly make you feel like you have contributed something to the class. Remember, if you are unclear about some point, it is likely that others share your lack of clarity.

  Finally, by asking questions in class, you serve as a role model for other students. Your questions may help break the ice in a class, making it easier for others to raise issues that they have about the material. And ultimately the answers that the instructor provides to *others'* questions may help *you* to better understand and evaluate your understanding of the material.

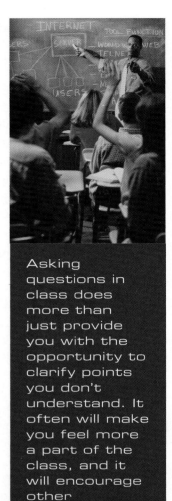

Asking questions in class does more than just provide you with the opportunity to clarify points you don't understand. It often will make you feel more a part of the class, and it will encourage other students to participate.

Breaking the Ice: Tips for Getting over Stage Fright and Asking Questions in Class

Raising your hand in class can be intimidating. You may be afraid that you'll say something dumb, making it clear to the whole class just how out of it you are; or that everyone will be staring at you; or that your instructor and fellow classmates will resent your wasting valuable class time with your own trivial questions.

Although it may not be possible to fully banish such self-defeating thoughts, you can follow three strategies to make it easier to raise questions.

1. **Sit in the front of the room.** Sitting close to the instructor will make it easier to ask questions. Moreover, if you sit in the back of the room and ask a question, the students in front of you will likely swivel around and look at you. In that case, if you already feel intimidated, your feelings of anxiety may rise off the charts.

2. **Write down your question.** If you anticipate that you'll stumble or forget what you want to say, write down your question before raising your hand. The idea is not to read it word for word, or even refer to it at all when you actually ask your question. But writing it will help you quickly organize your thoughts, and having it handy in written form will reduce your anxiety because you know you have a safety net.

3. **Be one of the first students to ask a question.** One reason people sometimes give for not having asked questions is that others have already asked so many questions that there's no time. Or that others have already addressed the issue. Or that others' questions were so good that they make yours look silly. To avoid this difficulty, be among the first to ask questions. Don't wait for others to break the ice; go for it.

The Problem Instructor

He talks too fast . . . she mumbles . . . he puts down people when they ask a question . . . she rambles and goes off on boring tangents . . . she explains things in a way that doesn't make much sense.

In the real world of the college or university classroom, not every instructor comes to class with a finely honed lecture that is clear, compelling, and interesting and presents it beautifully. As we first discussed when we considered strategies for taking notes in Chapter 5, we have all suffered through instruction that is deficient in one or more ways. What should you do when you find yourself in such a situation?

1. *Remember that this too shall pass.* First, keep in mind that this is a temporary condition; your experience usually won't last more than one term. Most instructors are conscientious and well prepared, and unless you have enormously bad luck, the unpleasant experience you're having now will not be routine.

2. *Ask questions about the material.* Even if you have no idea what is going on in class—or *especially* if you have no idea—ask questions. You are not the only one struggling with the instructor's shortcomings. You will be doing everyone in the class a favour if you admit you're not following what an instructor is saying and ask for clarification.

Speaking of Success

Rachel Trail

University of King's College

Rachel Trail attends one of the oldest and smallest universities in Canada—The University of King's College in Halifax. However, the diversity of the people at King's and their range of interests and reasons for attending university fascinate her. She finds greater freedom and increased autonomy to be major appeals associated with the postsecondary experience. She especially values how classes are organized time wise and work wise, and while there is additional responsibility related to going to university, Rachel appreciates the control she has in choosing what to do and when to do it.

Rachel loves to read but the reading list associated with the study of western thought in the Foundation Year Program at The University of King's College in Halifax is formidable—over 30 classic texts by Plato, Kant, Darwin, Freud, and Shakespeare to name just a few authors. In addition, most of the texts are difficult, so Rachel has developed a few strategies to help with the level and volume of reading she is required to do.

First, she thinks of paragraphs as mini essays with a structure that can help her anticipate the reading's message and prepare for the ideas and concepts of the material. She looks for the structure as

UNIVERSITY OF KING'S COLLEGE•HALIFAX

she reads the passage briefly and then reads the piece again one or two more times to capture the main points. This technique is also essential when reading poetry, especially when the imagery doesn't really cohere well.

With so many books to read and understand, the volume of reading can be somewhat overwhelming. Rachel finds that breaking large reading assignments into manageable chunks works well for her. In addition, at King's students focus on developing critical thinking skills by questioning, contemplating, and evaluating topics in a larger context and from several perspectives. So, by talking about the assigned works in small discussion groups, the information and learning are reinforced.

As far as future studies are concerned, Rachel Trail is thinking about majoring in Spanish. The development of solid reading skills early on in her academic career will serve her well as she moves on to read classic literature in a foreign language.

3. *Ask—privately—for the instructor to change her behaviour.* It is not bad classroom etiquette to ask an instructor to speak a little slower. Instructors sometimes get carried away with enthusiasm and begin speaking faster and faster without even being aware of it. Very often a reality check from a student will be welcome. But don't couch your comment in way that makes the instructor feel inept ("Could you slow down; you're going too fast and losing me"). Instead, keep the comment neutral, without placing blame. For instance, you might simply say, "I'm having trouble keeping up with you; would it be possible for you to speak a little more slowly?"

4. *Pool your resources.* Get together with other students in the class and work out a strategy for dealing with the situation. If an instructor speaks too fast and you just can't keep up with the flow of information, meet with your fellow students and compare what you've gleaned from the class. They may have understood or noted material that you missed, and vice versa. Together, you may be able to put the pieces of the puzzle together and get a fuller understanding of the material.

5. *Listen to the lecture again.* You might bring a tape recorder to class (but request the instructor's permission first!). Then, after class, you can play back the tape at your leisure.

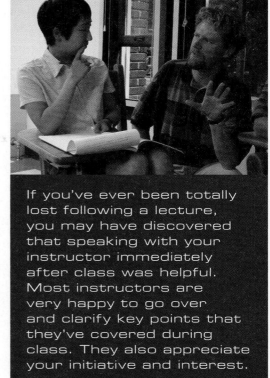

If you've ever been totally lost following a lecture, you may have discovered that speaking with your instructor immediately after class was helpful. Most instructors are very happy to go over and clarify key points that they've covered during class. They also appreciate your initiative and interest.

There's another option: Many instructors teach multiple sections of the same course. If this is the case, you might, schedule permitting, sit in on an additional section of the course. The second time around the information may become much clearer.

6. *Talk* with the instructor after class. If you feel totally lost after a lecture, or even if you've missed only a few points, speak with the instructor after class. Ask for clarification and get her to re-explain points that you missed. Such a dialogue will help you to understand the material better. But it will also do something more: help build your relationship with your instructor.

Looking Back

How do my reading style and attention span affect my reading?

- The most important aspect of reading is understanding, not speed. People have different reading styles that can be modified to improve their ability to read with understanding.

- One problem people have with reading is a limited attention span. However, attention span can be increased with self-awareness and practice.

How can I improve my concentration and read more effectively?

- Reading should be approached with a clear sense of purpose and goals, which will vary from assignment to assignment. Examining the frontmatter of a book and creating advance organizers are also useful activities.

- Maintain focus by breaking down the reading into small chunks, taking breaks as needed, dealing with distractions, and writing while reading. It is also helpful to identify the main ideas, prioritize them, think critically about the arguments, and explain the writer's ideas to someone else.
- Concept maps that structure and relate ideas can aid rethinking.

What is active listening, and what is the difference between hearing and listening?

- Listening is a voluntary act that involves focusing on what is being said, making sense of it, and thinking about it. In contrast, hearing is the involuntary act of sensing sounds.
- Active listening involves paying attention to what is being heard. It permits the mastery of material, facilitates class participation, and enables cooperation with other students.

How can I improve my listening skills?

- Active listening involves focusing on what is being said, including the speaker's meta-message, paying attention to nonverbal messages, listening for what is not being said, and taking notes.
- Asking questions in class clarifies ambiguous information, helps to personalize the material being covered, increases your level of involvement in the class, and makes it easier for other students to ask questions.
- Active listening also involves carefully analyzing the speaker's message, presentation, arguments, and nonverbal behaviour, and examining your own listening behaviour and reactions.

P.O.W.E.R. Portfolio

Reading and Listening

1. Develop your vocabulary. Keep a list of new words you encounter and review them periodically.
2. Consider becoming a conversation partner with a person whose first language is not English. This experience will demonstrate how difficult and how important the art of listening is. Consider including a log and reflective comments in the "Volunteer" or "Interests" section of your portfolio!

Resources

On Campus

If you are experiencing unusual difficulties in reading and the problem is one you encountered in high school, you may have a learning disability. If you suspect this is the case, take action. Many colleges and universities have offices that deal specifically with learning disabilities. You can also talk to someone at your school's counselling centre who can arrange for you to be tested.

In Print

The third edition of Kathleen McWhorter's book *Academic Reading* (Longman, 5th edition, 2003) provides a complete set of guidelines for reading textbooks and other kinds of writing you will encounter during college or university. Another useful volume is *Breaking Through: College Reading* (Longman Publishing Group, 6th edition, 2001), by Brenda Smith.

Integrating College Study Skills: Reasoning in Reading, Listening, and Writing (Wadsworth Publishing, 6th edition, 2001), by Peter Elias Sotiriou, advises and demonstrates how to use reasoning to connect students' reading, writing, and listening skills. Sotiriou uses a thoughtful, measured approach, with specific strategies for studying, reading, notetaking, and exam-taking.

On the Web

The following sites on the World Wide Web provide the opportunity to extend your learning about the material in this chapter. Although the Web addresses were accurate at the time the book was printed, check the P.O.W.E.R. Learning website, <www.mcgrawhill.ca/olc/power>, for any changes that may have occurred.

www.ucc.vt.edu
This site has links to several helpful reading resources, including sections on how to analyze essays, skimming and scanning, how to read a difficult book, and SQ3R, an approach to reading, and retaining, textual material.

www.ldonline.org/ld_indepth/postsecondary/index.html
This site has information to assist students with learning disabilities in the planning and selection process, plus lots of advice on creating a successful postsecondary education experience.

www.ucc.vt.edu/stdysk/addhandbook.html
This site offers a handbook for students with ADHD (attention deficit hyperactivity disorder).

The Case Of...

What's Wrong with this Picture?

Rahman Ali groaned in frustration as he left his Elements of Design course. He guessed he'd only understood about 50 percent of what the instructor had said. In general, Rahman felt his Photography program was going well, but this course was impossible.

Part of the problem was the size of the class—it was a common course for visual arts students and there were about 150 students in the class. Part of the problem was the type of class—every class was a PowerPoint presentation. And the third part of the problem was sheer volume—their instructor showed at least 30 slides a class, so there wasn't a lot of time for discussion. Rahman felt that he couldn't take up class time asking the teacher to speak a little slower or to re-explain points he didn't understand. It didn't make matters any better when his classmates whose first language was English said they were having trouble understanding their teacher as well.

As Rahman considered his options, no clear answer was obvious. He'd worked for a year after high school to save money for college and he wasn't going to quit. And the design course was compulsory—he couldn't drop it. Rahman tried to consider his options, but he couldn't focus on a clear solution.

1. How would you advise Rahman to prepare for his design course? What could he do in advance of each class?

2. What organizational strategies could Rahman apply to his listening skills for this course? How could he and his classmates help themselves to feel more successful in this course?

3. Why is listening such a hard skill for English-as-a-second-language learners? Is it as difficult for students whose first language is English? Why or why not?

4. A design course has lots of terms borrowed from French, Italian, Latin, or Greek. What other courses or programs have particularly difficult vocabulary?

5. Why is evaluation important for listening? How could Rahman evaluate his listening comprehension?

6. In what ways can Rahman use rethinking techniques to improve his understanding in his Elements of Design course?

Taking Tests

8

Ginette Berger looked at her trembling hands and told herself to breathe in . . . one, two, three . . . and out . . . one, two, three . . . . In high school Ginette used to get stomach aches and shortness of breath around exam time. Her guidance counsellor suggested she might have test anxiety and so she learned some relaxation techniques. When Ginette started her interior design program, she was so excited. She loved her program, but postsecondary was a lot harder than high school. As a familiar sense of dread came over her, Ginette reminded herself to breathe . . . .

Looking ▶▶
Ahead

Ginette is not alone in her dread of exams. For many students, tests represent the most anxiety-producing events in their postsecondary careers.

They needn't be *so* bad. There are strategies and techniques you can learn to reduce the fearsomeness of tests. In fact, in some ways learning *how* to take tests is as important as learning the content that they cover.

Taking tests effectively is an academic skill. It does not just involve mastering a body of information; it also requires mastering specific test-taking skills.

It is those skills we consider in this chapter. One of the first steps is to demystify tests. You will learn about the different types of tests and strategies that you can apply before you even take a test. You will become familiar with various types of test questions and learn a strategy that matches each type of question.

We will also explore two aspects of test taking that may affect your performance: test anxiety and cramming for a test. You will learn ways to deal with anxiety, keep your cramming to a minimum, and make the most of cramming if you *do* have to resort to it.

The chapter ends with suggestions for evaluating your performance toward the end of a test session and for using your test results to improve your performance the next time you take a test.

After reading this chapter, you'll be able to answer these questions:

- **What kinds of tests will I encounter in college or university?**

- **What are the best ways to prepare for and take various kinds of tests?**

- **What are the best strategies for answering specific kinds of test questions?**

Although tests are a fact of academic life, there are aspects of them that those who give tests—as well as those who take them—don't like very much.

Students hate tests because they produce fear, anxiety, apprehension about being evaluated, and a focus on grades instead of learning for learning's sake. Instructors hate tests because they produce fear, anxiety, apprehension about being evaluated, and a focus on grades instead of learning for learning's sake. That's right: Students and instructors dislike tests for the very same reasons.

However, tests are also valuable. A well-constructed test identifies what you know (and don't know) and where the gaps in your knowledge are. They help you see how your performance compares to that of others. Knowing that you'll be tested on a body of material is likely to motivate you to learn material more thoroughly.

But there's another reason why you may dislike tests: You may assume that tests have the power to define your worth as a person. However, *tests are not a measure of your value as an individual—just how well (and how much) you studied, how well you learned the material, and whether you knew how to write tests.*

If you do badly on a test, you may be tempted to believe that you've received some fundamental information about yourself from the professor and the college or university, information that says you're a failure in some significant way.

This is a dangerous—and wrong-headed—assumption. If you do poorly on a test, it doesn't mean you're a bad person, or stupid, or that you'll never do better again and that your life is ruined. If you don't do well on a test, you're the same person you were before you took the test—no better, no worse. You just did poorly on a test, period.

Journal REFLECTIONS REFLECTIONS

How I Feel about Tests

1. What general feelings do you have about tests?

2. What are your first memories of being in a testing situation? What were your feelings, and why?

3. What uses do you think tests serve?

4. Do you think tests are ever misused? In what ways?

5. In general, what makes a test "good" from your perspective?

6. What *specific* characteristics does a good test have?

7. In general, what makes a test "bad" from your perspective?

8. What *specific* characteristics does a bad test have?

9. What factors contribute to your success or failure on a particular exam? Which of these factors are under your control?

Tests are tools; they are indirect and imperfect measures of what we know. Someone with a great deal of knowledge can do poorly on a test; perhaps anxiety made her blank out or she went too slowly early on and was unable to complete the test. Another person may know considerably less and still do better on the test simply because he may have learned some test-taking skills along the way.

How much we reap the benefits of a test depends on several considerations: the kind of test it is, the subject matter involved, and above all how well we prepare for it. Let's turn, then, to the first step in test taking: preparation. (The five steps are summarized in the P.O.W.E.R. Plan below.)

P repare: Readying Your Test-Taking Strategies

Complete Try It! 1, "Test Preparation and Learning Style," to develop a test-preparation strategy that matches your learning style.

Preparation for tests requires several strategies. Among the most important are the following:

PREPARE
Review your work regularly

ORGANIZE
Bring the right tools to the test; follow directions carefully

WORK
Tackle the test

EVALUATE
Save time to check your work; know when to stop

RETHINK
Reflect on what you've learned when you get a test back

P.O.W.E.R. Plan

Remember Everything You Do in a Course Is Preparation for a Test Completing a reading assignment, writing a paper, filling out a worksheet—everything you do during a course helps to prepare you for a test. There is no surer way to get good grades on tests than to attend class faithfully, to take good notes, and to complete all class assignments seriously and on time.

Preparing for tests is a long-term proposition. It's not a matter of giving your all the night before the test. Instead, it's a matter of giving your all to every aspect of the course.

Know What You Are Preparing For Determine as much as you can about the test before you begin to prepare for it. The more you know about a test, the better you'll be able to get ready.

To find out about an upcoming test, ask these questions:

* Is the test called a "test," "exam," "quiz," or something else? As you can see in Table 8.1, the names imply different things. For simplicity's sake, we'll use the term test throughout this chapter, but know that these distinctions exist and they should affect the way you prepare.
* What material will the test cover or not cover?
* How many questions will be on it?
* How much time is it expected to take? a full class period? only part of a period?
* What kinds of questions will be on the test?
* How will it be graded?
* Will sample questions be provided?
* Are tests from previous terms available?

See Try It! 2, "Complete a Test-Preparation Checklist."

Test Preparation and Learning Style

Just as everyone doesn't learn the same way, not everyone uses the same approach to prepare for tests. What is the most effective way for you to prepare for tests?

Prepare: Identify your most effective test preparation strategy.

Organize: Review the results of your learning styles analysis in Chapter 2, Try It! 5. If you haven't completed this exercise, please do it now.

Work: Use the chart below to help you summarize a test-preparation strategy that best matches your learning style.

Evaluate: Use the strategy for an upcoming test to assess its usefulness.

Rethink: How did your strategy work? What other steps are required to improve your marks?

Preferred Learning Style	Description of Style	Preferred Test Preparation Strategy

If your preferred learning style is Bodily–Kinesthetic an example would be:

Preferred Learning Style	Description of Style	Preferred Test Preparation Strategy
Bodily–Kinesthetic	Move around. Touch and talk. Use physical activities to reinforce learning.	Read or answer questions out loud. Study standing up or moving around. Act out answers. Draw diagrams or charts.

Complete a Test-Preparation Checklist

Prepare: Learn to use a test-preparation checklist.

Organize: Use the checklist below.

Work: Complete the checklist below.

Evaluate: Were you able to complete the checklist?

Rethink: Are there items on the checklist that you don't do and should to improve your test-taking effectiveness?

Before taking your next test, complete the following test-preparation checklist.

Test-Preparation Checklist

- ☐ I checked whether it's a quiz, test, or exam.
- ☐ I began preparation long before the test (e.g., by taking notes in class).
- ☐ I understand what material will be covered.
- ☐ I have reviewed my textbook and have completed the review questions at the end of the chapter.
- ☐ I have done sample tests on the textbook's CD-ROM or website.
- ☐ I know how long it will take.
- ☐ I know what kinds of questions will be on the test.
- ☐ I know how it will be graded.
- ☐ I obtained sample questions or previous tests, if available.
- ☐ I formed or participated in a study group.
- ☐ I studied with my study group more than once.
- ☐ I used different and appropriate preparation strategies for each type of question.
- ☐ I read my class notes.
- ☐ I composed some essay questions.
- ☐ I answered essay questions aloud.
- ☐ I actively memorized facts and details.
- ☐ I made and used note cards.
- ☐ I created and used a test like the real test.

Table 8.1

Quizzes, Tests, Exams . . . What's in a Name?

Although they may vary from one instructor to another, the following definitions are the ones most frequently used:

Quizzes. A **quiz** is a brief assessment, usually covering a relatively small amount of material. Some quizzes cover as little as one class's worth of reading. Although a single quiz usually doesn't count for very much, instructors often add quiz scores together, and collectively they can become a significant part of your final course grade.

Tests. A **test** is a more extensive, more heavily weighted assessment than a quiz, covering more material. A test may come every few weeks of the term, often after each third or quarter of the term has passed, but this varies with the instructor and the course.

Exams. An **exam** is the most substantial kind of assessment. In many classes, just one exam is given—*a final exam* at the end of the term. Sometimes there are two exams, one at the midpoint of the term (called, of course, a midterm) and the other at the end. Exams are usually weighted quite heavily because they are meant to assess your knowledge of all the course material up to that point.

Review Your Notes If you have regularly taken notes and reviewed them, you have a great start on preparing for your test. If you have already done the work you may only have to review your notes and flashcards or ask some questions to study for the test.

Form a Study Group **Study groups** are small, informal groups of students who work together to learn the course material and study for a test. Forming such a group can be an excellent way to prepare. Some study groups are formed for particular tests, while others meet regularly throughout the term.

The typical study group meets a week or two before a test and plans a strategy for studying. Members share their understanding of what will be on the test, based on their own perceptions of what an instructor has said in class about the upcoming test. Together, they develop a list of review questions to guide their individual study. The group breaks up, and the members study on their own.

A few days before the test, members of the study group meet again. They discuss answers to the review questions, go over the material, and share any new information they may have about the test. They may also quiz one another about the material to identify any weaknesses or gaps in their knowledge.

Study groups, made up of a few students who study together for a test, can help organize material, provide new perspectives, and motivate members to do their best.

Study groups can be extremely powerful because they help accomplish several things:

- They help members to organize and structure the material, which forces members to approach the material in a systematic and logical way.
- They aid in the sharing of different perspectives on the material.
- They help prevent students from overlooking any potentially important information.
- They force their members to rethink the course material, explaining it in words that they and the other group members will understand. As we discussed in Chapter 6, this helps both understanding and recall of the information when it is needed on the test.
- They help motivate members to do their best. When you're part of a study group, you're no longer working just for yourself; your studying also benefits the other study-group members. Not wanting to let down your classmates in a study group may sometimes give more of a push to your study habits than you get from working only for yourself.

There are some some potential drawbacks to keep in mind. Study groups don't always work well for students with certain kinds of learning styles who prefer to work independently. In addition, "problem" members who don't pull their weight, may cause difficulties for the group. In general, though, the advantages of study groups usually far outweigh their possible disadvantages.

Review Your Textbook and Do Sample Tests Most textbooks come with sample test questions at the end of every chapter and many have accompanying CD-ROMs or online learning centres with sample tests. These resources are tremendously helpful in determining what you need to study—as well as where you don't need to focus your attention.

Study groups

Small, informal groups of students whose purpose is to help members study for a test

Match Test Preparation to Question Types Test questions come in different types (see Table 8.2), and each requires a somewhat different style of preparation.

- **Essay questions.** Essay questions are meant to see whether you have a broad knowledge of the material being tested. You'll need to know not just a series of facts but also the connections between them, and you will have to be able to discuss these ideas in an organized and logical way. Essay exams focus on the ways in which the various pieces of information on a topic fit together.

  The best approach to studying for an essay exam involves four steps:

  1. Carefully read your class notes and any notes you've made on assigned readings that will be covered on the upcoming exam. Also go through the readings themselves, reviewing underlined or highlighted material and marginal notes.

  2. Play professor: Think of likely exam questions. To do this, you can use the keywords, phrases, concepts, and questions you've earlier created in your notes. In addition, your class instructor may have given you a list of possible essay topics.

  3. Without looking at your notes or your readings, answer each potential essay question—aloud. Don't feel embarrassed about doing this. Talking aloud is often more useful than answering the question silently in your head.

     You can also write down the main points that any answer should cover. Don't write out complete and full answers to the questions, because your time is probably better spent learning the material you'll be tested on. The one exception is if your instructor tells you exactly what essay question is going to be on the exam. In that case, it pays to write out the answer.

Table 8.2

Types of Test Questions

Essay

Requires a fairly extensive, on-the-spot composition about some topic. An essay question may call on you to describe some person, process, or event, or it may ask you to compare or contrast two separate sets of material.

Multiple-choice

Usually contains a question or statement, followed by a number of (usually four or five) response choices. You are supposed to choose the most correct response from the possible response choices that are offered.

True–false

Presents statements about a topic that are either accurate or inaccurate. You are to indicate whether each statement is accurate (true) or inaccurate (false).

Matching

Presents two lists of related information, arranged in column form. Typically you are asked to pair terms, concepts, and definitions with one another.

Short-answer

Requires brief responses (at most a few sentences) in a kind of mini-essay.

Fill-in

Requires you to add one or more missing words to a sentence or series of sentences.

4. After you've answered the questions, check yourself by looking at the notes and readings once again. If you feel confident that you've answered particular questions adequately, check them off. You can go back later for a quick review.

If there are questions that you had trouble with, review that material immediately. Then repeat the third step above, answering the questions again.

- **Multiple-choice, true–false,** and **matching questions.** While the focus of review for essay questions should be on major issues and controversies, and on integration of the material—more of a big picture focus—studying for multiple-choice, true–false, and matching questions requires more attention to the details.

   Almost anything is fair game for multiple-choice, true–false, and matching questions, so you can't afford to overlook anything when studying. This means that your studying needs to be detail-oriented. And it means that you must put your memory into high gear and master a great many facts.

   It's a particularly good idea to write down important facts on index cards like those below. Remember the advantages of these cards: They're portable and available all the time, and the act of creating them helps drive the material into your memory. Furthermore, you can shuffle them and test yourself repeatedly until you know you've mastered the material.

- **Short-answer** and **fill-in questions.** Short-answer and fill-in questions are similar to essays in that they require you to recall key pieces of information; that is, you have to dredge the information up from your memory rather than, as is the case with multiple-choice, true–false, and matching questions, finding it on the page in front of you. However, short-answer and fill-in questions—unlike essay questions—typically don't demand that you integrate or compare different types of information. Consequently, the focus of your study should be on the recall of specific, detailed information.

Test Yourself Once you feel you've mastered the material, test yourself on it. There are several ways to do this. One is to create a complete test for yourself, in writing, making its form as close as possible to what you expect the actual test to be. For instance, if your instructor has told you the classroom test will be primarily made up of short-answer questions, your test should be too. One bonus: Constructing a test is actually an excellent way of studying the material and cementing it into memory.

You might also construct a test and administer it to a classmate or a member of your study group. In turn, you could take a test that someone else has constructed. The combined experience of making and taking a test on the same general subject matter is among the very best ways to prepare for the real thing.

Avro Arrow—CF-105 (1949)
–advanced, supersonic, twin-engine, all-weather interceptor jet aircraft
–2 prototype airframes—$2 million apiece
–engine/fire-control & missile systems costs rose— $12.5 million per aircraft
–test flights indicated plane could be world's fastest & most advanced
–project cancelled on 20 February 1959—all plans and prototypes destroyed

Endoplasmic reticulum (ER):
Smooth ER—makes fats (lipids)
Rough ER—has ribosomes, which make proteins
Together, they make membranes for whole cell (for plasma membrane, mitochondrion, etc.). Also make more of themselves.

Many students now take tests online. These tests are most often multiple-choice, true–false, or matching labels and definitions. There are four things to remember about these tests:

1. The time is usually fixed so plan your time to answer the questions.
2. Make sure you understand if you can change an answer. Most questions allow you to select an answer and then submit the answer. You can change your answers until you submit.
3. If you are anxious about online tests, ask to take a sample online test for practise.
4. The same recommendations for test taking apply to online tests as to paper tests.

Deal with Test Anxiety What does the anticipation of a test do to you? Do you feel shaky or frantic, as though there's not enough time to get it all done? Do you feel as if there's a knot in your stomach? Do you grit your teeth?

Fortunately, **test anxiety** is a temporary condition characterized by fears and concerns about test taking. Almost everyone experiences it to some degree; but if it is too great, it can make it harder for you to study and do your best on a test.

You'll never eliminate test anxiety completely, nor do you want to. A little bit of nervousness can energize us, making us more attentive and vigilant. Like any competitive event, testing can motivate us to do our best. So think of test anxiety as a desire to perform at your peak—an ally at test time.

For many people, however, anxiety can spiral into the kind of paralyzing fear that makes your mind go blank. So you definitely want to keep it in its place. There are several ways to do this:

1. *Prepare thoroughly.* The more you prepare, the less test anxiety you'll feel. Good preparation can give you a sense of control and mastery, and it will prevent test anxiety from overwhelming you.
2. *Take a realistic view of the test.* Remember that no single test determines how you'll do for the rest of your life. Your future success does not hinge on your performance on any single exam.
3. *Learn relaxation techniques.* You can learn to reduce or even eliminate the jittery physical symptoms of test anxiety by using relaxation techniques. These techniques are covered in Chapter 13, but the basic process is straightforward: You want to breathe evenly, gently inhaling and exhaling. Focus your mind on a pleasant, relaxing scene such as a beautiful forest or a peaceful spread of farmland, or on a sound such as ocean waves.
4. *Visualize success.* Think of an image of your instructor handing back your test, on which you've received an A. Or imagine your instructor congratulating you on your fine performance the moment you walk into your classroom on the day after the test. Positive visualizations such as these, which highlight your potential success, can help replace negative images of failure that may be fuelling your test anxiety.
5. *Set up a special testing arrangement.* If your test anxiety is severe, visit the counselling or student learning centre at your school. You may be able to set up a special testing arrangement that can accommodate your test anxiety.

Cramming: You Shouldn't, But . . . You know, of course, that **cramming,** hurried, last-minute studying, is not the way to go. You know that

---

Test anxiety

A temporary condition characterized by fears and concerns about test taking

---

Cramming

Hurried, last-minute studying

you're likely to forget the material the moment the test is over because long-term retention is nearly impossible without thoughtful study. But . . .

> . . . it's been one of those weeks where everything went wrong.

> . . . the instructor sprang the test on you at the last minute.

> . . . you forgot about the test until the night before it was scheduled.

Whatever the reason, there may be times when you can't study properly. What do you do if you have to cram for an exam?

The first thing to do is choose what you really need to study. You won't be able to learn everything, so you have to make choices. Figure out the main focus of the course, and concentrate on it. Don't spend a lot of time on what you're unable to do. Beating yourself up about your failings as a student will only hinder your efforts.

Instead, admit you're human and fallible like everyone else. Then spend a few minutes developing a plan for what you can accomplish in the limited time you've got.

Once you have a strategy, prepare a one-page summary sheet with hard-to-remember information. Just writing the material down will help you remember it, and you can refer to the summary sheet frequently over the limited time you do have to study.

Have you ever crammed for a test? If so, you know how exhausting it can be, and how easy it is to overlook crucial material. However, time pressures sometimes make cramming your only option. When that happens, there are strategies you can use to help you make the best use of limited time.

Next, read through your class notes, concentrating on the material you've underlined and the key concepts and ideas that you've already noted. Forget about reading all the material in the books and articles you're being tested on. Instead, only read the passages that you've underlined and the notes you've taken on the readings. Finally, maximize your study time. Using your notes, note cards, and concept maps, go over the information. Read it. Say it aloud. Say it aloud again. Think about it and the way it relates to other information. In short, use all the techniques we've talked about for learning and recalling information.

Just remember: When the exam is over, material that you have crammed into your head is destined to leave your mind as quickly as it entered. If you've crammed for a midterm, don't assume that the information will still be there when you study for the final. In the end, cramming often ends up taking more time for worse results than does studying with more appropriate techniques.

Organize: Facing the Day of the Test

You've studied a lot, and you're happy with your level of mastery. Or perhaps you have the nagging feeling that there's something you haven't quite gotten to. Or maybe you know you haven't had enough time to study as much as you would have liked, and you're expecting a disaster.

Whatever your frame of mind, it will help to organize your plan of attack on the day of the test. What's included on the test is out of your hands, but what you bring to it, you can control.

For starters, bring the right tools to the test. Have at least two pens and two pencils with you. It's usually best to write in pen because, in general, writing tends to be easier to read in pen than pencil. But you also might want to have pencils ready. Sometimes instructors will use machine-scorable tests, which require the use of pencil. Or there may be test questions that involve computations, and solving them may entail frequent reworking of calculations.

You should also be sure to bring a watch to the test, even if there will be a clock on the wall of the classroom. You will want to be able to pace yourself properly during the test. Having your own watch will help you feel more in control of your time during the test.

Sometimes instructors permit you to use notes and books during the test. If you haven't brought them with you, they're not going to be of much help. So make sure you bring them if you are allowed. Even for closed-book tests, having such material available before the test actually starts may allow you a few minutes of review after you arrive in the classroom.

"A gem cannot be polished without friction, nor a person perfected without trials."

Chinese Proverb

On the day of a test, avoid the temptation to compare notes with your friends about how much they've studied. Yes, you might end up feeling good because many of your fellow classmates studied less than you. But chances are you'll find others who sound like they have spent significantly *more* time studying than you, and this will do little to encourage you.

Plan on panicking. Although it sounds like the worst possible approach, permitting yourself the option of spending a minute feeling panicky will help you to recover from your initial fears.

Finally, listen carefully to what an instructor says before the test is handed out. The instructor may tell you about a question that is optional or worth more points or inform you of a typographical error on the test. Whatever the instructor says just before the test, you can be sure it's information that you don't want to ignore.

Taking the Test

Work: Tackling the Test

Take a deep breath—literally.

There's no better way to start work on a test than by taking a deep breath, followed by several more. The deep breaths will help you to overcome any initial panic and anxiety you may be experiencing. It's okay to give yourself over for a moment to panic and anxiety, but, to work at your best, use the relaxation techniques that we spoke about earlier to displace those initial feelings. Tell yourself, "It's okay. I am going to do my best on this." Don't let your mind get sidetracked by panicky thoughts.

Read the test instructions and *then skim through the entire exam.* Look at the kinds of questions that are asked and pay attention to the way they will be scored. If the point weighting of the various parts of the exam is not clear, ask the instructor to clarify it. Your goal is to know how to allocate your time. You don't want to spend 90 percent of your time on an essay that's worth only 10 percent of the marks, and you want to be sure to leave time at the end of the test to check your answers. An initial read-through also helps you verify that you have every page of the exam and that there is no other physical problem with it, such as badly copied pages or ink marks that partially obscure some of the questions.

If there are any lists, formulas, or other key facts that you're concerned you may forget, jot them down now on the back of a test page. You may want to refer to this material later during the test.

Once this background work is out of the way, you'll be ready to proceed to actually answering the questions. These principles will help you to do your best on the test:

- **Answer the easiest questions first.** By initially getting the questions out of the way that are easiest for you, you accomplish several important things. First, you'll be leaving yourself more time to think about the tougher questions later. In addition, moving through a series of questions without a struggle will build your confidence. Finally, working through several questions will build a base of points that may be enough to earn you at least a passing grade.

- **Write legibly on one side of the paper.** If an instructor can't read what you've written, you're not going to get credit for it, no matter how brilliant your answer. So be sure to keep your handwriting or printing legible.

  It's also a good idea to write your answers to essay questions on only one side of a page. This will allow you to go back later and add or revise information.

- **Master machine-scored tests.** Tests will sometimes be scored, in part, by computer. In such cases, you'll usually have to indicate your answers by filling in—with a pencil— circles or squares on a computer answer sheet.

  Be careful! A stray mark or smudge can cause the computer scanner to misread your answer sheet, producing errors in grading. Be sure to bring a good eraser in addition to a pencil; the biggest source of mistakes in machine grading is incomplete erasing on a test.

> "The biggest problem I have with tests is the course gives you a lot of general info, but the exam has very specific questions. I keep reviewing, cram as much in my head as possible, and make educated guesses as to what the exam question will be."
>
> Scott Acorn, Student, Capilano College

It's best to write your answers not only on the answer sheet but also on the test itself (if the test is not intended for future reuse). That way you can go back and check your answers easily—a step you should take frequently.

Use Strategies Targeted to Answering Specific Types of Test Items

Every type of item requires a particular approach. Use these strategies to tailor your approach to specific kinds of questions:

- **Essay Questions.** Essay questions, with their emphasis on description and analysis, often present challenges because they are relatively unstructured. Unless you're careful, it's easy to wander off and begin to answer questions that were never asked. To prevent that problem, the first thing to do is read the question carefully, noting what specifically is being asked. If your essay will be lengthy, you might even want to write a short outline.

  Pay attention to key words that indicate what, specifically, the instructor is looking for in an answer. Certain action words are commonly used in essays, and you should understand them fully. For instance, knowing the distinction between "compare" and "contrast" can spell the difference between

Table 8.3

Action Words for Essays

These words are commonly used in essay questions. Learning the distinctions among them will help you during tests.

Analyze: Examine and break into component parts.

Clarify: Explain with significant detail.

Compare: Describe similarities and differences.

Compare and contrast: Describe and distinguish similarities and differences.

Contrast: Explain and distinguish differences.

Critique: Judge and analyze, explaining what is wrong—and right—about a concept.

Define: Provide the meaning.

Discuss: Explain, review, and consider.

Enumerate: Provide a listing of ideas, concepts, reasons, items, etc.

Evaluate: Provide pros and cons of something; provide an opinion, and justify it.

Explain: Give reasons why or how; clarify, justify, and illustrate.

Illustrate: Provide examples; show instances.

Interpret: Explain the meaning of something.

Justify: Explain why a concept can be supported, typically by using examples and other types of support.

Outline: Provide a framework or explanation—usually in narrative form—of a concept, idea, event, or phenomenon.

Prove: Using evidence and arguments, convince the reader of a particular point.

Relate: Show how things fit together; provide analogies.

Review: Describe or summarize, often with an evaluation.

State: Assert or explain.

Summarize: Provide a condensed, precise list or narrative.

Trace: Track or sketch out how events or circumstances have evolved; provide a history or time line.

success and failure. Table 8.3 defines common action words. Also refer to Try It! 3, "Understand Action Verbs in Essay Questions."

Use the right language in essays. Be brief and to the point in your essay. Avoid flowery introductory language. Compare the two sentences that follow:

"In our study of Canadian engineering triumphs, it may be useful to ponder how the completion of the Canadian Pacific Railway came to represent such an important milestone in the field, and it will be seen that there are several critical reasons why it did have such an impact."

"The completion of the Canadian Pacific Railway was momentous for several reasons."

This second sentence says the same thing much more effectively and economically.

Essays are improved when they include examples and point out differences. Your response should follow a logical sequence, moving from major points to minor ones, or following a time sequence. Above all, your answer should address every aspect of the question posed on the test. Because essays often contain several different, embedded questions, you have to be certain that you have answered every part to receive full credit.

- **Multiple-Choice Questions.** If you've ever looked at a multiple-choice question and said to yourself, "But every choice seems right," you understand what can be tricky about this type of question. However, there are some simple strategies that can help you deal with multiple-choice questions.

  First, read the instructions carefully to determine whether only one response choice will be correct, or whether more than one of the choices may be correct. In some cases, the most correct answer is the right choice. Almost always only one choice is right, but in some cases instructors may permit you to check off more than one answer.

Turn to the first question and read the question part—the part before the response choices. *Before you look at the choices, try to answer the question in your head.* This can help you avoid being confused by inappropriate choices.

Next, *carefully read through every choice.* Even if you come to one that you think is right, keep reading—there may be a subsequent answer that is better.

Look for absolutes like "every," "always," "only," "none," and "never." Choices that contain such absolute words are rarely correct. Less absolute words, such as "generally," "usually," "often," "rarely," "seldom," and "typically" may indicate a correct response.

Be especially on guard for the word "not," which negates the sentence ("The one key concept that is not embodied in the Canadian Charter of Rights and Freedoms is . . . "). It's easy to gloss over "not," and if you have the misfortune of doing so, it will be nearly impossible to answer the item correctly.

If you're having trouble understanding a question, underline key words or phrases, or try to break the question into different short sections. Sometimes it is helpful to work backward and look at the response choices first to see whether you can find one that is clearly accurate or clearly inaccurate. Read the stem of the question with each alternative attached to see if it has the correct sound or flow. Do this by changing the question to a statement followed by the alternative. For example, change "Which of the following is the definition of a project?" to "A project is," followed by one or more of the choices for an answer.

*Use an **educated guessing** strategy*—which is very different from wild or random guessing. Unless you are penalized for wrong answers (a scoring rule by which wrong answers are deducted from the points you have earned on other questions, rather than merely not counting at all toward your score), it always pays to guess.

The first step in educated guessing is to eliminate any obviously false answers. The next step is to examine the remaining choices closely. Does one response choice include a qualifier that makes it unlikely ("the probability of war always increases when a South Asian leader is facing political difficulties")? Does one choice include a subtle factual error ("Prime Minister Pierre Trudeau imposed the *War Measures Act* in 1970 after the FLQ murdered a British diplomat")? In such cases, you may be able to figure out the correct response by eliminating the others.

- **True–False Questions.** Although most of the principles we've already discussed apply equally well to true–false questions, a few additional tricks of the trade may help you with this question type.

    Begin a set of true–false questions by marking the items you're sure you know the answer to. But don't rush; it's important to read every part of a true–false question, because key words such as "never," "always," and "sometimes" often determine the appropriate response.

    If you don't have a clue about whether a statement is true or false, here's another last-resort principle: Choose "true," if you won't be penalized for guessing. In general, more statements on a true–false test are likely to be true than false.

- **Matching Questions.** Matching questions typically present you with two columns of related information, which you must link using a process of elimination. For example, a list of terms or concepts may be presented in

Educated guessing

The practice of eliminating obviously false multiple-choice answers and selecting the most likely answer from the remaining choices

TRY IT!

www.mcgrawhill.ca/olc/power

Understand Action Verbs in Essay Questions

Prepare: Discover the importance of action verbs in essay questions.

Organize: Use the questions provided and if needed, a dictionary.

Work: How would you answer the following questions about the *Charter?* Define the action verb for each question.

Evaluate: Were you able to see the different requirements associated with different verbs?

Rethink: Do you think it's a good idea to ask what your instructor means when he or she uses the different verbs?

Answer the following questions about Section 2 of the *Canadian Charter of Rights and Freedoms* by outlining your responses, paying attention to the various action verbs that introduce the questions. The key is defining the action verb.

Section 2 of the *Canadian Charter of Rights and Freedoms* states:

Everyone has the following fundamental freedoms:

1. freedom of conscience and religion
2. freedom of thought, belief, opinion, and expression, including freedom of the press and other media of communication
3. freedom of peaceful assembly
4. freedom of association

1. (a) Summarize Section 2 of the *Canadian Charter of Rights and Freedoms.*
    (b) Define the verb "Summarize."

one column, along with a list of corresponding definitions or explanations in the second column. The best strategy is to reduce the size of both columns by matching the items you're most confident about first; this will leave a short list in each column, and the final matching may become apparent.

- **Short-Answer and Fill-In Questions.** Short-answer and fill-in questions basically require you to *generate and supply* specific information in your own words. Unlike essays, which are more free-form and may have several possible answers, short-answer and fill-in questions are quite specific. There is usually only one answer, which you must come up with on your own. Responding to them requires that you pay special attention to what, in particular, you are being asked.

  Use both the instructions for the questions and the questions themselves to determine the level of specificity that is needed in an answer. Try not to provide too much or too little information. Usually, brevity is best.

2. (a) Interpret Section 2 of the *Canadian Charter of Rights and Freedoms.*
   (b) Define the verb "Interpret."

3. (a) Evaluate Section 2 of the *Canadian Charter of Rights and Freedoms.*
   (b) Define the verb "Evaluate."

4. (a) Discuss Section 2 of the *Canadian Charter of Rights and Freedoms.*
   (b) Define the verb "Discuss."

5. (a) Analyze Section 2 of the *Canadian Charter of Rights and Freedoms.*
   (b) Define the verb "Analyze."

How do your answers differ for each question? Which of the questions provoked the lengthiest response? Which of the questions could you answer best?

About Academic Honesty Perhaps it's a tempting thought: A glance at a classmate's test may provide the one piece of information that you just can't remember.

You owe it to yourself not to do it. **Academic honesty**—completing and turning in only your own work under your own name—is the foundation of postsecondary life and your personal life. Copying from a classmate's paper is no different from reaching over and stealing that classmate's calculator or watch.

Cheating can take several forms. It may involve copying another's work, using a calculator when it's not allowed, discussing the answer to a question, copying a computer file when it's unauthorized, taking an exam for another person, or stealing an exam. Whatever the form, academic dishonesty is wrong. It diminishes the academic community, it makes the grading system unfair, and it ultimately reduces the meaning of your grade. It certainly damages academic and personal growth. It can't help but reduce self-esteem, and it robs the

Academic honesty
Completing and turning in only your own work under your own name

Career Connections

Professional Tests: More Exams and Tests

Accreditation Exams

Careers in paramedicine, nursing, business, computers, and technology have standardized tests you must pass to be accredited in your field. Furthermore, many professions require practitioners to regularly pass similar exams. Accreditation exams may be paper or computer and they may involve a practical demonstration.

Competency Assessments

Many companies now assess employees on competencies, which are the knowledge, skills, and abilities that demonstrate successful performance in the workplace. Competency testing can occur in many ways, but two common methods are testing employees at an assessment centre and 360-degree feedback.

At an assessment centre, employees are evaluated based on the behaviours demonstrated in situational tests or scenarios. There is a high correlation between assessment centre scores on high-performance competencies and actual performance in jobs. This 360-degree feedback (a process where feedback is elicited from a person's manager, the person's peers, staff reporting to that person, and the person) is commonly used for developmental purposes in an organization.

As can be seen from the Toyota model, your portfolio (where you always link knowledge, skills, and ability to demonstrate) can be helpful preparation for workplace assessments.

> At Toyota, competencies are linked to performance and business strategy. Skills necessary in cultivating the behaviours that support business objectives are targeted and encouraged to grow. Toyota appraises as its core competencies (knowledge, skills, and abilities that are critical to an organization) customer satisfaction, teamwork, problem solving, efficiency, quality, and quantity of work. Pay increases are available to those willing to learn new skills, as opposed to just those with seniority or experience.

cheater of self-respect. Finally, getting caught leads to many unpleasant scenarios: failing the exam on which the cheating has taken place, failing the entire course, being brought before an academic honesty or review committee, having a note placed in your academic file, being placed on academic probation, or even being thrown out of school. Cheating is simply not worth it.

E valuate: Taking Your Own Final Examination

The last few minutes of a test may feel like the final moments of a marathon. You need to focus your energy and push forward harder. It can be make-or-break time.

Save some time at the end of a test so you can check your work. You should have been keeping track of your time all along, so plan on stopping a few minutes before the end of the test period to review what you've done. It's a critical step, and it can make the difference between a terrific grade and a mediocre one. It's a rare person who can work uninterrupted on a test and commit absolutely no errors—even if he or she knows the material backward and forward. Consequently, checking what you've done is crucial.

Start evaluating your test by looking for obvious mistakes. Make sure you've answered every question and haven't skipped any parts of questions. If there is a separate answer sheet, check to see that all your answers have been recorded on the answer sheet and in the right spot.

If the test has included essay and short-answer questions, proofread your responses. Check for obvious errors—misspellings, missing words, and repetitions. Make sure you've responded to every part of each question and that each essay, as a whole, makes sense.

Check your responses to multiple-choice, true–false, and matching questions. If there are some items that you haven't yet answered because you couldn't remember the necessary information, now is the time to take a stab at them. As we discussed earlier, it usually pays to guess, even randomly if you must. On most tests, no answer and a wrong answer are worth the same amount—nothing! Only occasionally will instructors deduct points for wrong answers, and you will know in advance if that is their policy.

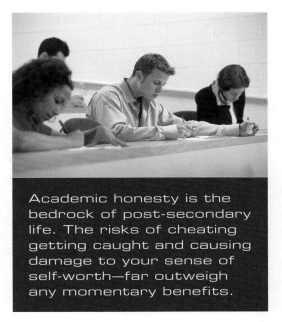

Academic honesty is the bedrock of post-secondary life. The risks of cheating getting caught and causing damage to your sense of self-worth—far outweigh any momentary benefits.

What about items that you initially were genuinely unsure about and for which you guessed at the answer? Unless you have a good reason to change your original answer—such as a new insight or a sudden recollection of some key information—your first guess is likely your best guess.

Know When to Stop After evaluating and checking your answers, you may reach a point when there is still some time left. What to do? If you're satisfied with your responses, it's simply time to tell yourself, *Let it go.*

Permit yourself the luxury of knowing that you've done your best and it's time to hand the test to your instructor. Just because there is time remaining in the class period and some of your classmates are still working on their tests, you don't have to continue reviewing your work over and over. In fact, such behaviour is often counterproductive, because it may lead you to start overinterpreting test items and reading things into questions that really aren't there.

Disaster! I've run out of time! It's a nightmarish feeling: The clock is ticking relentlessly, and it's clear that you don't have enough time to finish the test. What should you do?

Stop work! Although this advice may sound foolish, the most important thing you can do is to take a minute to calm yourself. Take some deep breaths to replace the feelings of panic that are likely welling up inside you. Collect your thoughts, and plan a strategy for the last moments of the test.

If there are essays that remain undone, consider how you'd answer them if you had more time. Then write an outline of each answer. If you don't have time even for that, write a few keywords. Writing anything is better than handing in a blank page, and you may get at least some credit for your response. The key principle here: Something is better than nothing, and even one point is worth more than zero points.

The same principle holds for other types of questions. Even wild guesses are almost always better than not responding at all to an item. So rather than telling yourself you've certainly failed and giving up, do as much as you can in the remaining moments of the exam.

Refer to Try It! 4, "Take a Test-Taking Test," and think of the strategies discussed so far in this chapter.

Take a Test-Taking Test

Prepare: Use test-taking strategies to take a test.

Organize: Use the test below and on the following pages.

Work: Try to employ as many test-taking strategies as possible to complete the test.

Evaluate: Were you able to employ some of the recommendations for test taking?

Rethink: Are you able to identify test-taking strategies you would use on an ongoing basis?

The following test on test-taking skills, illustrates every question type discussed in this chapter. Answers to all questions except short-answer and essay questions are provided at the end of the test.

Before taking the test, think of the test-taking strategies we've discussed in the chapter, and try to employ as many of them as possible.

Multiple-choice section

1. Tests are useful tools for which of the following purposes?
   a. determining people's likely level of future career success
   b. indicating strengths and gaps in people's knowledge
   c. defining people's fundamental abilities and potentials
   d. evaluating people's individual worth and contributions

2. One of the main advantages of study groups is that
   a. every individual must contribute equally to the group.
   b. group members can help each other during the test.
   c. each member has to memorize only a fraction of the material.
   d. groups motivate their members to do good work.

3. Which of the following is a good way to deal with test anxiety?
   a. visualizing success on the test
   b. drinking coffee or other stimulants
   c. telling yourself to stop worrying
   d. focusing on the importance of the test

4. Which of the following is likely to be the most effective cramming technique?
   a. preparing a one-page summary of the most important information
   b. quickly reading all articles and textbook chapters covered on the test
   c. neatly recopying all class notes and note cards while reading them aloud
   d. underlining or highlighting key information in the textbook and other resources

Matching section

____ 1. Essay question	A. A question in which the student supplies brief missing information to complete a statement
____ 2. Quiz	B. Hurried, last-minute studying
____ 3. Multiple-choice question	C. An informed attempt to select an answer by eliminating clearly incorrect answers
____ 4. Matching question	D. A question in which the student must link information in two columns

www.mcgrawhill.ca/olc/power

___ 5. True–false question   E. A brief test

___ 6. Fill-in question   F. A question requiring a lengthy response in the
                                       student's own words

___ 7. Short-answer question   G. Deduction of points for incorrect responses

___ 8. Guessing penalty   H. Representing another's work as one's own

___ 9. Test anxiety   I. A question requiring a brief response in the
                                       student's own words

___10. Cramming   J. A question that requires selection from several
                                       response options

___11. Academic dishonesty   K. A feeling of fear induced by testing

___12. Educated guess   L. A question requiring students to distinguish
                                       accurate and inaccurate statements

Fill-in section

1. Fear of testing that can interfere with test performance is called _____.
2. Last-minute studying is called _____.
3. The primary source of error on machine-scored tests is incomplete _____.
4. After inspecting the test and identifying areas that will be easy and those that will be hard,
    a reasonable test-taking strategy is to answer the _____ questions first.

True–false section

1. The best way to prepare for an essay test is to review detailed factual information about
    the topic. T _____ F _____
2. True–false questions require students to determine whether given statements are ac-
    curate or inaccurate. T _____ F _____
3. You should never permit yourself to feel panicky during a test. T _____ F _____
4. A good evaluation strategy toward the end of a test is to redo as many questions as time
    permits. T _____ F _____
5. For short-answer questions, students must select brief responses from response choices
    listed on the test form. T _____ F _____
6. In responding to essay questions, you should answer briefly and use plain language.
    T _____ F _____
7. In a multiple-choice question, the words "always" and "never" usually signal the correct
    response. T _____ F _____
8. It is usually unwise to guess on a multiple-choice test. T _____ F _____
9. If you run out of time at the end of a test, it is best to write brief notes and ideas down in
    response to essay questions, rather than leave them completely blank. T _____ F _____
10. Students' comments on the amount of studying they have done before a test are gener-
    ally accurate. T _____ F _____

(continued on next page)

Take a Test-Taking Test—Continued

Short-answer section

1. What are five things you should find out about a test before you take it?

2. What is academic honesty?

Essay section (write your answers on a separate sheet of paper)

1. Explain how tests can be useful to students and teachers.
2. Discuss the advantages of using a study group to prepare for an examination.
3. Why is academic honesty important?

Answers. Multiple-choice: 1B, 2D, 3A, 4A; Matching: 1F, 2E, 3J, 4D, 5L, 6A, 7I, 8G, 9K, 10B, 11H, 12C; Fill-in: test anxiety, cramming, erasing, easy; True–False: 1F, 2T, 3F, 4F, 5F, 6T, 7F, 8F, 9T, 10F; Short-answer: See page 162 and pages 174 and 175.

After you have completed the test, consider these questions: Did you learn anything from taking the test that you might not have learned if you hadn't been tested on the material? How effective were the test-taking strategies you employed? Were any types of strategies easier for you to employ than others, and were any types of questions easier for you to use them on than others? Exchange your essay responses with a classmate, and critique the essays. How do the responses of your partner compare to your own?

R ethink: Reflecting on the Real Test of Learning

Your instructor is about to hand the graded exams back. All sorts of thoughts run through your head: How did I do? Did I perform as well as my classmates? Will I be pleased with my results? Will the results reflect the amount of effort I put into studying? Will I be embarrassed by my grade?

Most of us focus on the evaluative aspects of tests. We look at the grade we've received on a test and take it to be a measure of something important. It's a natural reaction.

There is another way to look at test results: They can help guide us toward future success. By looking at what we've learned (and haven't learned) about a given subject, we'll be in a better position to know what to focus on when we take future exams. Furthermore, by examining the kinds of mistakes we make, it's more likely that we can do better in the future. Use Try It! 5, "Analyze Returned Tests," to evaluate your strengths and weaknesses as a test-taker.

When you get your test back, you have the opportunity to reflect on what you've learned and to consider your performance. Begin by looking at your

TRY IT!

www.mcgrawhill.ca/olc/power

Analyze Returned Tests

Prepare: Use a process for improving your test results by analyzing returned tests.

Organize: Use the questions and the form provided to record your answers.

Work: Use a recent test or the test you just took in Try It! 4 and analyze how you could have done better. Follow the directions below to complete your analysis.

Evaluate: Were you able to use the recommended process for analyzing your test results?

Rethink: Would you use this process to improve your test-taking performance?

You can help yourself to perform better on tests by evaluating your strengths and weaknesses as a test-taker. Complete the chart and follow the directions to analyze the information about a test you didn't do as well on as you'd expected.

Directions

1. Complete the top portion of the form. Be as specific and honest as possible in describing the way you studied (or didn't study).

2. Under questions missed, write in the numbers of the actual test questions that were incorrect on your test. If you missed questions 5, 8, 13, and 29, those are the numbers you should write in that column.

3. Now go across the rows of the chart. For example, if you got question 5 wrong, determine:
   - How many points were taken off?
   - What kind of question or problem was it?
   - What do you think was the reason that you got it wrong?

4. Look for patterns. Ask:
   - What kinds of questions did you have the most difficulty with?
   - Which questions were worth the most points?
   - What can you do to improve yourself on your next test?

5. Ask yourself what you still don't understand about the test or test question(s) that you answered incorrectly.
   - Did you have difficulty understanding the instructor's comments?
   - Write down any questions that you need to ask your instructor.
   - If you have questions for the professor, or want to clarify how you can improve in your next test, make an appointment to discuss these issues.

6. Make a list of the things you need to do to be more successful on your next test. Ask questions like:
   - How can I make sure I understand the material?
   - Do I need to manage my time better so I can spend more time studying?
   - How can I determine what is important to study?

7. Look at tests from other courses and see if there is a pattern. What can you learn from your successes and failures?

(continued on next page)

Analyze Returned Tests— Continued

Course: _____			Date of exam: _____			

Predicted grade: _____ **Actual grade:** _____ **% of total grade:** _____

Relevant details of the study process: (# of days/time spent studying, special methods used, etc.)

_____

_____

_____

Question Profile			Reason that Answer was Incorrect			
Question Missed	Points Lost	Type of Question*	Carelessness	Material Unfamiliar	Mis- interpreted	Not Complete

* MC = multiple choice T/F = True/False COM = completion
MA = Matching ESS = Essay

You may want to use other categories, i.e., for math: calculation, word problem, formula, etc.

mistakes. Chances are they'll jump out at you since they will be marked incorrect. Did you misunderstand or misapply some principle? Was there a certain aspect of the material covered on the test that you missed? Were there particular kinds of information that you didn't realize you needed to know? Or did you lose some points because of your test-taking skills? Did you make careless errors, such as forgetting to fill in a question or misreading the directions? Was your handwriting so sloppy that your instructor had trouble reading it?

Whatever your results, and especially if you crammed, think about the time you spent studying for the test. Next, think about how many hours you would have needed to study to get the mark you wanted. Almost always, you could have found those hours in the week or so before the test. Was the pressure and the anxiety really worth it or could you solve the problem with more effective time management?

Once you have a good idea of what material you didn't fully understand or remember, get the correct answers to the items you missed—from your instructor, fellow classmates, or your book. If it's a math exam, rework problems you've missed. Finally, summarize—in writing—the material you had trouble with. This will help you study for future exams that cover the same material.

Finally, if you're dissatisfied with your performance, talk to your instructor—not to complain but to seek help. Instructors don't like to give bad grades, and they may be able to point out problems in your test that you can address readily so you can do better in the future. Demonstrate to your instructor that you want to do better and are willing to put in the work to get there. The worst thing to do is crumple up the test and quickly leave the class in embarrassment. Remember, you're not the first person to get a bad grade, and the power to improve your test-taking performance lies within you.

What If You Fail?

If you have put forth your best effort in preparing for a test or exam—you have consistently attended class, taken good notes and reviewed them, kept up with the reading, asked questions in class, and participated in a study group—and you failed, approach your instructor and ask for some feedback and advice on how to improve your results for the next test or exam. If you feel out of your depth, let your instructor know—he may be able to advise you on your options. In addition, approach your academic advisor *early* if your first batch of test scores are poor or below your usual level. Your college or university undoubtedly has resources, ranging from peer mentors to learning resource centres, that can help those motivated to help themselves.

If those resources don't help, ask what the date is for withdrawing from the course without academic penalty. It is better to drop a course than to fail it. However, withdrawing from a course may affect your full-time status or student loan, so be sure you know the consequences.

If you have not put forth the effort needed to succeed in college or university, you should reflect on your behaviour. Has the transition to postsecondary life been more difficult than you expected? Are you preoccupied with your social life? Are you having roommate or family problems that interfere with your ability to concentrate? Are you emotionally, mentally, and physically ready for college or university? For some students, taking a year off to work, travel, and mature is the best way to ready themselves for higher education. Some students and their parents may resist putting off school, knowing graduation is delayed by a year, but in the end, it could save a lot of money (for lost tuition, books, living expenses) and prevent your ending up with a poor academic record. Students who are unmotivated to succeed should seek academic counselling early to help make the best decisions for their futures.

Students who have experienced academic failure in the past may become academically frustrated or defeated, which in turn, can lead to lack of confidence or unrealistic academic expectations. If you give up easily or approach assignments and tests with low expectations of success, your campus counselling centre may be able to help you with techniques and coping strategies. However, it is up to you to recognize that you need assistance and seek it.

Speaking of Success

Asta Kovanen

The Okanogan Valley College of Massage Therapy

Working with people and travelling are two of Asta Kovanen's passions and she believes she will be able to pursue both of those interests after completing her studies at The Okanogan Valley College of Massage Therapy, in Vernon, British Columbia.

The OVCMT is Asta's third post-secondary school. After graduation from high school, she entered college because "that was what you were supposed to do," but without a clear direction and too much partying, she left. She realized she wasn't committed and didn't love what she was doing—she felt she was wasting her time.

After some time away from school, including spending a year volunteering in Mexico and Honduras, she developed a different perspective. Asta realized how many resources are to be had for students in Canada and decided she was ready to take advantage of the educational opportunities available to her.

Asta then began to study international relations at a large university, but the huge impersonal classes and big city didn't appeal to her—she realized a largely theoretical approach to education would not give her the people contact she wanted and she realized she was unhappy in what she calls the "bubble world" of academics.

Asta now feels she is in a perfect place for her; massage therapists both work with people and have the opportunity to

travel the world. In addition, she loves that her program at OVCMT is extremely practical—after the first year she is qualified to work in a spa; after the second year, she is eligible to work in most provinces; and after year three she can be a registered massage therapist in British Columbia. This career will allow her to work almost anyplace in the world.

Asta says she has to work extremely hard to stay on top of all the work expected in her intensive program, especially tests and exams. Oral, practical, and conventional academic evaluations are given on a frequent basis. She and others in her courses have formed study groups and work collaboratively to reinforce the large quantities of material associated with anatomy, physiology, and the musculoskeletal system. With likeminded classmates who want the same level of experience as she does, Asta focuses on being super-prepared, but she is aware that stress can take a toll on students in her program, so she insists on being well-rested for tests and exams.

While Asta is fully committed to being a successful student, she recognizes that her whole identity is much more than that, so she makes time for friends, family, other activities and especially fun and laughter, both of which are great stress busters.

What kinds of tests will I encounter in college or university?

- Although tests are an unpopular fact of academic life, they can provide useful evaluative information about your level of knowledge and understanding about a subject.

- There are several types of tests, including brief, informal quizzes; more substantial tests; and even more weighty exams, which tend to be administered at the midpoint and end of a course.

What are the best ways to prepare for and take various kinds of tests?

- Good test preparation begins with completing the course assignments, attending class regularly, and paying attention in class. It also helps to find out as much as possible about a test beforehand and to form a study group to review material.

- If cramming becomes necessary, focus on summarizing factual information broadly, identifying key concepts and ideas, and rehearsing information orally.

- When you first receive the test, skim it to see what kinds of questions are being asked; figure out how the different questions and sections will be weighted; and jot down complex factual information that is likely to be needed for the test.

- Answer the easiest questions first, write legibly, use only one side of each sheet of paper, mark answer sheets carefully, and record answers in the test book as well as the answer sheet.

What are the best strategies for answering specific kinds of test questions?

- For essay questions, be sure to understand each question and each of its parts, interpret action words correctly, write concisely, organize the essay logically, and include examples.

- For multiple-choice questions, read the question very carefully and then read all response choices. Educated guessing based on eliminating incorrect response choices is usually a reasonable strategy.

- For true–false and matching questions, quickly answer all the items that you are sure of and then go back to the remaining items.

- The best strategy for short-answer and fill-in questions is to be very sure about what is being asked. Keep answers complete but brief.

P.O.W.E.R. Portfolio

Put It to the Test

Consider including in a portfolio a successful test from your current semester along with a reflection on what skill set or competency it relates to. *For example, a dental assistant student could put in a test from his dental records course, indicating the ways in which it relates to development of a professional-level dental vocabulary, communication skills, teamwork, or accuracy and detail.* Or put two tests in your portfolio, indicating why you may have done better on the second test and how you improved your test-taking strategy.

Resources

On Campus

Colleges and universities often provide a variety of resources for students having difficulties with test taking. Some offer general workshops for students, reviewing test-taking strategies.

If you find that you are experiencing significant test anxiety when taking a test or in the days leading up to it, talk to someone at your campus counselling centre or health centre. They can help you learn relaxation techniques and can provide psychological counselling to help make your anxiety manageable.

In Print

Test Taking Strategies & Study Skills for the Utterly Confused by Laurie Rozakis (McGraw-Hill; 1st edition, 2002) is a useful book that includes chapters about taking specific kinds of tests such as true–false, multiple-choice, fill-in-the-blank, matching, and math tests.

A book specifically designed for adults who need work-related training or a certificate/degree to become more successful in their careers but who are held back by poor study habits is *The Secrets Of Taking Any Test: Learn the Techniques Successful Test-Takers Know* by Judith Meyers, published by Learning Express (2000). Other postsecondary students can also use the author's simple 20-step program to discover their own style. This book contains information about how to make your own learning style work for you.

On the Web

The following sites on the World Wide Web provide the opportunity to extend your learning about the material in this chapter. Although the Web addresses were accurate at the time the book was printed, check the P.O.W.E.R. Learning website, <www.mcgrawhill.ca/olc/power>, for any changes that may have occurred.

www.coun.uvic.ca/learn/program/hndouts/simple.html
This page gives examples of question words that are often found in essay assignments or in essay questions on exams. Possible plans of action for each question type are outlined. These outlines are useful as a starting point for understanding how to approach essay questions.

www.iss.stthomas.edu/studyguides/tstprp1.htm
This website from St. Thomas University gives helpful tips on how to prepare for tests; a companion page at <www.iss.stthomas.edu/studyguides/tsttak1.htm> gives hints on how to take tests.

www.mentalhealthscreening.org/college/
This anonymous online screening test from Virginia Tech gives students an idea of whether they should contact a counsellor for assistance with anxiety, depression, alcohol, or eating disorders. To do this test, click on the link "Take a Sample Test."

The Case Of...

Too Many Questions, Too Little Time

There was no reason to panic, said Mia Varela to herself at the start of the test. The exam, a midterm in her computer programming course, contained 50 multiple-choice questions (each worth 1 point) and two case studies (worth a total of 50 points). And she did have 75 minutes to complete the test.

"Let's see," she said to herself. "At $1\frac{1}{2}$ minutes per multiple-choice question, that would take 75 minutes. Hmm . . . that's no good. How about a minute for each one? Fifty minutes for the multiple-choice questions, leaving 25 minutes for the case studies. That ought to work. I'll get the multiple-choice questions out of the way first."

But things didn't work out the way she planned. After an hour she had completed only 40 of the multiple-choice questions and hadn't even started on the case studies. With only 15 minutes left, panic began to set in. She had trouble thinking. She began to feel certain that she'd fail the test. She thought about how she hadn't studied enough. If only she'd worked harder. How could she explain this failure to her friends . . . to her parents . . . to herself. The thoughts kept coming, and time kept ticking away.

1. Is there evidence that Mia didn't study effectively for this type of test?

2, What was right about Mia's initial approach to the test?

3. What should Mia have done differently in calculating the amount of time to devote to each portion of the test? Why?

4. What should Mia have done to be aware of and address her timing problem sooner?

5. How should Mia have dealt with her panic? Were her thoughts productive or counterproductive? Why?

6. If you were in Mia's shoes, what would you do now, with only 15 minutes left in the test?

Writing

9

Jonathan just couldn't get started. The essay was due tomorrow but every time he sat down to write, nothing would come. He just sat and stared at the paper becoming more and more frustrated. Writing had never been easy, but this seemed to be the worst. He couldn't lose the marks for this assignment and get the grade he wanted in the course.

He had never tried any of the suggestions for writing a paper in college or university, but at this stage he felt he had nothing to lose. He started working through the process. On occasion he had to put aside some negative self-talk about his writing and keep going. He set a goal for the essay and started doing some freewriting. He just wrote for five minutes about the topic of his essay. Some of the words or phrases made sense so he decided to freewrite for another session lasting 10 minutes this time. After the second freewriting session he had a number of ideas he thought he could organize into a really good essay.

He followed the process until he had an essay he was willing to hand in. He actually thought it was pretty good. He passed the assignment and got the mark he wanted. In the end it wasn't as hard as he first thought. Jonathan's confidence in his writing ability has grown and while he still doesn't like to write, he can do it when required if he follows the process. At least he no longer sits and stares at a blank page becoming more frustrated by the minute.

Looking ▶▶ Ahead

Writing can be very rewarding, but few activities can create so much anxiety and frustration. A blank page can be intimidating, yet it doesn't have to be. You can learn to improve your writing skills. Being able to write is an essential skill, not only in college or university but also in the world of work after graduation. The ability to express yourself in writing about things such as ideas, instructions, research findings, and justifications for proposals is the mark of a professional.

This chapter provides a framework for writing college or university level papers. Suggestions are provided for confronting the blank page, generating thoughts and ideas, and polishing your first draft. How do you get started? Who is your audience?

What framework do you use for writing a paper and how do you move from a rough first draft to a final draft that hits the mark?

After reading this chapter, you'll be able to answer these questions:

- **What are the best techniques for getting started and writing a first draft?**

- **What are the five parts to a typical research paper?**

- **How do I move from a first draft to a final draft?**

The Writing Process

What happens when you sit down to write? Does the sight of a blank page or blank screen leave your mind similarly blank? Do your fingers, which move so quickly when you're playing a game on the computer, become sluggish when poised over a keyboard to write a paper?

Writing is not easy, and for many students, writing assignments raise more anxieties than any other academic task. This anxiety has many causes. For one thing, papers often compose a large part of your final course grades, putting pressure on you to do well. Maybe you always do all your writing at the last minute, with a deadline looming. Perhaps you've never really been taught how to write well. Or maybe you believe that there's some sort of special writing gene that you just weren't born with.

Stop! Delete from your memory any negative self-talk you may have about writing. There is no mystery to writing; it's a skill that can be taught, and a skill that, with practice, anybody can learn. *Writing is not a product you read; it is a thinking and reasoning process that is the means of producing that product*, a skill that can be learned like any other, not a talent you are born with or without.

Using strategies based on P.O.W.E.R. Learning (summarized in the P.O.W.E.R. Plan), you will be able to achieve the goal of writing clearly and competently. These strategies will help you to build on your strengths and maximize your abilities. They will permit you to translate what's inside your head into words that communicate your experience or thoughts directly.

P repare: Confronting the Blank Page

Nothing has the potential to be more liberating than a blank page. It offers every possibility, and it gives you the freedom to say whatever you want to say. And therein lies the key to good writing: deciding what it is you want to say.

Preparation is a central aspect of successful writing. Writing is a process, and preparation for it encompasses the following steps.

Decide What Your Goal Is To write successfully, you need to think about the end product. Is it a long research paper, based on information you must gather? an essay arguing a particular point of view? a fictional short story? a critique of someone else's work or argument? a book or movie review?

Most often, you'll be working to complete a class assignment that will explain what the goal is. But sometimes the assignment will provide you with several choices; it may even be vague or imprecise. If this is the case, your first step will be to decide just what you'll be doing through your writing.

If there is a choice among different types of writing, decide which will make you most comfortable. If one choice is to prepare

PREPARE

Approach writing as a process

ORGANIZE

Write a flexible outline and construct a thesis statement

WORK

Get it down in the first draft; Refine it in the second draft

EVALUATE

Be your own best critic: finetune your work

RETHINK

Reflect on the writing process: what worked, what didn't?

P.O.W.E.R. Plan

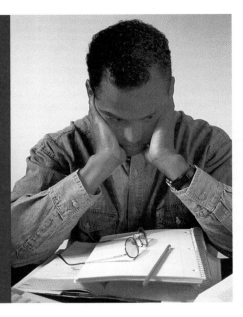

Nothing is more intimidating than a blank piece of paper—or a blank computer screen. On the other hand, it can also be liberating, offering you the freedom and opportunity to say what *you* want to say.

an essay and you are creative and enjoy expressing your opinions, choose that option. If you enjoy gathering information and drawing a conclusion from your findings, a research paper might be the best choice.

Choose Your Topic Once you've determined the specific type of writing you are going to do, the next step is to choose a topic. Although instructors usually assign a particular topic, in some cases the choice will be left to you. However, the freedom to choose a topic does not come without a price. In fact, many students find that choosing what to write about is harder than actually writing the paper itself. Here are some things you can do to choose an appropriate topic:

- **Use "freewriting."** According to Peter Elbow, a writing expert who has revolutionized the teaching of writing, one of the reasons we find writing so hard is that we have a set of censors inside our heads.[1] At a moment's notice, those censors are ready to spring up and whisper, "That's no good," when we set pen to paper.

    However, you can keep these internal voices at bay using a technique called "freewriting." In **freewriting,** you write continually for a fixed period, such as 5 or 10 minutes. The only rule that governs freewriting is to write continually, without stopping. It doesn't matter whether the product is bad; it doesn't matter whether it's good. The only principle you must follow in freewriting is to get something—anything—down on paper.

    Try it, and you'll see how liberating freewriting can be. Of course, the product will not be perfect, but you'll most likely find that you've written something of value to you.

    Suppose, for example, you are stuck for a topic. Through freewriting you can explore your feelings about the course you are going to be writing for, what you like and don't like, and get some rough ideas down on paper. What's more, you'll probably form an "attitude" toward one or more potential topics, which can be used to add a personal voice and authenticity to your writing.

    Once the freewriting session is completed, you may want to write a single sentence that captures the main point of what you have written—the "centre of gravity," Elbow calls it. You can then use this sentence as a springboard for further exploration of ideas the next time you write. See Try It! 1, "Set Yourself Free: Freewriting."

Freewriting

A technique involving continual, nonstop writing, without self-criticism, for a fixed time

"How do I know what I think 'til I see what I say?"

character in an E.M. Forster novel

- **Use brainstorming.** The oral equivalent of freewriting is brainstorming. While freewriting is done alone, brainstorming is often done with others. In **brainstorming,** you say out loud as many ideas as you can think of in a fixed time. Although brainstorming works best when you do it in a group, you can do it by yourself. (This is one of those times when talking to yourself has its benefits.) Initially, the goal is simply to produce as many ideas as possible, no matter how implausible, silly, or irrelevant. Jot down the ideas that intrigue you as they come up, so you don't forget them.

Brainstorming

A technique for generating ideas by saying out loud as many ideas as can be thought of in a fixed time

Set Yourself Free: Freewriting

Prepare: The purpose of this exercise is to learn the benefits of freewriting.

Organize: Use the space provided to practise freewriting for five minutes. Optional guidance is offered below, but if you want to go ahead and "just do it," simply start writing.

Work: Be sure to keep your hand moving; stop controlling yourself. Write only for yourself; forget about what others might think—be frank.

Evaluate: What is the main point of what you wrote? Was freewriting effective in helping you get something down on paper? Was it easy or difficult for you?

Rethink: Do you think the process of freewriting might help you when it's time to write a paper?

If you need a little more guidance, you are not alone; most people need help the first time they try it. There are actually two kinds of freewriting: plain vanilla freewriting (like that above) and *focused* freewriting. Focused freewriting gives you a starting point.

Here are some starting points for focused freewriting:

Today I feel . . .	I get sick when . . .
I remember . . .	I know . . .
I don't like . . .	I am . . .
I really like . . .	I am not . . .

Using one of these lead-in phrases as a starting point, return to the blank space and begin your freewriting.

How I Feel About Writing

Reflect on the feelings you have about writing by answering the following questions:

1.   When I receive a writing assignment, my initial reaction is . . .

2.   Do you ever write for pleasure? when? under what circumstances?

3.   Which writing experiences are particularly pleasant for you? Which are unpleasant?

4.   What tools do you need to gather when preparing for a lengthy writing assignment? Do you have special pencils or pens? a favourite chair? Do you prefer to use a computer?

5.   Are you particularly good at finding ways to put off writing tasks? Do you do anything to prevent this?

6.   When faced with a lengthy writing assignment, how do you decide what to write? How do you organize your thoughts?

7.   When you take a test that involves writing, such as an essay test, how do you approach it? Do you outline your responses? Do you do anything to gather your ideas?

As with freewriting, the idea is to temporarily silence the censors that prevent us from saying whatever comes into our heads. In brainstorming, the initial goal is not to produce high-quality ideas, but a high quantity of ideas. You can revisit and evaluate the ideas later. Refer to Try It! 2, "Get Your Brain Storming: Using Brainstorming to Generate Ideas," on page 225.

Decide Who Your Audience Is That's easy, you may be thinking; it's my instructor. *Not so fast.* Although the instructor is the most obvious reader for what you write, you should think of your audience in terms of the ultimate purpose of the writing assignment. For example, if you're writing a paper about the dangers of global warming, are you directing it to a layperson who knows little about the issue? Or are you writing it for someone with a good understanding of science, someone who already knows about atmospheric pressure, *El Niño*, and the ozone layer? Clearly, the answer to this question will make a difference in how and what you write.

In short, it's crucial to know—and to keep in mind—the people who may read your paper. What is their level of knowledge about the topic? Are they already predisposed to a particular position? What do you think they would like to take away with them after reading what you've written?

Keeping an audience in mind serves another purpose: It personalizes your writing. Rather than targeting your writing to a nondescript group of individuals

🏃 Working In a Group: Get Your Brain Storming: Using Brainstorming to Generate Ideas

Prepare: The purpose of this exercise is to learn to use brainstorming to generate ideas.

Organize: Your sociology instructor has asked you to come up with 10 ideas for a five-page paper on crime in Canada. Brainstorm in a group and come up with a list of possible topics, assigning one member of the group to record ideas below.

Work: As you brainstorm, keep the length of the paper assigned and the sort of topic suited to sociology generally in mind. Remember, the idea is to produce as many possibilities as you can, without evaluating how realistic or feasible they may be. Think quantity over quality.

Evaluate: After your group has finished brainstorming, go back to your answers and circle each that you think is realistic for a paper topic.

Rethink: Did brainstorming work? Did you surprise yourself with the number of possibilities you generated?

TRY IT!

www.mcgrawhill.ca/olc/power

("all the people who might be worried about global warming"), you individualize your audience. Think of the reader as your sister, or a friend, or your next-door neighbour. Think of how that individual would feel after reading what you've written, and what you would say to convince him or her. Remember, your writing is a representation of you as an individual. It means something to you, and you want its impact to be felt just as personally by another individual.

Research the Topic To write most papers, you must do research, which can also help you further refine your topic. We discuss methods of doing research later in this chapter.

Break the Task Down into Pieces If authors planning to write a book sat down at their word processor and thought about the 500 pages that they needed to write to complete it, they probably would never finish the book. Such thoughts are at best mind numbing and at worst totally unproductive and paralyzing. Instead, professional writers break their task down into smaller, manageable pieces. Maybe they decide that they'll write a certain number of pages in a given time, such as four or five pages a day. Or maybe they plan on writing a chapter each week.

You probably don't have as much time to devote to your writing as a professional writer, so the chunks you break your writing into should be shorter. For instance, if you have to write a 10-page paper, don't think of it as 10 pages. Instead, break it down into chunks of two pages a day, spread out over five days. Or think of it in terms of the major sections: an introduction, a description of the background of an issue, arguments in favour of a position, arguments against a position, and a conclusion. You could then schedule the writing of each section on a different day.

Organize: Constructing a Scaffold

When we read and listen to information, the organization phase is easy: The author or speaker has (we hope) already constructed a framework for presenting the information to us. Our job as readers and listeners is to figure out what that organization is, like detectives following a trail of clues.

When we're writing, however, we're creating something that hasn't existed before. Consequently, it's up to us to come up with the scaffolding on which to place our written product.

Construct an Outline (and Be Ready to Change It) The fundamental key to organizing an extended piece of writing is the outline. An outline provides a roadmap to follow when we're writing, a set of sequential steps that show us where we are heading and how we are going to get there.

The secret of successful outlining is flexibility. It is essential to keep an open mind about sequencing and to avoid getting locked in too early to a pattern that might later prove unworkable. The best approach is to place possible outline topics, based on your research, on index cards. Then read through all the cards and try to place them in a logical order. Ask yourself how the information represented by the cards builds up into a complete and convincing presentation. Remember your audience and treat your readers courteously. Ask yourself what a reader would have to know already in order to understand a given fact or argument. Try out several sequences, and determine which order works best.

You can do the same thing on a computer screen using a word-processing program. List all your topics and rearrange them to your heart's content. If you use the program's outlining feature, it will even renumber the outline as you make changes.

Develop the Paper's Structure Although sometimes instructors provide a structure for a paper, you may have to construct one yourself. One way to do this is to follow the **ABBCC structure.** "ABBCC" stands for the five parts of a typical research paper: argument, background, body, counterarguments, and conclusion. Other papers such as proposals, reports, and research papers will have their own structure. Each part plays a specific role in the overall paper:

- **Argument.** Just as we introduce ourselves when we meet someone for the first time, a writer needs to introduce a reader to the main argument being put forward in the paper. Every paper should have a main argument or **thesis,** a one- or two-sentence description of the main point or stand that is being taken in the paper. For instance, your thesis might make the argument that "Personal character does not matter in leaders; what matters is their effectiveness in accomplishing the goals for which they were elected."

  A thesis should be stated as a contention ("people are their own worst enemies") or in terms of some action verb ("the technological revolution requires that people receive more education"). An effective thesis statement takes a position on some issue and includes such key words as "should" or "ought." For instance, "Smoking should be banned from restaurants and bars" presents a thesis statement. However, "This paper will discuss smoking in restaurants and bars" is simply stating the topic.

  The argument need not be the first sentence of the paper—it is usually wise to start off with something that grabs readers' attention. Begin with a controversial quote, an illustrative story, or a personal encounter—anything that is likely to make a reader sit up and take notice.

  In addition to presenting the main thesis of the paper, the argument section should lay out the areas that you will cover and the general scope of the paper. You should use this section to present the paper's overall perspective and point of view. However, you shouldn't provide evidence yet for why your arguments are correct; save that for the body of the paper. Refer to Try It! 3, "Make Your Point: Write a Thesis Statement."

- **Background.** You'll need to provide readers with a context in which to place your paper's arguments, and the background section is the place to do it. Provide a brief history of the topic, talking about different approaches that have been taken and different schools of thought. Introduce any unusual terminology you might need to employ. If the topic is highly controversial, trace the controversy, and discuss why people have found the topic so controversial. For example if you are arguing that young offenders are treated too leniently by the court system, you should review major components of the *Youth Justice Act*.

- **Body.** The body makes up the bulk of most papers. In the paper's body, you restate your thesis and provide evidence as to why the thesis is correct.

  This evidence should be presented in a logical order. Exactly what this means depends on your topic. You may need to work chronologically if you are discussing a historical event. In other cases, you will want to start with

ABBCC structure
The structure of the typical research paper, consisting of argument, background, body, counterarguments, and conclusion

Thesis
The main point or position being argued in a paper, typically stating the writer's opinion about the paper's topic

Make Your Point: Write a Thesis Statement

Prepare: The purpose of this exercise is to help you learn to support your written argument by writing an effective thesis statements.

Organize: Use the topics listed below to complete this exercise.

Work: Write a thesis statement for each topic below. Remember that the thesis should be a contention or should use an action verb. See example below.

Evaluate: Evaluate each thesis statement that you wrote. Do they all contain a contention or action verb?

Rethink: Is there a relationship between how controversial a topic is and how easy it is to write a thesis statement?

global warming and modern technology: Modern technology will not be able to solve global warning. Only changes in behaviours will work.

drinking and driving

euthanasia

service charges for using bank machines

graduated drivers' licences

sovereignty for Quebec

same-sex marriages

Working in a Group: Each group member should generate three potential topics for a paper and compose a thesis statement for each. As a group, evaluate each thesis statement.

the least controversial arguments and gradually move into the ones that are the most debatable.

When deciding the order in which to present information, keep your audience firmly in mind. For instance, a paper on the dangers of electromagnetic radiation written for a Community Law class would be very different from one written for a Physics class.

- **Counterarguments.** You will also need to touch on information that runs counter to your own thesis. Acknowledge the counterarguments to your position, and then go on to systematically refute each one. This section need not be long, but it is crucial. By doing this you help reinforce your own position and strengthen your argument, showing that you have arrived at your point of view fully aware of—and unconvinced by—opposing views.

- **Conclusion.** A good ending to a paper is as important as a good beginning. It's where you pull everything together, and it is your last chance to drive home your thesis.

  The conclusion should summarize the thesis and the arguments that you have made regarding it. Do not introduce new information; all information should have been introduced earlier. The conclusion is a recap of the information and ideas in the paper. Close with a flourish. You might cite a quotation, present an anecdote that is linked to one you presented at the start of the paper, or pose a question ("If the government turns its back on welfare recipients, how can we claim to have a just society?"). However you choose to conclude the paper, make sure that it ties the various pieces together.

W ork: Writing the Work

Now comes the moment that so many dread. It's time to face that blank page or screen and actually start writing. However, if you've followed the steps above and carefully prepared and organized, this phase is likely to be easier than you expect. In fact, you should be so well prepared that you know just how to proceed; your outline provides a clear roadmap of where you are headed, and your research note cards will permit you to flesh out the points of your outline. One way to look at your outline is that it provides you with the major headings of your paper. The job of writing the paper then becomes a matter of matching the research to the appropriate outline heading, rather than starting with a blank sheet of paper.

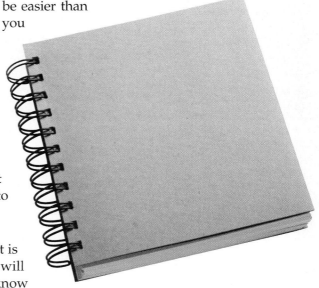

Still, the work of writing is rarely problem-free. The best way to proceed is to divide the actual work of writing into two stages: writing the first draft and revising your draft.

Writing the First Draft Starting a first draft is like diving into a cold lake. You know the initial plunge will be painful because the water is icy cold, but you also know that once you're in the lake it won't be so bad.

It's the same thing with writing a first draft. Getting started is often the hardest part. However, once you've put even a few words on paper, it gets easier.

When you set pen to paper or fingers to keyboard to begin writing, don't feel that you are carving your words in stone. Permit yourself to be less than perfect. Don't worry about word choice, grammar, sentence structure, spelling, or punctuation.

If you've ever gone white-water rafting, you know that following the water's rhythm permits you to remain afloat. In the same way, on those occasions when you achieve a steady rhythm while writing and the words are coming rapidly, stick with it and go with the flow. Revising can come later.

That can come later. The first draft is meant to give you something to move on from. The important thing is to fill up that blank space with *something*.

What's the rationale for such an approach? It's considerably easier to work from an existing draft—even one that is far from perfect—than to work from nothing. In most ways, the first draft is the hardest work you'll have to do, and it's important to get the process underway. By liberating yourself from the constraints of getting things perfect the first time, you will make the process—that of translating what's in your head into a final form that others can see—far easier.

There are several strategies you can use to make writing the first draft less painful:

- **Start where you like.** You need not follow the order of the outline when you write. For example, some writers start a paper by writing the conclusion section first. By keeping the end in mind, they know just where they are headed, making the journey a little easier. Similarly, other writers save the beginning of the paper for last, reasoning that they'll be better able to tell their readers where the paper is going after it has actually gotten there.

  What's most important is that you start writing *something*. Write whatever part of the paper you feel most comfortable writing, because just having something on paper is a comforting feeling and will encourage you to write the rest.

- **Turn off your inner critic.** If you're anything like most people, with every word you write, there'sprobably a voice somewhere in your head that's whispering, "Terrible sentence. Dumb idea. Forget it, you'll never finish this paper." That's the voice of your inner critic, and it's a voice that keeps many of us from reaching our potential as good writers.

  Your job is to turn that voice off, at least for now. (You'll want to use it later, when the nagging may come in handy as you revise your work.) While you're working on your first draft, you want to give yourself permission to let your creative processes put words on paper. As long as you write things down, you'll be able to go back, change things, and make your paper better. But you can't revise what isn't there.

- **Go with the flow.** When you're writing your first draft, try to write quickly. Writing often takes on a rhythm, and you should try to write in sync with the flow of that rhythm. If you're on a roll, go with it. Don't stop to edit your work; that will happen later.

  If you're having trouble getting into a rhythm and each word is like pulling teeth, take a break. Do something entirely different for a few minutes and then return with a fresh mind.

  If you're really having trouble, try rearranging your note cards. You might even shuffle them (after you've first numbered them so you can go back to the original order). Placing them in a random order may provide a fresh way of looking at your topic, and this may in turn free you enough to get your writing started.

- **Don't be afraid to modify your outline.** When you start writing, it's easy to fall into the trap of viewing an outline as a rigid, unbending framework. But this is not what an outline is; your outline is a living document, and you should feel free to rearrange headings and even to deviate from it as you're creating your first draft. You'll have the opportunity later to check that the writing still follows a logical course.

  Many writers find that their outlines need to be revised, and so might yours. The outline you started with may be incomplete, or the topics may have to be presented in a different order. As you're writing your draft, you may uncover gaps in the outline. That's fine; that's why you're writing a first draft and not pretending to start with a final one. Don't forget to plan your time to include editing and revisions.

- **Use your own voice.** Just as we all have distinctive speaking voices, each of us has a distinct *writing* voice. That voice represents our own unique style, a reflection of our outlook on life and of our past writing experiences.

  Novice writers sometimes get hung up trying to use a voice that isn't their own. For example, they may use words they would never normally use when speaking to someone else.

  Avoid the temptation to write as if you were someone else. Instead, use your own natural voice and vocabulary, and don't use big words in an effort to impress your audience. If you'd feel foolish saying "heretofore" in a conversation, you shouldn't use it when you're writing a paper. Don't scan the thesaurus in search of unusual words, and don't give in to the temptation that word-processor thesauruses offer of plugging in new and unusual words for simple ones. Just because you *can* do something doesn't mean you should.

> **Voice**
>
> The unique style of a writer, expressing the writer's outlook on life and past writing experiences

> "In university-level writing or even reading, you cannot possibly finish it all in one sitting or in the last minute. You have to go through it thoroughly and take certain steps to complete it."
>
> Mary Xavier, Student, University of Windsor

- **Forget about it.** The last step in creating a first draft is the easiest. When you have finished your sketch of the entire paper, from introduction through conclusion, put it aside. To revise your draft effectively—the next step in writing—it's necessary to mentally remove yourself from the situation. Like waiting for tea to steep to reach its full potency, you need to let your mind idle in neutral for a while so that it will be at full strength when you move on to the next phase of writing: revision.

Revising Your Draft Remember that inner critic—that voice in your head—that you tuned out while you were writing the first draft? It's time to tune it back in.

The fact is that most of writing is *rewriting*. That's why you should not torture yourself over your first draft too much. The difference between success and failure in writing rests in the revision process. Sure, it's possible to hand in a first draft, and sometimes you'll even get a passable grade. But if you want to reach your own potential as a writer, you *must* revise.

Don't feel that revising is something that only students have to do. Professional writers may go through dozens of drafts—and still not be completely satisfied. Virtually no one has the ability to write a first-draft paper that is so lucid and compelling that it stands on its own.

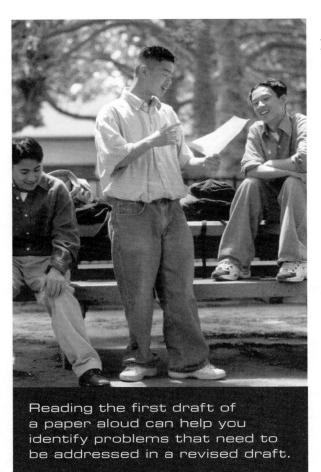

Reading the first draft of a paper aloud can help you identify problems that need to be addressed in a revised draft.

Following several basic rules can make the revision process work smoothly for you:

- **Read the first draft out loud.** Read your paper out loud—to yourself, a friend, or your computer. It doesn't matter who's listening.

  Reading out loud does several things. You'll more easily discover missing words, verbs that don't match the subject of the sentence, shifts in tense, missing transitions, and other things that you might have to fix. The combination of speaking and reading helps make problems more apparent than if you were simply reading the first draft to yourself silently.

  But reading aloud does something more. It slows you down. Speaking takes longer than silent reading, and the slowed pace of oral reading can help you identify things that need revising that you'd otherwise miss.

- **Take the long view.** Start off by taking the broadest perspective possible and asking yourself a series of questions:

  What is the purpose of my paper and has that purpose been fulfilled?

  Have I addressed every aspect of the assignment?

  Does the paper tell its readers everything they need to know?

  Will the audience be able to follow the paper's logic?

  Does the paper make its points clearly?

  Are the transitions between sections clear?

- **Be ruthless.** Remember, writing isn't etched in stone. The tendency is to feel that once we've put words on paper, they are something more than just words. They tend to take on a life of their own—a life that we have created and are often reluctant to change or part with.

  It is natural to feel a bit parental toward our first draft, but it is important to fight this instinct. Now is the time to give full voice to your inner critic. You need to be merciless and unforgiving with passages, paragraphs, phrases, and words that don't sound right or that do not ultimately add to the arguments you're trying to make. Don't tear yourself down; however, like a coach demanding the best from his or her players, be demanding of your performance.

  Start pruning at the paragraph level. Assess each paragraph to make sure that it adds to the final message, that it flows from the previous paragraph logically, and that it is consistent with what you are trying to accomplish in the section of the paper in which it is located.

  Then move to the level of sentences and words. Evaluate each sentence, and then each word, to make sure that it adds to the clarity of your message.

  By paring down your writing, you let your ideas stay closer to the surface, rather than being obscured by repetition and excess words. If you are extremely fond of a phrase or a group of words that seem to be unnecessary, start by cutting them out and setting them aside. You can ease the pain by saving what you've cut. Write down or print out the sections and phrases of which you're particularly proud, put them into an envelope, and toss the envelope into the top drawer of your dresser. You never know when you might need it. More important, knowing that you can save the cut material may make it easier to do the necessary cutting.

- **Check sequence and logic.** It's now time to reverse course. Whereas before the focus was on cutting extraneous material, you now need to check what's left with a view toward *adding* material.

   For example, because of earlier deletions, it may be necessary to add or modify transitions between sections and paragraphs. Ideas should flow logically, and the reader should be able to understand the structure in which they are set.

   If the logic or the structure of the paper has been lost, restore it by reordering the ideas you've presented. You can reorder sentences within paragraphs, and you can reorder paragraphs within sections.

- **Check punctuation and spelling.** Make sure you've fulfilled the basic requirements of punctuation that have been drummed into you since elementary school. Check for the obvious stuff; sentences should start with capital letters and end with the appropriate punctuation, commas should set off nonrestrictive clauses, and the like. Use a style manual if you're unsure.

   Check spelling carefully. This is one of the areas in which word processors earn their keep best, by checking the spelling of every word. The spellcheck feature not only will identify every misspelled word (that is, every word not in its dictionary), but it will prompt you with alternatives for those words that are misspelled.

   Don't rely completely on the spellchecker, however. Such programs can find only misspellings that do not happen to form actual words; if what you typed forms words, the spellchecker will leave it alone, even if the words you typed were not the ones you wanted to use.

- **Make it pleasing to the eye.** Instructors are human. They can't help but react differently to a paper that is neatly typed compared with one that is handwritten in a difficult-to-read scrawl.

   A neat paper conveys a message: I'm proud of this paper. I've put time and effort into it. This is my best work. A sloppy paper says something different.

   Take the time, then, to make sure your paper looks good. This doesn't mean that you need to invest in a fancy plastic cover, or worry about the alignment of the staples, or spend a lot of time deciding which font to use on your word processor. But it does mean that you should make sure the quality of the essay's appearance matches the quality of the writing.

E valuate: Acting as Your Own Best Critic

Because you've already put so much work into your paper, you might be tempted to rush through the final stages of the P.O.W.E.R. process. Avoid the temptation. If you've carefully revised your paper, the last stages will not be time-consuming, and they may have a significant effect on your paper's ultimate quality—and your success.

Take these steps to *evaluate* what you've written:

- **Ask yourself whether your paper accomplishes what you set out to do.** The beginning of your paper contains a thesis statement and the argument that you intended to make. Does your paper support the thesis? Are the arguments upheld by the evidence you've reported? Would an impartial reader be convinced by what you've written?

- **Put yourself in your instructor's shoes.** Does the paper precisely fit the assignment requirements? Does it meet the instructor's underlying goals in giving the assignment?

- **Check the mechanical aspects of the paper.** Make certain the paper represents you the way you want to be represented. Not only should the grammar and spelling be correct, but the paper should also look good. If your instructor requires that citations or references be reported in a certain style, make sure you've followed that style. Later in this chapter, we will discuss the different referencing systems in more detail. The four main styles are MLA (for arts and humanities), APA (for social sciences), CBE (for natural science), and Chicago or Turabian style (for humanities, computer science, health, and business).

If you've revised the paper with care, it will likely pass muster. If it doesn't, though, go back and work on it again. By this point, it should require only minor tinkering to get it into shape.

R ethink: Reflecting on Your Accomplishment

Rethinking is the homestretch of the writing process. It's a moment to savour, because it permits you take a long view of what you've accomplished. You've gone from a blank page to words on paper that tell a story—a story that you've put together. You've turned nothing into something—an achievement in and of itself.

Rethinking occurs on several levels: rethinking the message, mechanics, and method. But don't address them until a little time has passed since you completed the evaluation of the paper. Wait a day or so, and then re-read the paper. Then, bringing your critical thinking skills to bear, reflect on the following:

- **Rethink the message.** Be sure that the overall message your paper conveys is appropriate. A paper is like an advertisement. In most papers, you are seeking to communicate information to convince someone of a particular opinion. Make sure that the message is the one you want to communicate, and that ultimately the paper is successful in making the case.

- **Rethink the mechanics.** A television commercial filled with fuzzy images and jerky camera shots would not be very compelling, no matter how good the underlying product. In the same way, a paper with mechanical errors will not impress your readers or persuade them that your arguments are correct. Take another look at your writing style, then, to make sure you are putting your best foot forward. Look at grammar, punctuation, and word usage to make sure the choices you've made are appropriate.

Thinking Critically about Writing

Read the following short composition and identify what style of writing the author has used. What were the author's goals for this short essay? What are its strengths and weaknesses? What mechanical errors has the author made (if any)? How would you improve this composition?

A Modest Pride

It's not that I'm a weak guy, just that I had been somewhat self-conscious about my strength early on in my high school career. My gym class didn't help too much, either. Thanks to a demeaning test of strength appropriately dubbed the "Grip Test," once each semester I was provided the opportunity to squeeze a gadget, get a score, and have my teacher announce it out loud, no matter how high or (as in my case) how low it was. No matter how hard I tried, the cruel and callous scale never registered above 40. Almost every other male in the class could boast of a high-40s or mid-50s score. I hated that test with a passion. Until the last one. When my final semester rolled around and I had the gripper placed in my palm, I was prepared for the same old same old. I had been improving slightly from semester to semester, but nothing impressive ever happened. I drew in a deep breath, squeezed, looked at the scale, and almost passed out. Sixty-six! In a way only a teen could appreciate, for an accomplishment only a teen would find meaningful, I thought I was in heaven. My success was even sweeter as I watched jocks pale in comparison when they took the test. Sure, to some people my academic accomplishments seem fairly impressive, and I would agree. Yet the grip test situation was much more personal and represented success in an area I normally don't pay attention to. Plus I learned two things. One: I can pride myself on the smallest triviality. Two: I'm glad we didn't measure strength in our gym classes with the bench press

- **Rethink the feedback.** Go back over your instructor's feedback to make sure you understand it and use it for improvements.

- **Rethink the method.** Every time you finish a paper, you learn something—something about the topic of your writing and something about yourself. Ask yourself what you have learned to help you become a better writer in the future. What might you have done to improve the writing process? What could have gone better? What will you do differently the next time you write? Keep in mind that the P.O.W.E.R. approach represents a general process and that you may choose to emphasize particular stages according to what works best for you.

Above all, remember what you've accomplished. You've transformed what's inside your head—your thoughts, your ideas, your values—into something that can reach and potentially influence other people. Through your writing, you have exercised the ability to move others and get them to think in new ways. You've made a difference. That's the real power of writing. Refer to Try It! 4, "Thinking Critically about Writing."

Becoming Acquainted with Information Sources

In most cases you will need to explore and add to your ideas with research. What information do you need to support your point?

In general, you'll find information stored in two distinct kinds of places—libraries and computer information networks.

Libraries No matter how humble or imposing its physical appearance, whether it contains only a few volumes or hundreds of thousands, the library is one good place to focus your efforts as you seek out and gather information.

Although every library is different, all share two key elements: the material they hold—their basic collections—and the tools to help you *locate* the material you need.

What Can Be Found in a Library's Basic Collections?
Libraries obviously contain books, but they typically have a lot more than that. In addition to the fiction and nonfiction books on their shelves, libraries usually have some or all of the following:

- **Periodicals.** *Periodicals* are popular magazines published for general audiences, specialized journals for professionals in a field, and newspapers. Magazines and journals are often bound and stored by year; newspapers are usually kept in **microform,** in which documents that have been photographed and greatly reduced in size are stored on either microfilm (reels of film) or microfiche (plastic sheets), which can be read with special microform readers.

- **Indexes to Periodicals and Other Information Sources.** How can you learn what articles have been published in magazines, newspapers, and journals? Indexes provide the information.

  An index provides a listing of journal articles by subject area and author. Some indexes also provide a short summary, or **abstract,** of the contents of each article.

  Many kinds of indexes can be found. Some are general, such as the *Reader's Guide to Periodical Literature,* and cover a variety of general circulation magazines of the type you'd find at a decent newsstand, such as *Newsweek, Maclean's,* and *Rolling Stone.* Others are more specialized and concentrate on a particular field. For instance, the *Music Index* is an index of articles about music, and the *Business Periodicals Index* provides information on articles about business.

  Indexes come in both book and computerized form. Although some people prefer to use indexes in book form, computerized indexes such as CD-ROM, web-based or electronic databases, are considerably easier and quicker to use. Furthermore, you can often download the results of computerized searches at a library onto your own floppy disks, which you can later load into your computer.

- **Encyclopedias.** Encyclopedias provide a broad overview of knowledge. Some encyclopedias, such as the *Encyclopaedia Britannica* or *World Book Encyclopedia,* attempt to cover the entire range of knowledge, and they may take up many volumes. Others are more specialized, covering only a particular field, such

Microform

A means of storing greatly reduced photographs of printed pages, which can be read using special microform readers; the two main types of microform are microfiche and microfilm

Abstract

A short summary of the contents of a journal article

as *the Encyclopedia of Human Behavior* or *The Canadian Encyclopedia*. Most are printed as multivolume sets of books, although an increasing number come in CD-ROM computerized versions. Wikipedia is available free online at www.wikipedia.org. Encyclopedias provide a good general view of a topic, raising key issues that can lead you to more specific and current sources, and as such are a good resource at the earliest stage of your information gathering. Although some encyclopedias lack depth, subject-specific encyclopedias, such as the *Encyclopedia of Sociology,* are comprehensive references with articles written by leading scholars and edited by advisory groups comprised of the top academics in their fields.

> "Knowledge is of two kinds: we know a subject ourselves, or we know where we can find information upon it."
>
> Samuel Johnson

- **Dictionaries.** The reference section of most libraries has a wide range of dictionaries, including specialized dictionaries, such as French–English or manufacturing dictionaries.
- **Government documents.**
- **Musical scores.**
- **Reserve collections.** Reserve collections hold heavily used items that instructors assign for a class. Sometimes reserve material can be checked out for only an hour or two and used in the same room; in other cases the material can be used overnight or for a few days.

Most libraries offer information sheets describing all the different kinds of materials they have available and how you can find them. Find one of these sheets (often they are at the main desk closest to the entrance) and you have the key to the library.

Using Catalogues Catalogues contain a listing of all materials that are held in the library. Because they list where the information is physically stored, they also help you find what you're looking for.

Traditionally, catalogues consisted of paper cards that were filed in trays. In large libraries, the card catalogue sometimes extended across several huge rooms. Today, however, the catalogues of an increasing number of libraries are computerized. Rather than physically sorting through cards, users conduct a catalogue search on a computer. In fact, you may be able to access your school's catalogue from home as well as from computers housed in the library itself.

Other libraries use microform media (microfiche or microfilm) for their catalogues. And many libraries are in transition, using a combination of forms.

Although traditional card catalogues (consisting of records of information on actual cards) and computer catalogues (consisting of electronic records) are physically very different, the basic information each contains is the same. Information is usually sorted by title, author name, and subject, which means that each book (or other library holding) actually can be found in three different ways: searching for its author (author listing), its title (title listing), or its subject (subject listing). Individual entries generally include additional information, such as the publisher, date of publication, and similar information pertaining to the item.

Say, for example, you're writing a paper on David Suzuki. To find his books in an electronic catalogue, you enter his name, searching the catalogue for author entries. You may be presented with the following listing:

The key piece of information is the book's call number. The **call number** is a classification unique to a book that tells you exactly where to find it. Most post-

Call number

A unique classification number assigned to every book (or other resource) in a library, which provides a key to locating it secondary libraries use the Library of Congress classification system for call numbers, a combination of letters and numbers. The first letter indicates a general topical area, and the numbers provide further classification information. But you don't need to know the system; all that's really important is that it pinpoints the book's location in the library.

Because the record illustrated above is from an electronic search, it contains further helpful information. The words "IN LIBRARY" under "STATUS" tell you that the book has not been checked out by another patron and should be sitting on the shelf. You'll need to familiarize yourself with your library's particular system to know what specific commands are available to you. Chances are there's a handout or posted set of instructions nearby.

Stacks

The shelves on which books and other materials are stored in a library

Recall

A way to request library materials from another user who has them

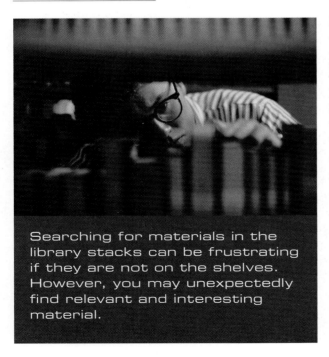

Searching for materials in the library stacks can be frustrating if they are not on the shelves. However, you may unexpectedly find relevant and interesting material.

Locating Information Once you have identified the information you're seeking by using the catalogue, you need to actually locate the work. In all but the biggest libraries, you can simply go into the **stacks,** the place containing shelves where the books and other materials are kept, and—using the call number—find what you're looking for. In some cases, however, you won't be permitted to enter the stacks. In libraries with closed stacks, you must fill out a form with the call numbers of the books you want. A library aide will find and deliver the material to a central location.

What if you go to the location in the stacks where the material is supposed to be and you can't find it? The most likely explanation is that the material is checked out or is in use by someone else at that time. It may also be incorrectly shelved or simply lost. Whatever the reason, don't give up. If the material is checked out to another user, ask a librarian if you can **recall** the material, a process by which the library contacts whoever has the book and asks him or her to return it because someone else needs to use it.

If the librarian informs you that the material is not checked out to someone else, wait a few days and see whether it appears on the shelf. Someone may have been using it while you were looking for it and then left it to be reshelved. If it was mis-shelved, the librarian may be able to find it. If the material is truly lost, you may be able to get it from another library through **interlibrary loan,** a system by which libraries share resources, making them available to patrons of different libraries. Ask the librarian for help; an interlibrary loan will take some time—between a few days and several weeks—but eventually you'll be able to get the material.

Finally, even if you do find exactly what you were looking for, take a moment to scan the shelves for related material. Because books and other materials are generally grouped by topic on library shelves, you may find other useful titles in the same place. One of the pleasures of libraries is the possibility of finding on the shelves an unexpected treasure—material that your catalogue search did not initially identify but that may provide you with exactly the kind of information you need.

The World Wide Web Want to know how to order flowers for your girlfriend in Ottawa? find a long-lost friend? the latest bulletin from Health Canada? biographical information on Jarome Iginla?

There is one place where you can look for all this information—and stand a good chance of finding it: the **World Wide Web.** The Web is a computer resource that links a vast array of information to the user's computer terminal. The information may be text, photos, graphs, or video or audio clips.

Like a library, the Web involves several essential components. They include a browser, Web pages, links, and search engines.

- **Browsers.** To use the World Wide Web, your computer has to have a browser. A **browser,** as its name implies, is a program that provides a way of moving around the Web. Among the major browsers are Netscape's Navigator and Microsoft's Internet Explorer.

   To use a browser, you indicate the location of the information that you're seeking by typing in an address. Web addresses are odd combinations of letters and symbols. They typically start off with "http://www" and then go on from there. The address identifies a unique location on the Web, known as a *Web page* (or sometimes *website*), that you are directing your browser to find. Another term for an Internet address is **URL (uniform resource locator).**

- **Web pages.** Also known as websites, Web pages are the heart of the World Wide Web. A **Web page** is a location on the World Wide Web that presents you with information. The information may appear as text on the screen, to be read like a book (or more accurately, like a scroll). Or it might be a video clip, an audio clip, a photo, a portrait, a graph, or a figure. It may be a news service photo of the prime minister of Canada or a backyard snapshot of someone's family reunion.

- **Links** (short for hyperlinks). Websites typically provide you with **links**—a means of automatically jumping—to other Web pages or to other places on that website. Just as an encyclopedia article on forests might say at the end, "See also *Trees*," Web pages often provide a means of reaching other sites on the Web—you just have to click on the link with your mouse and you are there.

- **Search engines.** A **search engine** is simply a computerized index to information on the Web. Among the most popular are Yahoo!, Google, AltaVista, and Excite! In fact,

Interlibrary loan

A system by which libraries share resources, making them available to patrons of different libraries

World Wide Web

A graphical interface that permits users to transmit and receive text and pictorial, video, and audio information

Browser

A program that provides a way of navigating the World Wide Web

URL (uniform resource locator)[2]

The address that defines the route to a file on the Web or any other Internet facility

Web page

A location (or site) on the World Wide Web housing information from a single source, and (typically) links to other pages

Link

A means of jumping automatically from one Web page to another

"First, they do an on-line search."

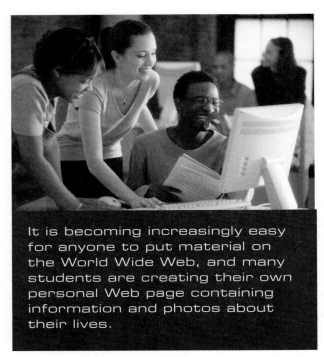

It is becoming increasingly easy for anyone to put material on the World Wide Web, and many students are creating their own personal Web page containing information and photos about their lives.

Search engine

A computerized index to information on the World Wide Web

Google has become such a popular search engine that it is now a verb, as in "I googled my basketball coach and found out all about his career!"

Search engines themselves are located on the Web, so you have to know their addresses. After you reach the specific Web address of a search engine, you enter the topic of the search. The search engine then provides a list of websites that may contain information relevant to your search.

Keep in mind that search engines cannot search subscription services such as ProQuest, EBSCO, or other scholarly, registered databases that might be available in your school's library—onsite or online.

Some search engines, such as Yahoo.ca, specialize in identifying general directories of information, such as sites from which to search for information on different dog breeds, the Islamic religion, and car repair. Using this type of search engine is analogous to searching for reference books devoted to general topics in a library, rather than searching for the specific facts contained in the reference books.

Other search engines, such as Google or AltaVista, are more useful when you are looking for specific pieces of information, such as who signed the *Canadian Charter of Rights and Freedoms,* what Viagra is, and who Ralph Klein is. This category of search engine identifies pages containing specific keywords, drawn from millions of individual Web pages.

Finally, a third type of search engine is exemplified by Ask Jeeves! and Dogpile. Known as *metasearch tools,* these sites send your search commands to other search engines, compiling the results into a single, unified list.

No single search engine works best. In fact, most people develop their own preferences. The best advice: Try out several of them and see which works best for you. To get started, use Try It! 5, "Information, Please!"

TRY IT!

www.mcgrawhill.ca/olc/power

5

Information, Please!

Prepare: The purpose of this exercise is to provide you with experience using search engines.

Organize: Use the questions below, which are also available online.

Work: Try to find the answers to the following questions, using at least three of the search engines described in the text.

Evaluate: Were you able to find the answers? Were some questions particularly easy or hard to answer? Do you have a preference for one search engine over another? Why?

Rethink: If you are not a regular user of the Internet to find information, would you use it more after this exercise? Why?

1. What was the French Revolution and when did it occur?
2. What is the title of a recent biography of Wayne Gretzky?
3. What are the words of Dr. Martin Luther King, Jr.'s "I Have a Dream" speech?
4. Is the birthrate in Quebec higher or lower than that in British Columbia?
5. What is the ecu?

The Far Reaches of the Web As its name implies, the Web is vast—sometimes frustratingly so.

Although search engines permit you to locate specific information, they do not provide a complete record of everything that is housed in cyberspace. In fact, no one knows how much material exists. Not only is more information added to the Web every day, but the information resides on thousands of individual computers. Anyone with a computer can set up a personal website.

The fact that anyone can put information on the Web is both the biggest asset and greatest disadvantage of using the Web as an information source. Because computer skill is the only expertise a person needs to set up a Web page, there may be as much *mis*information on the Web as there is information. Consequently, keep the usual consumer rule in mind: Buyer beware. Unless the website has been established and is maintained by a reliable organization, the information it contains may not be accurate. (We'll talk more about how to determine the trustworthiness of information on the Web when we discuss evaluating information sources later in the chapter.)

Searching the World Wide Web Using the World Wide Web to find information couldn't be easier—or more difficult. The ease of navigation around the Web makes finding information quite simple. At the same time, though, the mass of information that is tied into the Web can make finding *appropriate* information very tricky. See Try It! 6, "Work the Web."

> "Usually, when doing research, I refer to all forms of information! I do this so that I can cross reference my information and rid my research of any bias, or opinionated info. A wide range of materials and references allows for a broader view on whatever you are trying to locate information for."
>
> Jessica Boffo, Student, Capilano College

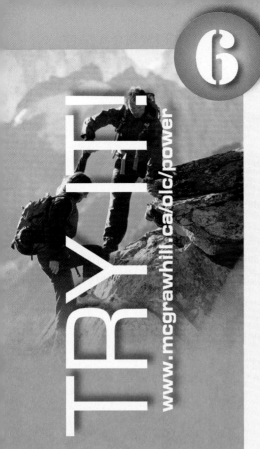

www.mcgrawhill.ca/olc/power

TRY IT!

6

Work the Web

Use the World Wide Web to locate information about the Canadian women's suffrage movement of the mid-nineteenth and early twentieth centuries. If you are doing it right, you should come across information about The Famous Five (Nellie McClung, Emily, Murphy, Irene Parlby, Louise McKinney, and Henrietta Edwards), the Toronto Literary Club, Emily Stowe, the Women's Christian Temperance Movement, Agnes Campbell Macphail, the Persons Case of 1929, the dates women in each province gained the right to vote, and a chronology of the women's suffrage movement in Canada.

Print out or write down what you find, including source documents, bibliographies, interesting links, and dead ends (you are sure to find some strange things out there!).

Evaluate your overall satisfaction with using the World Wide Web for research on this topic. What are the advantages and disadvantages of using the Web compared with traditional, noncomputerized methods?

Using the list of sites generated by a search is simple. With a computer mouse, click on the site address of the relevant document, and the home page of the site will (eventually) appear on your computer screen. You can then take notes on the material, in the same way you'd take notes on material in a book.

The simplicity by which you can navigate great "distances" through the Web also can make it difficult to find exactly the material that will be most helpful. Most of what you will come across may well be of little use. In fact, it's easy to end up in a virtual dead end, in which the information you have found is only minimally related to the topic you're researching. In that case, use the "Back" command on the browser, which will allow you to retrace the route that led to the site on which you currently find yourself.

The other danger with Web searches is that you may come across information that is so fascinating that you stray off track and lose sight of what you should be doing. It's important, then, to keep in mind what you're supposed to be doing and resist the temptations that the Web offers.

You and Computers: A Word to the Cyber-wary To make use of the Internet and the World Wide Web, you'll need to be familiar with computers—devices about which most of us have strong reactions.

If you are not yet at ease with computers, relax. With sufficient practice, using a computer will become second nature. No one is born with computer skills. Those computer wizards we're all familiar with, fearlessly sitting at a keyboard and tapping away, they, too, at some point knew nothing about computers. But they learned, and so can you. In fact, it's as much a necessity to learn to use a computer as it was for you to learn to use a calculator earlier in your schooling. No one facing the job market in the twenty-first century will want to leave school without basic computer skills.

Career Connections

Write Away

The first and most memorable pieces of writing your prospective employer sees from you are a cover letter and your résumé. Remember these three key points:

1. In your cover letter, emphasize what you can do for the employer, not what the employer can do for you.

2. Summarize your qualifications. Learn the core competencies of the job you are applying for and highlight the ones that match your skill set.

3. Request an interview; the purpose of sending a cover letter and résumé is to get an interview.

Instead of ending your résumé with "References available on request," why not let the employer know you have a portfolio by closing with, "Portfolio available for review."

Preparation and confidence are key to any successful interview. Creating a portfolio is an intensive review of your skills and abilities, which ensures you are prepared. When you see all the demonstrations you have compiled, you will feel more confident and capable.

> Logistics processes—such as supply chain management, transport, distribution, and inventory control—consume anywhere from 10 to 70 percent of company operating budgets and contribute roughly 10 percent to Canada's gross national product. The Canadian Professional Logistics Institute's unique website at <www.loginstitute.ca/prolog/infokit/> is a forum for logistics professionals and employers to communicate. Logistics professionals can create and maintain their own portfolios online with specialized software, for job searches and for career planning. At the same time, employers can post positions on the site. Based on the information given, the website will match portfolios and postings.

Using Computers to Present and Gather Information What can computers do for you, aside from providing the gateway to library catalogues, e-mail, and the World Wide Web? Probably the most common use of computers by students is for writing. *Word-processing programs* turn a computer into a smart typewriter—a *very* smart typewriter. With a word-processing program, you can check the spelling of words you type, but beware! Canadian spellcheckers are not always available or reliable; keep your spellchecker on but use it with caution. You must proofread your work closely to make sure the spelling is correct. No spellchecker can replace a good read-through.

If you aren't yet at ease with computers, consider taking a workshop or class on the topic, offered by almost every college or university. In just a few hours, you'll be able to learn word processing and other basic computing skills. It doesn't take long to become proficient, and your mastery of basic computer skills is a prerequisite for achieving postsecondary—and, ultimately, occupational—success.

Narrowing Your Search

Finding information is not the biggest information management task most of us face. After taking advantage of the library and Web, we typically have just the opposite problem: too much information. For instance, if you enter "bananas" into Yahoo! you get 17, 900 entries.

How you select and organize what you've found often makes the difference between success and failure. Keep in mind these tips for organizing information effectively:

- **Determine what you're looking for.** Suppose you have to write a paper for your biology class, and, because you have a good friend with AIDS, you decide to write about the disease. You go to the library card catalogue and find that your school has dozens of books about AIDS. You take a look at the World Wide Web and the situation is even worse, with literally thousands of references to AIDS. What do you do next?

  You need to refine your topic, transforming it from a broad, open-ended domain to something more restricted and manageable. Look at a few of the sources you've found and consider the major issues surrounding AIDS. Perhaps some of the books have chapters on particular subtopics, such as research into cures for the disease or its effects on the population in Africa. Because these topics are narrower, they make a more manageable topic for a paper.

- **Identify the key sources of information.** Every field has experts, and you need to make sure that you consider what they have said about your topic. How do you identify the experts? One way is to read through several books and see whose names keep popping up. Another way is to use an encyclopedia to get an overview of your topic. Encyclopedia articles often end with suggested readings; these can guide you to the appropriate sources of information.

- **Keep in mind what you're going to do with the information.** As you begin to do your research, keep your goal in mind. Are you writing a short, two-page paper giving your opinion? a longer term paper? a speech? a worksheet? Knowing what you need to do with the information will help you to organize your information search appropriately.

- **Learn the key issues and controversies.** Every field has key issues and certain controversies that remain unresolved. For example, in psychology, one key issue is whether human nature is the product of biology in the form of genes and biochemical processes or the result of the influence of environment—the culture, religion, and historical events of a particular time and place. Identifying these sorts of issues and controversies in the earliest stages of your research will ensure that you cover what is most important. They can also make the assignment you're seeking to complete—whether it's a paper, a speech, or a report—far more interesting than a mere recitation of facts. For instance, a paper on the treatment of cancer could focus on the use of herbal remedies and other nontraditional treatments that arouse great disagreement among physicians.

- **Use librarians effectively.** The stereotype of a librarian as someone whose main job is to stop people from talking in the library is dead. Librarians today are masters of information management—people who can help you find your way through a huge range of data sources and steer you to the right material.

  Make use of librarians—but do it properly. Start by looking for the information yourself. Then, if you're having trouble sorting through what you've found (or can't find material in the first place), ask for help.

  The better the question, the better the answer. Ask a precise question, such as, "I'm writing a paper on the environmental effects of using nuclear power to generate electricity. I've found two books, but they're not quite right. I wonder if you have any ideas about where I might find additional material?"

  Don't be afraid to ask. Think of librarians as highly trained guides who can save you hours of aimless wandering in an increasingly dense forest of information.

Using the Information You Find

You've found the information that you've been seeking, and you've selected and organized it, focusing on the topic of your research. Now what?

Although we'll be concentrating in future chapters on how to prepare written and oral reports using the sources you have located, it's important to begin the process of putting the information you've gathered into a form that you can use in the future. One time-honoured technique is using file folders and note cards.

Assembling Information Folders After you have gathered information, break it down into subtopics by placing the raw information you've located (photocopies, computer printouts, and computer disks) into different-coloured file folders, one folder for each subtopic. Label each folder with a stick-on label or note, which will permit you to easily modify the topic of the folder if necessary in the future. This initial sorting will permit you to take the next step in information management: creating note cards.

Note Cards: The Researcher's Basic Tool Making notes on index cards is the best way of transforming information into a form that can easily be used. They may be low-tech, but they are the best way to note, and later recall, what your research has uncovered. Best of all, they can be sorted an endless number of ways. As you narrow your topic, all you have to do is sort them differently. Note cards have other advantages, too. Even though you gathered your information from six different books, three magazine articles, and a couple of websites, you can place all note cards containing information about the same subtopic together in a stack, even though they came from different sources.

The key is to place no more than one major idea on each card. Sometimes that major idea will take a few words; other times it will consist of several sentences. If you avoid including more than one major idea on a card, you will later find it easy to arrange them and to place related pieces of information together. It often helps to put, in the top corner of the card, the subtopic (such as "Early Influences" or "Husband" or "Customer Service") that the idea fits into; this way you can see it easily.

One other important point about note cards: Make sure every note card contains information that clearly identifies its source. It is extremely important that you know where the idea on the note card came from so you can credit this source later when you write your paper and use the idea. This will also save you a lot of trouble if you need to return to the source of the idea. Although you don't need to include complete biographical information on every note card, you should keep a master list—either on a separate set of note cards or in a computer file—with the full citation.

Finally, you *must* write the ideas you place on the note cards in your own words. Unless you find some particularly compelling phrases that you think you might want to include in the final paper—which you should set off with quotation marks—always use your own words on note cards. Using your own words will prevent you from accidentally copying others' words and passing them off as your own—which, as we'll discuss next, is the gravest of academic sins. Using your own words also helps ensure that you really understand a concept yourself.

You also can use a word-processing program to take notes. Instead of note cards, place each idea in a separate paragraph, which can then be sorted and shifted around. In fact, some word-processing programs have built-in features to help you organize your research.

Citing Sources Although there are numerous citation systems for documenting and citing reference materials, the most commonly used style guides are those of the APA (American Psychological Association), MLA (Modern Languages Association), CBE (Council of Biology Editors) and CS (Chicago or Turabian Style). Because of the vast amount of research material on the Internet, all style guides have been adapted to cover citation of electronic sources.

Psychology and social science papers are written in *APA style*. Reference citations are used to document the source of ideas, paraphrases, and direct quotes. Parenthetical references within the text are used and allow the reader to locate the source of information in a reference section at the end of the paper. Footnotes are not used and there is no bibliography.

English and humanities students use *MLA style*. Documenting sources means telling the reader where research sources are located, whether facts, opinions, or quotations. A list of works cited and parenthetical references within the text compose the two parts of documentation.

Natural science writing is frequently referenced or documented using *CBE style*.

The *Chicago or Turabian Style* is used for writing humanities papers and computer papers and articles, and for business writing. To mark citations throughout an essay or article, a writer using the *Chicago Manual's* note-bibliography style inserts a superscript number after each quotation, paraphrase, or summary. Each citation corresponds to a numbered note containing publication information about the source cited. Such notes are called footnotes when printed at the foot of a page and endnotes when printed at the end of an essay, chapter, or book.

Find out what format your instructor wants you to use. If no particular style is required, choose one and apply it consistently. You'll find an excellent online reference with detailed information about these four styles at <www.bedfordstmartins.com/online/shrttoc.html>.

Plagiarism

Using another author's ideas or words without proper documentation; representing someone else's creative work (ideas, words, images, etc.) as one's own, whether intentional or not

Acknowledging Others' Ideas As you gather information you will begin to appreciate just how valuable ideas are. In fact, ideas are so valuable that there's no greater sin in the world of academics than **plagiarism,** taking credit for someone else's words, thoughts, or ideas. In the academic world, plagiarism is about the equivalent of stealing a car. Even if you just mean to "borrow" a passage, passing another person's work off as your own is entirely unacceptable.

Furthermore, if you do plagiarize and get caught, the penalty can be severe: In many schools, plagiarism results in dismissal. You could even face legal charges, because almost all published material is copyrighted, which means that it is someone's intellectual property. If an author learns that you have used his or her writing as your own, the author has the right to take you to court and sue for damages.

The best way to avoid plagiarism is to be scrupulous while doing your research. Make sure you put everything you write down into your own words, except for direct quotes. And when you quote directly from someone's work, use quotation marks. In addition, always include complete information about your source. This information should include the author, title, publisher, year of publication, and page numbers.

Be careful when you put ideas into your own words. It's not just a matter of rearranging the words and choosing synonyms for them. For instance, consider the following passage from the book Canadian Heritage:[3]

For over a century, Portuguese have been migrating from their homeland in search of work. Three epochs of migration are discernible for Portuguese men and women. Over one million people left Portugal for Brazil between 1886 and 1950. It was not until the Canadian and Portuguese governments signed labour contract agreements to supply railway construction and agricultural workers after World War II that Canada became a popular option for Portuguese immigrants for the first three decades following the war. The third epoch saw large numbers choose migration targets closer to home in Western Europe.

Here's one way of rephrasing the passage, but one that is so close to the original that it amounts to plagiarism:

For over a hundred years, Portuguese have been emigrating from their native land to look for employment. Three eras of Portuguese emigration can be seen. More than a million people immigrated to Brazil from 1886 to 1950. For thirty years following the Second World War, after Canada and Portugal agreed on labour contracts supplying workers for railways and farms, thousands of Portuguese immigrated to Canada. The third wave of immigration was to Western European countries nearer to Portugal.

A more appropriate rewording of the original passage would be the following, which more clearly rephrases the authors' ideas:

In Portugal, three distinct patterns of immigration can be identified over the past century, driven by Portuguese workers seeking employment abroad. First, from 1886 to 1950, more than a million Portuguese emigrated to Brazil. Second, for three decades after the Second World War, thousands of Portuguese settled in Canada, after labour agreements allowing Portuguese workers access to jobs in the railroad and agricultural sectors were signed. Third, the prospect of jobs in Western Europe resulted in emigration to countries nearer Portugal.

Even in this case, it is still necessary to cite the source of the facts or ideas that you are rephrasing by adding a footnote reference to the original work. The keys to avoiding plagiarism are to use your own words and, if you use the words, ideas, or thoughts of others, to be sure to cite the source. However, it is not necessary to have a citation after every sentence. Some facts are so basic ("Japan and Germany were Canada's enemies in World War II") that no source is necessary.

Keep in mind, too, that you must cite material that you find on the World Wide Web. Just because the material may appear on your home computer screen, it still was produced by someone else, and the author must be given credit. Although the rules for how to cite material found on the Web are still developing, it is still necessary to provide the source of anything you come across on the Web. At the very least include the site name, Web address, and author. (Complete Try It! 7, "Summarize, Don't Plagiarize," on page 248 to get some practice in the art of gathering information and ideas without stealing them.)

Copy-and-Paste Plagiarism or Cyber-Cheating Using the Internet has made researching papers and essays easier and more convenient, but it has also led to an increase in plagiarism and cheating. For students who are short of time or who haven't researched their topics thoroughly, it may be tempting to copy and paste online articles or to download essays posted on sites such as "School Sucks." However, these tactics are counterproductive and very risky. Not only are these students *not* reading, thinking, analyzing, writing, or learning about their topics; cheating is an intellectually dishonest activity and subject to harsh academic penalties. It is just not worth it to cheat.

Working in a Group:
Summarize, Don't Plagiarize

Prepare: The purpose of this exercise is to provide experience determining when to use references or cite information you obtain from other sources.

Organize: Use the excerpt below, which is also available online.

Work: Use your own words to capture the overall meaning of the quoted passage without copying or plagiarizing. Assume that you want to reflect the main points of the passage in an article of your own. Decide whether you would cite the work in a footnote or reference. Try to make your summary 10 to 15 percent of the original length.

Evaluate: Were you able to complete the summary and decide the requirement for references? Compare your summary to that of other students. Is there agreement on the requirement for references?

Rethink: Were you able to distinguish between a summary and using someone else's work? When in doubt, summarize don't plagiarize.

1. Excerpted from Granatstein, J. L. (1998, July 1). Mackenzie King. *Maclean's, 111,* pp. 24–25, on William Lyon Mackenzie King's political career:

   [William Lyon Mackenzie] King was the first "expert" to become prime minister, a genuine student of labour conditions and the need to reconcile the conflict between, as the title of his unreadable 1918 book put it, Industry and Humanity. He took over the reins of government in 1921 when the farmers of Canada were united in revolt against the old party system and its dominance by eastern interests. Within five or six years, he had almost completely absorbed them back into his Liberal party.

   In his first term, he found the British government trying to whipsaw him into unconditional military support for London's interests in the Middle East, but he evaded the attempt skilfully and lost no support in doing so. In the 1926 King-Byng constitutional crisis—provoked when Lord Byng, the governor general, refused King's request to dissolve Parliament— King was likely in the wrong in seeking to cling to office and in resigning so precipitously that he left Canada briefly without a government. But he succeeded in clipping the wings of the British-appointed governor general. Canadian autonomy—and King—benefited.

   During the Great Depression, when he was out of office for five years, he dabbled in spiritualism so much that we might think him addled. But when he was re-elected in 1935, his first act was to conclude a major trade agreement with the United States, a step of huge importance. And through skilful practice of his "on the one hand, on the other hand" policies, he brought Canada united into the Second World War in 1939, a feat that seemed unimaginable in 1937. Addled? Hardly.

   This most pacific of men surprisingly proved himself a great war leader. Under his direction, a strong cabinet mobilized a gigantic war effort. Canada's military was a million strong with the First Canadian Army overseas, a navy of 100 000 and the British Commonwealth Air Training Plan. Astonishingly, this mobilization was accomplished without a huge and divisive split over manpower, although overseas conscription was imposed for a few thousand infantry in November 1944. At the same time, the agricultural and industrial resources of the nation poured forth in unprecedented quantities. Canada became rich during the war, one of the very few beneficiaries of a global tragedy.

   After peace had come, King, by now over 70 years old, hung on. He took his nation into the discussion that led to NATO, and he ensured a smooth transition to his chosen successor, Louis Saint-Laurent. For 27 years, King dominated Canada.

Professors are becoming more attuned to copy-and-paste plagiarism; it is usually easy to detect differences in writing styles or essays that do not match the topic given. Wayne Petrozzi, who teaches political science at Ryerson University, suspects approximately 8 to 12 percent of student papers he receives have elements of academic dishonesty. Petrozzi doesn't believe the majority of student researchers are wilfully cheating; rather they ". . . just don't know how to write an academic paper."[4] Many instructors routinely inspect student-cheating sites to detect what essays are available (for free or for money). Remember, there is no quality control in cyber-cheating—many online essays are riddled with mistakes!

Aside from plagiarism, some students are using new technologies, such as PDAs (personal digital assistants), graphing calculators, and cell phones with text-messaging features to their advantage by using them as tools to cheat on exams. These tools are the electronic form of note passing. Cheaters using high-tech methods face the same consequences as ever: an inferior academic record, possible suspension or expulsion, and an unproductive learning experience in higher education.

10 + 1 Ways You Can Avoid Plagiarizing

1. Be aware of what plagiarism is, so you can prevent it.
2. Recognize, admit, and accept that plagiarism is dishonest and that it is wrong to lie, steal, and cheat.
3. Acknowledge that academic work takes time and effort. Make a commitment to your studies.
4. Understand what your essay assignment is asking you to do. The clearer you are on your topic, the easier it will be to do a good job without plagiarizing.
5. Begin your assignment in time to finish it without panicking (or plagiarizing).
6. Learn to research properly . . . ask your school librarian, your professors, or peer tutors for help. Or check the Internet.
7. Go to your school's writing centre or learning centre for help if you are not confident of your writing skills.
8. Understand that there is a difference between plagiarism and incorrectly citing your sources. Check and recheck your citations.
9. Put other people's exact words in quotations. There is nothing wrong in using other people's thoughts or words if you acknowledge them!
10. Work with others in a study or writing group and peer edit your work.
11. Learn to **paraphrase**!

Remembering That Not All Sources of Information Are Equal

Paraphrase
Use the ideas in the original passage but put them in your own words, often because you want them to be clearer to your readers

You have gathered and organized a great deal of information, and as you begin to work it into your final product, you must use your critical thinking skills to evaluate that information. Some of the important critical thinking questions you must address before you can feel confident about what you've found include the following:

- **How authoritative is the information?** It is absolutely essential to consider the source of the material. Approach every piece of information with a critical eye, trying to determine what the author's biases might be. The best approach is to use multiple sources of information. If one source is divergent from the others, you may reasonably question the reliability of that source.

Another approach is to consider the publisher of the material. For instance, books published by well-established publishers are carefully reviewed before publication to ensure their accuracy.

Be especially critical of information you find on the World Wide Web. It's important to keep in mind that the Web is completely unregulated and that *anyone* can put *anything* on the Web.

One way of evaluating Web information is to consider a site's sponsor. Commercial Web pages (whose address includes the letters *.com,* short for commercial) often include the least objective material. Addresses including letters such as *.gc.ca* (Canadian government) or *.bc.ca* (site from British Columbia) generally include information that is more objective. Still, each site must be evaluated on its own merits. Note that much information on the Internet is American and may not be relevant to your research.

- **How current is the information?** No matter what the discipline, information is changing at a rapid rate. Even a field like Chaucerian English, which concentrates on poetry written in the fourteenth century, advances significantly year by year as scholars make new discoveries, come to new insights, and reach new conclusions.

  Consequently, don't assume that, because you're researching a historically old topic, old sources will suffice. Consider whether what you've found is the most recent and up-to-date approach. Compare older sources to newer ones to identify changes in the ways in which the topic is considered.

- **Is anything missing?** One of the hardest questions to answer is whether your research is complete. Have you found all the relevant sources? Have you missed anything that is important?

  Although there is no way to answer these questions definitively, you can do a couple of things. The best way to ensure that you haven't missed anything important is to check out the sources that you have found. Many will have bibliographies and lists of suggested additional readings. By carefully considering this information, you'll be able to get a good sense of the important work in your topic area and to verify that you haven't overlooked some critical source.

  You can also talk to your course instructor, describing generally what you've found. Librarians can also be extremely helpful; they may be acquainted with the general topic and know the most definitive sources in the field, including online and electronic sources.

Placing Information in Context

The Information Age presents us with great promise and opportunity. Through the use of media such as e-mail and the World Wide Web, we have at our fingertips the ability to communicate with others around the world. The computer keyboard truly can be said to contain "keys"—to the entire earth and its peoples.

At the same time, the world of information can be overwhelming. It's important, then, to revisit our information-seeking strategies by taking the following points into account:

- **Consider alternative types of information.** Information comes in many forms, and you should make sure that you have exhausted every potential source on your topic. For example, libraries sometimes house graphics and audiovisual material, such as videotapes, audiotapes, and CD-ROMs. Television, which includes both daily news programs and newsmagazines such as *CBC Newsworld* and *The Fifth Estate,* can provide useful information. Finally, once you identify experts in a field, you might try to contact them via letter, phone, or e-mail if you have a specific question. They won't always have the time to respond in a detailed fashion, but it's worth a try.

"Knowledge, in truth, is the great sun in the firmament. Life and power are scattered with all its beams."

Daniel Webster

- **Gather information from more than one point of view.** Don't settle for one viewpoint. Even if consensus exists on an issue, some dissenters from the predominant view are sure to exist. Seek them out and try to figure out why they hold the views they do. This can help you to better understand the dominant view and may even spur you to reconsider your own opinion or to express it in a new way.

- **Identify your own biases and assumptions about a topic.** We are not empty-headed vessels into which information simply flows, like coffee into a cup. Instead, we consider information in terms of the considerable amount of knowledge we already have. Ask yourself whether your prior knowledge is affecting the way you view the new information to which you're exposed. Have you looked at it as objectively as possible? Do you know what your own biases are? Are you open to new information that might contradict your existing beliefs and feelings?

- **Use information to improve your own life.** Finally, don't get so caught up in gathering material for course assignments that you neglect thinking about how you can use information on a personal level. Wander around the stacks of the library and find a book you want to read. Surf the Web and see what you come across. Taking a break from the serious business of higher education will help you to concentrate more when you do go back to work.

Looking ◀◀
Back ◀

What are the best techniques for getting started and writing a first draft?

- Freewriting and brainstorming can help you choose a topic.
- Identifying the audience for writing is essential.
- Breaking down large writing tasks into smaller, more-manageable pieces helps pave the way for completing a writing assignment.
- Good organization, which is essential to both writer and reader, often follows the ABBCC structure: argument, background, body, counterarguments, and conclusion.

How can I move from my first draft to my final draft?

- Use your outline as your roadmap.
- Begin the first draft by plunging in, starting anywhere in the paper.
- Revision is an essential part of writing; most of writing is rewriting.

Speaking of Success

Shawn Thomson

General Arts and Science Diploma, Cambrian College, Sudbury, Ontario

It is not often that a 27-year-old is declared a hero and has his hometown proclaim a day in his honour, but it happened to Shawn Thomson on May 20, 2004, as he completed a 18-day, 740-kilometre bike ride from Ottawa to Goderich, Ontario. What made this remarkable feat all the more exceptional is that Shawn, who has cerebral palsy and normally uses an electric wheelchair, rode a bike specially equipped with hand pedals. Shawn made the trip to raise attention and money for the group Mothers Against Drunk Driving (MADD). Shawn spent five years dreaming about the project and six months planning the "Shawn 'MADD Man' Thomson Bike Tour." So the trip, while difficult and exhausting, was the achievement of a very important goal.

Due to a lack of balance, Shawn, whose disability is incurable, cannot walk by himself. However, he refuses to let cerebral palsy keep him from reaching his goals. He credits his parents with instilling him with the motivation to set goals and not to give up. One of his key objectives was to graduate from college.

When investigating postsecondary institutions, Shawn discovered that Cambrian College in Sudbury, Ontario, Canada, through its Glenn Crombie

CAMBRIAN COLLEGE

Sudbury • Ontario
www.cambrianc.on.ca

Centre for disability services, provided support for students with disabilities, especially in the area of adaptive technology. He took advantage of a special needs grant to purchase equipment to make attending college easier. Because Shawn has difficulty controlling and coordinating movement and is subjected to frequent involuntary movements in all four limbs, he used the services of a notetaker who typed notes into a computer and then e-mailed them to him. In addition, Shawn was able to e-mail some of his assignments to his professors, which allowed him to be more independent in his academic work.

Since graduating from Cambrian, Shawn, like many other people with physical disabilities, has had a hard time finding a job. Shawn is hoping that technology might again help him achieve his goal of a satisfying career. He is currently taking courses in entrepreneurship to develop an online business on eBay. If his business plan is viable, he will have some assistance to get started. If successful, Shawn hopes to teach other people with disabilities how to do business online. Shawn, a self-described "people person," has a great desire to help others and refuses to believe cerebral palsy should prevent him from aiding other people who need assistance.

What are the basic sources for finding and gathering information?

- The World Wide Web is a computer resource that links a vast array of electronic information to users' computer terminals. Web users access Web "pages" (or sites) by using a browser, and may move from site to site by following links on each Web page.

What are the most effective ways to use information sources?

- The easiest procedure for translating raw information into a usable form is to take notes on index cards. Computers may also be used as a replacement for actual cards.

What do I need to keep in mind as I use information from reference resources?

- It is crucial to avoid plagiarism—passing off someone else's words or ideas as your own.

- An important step in using information for research is evaluating the worth of the information that has been gathered by considering how authoritative the source is, whether the author has any potential biases, how recent the information is, and whether anything important is missing from the research.

P.O.W.E.R. Portfolio

Writing and High-Tech Skills

1. Writing samples are frequently included in portfolios to demonstrate competence, skills, and range of experience. Consider including writing samples that closely relate to your academic or career goals. For example, if you were headed toward a health-related career, objective description, accurate summaries, case histories, and daily charts or logs would be appropriate inclusions. If you were considering a career in communication arts, suitable entries would be scripts, articles, stories, press releases, brochures, newsletters, and printouts from Web pages. If your goals are primarily academic, include samples of your best analytical essays, reports, or critiques, and keep adding submissions as your writing skills develop. Remember to include your reasons for including specific writing samples and what they signify about you.

2. Information technology (IT) and knowledge management (KM) skills have become crucial in academic and work settings. Consider including a section on IT or KM in your portfolio. An essay in which you have used several methods of gathering information and paraphrased or quoted accurately would be an ideal submission. Or consider developing an intensive bibliography of print and online sources on a particular topic. Or include a critique of a particular website; the critique allows you to summarize the contents and the source objectively. In your observations, be sure to indicate why you chose the selection, what skills, talents, or experiences it demonstrates, and what you learned.

Resources

On Campus

If you are having difficulties with writing, the first place to turn is to a cooperative classmate. Ask someone to read a draft of a writing assignment. He or she may be able to make enough constructive comments to allow subsequent drafts to come more easily. In addition, some colleges and universities have writing clinics where you can bring a draft of your paper and work with a counsellor or peer tutor. Finally, your instructors may be willing to read preliminary drafts of your work.

The librarians at your college or university library are the people to whom you should turn first if you need help in locating information. In recent years, librarians—most of whom hold advanced degrees—have significantly changed what they do, and most are now equally at home using traditional print material and searching electronic information storehouses.

If you are having difficulty gaining access to the World Wide Web, you may also find help at your school's computer centre. Most campuses have consultants who can help you with the technical aspects of computer usage.

In Print

Michael Harvey's book, *The Nuts and Bolts of College Writing* (Hackett Publishing Company, 2003), provides useful information for postsecondary writers.

Robert Berkman's *Find It Fast: How to Uncover Expert Information on Any Subject Online or in Print* (HarperResource, 5th edition, 2000) provides a step-by-step guide to locating information of all sorts.

On the Web

The following sites on the World Wide Web provide the opportunity to extend your learning about the material in this chapter. Although the Web addresses were accurate at the time the book was printed, check the P.O.W.E.R. Learning website, <www.mcgrawhill.ca/olc/power>, for any changes that may have occurred.

www.utoronto.ca/writing/other4.html
The University of Toronto has an excellent online writing support site. A particularly useful Web page is the Online Resources for Students of English as a Second Language, which provides links to many helpful sites.

http://web.uvic.ca/wguide/Pages/MasterToc.html
A very comprehensive site, the University of Victoria's Writer's Guide provides sample essays, a complete list of literary terms, and helpful information on topics such as citing sources, grammar, and spelling.

http://wombat.doc.ic.ac.uk/foldoc/index.html
You'll find a free online dictionary of computing at this site. Topics are listed alphabetically, and a search engine helps locate specific information.

www.ipl.org
This is the first Internet Public Library. Its mission is to discover and organize high-quality information resources. It offers an online text collection of more than 7000 titles, with a search engine to help you find what you're looking for, plus guides to periodicals and newspapers.

www.hamilton.edu/academics/resource/wc/AvoidingPlagiarism.html
A very thorough and informative site illustrates how to recognize and avoid plagiarism.

www.sosig.ac.uk/desire/internet-detective.html
The Internet Detective is a hands-on tutorial to evaluating websites. It includes interactive exercises and tests.

http://library.queensu.ca./inforef/guides/evalchart.htm
This site from Queen's University is a checklist for evaluating Web resources.

www.sc.edu/beaufort/library/pages/bones/bones.shtml
"Bare Bones 101: A Basic Tutorial on Searching the Web" is a primer that helps a new Internet user manage search engines, create search strategies, and practise searching on the main search engines. Includes links to sites helpful for more complex searching.

www.thecanadianencyclopedia.com
The Canadian Encyclopedia Online contains the full text of the printed volumes and junior edition articles, as well.

The Case Of...

The Unsuspecting Plagiarist

Trisha Cunningham's heart started to beat harder and she blinked back tears when she read her Business Communication teacher's comments scrawled at the bottom of her informal report, *No mark given. Please see me during office hours about this paper.* What could the problem be? This report, a corporate history of Sony Music, was worth 25 percent of her course mark! When she had sent the report by e-mail the previous week, she had felt she had done a good job.

When Trisha met with her professor the next day, she was shocked to learn that large portions of her report were highlighted by *turnitin.com,* an online service teachers at her college regularly used to detect "cut and paste" plagiarism. Trisha had consulted lots of websites during the research stage of her project and she had kept a pretty accurate list of her sources, which she had included in her "Works Cited" list, but it was really hard to know what she could or couldn't use.

Trisha knew she was in trouble when her professor seemed totally unsympathetic about her ignorance of how to include, document, and cite Internet sources in the report. Plagiarism had been covered in class—no excuses!

1. What are some potential consequences of Trisha's plagiarism? Do you agree with the penalties? Why or why not?

2. What do you think Trisha should do about this situation? What are her options? Is there any possibility of a positive ending to this case?

3. Where can Trisha go for help so this will never happen again? How could teachers help students avoid charges of plagiarism?

4. Should online plagiarism (like Trisha's case) be treated the same or differently from cases involving purchased or downloaded essays and research papers? Why or why not?

5. How have cases of plagiarism in the newspaper industry been handled recently? Why are workplace penalties so severe? Or are they severe enough?

Speaking

L eung told his study group he was ready to present their group project. He urged them not to worry. He was outgoing and popular. He could do this with his eyes closed. He thought giving good presentations was easy.

On the day of the presentation, Leung forgot to get the handout printed for distribution to the class. He didn't prepare any visual aids so he just read from a few notes. Several times he seemed lost and not sure of the next step in the presentation. Although he gave several points, he did not identify the source and he made them sound like they were his own opinions. He did not make any eye contact with the audience and failed to introduce or acknowledge the role of the group in the project. He left no time for questions or discussion, and appeared greatly relieved when the process was over. In the end, the group received a poor score and felt let down by Leung.

Leung grew from his mistake and went on to learn how to give presentations that have a purpose, a logical flow, and meet the needs of his audience. He no longer thinks that giving a good presentation is easy and he understands charm or charisma alone won't carry the day. Preparation is the key.

Looking ▶▶
Ahead

Some people feel totally exposed when they are speaking in front of people, and count it as one of their biggest fears. This chapter deals with how to give effective oral presentations, how to get over presentation anxiety, and how to effectively engage the audience. We'll consider the importance of preparation, and how you can learn to give both off-the-cuff and formal presentations effectively.

Learning to give effective presentations will contribute to your success in college or university and will likely be a major part of your career or professional success. At the very least, it will save you a lot of anxiety and stage fright.

After reading this chapter, you'll be able to answer these questions:

- **How can I deal with stage fright?**

- **How can I engage my audience?**

- **How can I give off-the-cuff answers to questions?**

Speaking Your Mind

Public speaking ranks right at the bottom of most first-year postsecondary students' rankings of their academic abilities.[1] In fact, surveys of the general population find that most people are more afraid of public speaking than of dying! It's not surprising. How often are we so totally exposed to others' scrutiny? Not only do we have to worry about the message we're communicating—just as with our writing—but in addition, each of us has to be concerned about nonverbal behaviour and the impression we are making: *Is my hair sticking up? This sweater was a big mistake. Are they bored? I wish my hands would stop shaking.*

Although you may always be a little nervous about public speaking, it's important to keep several points in mind:

- Audiences are generally sympathetic. They've all been where you are and probably share your fears about public speaking. They're on your side and are rooting for you to succeed.
- Once you start speaking, it will become easier. Anxiety tends to be highest *before* you start talking. Most people find that after they start a talk, their nervousness tends to decline.
- Practice helps. Practice and preparation for the talk will go a long way toward easing your tension.

Keep in mind, too, that in many fundamental ways, speaking is like writing. You need to consider who your audience is, muster your arguments, and decide how to sequence those arguments. Consequently, the P.O.W.E.R. writing framework that we presented in Chapter 9 applies to speaking as well.

Prepare: Deciding What You Want to Say

As with writing, *preparation* is crucial to speaking successfully. Speaking is a process, and preparation for it encompasses the following steps:

- **Decide what your goal is.** To speak successfully, you need to think about the end product. Who is your audience? Why have you been asked to speak? How long do you need to speak for?
- **Choose your topic.** Once you've determined who you are speaking to and why, you will need to choose a topic that is relevant to both your audience and the occasion. Although instructors will assign a specific topic or a list from which you can choose, in professional environments the choice will usually be left to you.

PREPARE

Decide what you want to say

ORGANIZE

Prepare a structured presentation with logical connections your audience can follow

WORK

Follow the 3 Ps: Preparation; Professionalism; Props

EVALUATE

Ask how you did: get feedback

RETHINK

Improve your performance: adapt your methods with each presentation

P.O.W.E.R. Plan

Meeting the Challenge of Public Speaking

Getting up to speak to a group is the most difficult thing many people can imagine. But the ability to present ideas and solutions to team members and customers is a must in many work environments. What are some things you can do to increase your ability to give presentations?

You may think that having the "gift of gab" or being charismatic is a must for public speaking. In truth, most participants like a speaker who has a clear purpose, is enthusiastic, believes in the message, provides a well-organized presentation, and is interested in helping the participants understand the message.

Organize: Prepare a Structured Presentation

Effective presentations communicate a message in a concise and organized manner. You can achieve this by using notes to cue you to the main parts of your presentation and by making logical connections for your audience to follow. To ensure that the purpose of your message is communicated clearly, follow some basic guidelines:

- **Always start with the purpose in mind.** Why are you giving the presentation? What do you want the participants to gain from your presentation or do differently as result?

- **Do more with less.** With few exceptions, it is better to deal with less information that is covered more thoroughly. Have a basic message that you want to deliver and stick to it.

- **Open/Input/Close.** Divide your presentation into three parts that are linked together.

  Open. *Explain the purpose of your presentation and what participants can expect to gain. Give people a reason to listen or arouse their curiosity by asking a question you will answer in your presentation.*

  Input. *Provide the information you have chosen to support your purpose. Help your listeners by being logical, well organized, and to the point.*

  Close. *Provide a brief summary, restate your purpose, and leave time for questions.*

- **Plan your use of time.** If you have 20 minutes for the complete presentation, you will only have about 8 to 10 minutes to provide information. The following is an example time line for a 20-minute presentation:

  5 minutes: Introduction/Open
  8 minutes: Input
  2 minutes: Close
  <u>5 minutes</u>: Questions
  20 minutes

- **Develop an outline.** Summarize your major points on a sheet of paper or on index cards. It will help you be more confident if you script your opening and closing statements. Use the notes as a prompt to keep you on track, but explain things in your own words so you sound more natural.

- **Rehearse.** When your plan is ready, try it out. Actually give your presentation to another person or to yourself using a mirror. Make sure you are familiar with the content and that you can deliver the presentation in the time allotted.

Work: Follow the 3 Ps: Preparation; Professionalism; Props

A successful presentation is about more than just the words you speak. The way you present yourself and the tools you use to back up your comments will directly impact the degree to which your audience accepts your message. Keep the following points in mind to ensure a successful presentation:

- **Make contact with your audience.** Draw the participants into the presentation by making eye contact, being energetic and enthusiastic, asking questions, and using examples that are likely to be a part of their lives. If stage fright is a problem for you, pick one person in the audience and speak to them.

- **Dress for the occasion.** Your clothes say a lot about the kind of person you want to portray and how confident and comfortable you are feeling. As a general rule try to dress just above the level of the audience. If the audience is likely to wear business casual, you should wear the upper end of business casual. Being overdressed is just as poor a choice as being underdressed.

- **Fight stage fright.** Some stage fright is natural. Even experienced presenters feel some anxiety before they give a presentation. If you are concerned about stage fright there are four things that can help:

  Don't worry. *Remember audiences are often understanding if you are genuine and sincere in your effort. Most people have been there. If need be, pick one person and speak to them for the first minute or so.*

  Be prepared. *Preparation is a key part of portraying purpose and confidence.*

  Visualize. *Imagine yourself giving an effective presentation. Imagine the best that could happen.*

  Calm yourself. *Practice taking deep breaths and relaxing your neck and shoulders for a few minutes before your begin.*

- **Use nonverbal behaviour to support your message.** Stand up straight. Avoid rocking back and forth on your feet. Make eye contact. Use gestures that support your message. Look left, right, and to the centre to include everyone.

- **The first minute counts—a lot.** If you can get your audience's attention, arouse their interest, and engage them in the first few minutes, you're on

Career Connections

Speak to the Point

Imagine in the future that your boss stops you in the hallway and asks if you have an answer for the missed customer delivery last week. He is obviously concerned that the problem is found and corrected so it doesn't happen again. He will judge your progress on the answer you provide and the how you provide it.

Almost any job whether it be a nurse, teacher, customer service representative, furnace technician, emergency dispatcher, or home renovator, has to be able to explain a problem and provide a solution to a customer. If your answer is rambling, sounds unsure or even worse, made up, the customer's confidence in your solution will be less and as well as his or her confidence in you. People will judge the quality of your ideas or your solutions by how you present and explain them.

Most professionals spend a significant portion of their time speaking to others. The suggestions provided in the chapter will help a lot. The key is practice. Find opportunities to practice giving off-the-cuff answers. Rehearse in front of a mirror. Ask friends or coworkers for feedback. Use opportunities to take training. Don't limit your career or let your good ideas go to waste because you weren't able to make them heard.

For instance, during a chat, a Heating and A/C contractor indicated that he was just about to hire his fourth new customer service representative in a row. This was a position for a new grad to book service calls and deal with customer issues. Each of the previous three were fired because the way they spoke to customers had caused customers to take their business somewhere else. He joked that in today's competitive environment if he kept people with poor communication skills he would be out of business in a year.

Go to a job board such as workopolis.com or monster .ca and look at jobs that might interest you. Make a note of the number that require strong communication skills or ability to talk with others.

your way to a successful speech. On the other hand, let them drift off early on and you've lost them—potentially for good.

How do you get them interested? There are several ways:

Begin with an anecdote. *"It was a scientist's dream, experienced as he dozed off in front of a fire, that led to one of the most important biological discoveries of all time."*

Start with a quotation. *"'I have seen the enemy, and he is us.' But are we really the enemy? I believe . . ."*

Arouse their curiosity. *"I have a secret, one that I've kept hidden for many years—until now."*

Talk about the significance of the topic. *"If you think that global warming is not a problem, take a look at the changes in weather patterns across North America this year."*

Ask a question. *"Have you ever wondered how you could save enough money to buy a new car?"*

Use humour. *"My introduction to gardening was not promising: Seeking to surprise my mother, I 'weeded' her garden so enthusiastically that I pulled up all her flower seedlings."*

See Try It! 1, "Let's Talk."

Let's Talk

Prepare: The purpose of this exercise is to practise writing an opening statement for a presentation.

Organize: To complete this exercise you will need a pencil or pen and a piece of paper, or if you prefer, a blank word-processing page on your computer. You will also need a partner to act as listener.

Work: Think of a topic you know something about. Write it down. Imagine you have been assigned to give a presentation on that topic to your fellow students. Write an opening that states your purpose, why it is important, or how it can help the audience. You may start with a brief story or a question to arouse curiosity. Give the opening statement to your partner. Ask for their feedback.

Evaluate: Were you able to write an opening that provided a positive start to your presentation and got the audience ready to listen?

Rethink: Would you use this method of opening a presentation in the future? Why?

- **Provide oral transition points.** When we're reading a textbook selection, we usually have the luxury of knowing exactly when a transition point occurs; it's marked by a title, section heading, or new paragraph. These markers help us construct a mental map that permits us to understand the overall structure of the piece we're reading.

  Listeners don't have the same advantage. Unless the speaker orally signals that he or she is moving to a new part of a talk, listeners will get lost. Not only will they be unable to understand the structure of the talk, they won't know where the talk is headed.

  However, there are several ways to erect verbal signposts throughout a speech. By using phrases such as the following, you can alert listeners that a twist in the journey lies ahead:

  "To understand the problem, we need to consider . . . "

  "The problems are clearly daunting. But there are solutions. Let's consider some of them. . . . "

  "Now that we've considered the solutions, we need to take a look at their costs. . . . "

  "Let's go back for a moment to an earlier point I made. . . . "

  "To sum up, the situation offers some unexpected advantages. . . . "

- **Avoid clichés.** "At the end of the day," "the bottom line," and "at this moment in time" are all examples of overused expressions that can irritate listeners and diminish the effectiveness of your presentation. Other sayings to avoid include "like," "24/7," "absolutely," "address the issue," "awesome," "ballpark figure," "basically," "bear with me," "I hear what you're saying," "in terms of," "it's not rocket science," "literally," "prioritize," "pushing the envelope," and "thinking outside the box."[2]

How I Feel About Public Speaking

Just how do you feel about speaking in public? Explore your feelings—both positive and negative—by considering these questions:

1. How, in general, do you feel about public speaking? How much experience have you had speaking to an audience?

2. Do you think other people feel better about speaking in public than you do? Do most people you know like or dislike it?

3. Ask a few of your friends how they feel about public speaking. What was their reaction to the question?

4. What was the best experience you ever had with public speaking? Why was it positive?

5. How do you think your audience felt about your speaking while it was occurring?

6. What was the worst experience you ever had with public speaking? Why was it bad?

7. How do you think your audience felt about your speaking while it was occurring?

8. What is the worst part of public speaking for you: before, during, or after speaking?

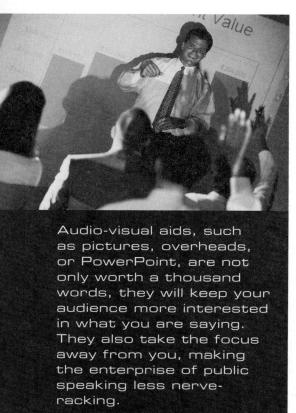

Audio-visual aids, such as pictures, overheads, or PowerPoint, are not only worth a thousand words, they will keep your audience more interested in what you are saying. They also take the focus away from you, making the enterprise of public speaking less nerve-racking.

- **Make your notes work for you, not against you.** A speaker is giving a talk, and suddenly she loses her place in her notes. She fumbles around, desperately trying to find her place and figure out what comes next.

It's a painful situation to watch—and even worse for the person experiencing the problem. How do you avoid finding yourself in such a predicament?

One way is by thoroughly acquainting yourself both with what you are going to say *and* with your notes. Once again, practice is your best friend, but the type of notes you have also makes a big difference.

There are as many forms of notes as there are speakers. Some speakers write out their entire talk in advance; others use no notes at all, counting on memorizing their talk. Avoid either extreme. If you write out your complete speech in advance, you'll experience an overwhelming urge to read it to your audience. Nothing could be more deadly. On the other hand, if you memorize your talk and have no notes at all, you'll be susceptible to a memory lapse that can make you feel completely foolish. Even if you can remember your talk successfully, you may end up sounding mechanical, like an amusement park guide who has given the same speech about the "jungle cruise" at least a thousand times.

The best approach is to choose a middle ground. Develop an outline that includes the major points you want to cover, and have this outline in front of you when you speak. It should be written or typed on a sheet of paper, or you might use index cards (number them!). In addition, write out and memorize your opening and closing statements.

By memorizing the opening and closing statements, you'll have the opportunity to look your audience in the eye and engage them nonverbally at two of the most crucial junctures in your talk—the beginning and the end. Using an outline for most of your talk permits you to sound natural as you speak. You'll probably use slightly different words every time you give your talk, which is fine.

- **A picture can save you a thousand words.** Maps, charts, photos, drawings, figures, and other illustrations add another dimension to a presentation, helping to engage listeners. Computer programs, such as PowerPoint, permit you to create graphics relatively painlessly.

You can even use props. For example, if you are talking about a series of Supreme Court of Canada rulings, you might incorporate a gavel into your talk. Visual aids make abstract concepts more concrete and immediate.

Visual aids serve another function. They can reduce your anxiety. You can be assured that when an audience is focusing on an illustration or prop, their attention is drawn away from you, at least temporarily. Just knowing this may be enough to lower your anxiety level. (Just resist the temptation to play with your props as you talk!) Refer to Try It! 2, "Prop Yourself Up."

Evaluate: How Did You Do? Ask For Feedback

After your presentation, review your performance. Was your message clear and concise? Did you engage your audience and keep their interest? Ask others to evaluate you as well and take notes on the feedback your receive.

TRY IT!

www.mcgrawhill.ca/olc/power

Prop Yourself Up

Prepare: The purpose of this exercise is to think of visual aids or props that would help selected presentation topics.

Organize: To complete this exercise you will need a pencil or pen and a piece of paper, or if you prefer, a blank word-processing page on your computer. A list of topics is included below:

- The presentation you chose for Try It !1
- A speech about the dangers of biological warfare
- Convincing others that at times it is O.K. to lie
- Using cell phones while you are driving
- Rating a movie you have seen lately

Work: Working as an individual or as a group select three of the above topics and develop ideas for visual aids or props that would help support your presentation.

Evaluate: Would the props or visual aids you selected add to the effectiveness of your presentation? How and why?

Rethink: When would you include the use of visual aids and props in future presentations?

ethink: Improve Your Performance

Review your current outlook on making presentations and the feedback you have received after making one more recently. Be prepared to revise your approach for preparing and delivering presentations each time you make one.

Speaking Off-the-Cuff:
Extemporaneous Speaking

What do you do when an instructor calls on you in class and asks, "What do you think the point of this poem is?" Just as anxiety producing as giving a prepared talk (and probably a lot more common) is public speaking that is extemporaneous.

www.mcgrawhill.ca/olc/power

3 Working in a Group:
Put Yourself on the Spot

Prepare: The purpose of this exercise is to practise using the PREP framework to develop and deliver an off-the-cuff response.

Organize: To complete this exercise you will need a pencil or pen and a piece of paper.

Work: Working as a group, prepare a list of topics to use as a focus for an off-the-cuff presentation. Put each topic on a separate piece of paper. Suggested topics might be: Are basketball players paid to much? What is the best way to wash dishes? How can we get people to exercise more? One at a time each group member chooses a topic from the pile and delivers an impromptu presentation. Presenters may have one minute to use the PREP framework to structure their answer.

Evaluate: Does the PREP framework help you prepare off-the-cuff answers? Do you feel more confident being able to respond to your feet?

Rethink: Would you use the PREP framework in the future? Why?

Extemporaneous talk

An unprepared, off-the-cuff oral presentation

Extemporaneous talks are unprepared presentations that require you to speak on a moment's notice.

Extemporaneous speaking happens far more frequently than you may like to think: your professor asks you to explain why organizations are moving to flatter structures; a coworker or classmate asks you to explain how a particular software program works; you visit your landlord to complain about the water heater that keeps breaking, and the landlord asks you for details about the problem. The response you give in each of these situations (and many others) is very much an exercise in extemporaneous speaking. Refer to Try It! 3, "Put Yourself on the Spot."

"PREPing" to Speak Extemporaneously Just because extemporaneous speaking is, by definition, unplanned, it does not have to be totally off the top of your head. There is a simple process that you can use when you're put on the spot. Known as the PREP formula, it consists[3] of breaking down an answer into four parts:

* **Point of view.** Initially provide your point of view, delineating a clear view of where you stand on the issue.

- **Reasons.** Provide the chief reasons why you believe your position is correct.
- **Evidence or examples.** Give specific evidence to support your point of view.
- **Point of view, restated.** Restate your point of view.

Here's an example:

Professor Fiske: Who can tell me whether First Nations land claims are a uniquely Canadian problem? Sylvie, why don't you take a stab at the answer?

Sylvie: I don't believe land claim issues are uniquely Canadian at all [**point of view**]. If *we* look at other times in history or at other parts of the world today, we find all sorts of land claims issues [**reasons**]. For example, consider the United States and Mexico. Or look at the difficulties that Zimbabwe is having. Or look at Australia or New Zealand [**evidence or examples**]. So, it's hard for me to understand how anyone could contend that land claims are uniquely Canadian. Settling Aboriginal land claims is a complicated issue many nations are now dealing with [**point of view, restated**].

Although using the PREP system may seem awkward at first, you'll find it easy to learn. And with sufficient practice, it will become automatic, saving you lots of mental scrambling the next time you're called on in class.

Remember: You're Already an Accomplished Public Speaker

Speaking in front of others is something you've done all your life. It may have been in moments of intimacy or friendship with just one other person present. It may have been with a group of friends deciding on what kind of pizza to order, with you arguing against anchovies and your friends arguing in favour. It may have been as an athlete, with you shouting encouragement to your teammates. The point is that you've already spoken in front of others—lots of times.

When you are faced with giving a formal presentation, then, give yourself credit for the times you've already spoken publicly. Let go of your fears and enjoy your moment in the spotlight. You may well find that the ability to impart what you know to others is a satisfying and rewarding experience.

"If you have an important point to make, don't try to be subtle or clever. Use a pile driver. Hit the point once. Then come back and hit it again. Then hit it a third time—a tremendous whack."

Sir Winston Churchill

Looking ◄◄ Back ◄

How do I meet the challenge of public speaking?

- Plan a logical flow that builds on a purpose.
- Involve the audience as much as possible.
- Rehearse in front of a minor or with a friend.

Speaking of Success

John Lu

B.A. Advanced, Economics, University of Manitoba; Creative Communications Program Diploma, Red River Community College

In April 1997, John Lu decided to turn his back on a stable, lucrative career in the financial industry to pursue his love of language. Armed with a B.A. in economics and with almost 11 years of experience working for a major Canadian bank, John enrolled in the Creative Communications program at Winnipeg's Red River College in 1998.

"It's great to dream and when you put that dream into action, it becomes a goal," John says of his dream of starting a career in TV journalism. Ironically, John says he wasn't particularly goal oriented in university, but when he returned to community college, he made the most of his opportunity at RRC. "I have never been more successful in an academic setting than I was in community college."

In his final year at RRC, John had an internship at Winnipeg's CTV affiliate, CKY5, which landed him a part-time job as a news reporter. However, a subsequent internship at The Sports Network (TSN) led to a full-time offer he couldn't refuse. John is a sports fan and plays sports as well, so a job offer with the nationwide sports network was doubly attractive.

In addition to sports reporting, John has now had several stints on the anchor desk, which allows him to develop his skill set into that of a complete broadcaster. Now that he has several years' experience at TSN, John says he has a greater comfort level in his job, but still retains the excitement and enthusiasm he has always had. John says there is a lot to be said for doing

what you enjoy, and that a bad day at TSN is better than most good days at other places!

Every career in journalism, whether print or broadcast, is based on writing. John was used to writing university essays, but in college he practised several different styles of writing, including scripts, poetry, and prose, to improve his skills. As for being in front of the camera, he admits he likes "hamming it up." He credits singing in choirs, being in a band, emceeing, and taking part in amateur drama productions with his

being comfortable in front of people. John says it was an easy adjustment to go from being in front of a live audience to reporting to thousands of sports fans on TV.

John says that while it is important to work hard in college, it is more important to work smart. To that end, he made the most of the intense and interactive program at Red River College, enjoying the sense of camaraderie he developed among his peers. Respect for his classmates has transferred to his coworkers; John's philosophy is to "treat them well." Sports has its share of big egos, but John believes in being humble.

John's career has had many highlights, including covering the 2003 World Series, the 2004 Toronto Maple Leafs training camp in Stockholm, Sweden, and the 2004 World Cup of Hockey. And who knows, perhaps he will be covering the 2008 Olympic Games from Beijing. John is brushing up on his Mandarin just in case.

- Dress for the occasion.
- Look confident.

How do I start my presentation?

- Begin with an story or a quotation to engage the audience.
- Let people know what they can expect to gain.
- Ask a question.
- Use humour carefully.
- Fight stage fright with preparation, relaxation techniques, and visualization.

P.O.W.E.R. Portfolio

Speaking

1. Consider including evidence from speeches, oral presentations, panel discussions, or other public speaking venues. You can include programs, scripts, printouts from PowerPoint presentations, photographs, and instructor's grade sheets and comments. So many jobs today require presentation skills that it is essential to prove your mastery in this area. Your reflective comments should indicate what you learned and your goals for the future.

Resources

On Campus

If you are having difficulties with oral presentations, ask a friend or classmate to be your audience while you rehearse. He or she may be able to provide you with feedback to improve the presentation content, your use of props, and any distracting nonverbal behaviour you were unaware of.

In Print

Canadian author Martin M. Antony addresses the anxiety that affects many people when considering public speaking in *10 Simple Solutions To Shyness: How To Overcome Shyness, Social Anxiety & Fear of Public Speaking* (New Harbinger Publications, 2004). This book also deals with social anxiety, a common problem that can affect school and workplace communication.

Hamilton Gregory's book, *Public Speaking for College and Career* (McGraw-Hill, 7th edition, 2005), provides an excellent introduction to public speaking. It is filled with tips for planning and delivering oral presentations.

On the Web

The following site on the World Wide Web provides the opportunity to extend your learning about the material in this chapter. Although the Web addresses were accurate at the time the book was printed, check the P.O.W.E.R. Learning website, <www.mcgrawhill.ca/olc/power>, for any changes that may have occurred.

http://people.hsc.edu/faculty-staff/cdeal/mainsections/student.html
Hampden-Sydney College's Online Speaking Centre is a very instructive site with lots of information on various types of oral presentations, including group presentations. It also includes a section on ethical speaking to help students avoid verbal plagiarism.

The Case Of...

The Reluctant Speaker

"No one," thought Maggie Ryan to herself, "could hate public speaking more than I do."

Maggie, who already thought of herself as somewhat shy, was horrified at the thought of giving a presentation. Not only did she not like talking in front of others, exposing herself to their scrutiny, but also she was conscious of her strong Newfoundland accent, which her friends at the Western community college she attended teased her about.

Maggie was sure she'd never be able to stand up in front of the class. She made up her mind to ask her instructor whether she could write a paper instead of making the oral presentation. But before she could, one of her friends in the class told her that he had already asked for an alternative assignment for himself and that the instructor had flatly refused. The instructor had merely said that it would be a "good experience" to give the talk.

Maggie was stuck.

1. How would you advise Maggie to prepare and organize for her talk?

2. Maggie expressed a willingness to write a paper instead of giving a talk. Should she prepare the paper and read it for her presentation? Why or why not? How might she use the research for her paper to help with her talk?

3. Maggie is especially nervous about speaking because she believes that her accent interferes with understanding. How might she deal with this particular anxiety? How could friends or classmates help her?

4. Do you think props would be helpful for Maggie? What purpose might they serve?

5. What advice would you give Maggie about what to do during her talk to reduce her anxiety?

6. What tips would you give Maggie to ensure her audience is engaged?

Making Decisions That Are Right for You

11

For Scott Gerofsky, the moment of truth was fast approaching. He had to make up his mind and decide what he was going to do when he graduated.

Throughout his university career, he had intended to go to law school, and he had majored in criminology. He had taken the LSAT, the pre-law standardized test, at the beginning of his fourth year and had done well. He had applied to law schools and been accepted at a decent one. It seemed that his future in law was well in hand.

Except for one thing: He was no longer sure he wanted to be a lawyer.

The reason for his indecision was a job that he had during the summer between his third and fourth years. Although he'd only been a glorified gofer on the film, *Mean Girls,* which was shot in Toronto, the director caught his attention. Directing looked like terrific fun, and the idea of becoming a film director had taken hold of him. Scott had spoken to the director, who had told him that it was a rewarding, although high-stress, job. He also told Scott that the sooner he started working in the film industry, the better.

Scott couldn't shake the idea that he might be able to build a career in the movie industry. However, his girlfriend and family were dead set against the idea. His father argued that Scott should consider working in the film industry only after he got his law degree. But Scott was unconvinced; he didn't want to give up the idea of becoming a director in Toronto, Vancouver, or even Hollywood.

As his last semester went by, Scott knew he had to make up his mind. But which decision was the right one?

Looking ▶▶ Ahead

Like Scott, we all face important decisions in our lives at one time or another. How can we make the right decisions and avoid making the wrong ones? The best way is to employ some systematic, basic techniques that can help improve the quality of our decision making.

This chapter will give you a sense of what decision making is and is not and discuss a structured process that can help make your decisions the right ones. We'll also consider the related issue of problem solving. You'll confront a variety of problems as you proceed through college or university, and solving them will often be challenging. We'll look at several proven techniques for approaching and ultimately solving problems.

Of course, making decisions and solving problems is never easy. Sometimes the best decision or solution to a problem is one that doesn't initially occur to us because of the mental blind spots we all have. The best problem solvers and decision makers have learned how to use critical thinking to see around these blind spots. Consequently, we'll examine some common problems that can affect our thinking and discuss several biases that can make us jump too quickly to conclusions.

After reading this chapter you'll be able to answer these questions:

- How can I improve the quality of my decisions?
- What strategies can I use for problem solving?
- What are some problems that affect critical thinking, and how can I avoid them?

Making Good Decisions: A Framework

Making choices is a constant part of everyday life. **Decision making** is the process of deciding among various alternatives. Whether you are trying to decide between buying a Ford or a Honda, between renting an apartment that is close to your job and farther from campus or renting one that is close to campus but farther from work, or simply between having a hamburger or pizza—every one of these choices requires a decision. Some decisions are easily made and have few consequences, but others, such as whether to major in music composition or business administration, can be gut-wrenching and involve the deepest examination of beliefs and values.

Whatever the decision, however, it is possible to map out a strategy for making the decision that is best for you. Even though some decisions require more thought than others, every decision can benefit from systematically thinking through the options involved, based on the P.O.W.E.R. Plan illustrated on the right below.

Decision making
The process of deciding among various alternatives

Prepare: Identifying Your Goals

Every decision starts with the end: what you want to accomplish by making the decision. Ask yourself why a decision is necessary and what you want to achieve by making it.

For example, suppose you are trying to decide between two alternative careers: either being a sales representative for a sporting goods manufacturer or working in and eventually running your own sporting goods store.

In such a case, the only way to make an appropriate decision is to know your goals. You need to consider both short- and long-term goals. For instance, becoming a sales representative would provide good benefits, such as health insurance, a company car, and a bonus plan. It would also allow you to meet colleagues with similar goals and interests and provide both opportunities to attend formal training programs and the chance to work your way up the corporate ladder.

On the other hand, although you might have a lower starting salary and fewer benefits working in a sporting goods store, there would probably be more job security. Even more important, it would give you the opportunity to achieve your long-term goal of learning how to run your own business. Both jobs might at first be equally rewarding in terms of satisfaction—new jobs tend to be exciting just because they are new—but one may grow stale, while the rewards of the other might continue to increase over the course of a career. In short, you need to consider both the short term and the long term when identifying your goals.

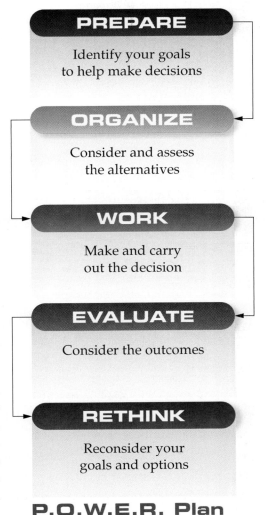

PREPARE
Identify your goals to help make decisions

ORGANIZE
Consider and assess the alternatives

WORK
Make and carry out the decision

EVALUATE
Consider the outcomes

RETHINK
Reconsider your goals and options

P.O.W.E.R. Plan

Thinking about the goals involved in decisions is an important process. Identifying the goals that underlie decisions ensures that we make our decisions in the context of our entire lives and not just to provide short-term answers to immediate problems.

Organize: Considering and Assessing the Alternatives

Every decision is based on weighing various alternatives. Determining what those alternatives are, and their possible consequences, is often the most difficult part of decision making. Once you have generated a list of alternatives or solutions the next step is to assess them. Some solutions may be too expensive or unrealistic and can be crossed off the list. How do you assess the solutions that remain? There are three techniques you can use to make better decisions:

- **The SWOT Analysis.** One technique that can help is the SWOT analysis. It is a common technique used to make decisions in organizations. For each possible decision list the Strengths, Weaknesses, Opportunities, and Threats of that alternative.

    One of the decisions you may have to make is buying a car. Put the decision to the SWOT test.

1. *What are the* Strengths *or benefits of this alternative?*
    a. Easier transportation
    b. More convenient
    c. Late less often
    d. Better social life

2. *What are the* Weaknesses *or drawbacks of this alternative?*
    a. Lots of expenses
    b. Unexpected repairs
    c. Insurance
    d. Parking fees

3. *What* Opportunities *would this alternative provide?*
    a. Opportunity to go to another school farther away
    b. Opportunity for a part-time job where there is no bus

4. *What Threats or risks come with this alternative?*
    a. Unexpected repairs drain budget for other essentials
    b. Get out more and go to more places means potential impact on time management and cost of social life
    c. Have an accident

Now review your analysis. Like most decisions some factors can have positive and negative effects. For example, the car likely leads to a more active social life but also has an impact on time for study and increased expenses.

We've all been there: facing a mind-boggling array of similar choices. However, by systematically assessing the alternatives, it's possible to make an informed decision that will satisfy us.

My Decision Crossroads

Have you ever made a decision that proved to be of great importance in terms of the direction your life would take? For example, perhaps you broke off a romantic relationship, or decided to quit a sports team because practice took up too much time, or participated in a deliberate act of civil disobedience during a protest rally. Reflect on that decision by answering these questions:

1. What was an important decision that you made that had significant effects on your life?

2. In what ways did that decision change your life?

3. What have been the main benefits (for yourself and others) that you derived from the decision?

4. What have been the main disadvantages (for yourself and others) of the decision?

5. Considering both the benefits and disadvantages of the decision, how would you judge your decision?

6. To what extent did you anticipate the effects the decision would have on your life?

7. Every decision to do something is also a decision not to do other things. What did your decision keep you from doing?

8. If you had it to do over again, would you make the same choice?

The important thing is that you have considered the issue. It will be up to you to manage the weaknesses and risks to achieve the most gain toward your goals. For example, if you are concerned about having on accident you may wish to take a course on defensive driving. It is likely to decrease the chances of being in on accident and you may get a reduction in your insurance premiums. In this way a potential risk can become, at least in part, a potential benefit.

- **Learn to manage your rational and emotional side.** All decisions involve some rational and some emotional factors. There are lots of decisions that may have felt right at the time, but didn't turn out very well. There are lots of decisions made by the numbers and the facts that didn't accomplish the goal.

  A common sales technique is to get the customer to want the product for status, fun, looking good, etc. Salespeople try to appeal to the impulsive or emotional side of the buyer: "Imagine how you will look in this," or "You'll look cool wearing this." Then once the customer likes the product, the salespeople give them all the logical reasons to buy it.

  Depending on your preferences and personality you may be prone to making impulsive, on-the-spot decisions or you may be prone to analysis paralysis where you feel like you never have the information and facts you need to make a decision. Both ends of this range are ineffective.

If you tend to be impulsive, make sure you sit down and complete a SWOT analysis before you make major decisions. If you tend to avoid making decisions, complete an analysis to detail the benefits and risks and use the best-and worst-case technique to put the decision in perspective.

- **Consider the best- and worst-case scenarios.** There are times when the best analysis doesn't provide a clear alternative or when you are concerned abut making a mistake. Sometimes it helps to ask:

    What is the best thing that can happen if I choose this alternative?
    What is the worst thing that can happen if I choose this alternative?

Maybe the best you can achieve is not worth the risk. More often you will find that the worst case is not so bad. You can recover from it and go on to achieve your goals.

Obviously, not every decision requires such an elaborate process. In fact, most won't. But when it comes to major decisions, ones that potentially will have a major effect on you and your life, it's worthwhile to follow a systematic process.

Take a look at *Career Connections* on the next page for another process that you can follow to help you make a career decision.

Work: Making and Carrying out the Decision

If all else fails, toss a coin to decide what alternative to follow. Tossing a coin at least brings you to a decision. Then, if you find you're unhappy with the result, you'll have gained important information about how you really feel regarding a particular choice.

Working through the recommended techniques will lead you to the point of decision: choosing one of the alternatives you've identified. Having carried out the steps will make the actual decision easier, but not necessarily easy.

Choosing among Alternatives The reason that important decisions are difficult is that the alternatives you have to choose from carry both benefits and costs. Choosing one alternative means that you have to accept the costs of that choice as the price for obtaining the benefits. And not choosing other alternatives means that you have to give up the benefits of the other alternatives, even though you have also avoided their costs.

What if, after going through the steps of the process laid out here, you still can't make up your mind? Try these strategies:

- **Give the decision time.** For everything there is a season. Timing plays a major role in good decision making. There are occasions when decisions may seem forced or uncomfortable. Some common advice is to give the decision some time. The passage of time often changes how we look at things and how outside factors influence our decisions. If you don't have to decide right away and you are not sure what to do, take some time.

- **Make a mental movie, acting out the various alternatives.** Many of us have difficulty seeing ourselves in the future and envisioning how various options would play out. One way to get around this difficulty is to cast yourself into a series of "mental movies"

Career Connections

Weighing Career Possibilities

Some of the most important decisions you'll ever make concern choosing a career. Here's one method that can help you choose between different possible careers:

- Generate a selection of choices to consider after graduation. Make a list of possibilities—including work possibilities (e.g., computer programming, banking, teaching, health sciences, business, computer software development, etc.), study possibilities (e.g., business school, grad school), and even some dream possibilities (e.g., jazz musician, overseas stint with Crossroads Canada).

- Determine your values—they are most important things to consider when choosing an occupation. If you don't consider your values when planning your career, there's a good chance you'll dislike your work and, therefore, not succeed in it. For example, someone who needs autonomy would not be happy in a job where every action is decided by someone else. Generate a list of factors to use in assessing after-graduation possibilities. For instance, consider how the following factors will affect your career satisfaction:

  - the benefit to society of what you are doing
  - a good income
  - your parents' opinions
  - interaction with people
  - achievement
  - status
  - autonomy

  - job security
  - freedom and spare time
  - the likelihood of success
  - the everyday working conditions

- Determine how well a particular option fulfills each value you consider important. Systematically consider how a potential career fulfills each your values. One easy way to do this is to create a chart like the one in Table 11.1.

- Compare different choices. Using the chart, evaluate which of your possible choices most closely matches your values. Keep in mind that this is just a rough guide and that it's only as accurate as (1) the degree to which you know what is important to you and (2) your understanding of a given choice. Use the results in conjunction with other things you find out about careers—and yourself.

> Workplaces have values as well. For Telus, Canada's second-largest telecommunications company, their values "inspire how we act and make decisions with each other as employees, with our customers, suppliers, and competitors, and in our communities." Telus's corporate values include (1) embracing change and initiating opportunity, (2) growth, (3) spirited teamwork, and (4) innovation. When considering a career, it is also important to know whether your values and your employer's values are in harmony.

that have different endings depending on the decision you make. Working through the different scripts in your head makes potential outcomes far more real and less abstract than they would be if you simply left them as items on a list of various options.

- **Toss a coin.** This isn't always as crazy or escapist as it sounds. If each alternative seems equally positive or negative to you, pull out a coin and assign each of the two alternatives to either side. Then flip it.

  The real power of the coin-toss strategy is that it sometimes will help you find out your true feelings. It may happen while the coin is in the air or it may be that when you see the result of the coin toss, you won't like the outcome and will say to yourself, "No way." In such a case, you've just found out how you *really* feel about which alternative to choose.

- **Learn to view indecision as a decision.** Sometimes we spend so much time making a decision that our indecision becomes a decision. It works like this: Suppose a friend asks you to help her work on a student government task force that is studying the use of alcohol on campus. You'd like to participate, but, because you'll have to commit to a term-long series of meetings, you're worried about the expenditure of time it will take.

Table 11.1

Making Career Decisions

Life-Satisfaction Considerations	Possible Choice #1	Possible Choice #2	Possible Choice #3	Possible Choice #4
	Computer programming			
Desire to benefit society	✓			
Good income	✓			
Parents' opinions	✓			
Friends' opinions				
Interest in the activity	✓			
Prestige of job				
Job security				
Good vacations				
A lot of spare time				
Likelihood of success	✓			
Working conditions				
Other:				
Other:				
Other:				
Other:				
Other:				

"Generally, I take life one day at a time. Recently, however, I have become more goal oriented. This comes with age, I'm sure. You realize that life is short, and if you do not plan for your goals, they may not get done."

Marlene Luscombe, Student, Trent University

Because the first meeting isn't going to occur for a few weeks, you have some time to make up your mind. But you just can't seem to decide, even though you think about the pros and cons every once in a while. Finally, it's the day of the meeting, and you still don't know what to do.

The truth is, you've made the decision: You don't really want to be on the committee. Your indecision is telling you that you don't have sufficient interest to make the commitment. In some cases, then, viewing your own behaviour gives you the response to your question.

- **Go with your gut feeling.** Call it what you like—gut feeling, intuition, superstition—but sometimes we need to go with our hearts and not our minds. If you've thought rationally about a decision and have been unable to determine the best course of action but have a gut feeling that one choice is better than another, then follow your feelings.

  Following a gut feeling does not mean that you don't need to consider the pros and cons of a decision rationally and carefully. In fact, generally our "intuitions" are best when informed by the thoughtfulness of a more-rational process.

Carrying out the Decision Ultimately, decisions must move from thought to action—they need to be carried out. Consequently, the final stage in making a decision is to act on it. You need to turn what you've decided on into behaviour.

valuate: Considering the Outcomes

Did you make the right decision?

Even if you've spent time and mental effort in thinking through a decision, you still need to consider the results. Even well-considered decisions can end up being wrong, either because you neglected to consider some aspect or alternative or because you or the situation changed.

For instance, suppose you were trying to decide between a major in management or information technology (IT). If you decide to go into management, it means that you'll be taking more courses related to finance and economics than if you had decided on an IT major. As you take these courses, you will be finding out whether you're enjoying them and how comfortable you feel with them. If you find you are consistently unhappy with these courses (and therefore your choice of major), you should allow yourself to re-evaluate your decision and reconsider the alternatives. It's not too late to change your mind about your decision.

> "Nothing is more difficult, and therefore more precious, than to be able to decide."
>
> Napoleon I, *Maxims* 15

In fact, even major decisions are often reversible. That's why it's so important to evaluate your choices. If you chose the wrong alternative, reverse course and reconsider your options.

It's not bad to change your mind. In fact, admitting that a decision was a mistake is often the wisest and most courageous course of action. You don't want to be so rigidly committed to a decision that you're unable to evaluate the consequences objectively. Give yourself permission to be wrong.

R ethink: Reconsidering Your Goals and Options

We can get to most places by multiple routes. There's the fastest and most direct route, which will get us to our destination in the least amount of time. Then there's the longer, more scenic route, where the trip itself provides pleasure. You can "take the long way home," as the song goes.

Is one route better than the other? Often not. Both take us to our destination, so we've succeeded no matter which way we've chosen. However, the experience of reaching our goal will have been very different.

Decisions are similar to travelling down different routes. There's often no single decision that is best for us, just as there's often no single road to a particular place. Consequently, it's important to periodically reconsider the major decisions that we've made about our lives.

Ask yourself these questions:

- Are my decisions still producing the desired consequences?
- Are my decisions still appropriate, given my circumstances and changes in my life?

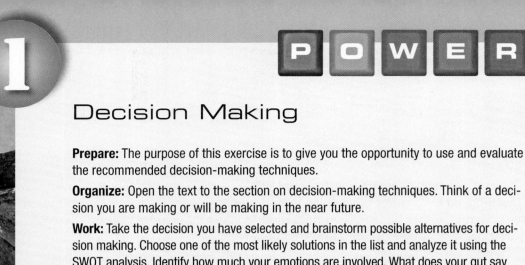

Decision Making

Prepare: The purpose of this exercise is to give you the opportunity to use and evaluate the recommended decision-making techniques.

Organize: Open the text to the section on decision-making techniques. Think of a decision you are making or will be making in the near future.

Work: Take the decision you have selected and brainstorm possible alternatives for decision making. Choose one of the most likely solutions in the list and analyze it using the SWOT analysis. Identify how much your emotions are involved. What does your gut say about this alternative? Finally, identify the best-case and worst-case scenario if you choose this alternative. Use this same three-part process to evaluate other alternatives on your list.

These techniques also work well in group decision-making situations. Get together with three or four other students and repeat the same three-part process you completed on your own.

Evaluate: Were you able to use the techniques to add value to your decision-making process?

Rethink: Would you use these techniques to make decisions in the future? Why or why not?

- Are my decisions consistent with what I want to get out of life?
- Do my decisions fit with my mission statement (a written guiding philosophy of life, discussed in Chapter 2)?

Periodically taking stock like this is the best way to make sure that your decisions are taking you where you want. Taking stock also helps you to be more effective in making future decisions that affect your life. Complete Try It! 1, "Decision Making," to review your techniques.

Problem Solving: Applying Critical Thinking to Find Solutions

Two trains are approaching one another, each moving at 100 kilometres an hour. If the trains continue moving at the same speed, how long will it be before . . .

Problem solving

The process of generating alternatives and finding solutions

If this is what comes to mind when you think of problem solving, think again. **Problem solving** encompasses more than the abstract, often unrealistic situations portrayed in math texts. It involves everyday, commonplace situations: How do we divide the grocery bill so that each person pays a fair share? How do I keep my one-year-old from tumbling down the stairs when there seems to be no way to fasten a gate at the top? How can I stop an annoying classmate from getting on my nerves? How do I manage to study for a test and complete a paper the same evening?

While decision making is most focused on *choosing* among various alternatives, the central issue in problem solving is *generating* alternatives. Since many problems require that decisions be made regarding alternatives, decision making and problem solving are often related.

What's the Problem?

The first step in solving any problem is to be as clear as you can about what the problem is. This may sound easy, but often it isn't. In fact, it may take some time to figure out just what is being asked. The reason is that some problems are big and hard to define, while others are quite precise, such as mathematical equations or the solution to a jigsaw puzzle. Determining how to stop the nuclear arms race between India and Pakistan and finding peace in the Middle East are big, ill-defined problems. Simply determining what information is required to solve such problems can be a major undertaking.

It's also necessary to determine what's important in coming to a solution. To determine what is critical in solving a problem, ask yourself these questions:

1. What is the initial set of facts?
2. What is it that you need to solve?
3. Which parts of the problem appear to be most critical to finding a solution?
4. Is there some information that can be ignored?

As you clarify what the problem is, you may find that you have encountered similar problems before. Your experience with them may suggest the means to the solution of the current problem. For example, consider the problem of the trains rushing toward one another. If you have worked on this kind of problem before and you know how quickly each train is moving and their starting points, there's a fairly simple equation you can write to determine how long it will take before they meet. On the other hand, to solve most of the problems we face in our daily lives, we have to do more than reach into our memories of prior situations. Instead, we need to devise novel approaches. How do you do this? There are several strategies you might use.

Strategies for Working on Life's Messier Problems

- **Trial and error.** Although it's a fairly primitive strategy, trial and error sometimes works. For instance, to invent a workable light bulb, Thomas Edison needed a good filament, the part of the bulb that actually glows. He tried out one material after another for the filament until he finally found one that worked.

- **Break the problem down into smaller, more-manageable pieces.** Break a problem down into a series of subgoals. As you reach each subgoal, you get closer to your overall goal of solving the problem. For example, if your goal were to spend your third year in your school's foreign exchange program in Ecuador, a subgoal would probably be to learn some basic Spanish. By reaching this subgoal, you move closer to reaching your ultimate goal—a year abroad in a country that interests you.

"Problems are only opportunities in work clothes."

Henry J. Kaiser, *Maxim*

• **Work backward.** Sometimes you know the answer to the problem, but not how to get there. Then it's best to work backward. A **working backward** strategy starts at the desired solution or goal and works backward, moving away from the goal. For example, consider this problem:

> Water lilies on a certain lake double in area every 24 hours. From the time the first water lily appears until the lake is completely covered takes 60 days. On what day is the lake half covered?

It's impossible to solve this problem by breaking it down into subgoals, but most people solve it almost immediately if they work backwards. Here's a hint: If the pond is fully covered on day 60, how much is it covered the day before? Because the water lilies double each day, there had to be half as many the day before day 60. The answer, then, is that half the lake is covered on day 59. Only by moving backward could you see the solution clearly.

• **Use a graph, chart, or drawing to redefine the problem.** Transforming words into pictures can often help us to devise solutions that otherwise would elude us. One good example is this problem:

> Sally lies on Wednesday, Thursday, Friday, Saturday, and Sunday, but tells the truth on all other days. John lies on Sunday, Monday, and Tuesday, but tells the truth on all other days. One day Sally and John had lunch together. One exclaimed: "I lied yesterday." The other replied: "Me too."
>
> Question: On which day did they have lunch together?
>
> Hint: Use a table (see Table 11.2 below).

> Answer: Wednesday—John lied on Tuesday and is telling her the truth, because he tells the truth on Wednesdays. Sally is lying to John as she lies on Wednesday, but told the truth on Tuesday.

• **Consider the opposite.** Problems can sometimes be solved by considering the opposite of the problem you're seeking to solve. For example, to define "good mental health" you might try to define "poor mental health."

• **Use analogies.** Some problems can be solved through the use of **analogies,** comparisons between concepts or objects that are alike in some respects, but dissimilar in most others. For instance, if you liken a disastrous experience attending summer camp to a voyage on the *Titanic,* you're using an analogy.

Analogies may help us gain additional insight into the problem at hand, and they may provide an alternative framework for interpreting the information that is provided. For instance, manufacturers of Pringles potato chips found that they could cut packaging costs if they slightly moistened the chips before packaging them—an idea that came when researchers noticed that dry tree leaves, which normally crumble easily, could be packed together tightly if they were wet.

Table 11.2

The Truth Table

	Monday	Tuesday	Wednesday	Thursday	Friday	Saturday	Sunday
Sally lies			X	X	X	X	X
John lies	X	X					X

- **Take another's perspective.** By viewing a problem from another person's point of view, it is often possible to obtain a new perspective on the problem that will make it easier to solve.
- **Forget about it.** Just as with decision making, sometimes it's best simply to walk away from a problem for a while. Just a few hours or days away from a problem may give us enough of a break to jar some hidden solutions from the recesses of our minds. The idea of "sleeping on it" also sometimes works; we may wake up refreshed and filled with new ideas.

Solve the problems in Try It! 2, "Exercise Your Problem-Solving Skills," on page 286.

Assessing Your Potential Solutions

If a problem clearly has only one answer, such as a math problem, this step in problem solving is relatively easy. You should be able to work the problem and figure out whether you've been successful. In contrast, messier problems have several possible solutions, some of which may be more involved and costly than others. In these cases, it's necessary to compare alternative solutions and choose the best one. For example, suppose you want to surprise your best friend on her birthday. She is working in Lethbridge, about 145 kilometres from you, and you need to find a way to get there. Perhaps you could rent a car, take a bus, or find some other way. Money is an issue. You will want to figure out how much each alternative costs before choosing one as your solution to the problem. Since every penny you spend getting there is a penny less that you will have to celebrate, you will want to weigh the options carefully.

Finally, spend a bit of time seeing where you can refine the solution. Is the solution you've devised adequate? Does it address all aspects of the problem? Are there alternative approaches that might be superior? Answering these questions, and refining your solution to address them, can give you confidence that the solution you've come up with is the best one. For example, if you're trying to get to Lethbridge, you might decide to try to find a ride with someone going to Lethbridge that day, using the ride board at your school. Maybe your friend's family is going to be driving in and could pick you up. Maybe someone could lend you a car for the trip.

Reflect on the Process of Problem Solving

It's natural to step back and bask in the satisfaction of solving a tough problem. That's fine—but take a moment to consider your success. Each time we solve a problem, we end up a couple steps ahead the next time around, but only if we've thought about the process we went through to solve it.

Go back and consider what it took to solve the problem and your emotional reactions along the way. Can the means you used to come up with your solution be applied to more complex kinds of problems? If you arrived at a solution by drawing a chart, would this work on similar problems in the future? Taking a moment to rethink your solution can provide you with an opportunity to become an expert problem solver and, more generally, to improve your critical thinking skills. Don't let the opportunity slip away.

Working in a Group: Exercise Your Problem-Solving Skills

Prepare: The purpose of this exercise is to give you the opportunity to practise the recommended strategies for problem solving in a group.

Organize: Open the text to the section on Strategies for Working on Life's Messier Problems (page 283), and review the list of sample problems provided here.

Work: Try various strategies for solving each of the selected problems. Build on each others' ideas in the group and use the *Hint* for choosing a strategy included after each problem. Try to use each of the strategies at least once.

Evaluate: Were you able to use and evaluate the problem-solving strategies?

Rethink: Would you use these techniques to increase your problem-solving abilities? Why or why not?

Working in a group, try to solve these problems.[1] To help you devise solutions, a hint regarding the best strategy to use is included after each problem.

1. One cold, dark, and rainy night, a motorist has a flat tire on a deserted stretch of country road. He pulls onto the shoulder to change it. After removing the four lug nuts and placing them into the hub cap, he removes the flat tire and takes his spare out of the trunk. As he is moving the spare tire into position, his hand slips and he upsets the hub cap with the lug nuts, which tumble off into the night where he can't find them. What should he do? (*Hint:* Instead of asking how he might find the *scattered* lug nuts, reframe the problem and ask where else he might find other lug nuts.)

2. A worker paving a walk needs to add water quickly to the concrete she has just poured. She reaches for her pail to get water from a spigot in the front of the house, but suddenly realizes the pail has a large rust hole in it and cannot be used. As the concrete dries prematurely, she fumbles through her toolbox for tools and materials with which to repair the pail. She finds many tools, but nothing that would serve to patch the pail. The house is locked and no one is home. What should she do? (*Hint:* When is a pail not a pail?)

3. What day follows the day before yesterday if two days from now will be Sunday? (*Hint:* Break it up, or draw a diagram.)

4. A caterpillar has to climb up the muddy wall of a well that is 12 metres deep. Each day the caterpillar advances four metres, but each night as he sleeps he slips back two metres. How many days will it take him to get out? (*Hint:* Draw it.)

5. A man has four chains, each three links long. He wants to join the four chains into a single, closed chain. Having a link opened costs two cents and having a link closed costs three cents. How can he have the chains joined for 15 cents? (*Hint:* Can only end links be opened?)

6. What is two-thirds of one-half? (*Hint:* Reverse course.)

7. I have three separate large boxes. Inside each large box are two separate medium-sized boxes, and inside each of the medium boxes are four small boxes. How many boxes do I have altogether? (*Hint:* Draw it.)

After working to solve these problems, consider these questions: Which problems were the easiest to solve, and which were the more difficult ones? Why? Were the hints helpful? Do you think there was more than one solution to any of the problems? Did your initial assumptions about the problem help or hinder your efforts to solve it? (*Note:* Answers to the problems are found at the bottom of the page.)

Answers to Try It! 2 problems: 1. Remove one lug nut from each of the other three tires on the car and use these three to attach the spare tire. This will hold until four more lug nuts can be purchased. 2. Dump the tools out of the toolbox and use it as a pail. 3. Thursday. 4. Five days; on the fifth day the caterpillar will reach the top and will not have to slide down again. 5. Open all three links on one chain (cost = 6 cents) and use them to fasten the other three chains together (cost = 9 cents; total cost = 15 cents). 6. It is the same as one-half of two-thirds, or one-third. 7. Thirty-three boxes (3 large, 6 medium, 24 small).

Don't Fool Yourself: Avoiding Everyday Problems in Critical Thinking

As you have probably noticed already, the quality of the thinking you do regarding problems and decisions plays a crucial role in determining how successful you are. Being able to think clearly and without bias is the basis for critical thinking.

Unfortunately, it is sometimes the alternative you *didn't* think of that can end up being the most satisfactory decision or solution. So how can we learn to think critically and avoid blind spots that hinder us in our decision making and problem solving? We can start by considering the common obstacles to critical thinking.

Here are some decision-making and problem-solving pitfalls to look out for. Avoiding them will improve your critical thinking greatly.

- **Don't assume that giving something a name explains it.** The mere fact that we can give an idea or problem a name doesn't mean we know its causes and can explain it. Yet we often confuse the two.

  For instance, consider the following sequences of questions and answers:

  Q. Why do I have so much trouble falling asleep?
  A. Because you have insomnia.

Q. Why is he so unsociable?
A. Because he's an introvert.

Q. Why did the defendant shoot those people?
A. Because he's insane.

Q. How do you know he's insane?
A. Because only someone who was insane would shoot people in that way.[2]

It's clear that none of these answers is satisfactory. All use circular reasoning, in which the explanation for the behaviour is simply the use of a label. But labels don't explain anything; they merely provide a convenient name.

- **Don't accept vague generalities dressed up as definitive statements.** Read the following personality analysis and think about how well it applies to you:

> You have a need for other people to like and admire you and a tendency to be critical of yourself. You also have a great deal of unused potential that you have not turned to your advantage, and although you have some personality weaknesses, you are generally able to compensate for them. Nonetheless, relating to members of the opposite sex has presented problems for you, and although you appear to be disciplined and self-controlled to others, you tend to be anxious and insecure inside.

If you believe that these statements provide an amazingly accurate description of your unique qualities, you're not alone: Most college or university students believe that the descriptions are tailored specifically to them.[3]

But how is that possible? It isn't. The reality is that the statements are so vague that they are virtually meaningless. The acceptance of vague but seemingly useful and significant statements about oneself and others has been called the *Barnum Effect,* after showman and circus master P.T. Barnum, who coined the phrase "there's a sucker born every minute."

- **Don't confuse opinion with fact.** Opinions are not fact. Although you may be aware of this simple formula, almost all of us can be fooled into thinking that someone's opinion is the same as a fact. Sometimes it occurs when we listen to so-called authorities. For instance, the fact that a person has a distinguished title, such as "Doctor" or "Professor," doesn't mean that his or her statements are facts, as opposed to opinions.

A fact is information that is proven to be true. In contrast, an opinion represents judgments, reasoning, beliefs, inferences, or conclusions. If we accept some bit of information as a fact, we can use it to build our opinions. But if we are presented with an opinion, we need to determine the facts on which it is built in order to judge its reliability.

The difference between fact and opinion can sometimes be subtle. For instance, compare these two statements:

1. All college and university students need to take a writing course during their first term.

2. Many college or university students need to take a writing course during their first term.

The first statement is most likely an opinion, because it is so absolute and unqualified. Words such as "every," "all," and "always" are evidence

Fact versus Opinion

Prepare: The purpose of this exercise is to give you the opportunity to learn more about distinguishing fact from opinion.

Organize: Open the text to the section on "Don't confuse opinion with fact," on page 288, and use the statements below.

Work: Take each statement and apply your own knowledge and skill and the techniques you have learned to determine if the statement is fact or opinion. This exercise can also be completed as a group.

Evaluate: Were you able to distinguish fact from opinion?

Rethink: Would you use this skill to determine what should be included in your decision making? Why or why not?

1. College or university students should get at least seven hours of sleep every night.
2. The average college or university student sleeps less than seven hours a night.
3. Nike offers better styling and comfort than any other brand of shoe.
4. Two out of five sports figures surveyed preferred Nike over Converse shoes.
5. Currently, women's earning power is equal to men's.
6. Canadian government figures show full-time female workers earn 72.2 cents for every dollar earned by male workers.
7. In general, Canadian high-school students receive less classroom instruction in math and sciences than their counterparts in Europe and Asia do.
8. No secondary-school student in Canada should graduate without having studied math and sciences for at least four years.
9. Wayne Gretzky is the most outstanding, most exciting, and certainly most successful hockey player who ever stepped onto a rink.

of opinion. The second statement is more likely a fact, since it contains the qualifier "many." In general, statements that are qualified in some way are more likely to be facts.

Try "Fact versus Opinion" (see Try It! 3) to see the difficulties in distinguishing between the two.

• **Avoid jumping to conclusions.** Read this riddle and try to answer it:

A father and his son were driving along the interstate highway when the father lost control of the car, swerved off the road, and crashed into a telephone pole. The father died instantly, and his son was critically injured. An ambulance rushed the boy to a nearby hospital. A prominent surgeon was summoned to provide immediate treatment. When the surgeon arrived and entered the operating room to examine the boy, a loud gasp was heard. "I can't operate on this boy," the surgeon said. "He is my son."[4]

How can this be?

If you find this puzzling, you've based your reasoning on the assumption that the surgeon is a male. But suppose you had assumed that the surgeon was a female. Suddenly, the riddle becomes a lot easier. It's far easier to guess that the surgeon is the boy's *mother* if we don't leap to embrace a faulty assumption.

Why is it so easy to jump to conclusions? One reason is that we sometimes aren't aware of the assumptions that underlie our thinking. Another is our reliance on "common sense."

- **Don't believe in the myth of common sense.** Much of what we call common sense makes contradictory claims. Which are we to believe? For example, if you subscribe to the notion "Absence makes the heart grow fonder," you may assume that your high-school girlfriend, now at school across the country from you, will arrive home at Christmas even more in love with you than before. But what about "Out of sight, out of mind," which suggests a less positive outcome?

  Truisms, as such statements are called, are not factually true. Sure, being away from a loved one for a few days or a week can make you aware of just how important that person is to you and make it seem as if your heart has grown fonder. But living away from someone for an extended time is more likely to produce distance than romance.

- **Don't assume that just because two events occur together one causes the other.** Just because two events appear to be associated with one another—or, in the language of social science, are *correlated* with one another—we cannot conclude that one event has caused the other to occur. It's a basic rule: *Correlation does not prove causation.*

  For example, suppose you read that a study showed that 89 percent of juvenile delinquents use marijuana. Does this mean that smoking marijuana *causes* juvenile delinquency? No, it doesn't. It is pretty safe to say that 100 percent of juvenile delinquents grew up drinking milk. Would you feel comfortable saying that milk causes delinquency? With correlations such as marijuana use and delinquent behaviour, it is very likely that there's some third factor—such as strife among family members—that causes people both to (1) try drugs and (2) engage in illegal acts. The bottom line: We don't know anything other than the fact that many young people charged with crimes said they had smoked marijuana. We do not know the cause of the correlation.

  In short, we need to be careful in assuming causality. Even if two events or other kinds of variables occur together, it does not mean that one causes the other. (To apply what we've been discussing to some actual situations, complete Try It! 4, "What's Wrong with This Picture?")

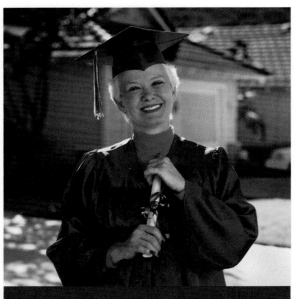

One impediment to critical thinking is difficulty in distinguishing fact from opinion. For example, although many people are of the opinion that older people have a hard time learning new material, age need not be a deterrent to learning.

4

What's Wrong with This Picture? Identify the Faulty Reasoning

Prepare: The purpose of this exercise is to give you the opportunity to use your critical thinking skills to identify faulty reasoning or conclusions.

Organize: Open the text to the section on "Avoiding Everyday Problems in Critical Thinking" and apply the material to the statements below.

Work: Take each statement and identify the faulty reasoning or wrong conclusion. Rewrite the statement to be more accurate or truthful.

Evaluate: Were you able to see faulty reasoning and identify how to improve the statements?

Rethink: Would you use this skill to determine what conclusions should be included in your decision making? Why or why not?

1. When asked why she often engages in shoplifting, Marian says, "I can't help it. I'm a kleptomaniac."

2. Zack reads in a newspaper horoscope that he "will have good luck toward the end of the week, especially in matters of chance, with a sharp downturn possible by early next week." He immediately buys 10 lottery tickets for Friday's drawing.

3. A political candidate makes this statement: "My party is 10 times more concerned about the lives and fortunes of the working person than is the opposing party."

4. Two students in a large lecture class—one evidently Asian and the other not—wait as their math professor grades their papers. The professor notes that Jackie Lee has done very well, while Darryl Roberts has not. As she finishes grading, the professor gives the good paper to the Asian-looking student and the other paper to the student who doesn't look Asian. The students look at the papers, and exchange them with the rightful owner.

TRY IT!

www.mcgrawhill.ca/olc/power

Speaking of Success

Jeff Goplin

Business Marketing Diploma, Northern Alberta Institute of Technology

When Jeff Goplin considered his postsecondary options, his foremost goal was to graduate and experience the world of work as soon as possible. With that end in mind, he was attracted to the Northern Alberta Institute of Technology and its practical hands-on two-year Business Marketing program. Jeff was extremely pleased with his courses, such as business statistics, marketing, market research, and selling, which he says were very relevant to achieving his goal.

Since shortly after graduation, Jeff has worked at Manpower Services, a world leader in the staffing industry, serving customers in more than 3700 offices in 59 countries. Now the regional marketing manager for Alberta, Jeff is responsible for Manpower's marketing throughout the province. Jeff is a strong proponent of his employer's global values and appreciates its corporate social responsibility, especially as it relates to Alberta's underemployed workers.

Although Alberta's economy is strong and its unemployment rate is the lowest in Canada, there is a shortage of skilled workers. There are employers whose needs are not being met and workers who, for lack of training or education, are not able to access higher-paying jobs.

THE NORTHERN ALBERTA INSTITUTE OF TECHNOLOGY

In addition to his work, Jeff is an active community member on behalf of underemployed persons. To this end, he sits on a number of workforce development and training boards and committees. In addition to the benefits gained by employers and workers, both Jeff and Manpower Services profit from this volunteer work. Jeff gains valuable experience and good contacts throughout the community; Manpower Services' profile is raised and goodwill is created for the organization.

When Jeff addresses college or university students, as he frequently does, he is an advocate for volunteer work in the community. He says this type of experience is very valuable for the workforce of tomorrow. However, Jeff also recommends taking some time before making the decision, to weigh the pros and cons of the situation. He advises students who want to offer their services in the community to get a clear understanding of the expectations and responsibilities associated with the position. He says that student volunteers need to know their limits before committing to a volunteer job so that they don't get too tired, their studies don't suffer, and the volunteer organizations and people served by them are not disappointed

How can I improve the quality of my decisions?

- A structured process of decision making can clarify the issues involved, expand our options, and improve the quality of our choices.

- Good decision making begins with understanding your short- and long-term goals.

- Decision making is improved if you have a large number of alternatives.

- For difficult decisions, strategies include giving the decision time, acting out alternatives, tossing a coin to test our feelings, understanding that indecision is often a decision itself, and acting on gut feelings.

What strategies can I use for problem solving?

- Problem solving entails the generation of alternatives to consider.

- We need to first understand and define the problem and to determine the important elements in coming to a solution to a problem.

- Approaches to generating solutions include using trial and error, breaking problems into pieces, working backward, using pictures, considering the opposite, using analogies, taking another's perspective, and "forgetting" the problem.

- Problem solving ultimately requires the evaluation and refinement of the solutions that have been generated.

What are some problems that affect critical thinking, and how can I avoid them?

- Several types of obstacles pose threats to critical thinking, such as faulty assumptions, vague generalities, jumping to conclusions, and the myth of common sense.

- Awareness of the biases that may affect our thinking can help us avoid them.

P.O.W.E.R. Portfolio

Decision Making and Critical Thinking

1. How can you demonstrate critical thinking, one of the most important skills employers expect from employees? Here are several suggestions! Write a letter to the editor about a topical or controversial issue in your community. Make sure your commentary shows a depth of reasoning. Or include a discussion thread from an e-mail group you participate in. The subject area doesn't matter as much as the quality of your arguments. Or consider including an op-ed piece you wrote for your school or local newspaper, an analytical essay, a case history, or a video of a debate you participated in. Your reflective comments should indicate what you learned and the thinking process you went through.

2. Consider including your journal reflections on decision making from this chapter in your portfolio. The "look back" approach to decision making can have positive implications for future decisions.

3. Use a formal decision-making technique, like SWOT (strengths, weaknesses, opportunities, and threats) analysis, a decision-making tree, or PMI (plus, minus, interesting) and work through a problem. Include your work in your portfolio, along with a commentary on the process. Information about these techniques is available at <www.psychwww.com/mtsite/page2.html>.

Resources

On Campus

Some colleges or universities offer courses in critical thinking, and they are a good bet to help increase decision-making and problem-solving skills. In addition, courses in logic and philosophy will help improve critical thinking skills.

If you are having a personal problem that is difficult to solve, you can turn to staff at the campus counselling centre, mental health centre, or residential life office. Even if the person with whom you speak initially is not the right one, he or she can direct you to someone who can help.

In Print

If you have trouble making good decisions, the H.W. Lewis book *Why Flip a Coin? The Art and Science of Good Decisions* (Wiley, 1998) is for you. The book shows how to make a rational decision based on the information at hand.

Thinking and Deciding by Jonathan Baron (Cambridge University Press, 3rd edition, 2000) is helpful for anyone interested in learning how to think and decide better. The book explores conventional ways of thinking and provides a toolkit for improved thought processing

Asking the Right Questions: A Guide to Critical Thinking, by M. Neil Browne and Stuart M. Keeley (Prentice Hall, 7th edition, 2003), focuses on the difference between memorization and the more difficult tasks of critical analysis and synthesis. It teaches students to respond to alternative points of view and develop a solid foundation for making personal choices about what information to accept and what to discard.

On the Web

The following sites on the World Wide Web provide the opportunity to extend your learning about the material in this chapter. Although the Web addresses were accurate at the time the book was printed, check the P.O.W.E.R. Learning website, <www.mcgrawhill.ca/olc/power>, for any changes that may have occurred.

www.psychwww.com/mtsite/index.html
This Web site offers links to other sites that can help you with setting goals, time management, and stress control, and to numerous other helpful sites. It also includes shareware for setting up life plans.

www.kcmetro.cc.mo.us/longview/ctac/toc.htm
Core concepts in critical thinking are presented here with exercises and examples. The site contains a short history of logic and answers the question: "What is the point of studying critical thinking?"

http://www2.sjsu.edu/depts/itl
This award-winning site has three interactive tutorials on critical thinking, with exercises and tests so that you can evaluate your analytical ability.

The Case Of...

Left Holding the Lease

Erica has a problem.

In the spring of her first year of college, she and her friend Jeri had found a two-bedroom apartment to share for the upcoming school year. The apartment was on the expensive side, but they had decided that it was worth it because it was so close to campus. She and Jeri had jointly paid the security deposit on the apartment. However, because Jeri hadn't been around when it came time to sign the lease, only Erica had signed it. Consequently, Erica was legally responsible for fulfilling the terms of the lease.

Now, only two weeks before the start of the fall term, Jeri tells Erica that she has realized she can't afford the rent on the apartment and that she has decided to live with her parents. Erica is simultaneously furious with Jeri and panicky at the thought of having to pay the rent herself, which she simply can't afford.

How is she going to deal with the problem?

1. Is the problem a purely financial and legal one, or are there personal and social considerations that should be taken into account in solving the problem?

2. Is the problem solely Erica's problem, or should Jeri take responsibility for solving it as well?

3. What alternatives does Erica have for dealing with the situation?

4. How should Erica go about evaluating the outcomes for each alternative?

5. Based on your analysis of the problem, what advice would you give Erica for dealing with the situation?

Making Academic Choices

F "REN257: Oral French."

Jesse Price's eyes skimmed over the title, automatically dismissing it from consideration. Then he returned to the course description in the list of general education options. Perhaps it was worth a try.

Although Jesse had gotten Bs and Cs in high-school French, he had dropped it as soon as he could, because he was focusing on sciences, where his marks were better. He needed the best grades possible to get into Aviation and Flight Technology—the competition to get into that program was fierce.

Now he was in AFT and he loved every minute of it, but he needed a general education elective, and the one he was considering was French! How would he survive postsecondary French? Could he even remember any vocabulary?

After talking it over with the course instructor, he felt a bit better; she indicated the course started with the basics and told him he would surprise himself with what he would remember. He'd heard the course was interactive and fun—why not give it a shot? He decided to enroll. After all, it *did* fit his schedule and it *was* a break from all the technical courses in his program.

It turned out to be one of the best decisions he had ever made; he loved the course. The instructor was terrific, making French seem fascinating. He had never spent any time in francophone areas of Canada, but now he started to consider it. He found he had a real flair for pronunciation and enjoyed giving simple presentations about the field of aviation in French. It turned out that much of the vocabulary he was developing related to his career.

Jesse enjoyed his French course and did so well that he actually took another French course in his third semester. At graduation, he applied for an aircrew position in the Canadian Forces. While not yet bilingual, Jesse's proficiency and confidence in using French made him a much stronger candidate than he would have been otherwise. His interviewers were very impressed when Jesse was enthusiastic about taking more French courses during his military training.

Looking ▶▶
▶ Ahead

Our academic and professional careers are propelled by many forces, not the least of which is chance. Jesse Price, like many other students, found a new direction while leafing through the general education course list. Although he never would have predicted at the start of college that he would end up taking two French courses and possibly take more, his willingness to take an academic chance led to a new passion and to a career opportunity.

In this chapter we focus on choosing an academic course of study, one of the central challenges of college or university. Not only do the choices we make colour our entire postsecondary experience, but they also may determine the path we follow once we graduate.

This chapter begins by considering the many choices you'll have to make as a routine part of attending college or university, including the choice of courses, instructors, and programs or majors—each of which has long-term implications. You'll learn ways to select courses that meet your needs and meet requirements for future courses or programs.

Ultimately, the degree to which your postsecondary education benefits you is in your hands. By learning various strategies, you can act decisively to get the most out of your postsecondary experience. After reading this chapter, you'll be able to answer these questions:

- **How can I prepare for the academic choices that college or university demands?**

- **What is the best way to choose courses and ensure I'm getting the most out of my studies?**

- **How can I choose a major or program?**

- **How can I deal with academic success and failure?**

Making Academic Choices

For some readers of P.O.W.E.R. Learning, there may be little in the way of academic choice. In some college or university programs, most courses are compulsory, with just a couple of electives to be chosen. For other programs, the course calendar is like an Ikea catalogue; course offerings are briefly described and you must match the ones that sound most interesting to you with your personal interests and goals, as well as with the requirements of your program.

Choosing the right set of courses can be intimidating. But if you approach the problem thoughtfully, your final choices will make the best of the possibilities offered. Let's consider how to proceed, using the P.O.W.E.R. system as a guide (see the P.O.W.E.R. Plan).

Prepare: Becoming Familiar with Your Options and Requirements

Choosing which courses to take requires that you take several significant preparatory steps before you jump in. In addition, many academic decisions are very school-specific, so it is extremely important for you to be familiar with the policies and procedures of your particular college or university.

Familiarize Yourself with Your College or University Calendar A college or university calendar, sometimes called a catalogue or program guide, provides information about courses, programs or majors, tuition fees, important details (add/drop guidelines, course withdrawal, exam schedules), and the steps you need to take to graduate with a college certificate or diploma or a university degree.

All this information is also included on the college or university Web site. In addition, websites are updated regularly and recent events or unexpected changes are added throughout the year. In addition to online calendars, many colleges and universities also

PREPARE

Become familiar with your options and requirements

ORGANIZE

Examine what you have done and what you need to do

WORK

Choose next term's courses

EVALUATE

Decide whether you are in the classes you need

RETHINK

Learn what you love and like what you learn

P.O.W.E.R. Plan

have online tracking where students can see the courses they have completed and the courses they require to graduate. In some cases, students can create their own timetable online. Use these resources to ensure your academic record is accurate and to assist you with any decisions about dropping or adding a course.

College or university calendars are actually legal documents that offer you a contract. If you are admitted to the college or university and you fulfill certain requirements (such as taking a particular set of courses, maintaining a certain level of grades, and—let us not forget—paying your tuition bills on time), you'll get something in return. That something is a diploma or degree.

Because they outline contractual obligations, college and university calendars are important documents. They provide an outline of what your institution expects and offers in a number of areas:

1. **Academic regulations.** Every college and university has strict rules, requirements, and policies; these are all spelled out in the college or university calendar. For example, to continue in school, you must maintain a particular grade average in all your courses; to drop a course, you need to do so by a certain date in the term; and to graduate, you need a certain number of courses or course credits.

2. **Academic programs.** Most of the college or university calendar is a description of the major areas of study offered by the school—its academic departments, programs or majors, and the requirements for each program or major.

   Requirements generally fall into two or three categories. First, typically, are schoolwide requirements that every student enrolled in a college or university must fulfill. Second are specific requirements for each particular program or major. A **major** is a specialization in a particular subject area, requiring a set course of study; to major in an area, you must take a specific number of courses or credits in that area. Finally, if the major falls within a broader academic unit (such as a school of education), that broader entity may have its own requirements for a degree. A **program** is typically found in colleges and involves a course of study with a set curriculum.

   For instance, an early childhood education major might be required to fulfill schoolwide requirements that apply to all students enrolled in the college or university, such as several English, writing, or general education courses. Then, because the early childhood education program may be housed in a more-general division of social sciences, there may be divisional requirements to fulfill (perhaps a course in social science methodology or a human services issues requirement). Finally, the early childhood education program will have its own separate requirements for its majors to complete, such as completing three field placements.

3. **Advance credit or transfer credit.** Most Canadian universities and colleges have transfer or articulation agreements that recognize academic knowledge and achievements undertaken at other postsecondary institutions. College and university calendars provide information for students transferring from other schools or intending to transfer to other colleges or universities in the future. Transfer students should pay careful attention to what courses they will and will not receive credit for. Partnership programs, offered by two separate institutions, may also have specific requirements students need to be aware of.

Major

A specialization in a particular subject area, requiring a set course of study (often found in universities)

Program

A course of study (often found in colleges and professional schools) with a set curriculum

4. **Prior learning assessment and recognition (PLAR).** PLAR is the process of identifying, assessing, and recognizing what a person knows and can do. The award of transfer credit in given courses or programs may be based on formal or informal learning experiences including work experience, life experience, unstructured educational experiences such as self-study, and structured educational activity. An individual is assessed through a combination of demonstration, portfolios, interviews, assignments, challenge exams, and other assessment methods. This method of gaining academic recognition for prior learning is particularly helpful for immigrants to Canada with training, skills, and experience from their home countries, as well as adult learners who are returning to college or university for formal credentials. Information about PLAR can be obtained from college or university calendars, school websites, or academic advisors.

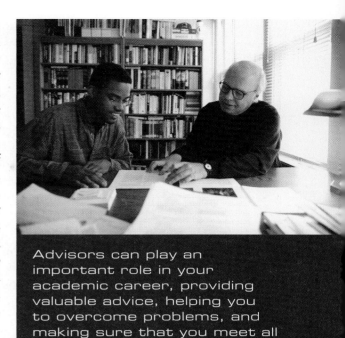

Advisors can play an important role in your academic career, providing valuable advice, helping you to overcome problems, and making sure that you meet all the requirements needed to graduate.

5. **Course listings.** The college or university website and course calendar list all the courses the school offers, even though not all of them may be offered every term. Courses are listed by department, and the descriptions typically include the course name, the number of credits it provides, and a short description. Some courses have **prerequisites**—requirements you must fulfill before you can enroll in them. If the course has a prerequisite, this will also be stated. Sometimes the description will also name the instructors who teach the course and the time and place the class meets, although this information may be published separately.

Prerequisites

Requirements that must be fulfilled before a student may enroll in a course, program, or discipline

Get Academic Advice Every college or university has its own way of doing things, so be sure to find out the best practice at your school. Get advice *before* you add or drop courses to make sure you understand the consequences of your decision. Sometimes students drop courses that are a prerequisite and can't continue the full course of study until the prerequisite is completed. In general, the following resources are very helpful:

- **Academic advisors** are important school employees. Most academic advisors want to empower students to do their own academic pathing. Your academic advisor performs many important functions within

"It can be no dishonor to learn from others when they speak good sense."

Sophocles, *Antigone*

the college or university community, such as providing assistance for students who are off-track academically, in addition to counselling for emotional concerns or major issues between students, peers, parents, or professors. Before consulting an academic advisor about course selection concerns, be sure you have tried to find the answer on the school website, in the school catalogue, or in your program guide.

- **Program coordinators** can provide information to students about program requirements as well as answer many career-related questions.

- **Student advisors** are voices of experience. They have gone through many of the same situations and solved many of the same problems as younger students and can give good clear-headed advice.

Organize: Examining What You Have Done and What You Need to Do

Where Are You? If you've prepared well, you have a basic understanding of the courses you have already taken that fulfill the requirements for the diploma or degree you are seeking. To figure out what you need to do, you'll need to organize a list of the requirements you must fulfill to graduate. Try It! 1, "Create a List of Course Requirements," provides a form that you can complete if your college or university doesn't provide one for you. Even if you have yet to decide on a program or major, you may be taking some courses that satisfy one of the requirements for a program or major you are considering. Noting this on your list will help you plan as your academic career progresses.

If this is just the start of your postsecondary career, you'll probably have completed only a few requirements. Don't let the blanks on the form get you down; this is typical, and the credits have a way of adding up quickly.

If you are further along in your college or university career, you may find that you have already fulfilled a significant number of requirements. In fact, you may not remember everything you've already done. If you have trouble remembering what courses you've taken, get a copy of your transcript from the **registrar,** the official designated to oversee the scheduling of courses, the maintenance of grades and transcripts, and the creation and retention of other official documents. A **transcript** is the official record of the courses you've taken and the grades you received in them. Many educational institutions charge a fee for official transcripts.

As you're recording the courses you've taken, remember that meeting graduation requirements may not be the same as meeting your major's requirements. For instance, some schools not only require that you take and pass certain courses, they require you to achieve a certain minimum grade in your courses as a whole. Or you may have to get a grade of C or better in a course for it to be counted toward your major. In this case, if you received a C− in the course, you'd still get credit toward graduation, but the course wouldn't count toward the number of credits you earned for your major.

Confusing? You bet. That's why it's important to keep track of where you stand from the very start of your postsecondary career. (It's a good idea to keep all relevant information together in a file folder or even a shoebox.) There's no worse surprise than finding out a month before you thought you'd be graduating that you lack some critical requirement. Don't count on others to keep track of this information for you. No one knows more about what you've done—or is more interested in it—than you.

Where Are You Going? You also need to determine what requirements you've yet to fulfill. Use this information to help determine which courses you should take in the upcoming term. Once you have declared a major you can add those requirements to your record.

Now that you know where you are and where you are going, you are ready to start selecting courses to take you there.

Work: Choosing Next Term's Courses

The course offerings for the next term are published in a *course schedule*. It is organized by department, with each course in the department having a number, such as "PSYC230: Sports Psychology." Generally, the higher the number, the more advanced the course. The course catalogue will usually tell you when and

---

Registrar

The college or university official designated to oversee the scheduling of courses, the maintenance of grades and transcripts, and the creation and retention of other official documents

Transcript

An official record of courses taken and grades received by students

Chapter 12 Making Academic Choices

1

Create a List of Course Requirements

Prepare: The purpose of this exercise is to review your academic record to ensure you have the credits you require to graduate.

Organize: You will need your transcript or academic record and the chart provided below or online.

Work: List the courses you require to graduate including any courses that are prerequisites. Mark the courses you have completed including the grade achieved.

Evaluate: Is your plan complete? Does this process help you set goals?

Rethink: Would you review your academic plan before each semester or before making significant decisions affecting your ability to graduate?

List of Course Requirements

Type of Course	Credits Required	Credits Completed	Grade Required	Grade Achieved	Whose Requirement?		
					School	Division	Department
I. Prerequisite Courses							
Total Prerequisite Courses							
II. Required Courses							
Total Required Courses							

where the class meets (for large introductory courses there may be several sections) and whether the course has any prerequisites—requirements that must be fulfilled before you can enroll in a course or discipline.

Go with What You Know Chances are, you already know of at least one or two courses you need to take in a given term. Perhaps this is the term you plan to fulfill your natural science or your foreign language requirement. There may be some courses you have been waiting to take, since some courses are only taught once a year. A good place to begin is to find out when these courses are given and where.

Draft a Personal Schedule for the Term First, write down when the courses you absolutely have to take are scheduled. If, as is the case for many introductory courses in large colleges or universities, you have a choice of times, choose one you prefer. In choosing times, take into consideration whether you are a "morning person" who is at your best first thing in the morning, or whether you usually must drag yourself out of bed in the morning and don't fully function until 11 A.M. This will be the beginning of your time management for the upcoming term.

Next, choose courses that are not required. Keep in mind broad considerations about the kinds of courses you need to take for your major and for graduation, but also explore possible courses that simply sound interesting to you. College or university offers the opportunity to discover who you are and what you like and do best, but the only way that can happen is by taking intellectual risks.

To get started in deciding what courses to take for the upcoming term, complete Try It! 2, "Choose Your Courses."

Register for Courses After laying the groundwork of course selection, the rest of the actual work of choosing courses for your classes consists of completing the school's paperwork to become formally enrolled in your chosen classes.

Meeting with your advisor is an essential step. Sometimes, in fact, it's mandatory, and you won't be allowed to register without your advisor's signature. But even if it's not required, it's a good idea to go over your proposed course of studies. You may have overlooked something, or your advisor may be able to suggest some alternative courses that will work better for you.

Remember, though, that the ultimate responsibility for taking the right courses rests with you. Not only can advisors sometimes make mistakes and overlook a requirement, but also only you ultimately know what's right for you.

Register
To enroll formally in courses

After meeting with your advisor, your next step will be to actually **register,** the formal act of enrolling in courses. Course registration varies significantly from one school to another. In some cases, it's a matter of listing course numbers on a form, along with some alternatives.

In some larger schools, you will be expected to register for your courses over the telephone or through the World Wide Web. If your college or university uses a telephone registration system, you will be given a specific time in which to call. When you do call, you'll receive voice prompts to enter your course choices using your telephone's touch-tone key pad (see Figure 12.1 on page 306).

If your college or university uses the newest form of registration, the World Wide Web, you will be prompted to enter course information on a Web form, and your registration will be accomplished completely online.

TRY IT!

www.mcgrawhill.ca/olc/power

Choose Your Courses

Prepare: The purpose of this exercise is to review your timetable for the coming semester to ensure that the classes you have enrolled in meet both your course requirements and your needs.

Organize: You will need your timetable for the coming semester and the chart provided below or online.

Work: Review your timetable and check off the courses you require for the coming semester. Identify scheduling conflicts and the classes or instructors you want.

Evaluate: Is your timetable complete? Are there any changes that would help you accomplish your goals?

Rethink: Would you complete a timetable review before each semester?

Course Selections

Term: _____

Course Name and Number	Credits	Required Course or Just for Fun?	Pre-requisites Met?	Grade Required	Meeting Days and Time	Schedule Conflicts	Instructor	Instructor Okay?

Evaluate: Deciding Whether You Are in the Classes You Need

Picture this horror story:

You receive your grade report from the previous term. You're excited because you know you've done well. You're especially looking forward to seeing your French grade because you know you were on the borderline between an A– and a B+. Instead you're astounded to see that not only is there no grade listed for the French class, but you've received an F in a Spanish class that you didn't even take. That F pulls down your grade average, and at the bottom of your grade report is an announcement that you are on academic probation.

Here's the explanation: Because of an error during registration, you were never formally enrolled in the French course, even though you actually spent the entire term attending classes in the course. To compound the mistake, your instructor never noticed that you weren't on her class roster. At the end of the term, when she was filling out her grade report, she didn't notice that your name wasn't listed. So no grade was reported for French.

Figure 12.1
Telephone Course Registration Worksheet

Before you begin your telephone call, fill in this entire worksheet, listing all courses you wish to add, drop, or change including laboratory and discussion sections, and the appropriate "action codes" you will enter. Be sure to fill in all boxed areas properly and to enter '##' at the end of your call.

1. Call the system at (555) 444-3214 (From On-Campus, call 4-3214)

2. Enter your student ID number ☐1☐2☐6 - ☐0☐4 - ☐9☐8☐1☐1

3. Enter your branch code ☐1 (Undergraduate = 1, Graduate = 2)

4. Enter your personal ID number (PIN) ☐6☐7☐7☐5

5. If the Schedule Confirmation you receive in the mail instructs you to get from your advisor a Registration Approval Code before
   add/drop, enter that code ☐ ☐ ☐ ☐

6. For each add, drop, or change you want to make, enter the appropriate action code from the list below and the schedule number for the course you want affected by that action.

Action Code*	Schedule Number of Course Requested	Dept	Course #	Section #	Crd	Day/Time
1 0	7 8 2 8 4 0	Psych	102	1	3	T-T 11:15-12:30
1 0	6 7 2 9 9 7	Engl	231	1	3	M-W-F 9:05-9:55
1 0	2 6 0 4 6 3	Phed	102	2	1	M 4:00-4:50
1 0	1 2 0 3 0 9	Latn	124	1	3	T-T 9:00-10:15
1 0	8 8 0 1 8 1	Hist	102	1	3	M-W-F 10:10-11:05
1 0	7 2 4 9 6 2	Phys	101	3	3	T-T 2:30-3:45
☐☐	☐☐☐☐☐☐					
☐☐	☐☐☐☐☐☐					
☐☐	☐☐☐☐☐☐					
☐☐	☐☐☐☐☐☐					

7. After entering your course requests, enter ## instead of an action code to terminate your call.

*Action Code	Action
10	ADD a course or Swap between sections of a course (To SWAP, simply add the new section; the old section will automatically be dropped from your schedule.)
30	ADD a course with **Pass/Fail** option or **CHANGE** existing course to **Pass/Fail**
90	**DROP** a course
80	REMOVE Pass/Fail or Audit option from existing course
50	CHANGE variable credit for an existing variable credit course
40	ADD a course with **AUDIT** grading option or **CHANGE** existing course to **AUDIT** grading
60	**LIST** your course schedule (press any key to end listing)
*	**ERASE** an entry error before completion

Note: Action Codes 30 and 80 are not available to graduate students. 40 is not available to undergraduates.

At the same time, the instructor of the Spanish class in which you were erroneously enrolled had to give you a grade at the end of the semester. Because you never completed any assignments or took any tests, your average for the semester was 0—warranting an F for the term. That F is what appeared on your grade report.

The situation—which is far more likely to occur at a large university than a small college—might be seen as a comedy of errors if it weren't so painful. Fortunately, if this were actually your story, it would most likely have a happy ending—eventually. You would go to your college or university registrar, who would be able to tell you what to do to get the F erased and the appropriate grade added. Still, undoing the cascade of errors would take time and a considerable amount of effort.

Difficulties such as these are encountered by a surprising number of students every term. Many problems, however, can be avoided with a bit of due diligence on the part of the student. One key is to evaluate your success in registering.

Before the term starts, your school will provide you with a list of courses in which you are enrolled for the upcoming term. Immediately look it over. Use the following checklist to determine how successful your efforts to register have been:

- Are the courses to which you are assigned the ones you wanted?
- Are the times accurate? Are there any conflicts?
- Have any substitutions been made?
- Are you registered for the number of credits that you wanted to be registered for?

If there are any problems, try to correct the situation immediately. If there has been a clerical error, you should pay a visit to the registrar's office. Sometimes, though, you'll find that there was no mistake. Class sizes are almost always limited, and not every student who wants to enroll can do so, either because of physical limitations (the room can hold only a certain number of students) or because of educational considerations (learning may be maximized when only a small number of students are in the class).

When a course is overbooked, you have several alternatives. One is to sign up for another section of the course that is not overbooked. Another is to attempt to register for an entirely different course.

Finally, you may appeal directly to the course instructor. Instructors sometimes will permit particularly interested or motivated students to enroll in the class, even if the official capacity has been reached. You may find that approaching an instructor with a polite request may yield you a slot in the course after all.

If none of these alternatives works, you will have to add a course to the ones you have already registered for. How do you add courses after the registration period has ended? Typically, you'll need to complete a special form. Depending on the timing of your request, the form may require the signature of the instructor whose course you are adding.

"Help—I Can't Get into the Courses That I Need to Graduate!" For some students, their efforts to register result in utter disaster. Sometimes most or all of their first choices are unavailable, and they end up enrolled in only a few of the courses they had requested. Or perhaps they cannot get into the one crucial course required for graduation.

Whatever the problem, there are several steps you can take to improve the situation:

- **Don't despair—act!** Virtually no academic problem exists that can't be solved in some way. Focus your energies on finding a creative solution to the problem.
- **Identify classes that are still available and enroll in them.** Many classes offered at your college or university are probably still available. Registrars or departments often maintain lists of classes that have openings.
- **Talk with your advisor.** Perhaps what you think of as an absolute requirement can be waived or appealed. Or maybe some other course can substitute for a particular required course.
- **Speak with individual course instructors.** It may be that the instructor of the course you need will make an exception and permit you to enroll, given that you must take the course for some pressing reason.
- **Consider taking a must-have, required course at another school.** If you live in an area where there are other schools in the vicinity, it may be possible

In distance education, you can take classes at another institution without physically having to be on that campus. David Morris and Marian Burdsall are both earning their M.B.A.s entirely online from Athabasca University in Alberta, while living in Kingston, Ontario. What do you think the future of distance education will be?

Distance learning

The teaching of courses at another institution, with student participation via video technology or the World Wide Web

to enroll in a course that you simply *must* take at another school. It also may be possible to take the course using distance learning. In **distance learning,** courses are taught at some other institution, and students participate via either video technology or the World Wide Web.

Before you take a course offered by a college or university other than your own, make sure that you'll receive credit for the course at your school. Also keep in mind that you'll probably have to pay for courses offered by other schools, over and above what you've already spent on your own school's tuition.

R ethink: Learning What You Love and Liking What You Learn

Take one step back. No, make that two steps back.

Stepping back and taking stock of where you are in your course of studies and where you're headed are absolutely essential tasks. In fact, they are among the most important things you can do during your postsecondary career. They can spell the difference between plodding through your courses, focused only on day-to-day deadlines and tribulations, and, alternatively, gaining a sense of satisfaction as you progress toward your own goals and see yourself growing as a person.

Taking stock of your course of studies is not something you need to do every day, or once a week, or even once a month. But you should do it, without fail, at least once every term. Circle a date on your calendar so you'll be sure to do it, and treat it no differently than any other deadline you simply can't miss.

When you do take stock, answer the questions in Try It! 3, "Reflect on Your College or University Experience." If you're satisfied with your answers, feel affirmed

TRY IT!

www.mcgrawhill.ca/olc/power

3

🏃 Working in a Group: Reflect on Your College or University Experience

Prepare: The purpose of this exercise is to take a time out to think about your postsecondary experience.

Organize: You will need the questions provided below.

Work: As an individual or a member of a group, think about and discuss these questions.

Evaluate: Are you able to identify value or payoff in your postsecondary experience? Is there anything you would change to help you achieve your goals?

Rethink: Would you reflect on your school experience each semester or at least once a year? Why?

Course Work

- Are my courses moving me toward my educational, career, and personal goals?
- Are the classes I'm taking helping me to meet my short-term and long-term goals?
- Are the classes I'm taking meeting my expectations?

Personal Commitment

- Am I working hard to get the most out of the classes I'm taking?
- Am I doing my best in every class?
- Am I keeping the goal of learning—apart from doing well in classes—in mind as I progress through my classes?

Personal Growth

- What personal growth am I experiencing?
- Am I becoming closer to the person I want to be?
- Are my critical-thinking abilities growing?

College

- Is my school providing me with the best educational experience possible?
- Am I learning not only in the classroom, but also outside the classroom?
- Am I learning from my fellow students as well as my instructors?

Changes

- Is there anything (my course selections, my major, or my school) that I should consider changing?
- Have I made the best choices in the past? How can I remedy mistakes that I have made?

in the choices you've made. You're on the right track, and you should feel secure in the knowledge that you're getting from college or university what you want and aspire to.

On the other hand, if you're less than satisfied with the answers you come up with, take action. Choose courses in the future that better match your goals. Consider changing your program or major to one that more closely reflects what you want to get out of your higher education. And, if you're truly unhappy with the way your postsecondary career is proceeding, consider changing schools.

Whichever course you choose, don't accept being dissatisfied with your college or university career. There are few times in our lives when we have the opportunity to partake of an experience that has the potential to raise us to new intellectual and emotional heights. Higher education should be intellectually enlightening and exciting. We should be able to see how our education is preparing us for the rest of our lives. The worst thing we can do is let the time slip away without being confident that our postsecondary experience is the best experience possible.

Taking stock of your courses and academic career also helps you with another important choice you will have to make: choosing your program or major.

Choosing a Program or Major

You attend a family gathering and encounter relatives you haven't seen for a while. What's the first question they ask when you say you're attending college or university? You can bet on it: "What's your major?"

Although you could argue that there are lots of other important questions that you could be asked—"What interesting things have you learned?" comes to mind—having a major focus of study *is* an important part of higher education. A program or a major, a field of specialization requiring a particular course of study, is important because it focuses what we study, leading us to become experts in a specific area.

Some students know what they want to major in when they begin college or university. In contrast, other students don't have a clue what they want to major in when they start school. That's fine. No one says you should know.

In fact, using your first year in college or university to explore a range of possibilities is a very good idea. You might find after taking a civics course that you have a passion for legal studies. Or a physics class may lead you to consider a program in engineering technology. College or university is meant to be a time of exploration, and leaving yourself open to the future—and the unknown—is a completely reasonable thing to do. (To begin your own exploration of majors, complete Try It! 4, "Identify Major Attractions," on page 312.)

But what if you don't have any idea which program or major you want to pursue? If you are still in your first year of school, you have plenty of time to decide. But here are some approaches that should help. You may also want to review the discussion of decision making in Chapter 11 as the time to declare a major (usually by the end of your second or the beginning of your third year) draws nearer.

1. **Celebrate your indecision.** If you don't have to make a decision for some time, take advantage of the situation. Enjoy the fact that you're uncommitted and that you have an uncommon degree of freedom.

2. **Focus on your interests.** Take a long look inward, paying attention to what your interests are. What do you most like to do in life? What are your strengths and weaknesses? What do you want to get out of life? The more you know about yourself, the easier it will be to narrow down the choices for a program or major.

3. **Seek the help of others.** College and university campuses provide many resources to help their students choose a program or major (and also to help narrow the choices for potential careers). Talk to other students majoring in areas that interest you. Find out what they like and don't like about the field and its requirements. You will probably find your interest grows or diminishes depending on how you feel about the issues they mention.

"He who hesitates is sometimes saved."

James Thurber, author

Speak with your advisor. If you've gotten to know your advisor, he or she can often provide reasonable, helpful information. For instance, you may be able to find out about the strengths and weaknesses of various departments.

You can also turn to your college or university counselling or career centre. Most schools have offices that can provide information about the various programs and majors, including information about career opportunities typically available to graduates. Sometimes it's possible to take tests that will help focus your choices, pinpointing your strengths and weaknesses.

4. **Be career-oriented, but not *too* career-oriented.** If you have a good idea about what career you want to embark on once you graduate, you can easily find out what skills are required to be successful in that field. Knowing what you'll need to gain entry into a field can help you determine a good major that will set you on the road toward your desired profession.

Don't narrow your options too much, however. Students sometimes fear signing up for classes that don't seem to lead directly toward a career. Or they may avoid courses that seem to point them in the direction of a career that would be "unacceptable" to their parents or friends. One of the greatest sources of indecision in choosing a major stems from the mistaken notion that when you choose your major, you're also choosing a career.

Don't fall into that trap. Follow your heart—not always your head—

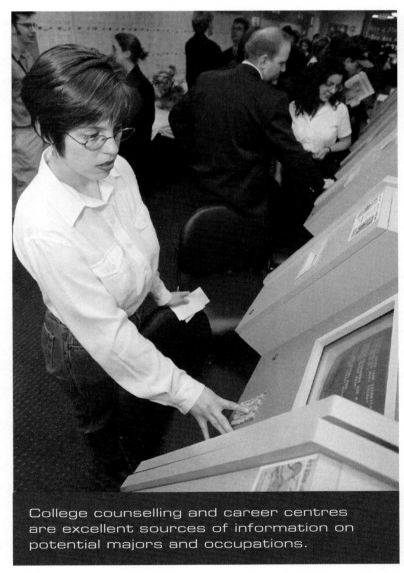

College counselling and career centres are excellent sources of information on potential majors and occupations.

Identify Major Attractions

Prepare: The purpose of this exercise is to identify or confirm your academic interests.

Organize: You will need the chart below or online.

Work: Examine the 10 areas of interest and check any that appeal to you. Then review your areas of interest to see if they are part of your academic plan. Be open to looking at unexplored territory or adding your own items to the list.

Evaluate: Are you able to identify or confirm academic interests that are part of your academic plan?

Rethink: Do your interests reflect your current program choices? Were there any surprises or areas that might need further exploration?

Field of Study	Characteristics	Is This Me?
Arts (e.g., dance, drama, music, art, creative writing, graphic design, interior decorating, fashion design)	• High interest in creative expression.	☐
	• Appreciation of nonverbal communication.	☐
	• Understanding of aesthetics.	☐
	• Commitment to perfection.	☐
	• Ability to manipulate form and shape.	☐
Business (e.g., marketing, financial planning, accounting, management, purchasing, logistics)	• Interest in organization and order.	☐
	• Ability to lead and manage people.	☐
	• Interest in practical problem solving.	☐
	• Ambition and interest in financial incentives.	☐
	• Can-do attitude.	☐
	• Ability to simplify complexity.	☐
Engineering sciences (e.g., engineering, computer science, tool and die maker)	• Intense interest in solving real problems.	☐
	• "Tinkerer" mentality a plus.	☐
	• Extreme ability to focus on minute details.	☐
	• Commitment to exactness and perfection.	☐
	• Strong logical ability.	☐
	• Ability to work alone for long stretches.	☐
Helping professions (e.g., nursing, counselling, child and youth work, teaching, and many areas of medicine such as psychiatry, art therapy, occupational therapy)	• Interest in people.	☐
	• Desire to solve real human problems.	☐
	• Commitment to people more than to money.	☐
	• Tolerance of "messy" situations with multiple, partial solutions.	☐
	• Insight and creativity.	☐
	• Ability to work with people.	☐
Humanities (e.g., English literature, history, theatre, film)	• Interest in human emotions and motivations.	☐
	• Interest in cultural phenomena.	☐
	• Ability to integrate broad areas of study and inquiry.	☐
	• Good skills of human observation.	☐
	• Interest in the panorama of human life.	☐

TRY IT!
www.mcgrawhill.ca/olc/power

Field of Study	Characteristics	Is This Me?
Languages and linguistics (e.g., translator, interpreter, journalist, anthropologist)	• Interest in words, word origins, and speech.	☐
	• View of language as a science.	☐
	• View of literature as human expression.	☐
	• Appreciation of cultural differences as scientific phenomena.	☐
Physical education (e.g., kinesiology, health and fitness, recreation and leisure studies, physiotherapist)	• Interest in physical performance.	☐
	• Enjoyment of sports and athletics.	☐
	• Commitment to helping others appreciate physical activity.	☐
	• Patience and perseverance.	☐
	• Commitment to perfection through practice.	☐
Physical, biological, and natural sciences (e.g., physics, astronomy, chemistry, biology, some areas of medicine such as paramedicine, laboratory technology, respiratory technology)	• Enjoyment of research questions; high level of curiosity about natural phenomena.	☐
	• Quantitative thinking a requirement; high comfort level with mathematics and statistics.	☐
	• Minute-problem-solving skills; attention at great level of detail.	☐
	• Strong logical ability.	☐
	• Ability to work with others.	☐
Social sciences (e.g., psychology, communications, sociology, education, political science, economics)	• Interest in people as individuals or groups.	☐
	• Ability to think quantitatively and qualitatively.	☐
	• High comfort level with mathematics and statistics.	☐
	• High level of creativity and curiosity.	☐
	• Ability to work with others.	☐
	• Interest in theory as much as problem solving.	☐
Spiritual and philosophical studies (e.g., grief counsellor, thanatology, pastoral counsellor, academic)	• Interest in the inner life.	☐
	• Interest in highly theoretical questions.	☐
	• Ability to think rigorously about abstract matters.	☐
	• Appreciation of the human search for meaning.	☐

It's a question nobody can resist asking, and one that you've probably asked: What kind of work are you going to do when you graduate?

While some postsecondary students wait until late to decide their careers, other students are focused on specific career paths right from the start. Whether you are undecided or wholeheartedly committed to a specific occupation, our world is changing rapidly and everyone should be prepared to continually develop their careers, whether that means changing jobs, being promoted, being downsized, or given special temporary projects.

Gathering and using information is a key skill area in the Conference Board of Canada's Employability Skills 2000+. As far as careers are concerned, the Internet is becoming increasingly important for searching out data on careers, posting résumés, and getting advice on job applications and human resource issues. As well, most Canadian workplaces will now accept job applications by fax or e-mail. In addition, the computer expertise you develop as you research companies, write and revise résumés and cover letters, and apply for jobs online will show potential employers you have the technological skills they are looking for.

Here, in summary, are some steps to take to identify a career:

1. **Start with what you know about yourself.** There's no single perfect career choice. Some people search for the ideal career, assuming that they need to identify the one career for which they are destined. The reality is that many careers would make them equally happy and satisfied. You've already done a lot of mental work toward narrowing down a profession. Do you hate the sight of blood? Then you're probably well aware you're not cut out to be a veterinarian. Does the sight of a column of numbers bring an immediate yawn? Forget about accounting and statistics. Awareness of your likes and dislikes puts you on the road to identifying a future career. Knowing what you don't want to do helps identify what you do want to do and to narrow down the occupations that suit you.

2. **Gather information.** The more you know about potential careers, the better. Examine career-planning materials, read industry profiles, and visit relevant websites. Talk with career counsellors. Discuss your options with people who work in professions in which you're interested. Find out how they chose their career, how they got their current job, and what advice they'd have for you. In addition, consider participating in an internship in a profession that you think might be attractive. As an intern, you'll gain first-hand experience—probably postsecondary credit as well—for the work that you do.

3. **Narrow down your choices.** Once you've gathered enough information to give yourself a reasonable comfort level, narrow down the choices. If it's early in your postsecondary career, you don't need to make up your mind. If it's late and you feel the pressure to choose, then make the decision. Just do it. Remember, there's no single, absolutely correct decision; there are many right decisions. There's nothing to prevent you from shifting careers later.

Whatever it is you ultimately choose as a career, think of it as only a first step. As the average life span continues to lengthen, most people will pass through several careers during their lives. By periodically taking stock of where you are and considering the things you want for your life, you'll be in a position to make career changes that bring you closer to your ideal. In short, any career choice you make now is likely to be just the first of many.

For over 10 years, the Bank of Montreal's Institute for Learning has been its corporate university, serving as the strategic training and education centre for North America and as a tangible symbol of BMO's dedication to lifelong learning. Tens of thousands of employees have received professional training and development in both face-to-face training and e-learning environments. Ranked as one of Canada's top 100 employers, BMO has spent more than half a billion dollars in the past decade on employee development.

and pursue courses without regard to how they may broaden or narrow your future job opportunities. You may discover a passion—and an aptitude—that you never knew you had.

5. **Always keep in mind that education is a lifelong enterprise.** Educational opportunities will continue to present themselves not just through the undergraduate years, but for the rest of your life as well.

Consequently, no matter what your choice of major, you're not precluding the possibility of taking courses in other areas in the future. You may eventually end up in a graduate school pursuing a master's degree, a doctorate, or a law degree. You also may take continuing education courses periodically at a local college or university even after you graduate, because they will help you advance in your career or simply because they interest you.

In short, choosing a major or a program is not a decision that sets your life on an unchangeable course. Instead, it's one step in what can be a lifetime of learning.

Dealing with Academic Failure—and Success

Experiencing failure is not easy. If we take a course and fail it, it hurts, though we may pretend for a moment that it doesn't. But even if you feel tempted to shrug it off publicly, don't make that mistake privately. It's important to take responsibility for and accept our failures.

However, there's a difference between accepting failure and blaming ourselves. When we fail, it's reasonable to seek to understand what went wrong. It's helpful to figure out how we can do better in the future and to take steps to avoid further failure.

However, it's not useful to spend time and energy blaming ourselves. Self-criticism, denunciation, and rebuke directed at ourselves are behaviours that don't take us forward; they keep us mired in the past.

It's important, then, to forgive ourselves for our failures.

We should not make failure a part of our lives, but it's important to learn from it. We need to consider why a failure occurred, to analyze what we could have done—or avoided doing—to prevent it, and to seek ways of preventing a similar outcome in the future. Real failure occurs when we don't learn from our mistakes.

If you have failed a test, exam, or course, you can take several steps to save your grade:

1. Check with your instructor. Politely request a meeting with your professor to discuss the issue. Ask about possibilities for rewriting or making up the work. If you have a concern about marking procedures or grading criteria, explore these topics diplomatically.

2. If you feel your grade is wrong or unfair and you have not achieved a satisfactory resolution to your problem, consider lodging an academic appeal. The process varies from school to school but usually involves further contact with your professor, the coordinator of the program, the chair of the department or division, and possibly the dean or an academic review committee. Make sure you have documentation and evidence that supports your claims. Don't throw anything away in anger

Focus on Your Interests

The following questions are intended to lead you to explore areas of personal preference and interest that should inform your choice of a major. These questions are informal and designed to be answered briefly. Extended and formal "interest inventories" are available in your school's counselling office. A useful online interest inventory is The Career Key, at <www.careerkey.org/english/>, which can help you with career choices, career changes, career planning, job searches, and much more. You may want to explore your interests further through the use of one of those inventories.

1. Do you think you would enjoy being told exactly what to do and how to do it, or would you rather work things out by yourself, without extensive instructions or supervision? What implications might your answer have for a choice of majors?

2. Do you think you would enjoy helping other people more than earning money? Why or why not? What implications might your answer have for a choice of majors?

3. Are you ambitious and success oriented and not ashamed to admit that you'd like to earn a lot of money, or are success and money of secondary importance to you? What implications might your answer have for a choice of majors?

4. Do you like exploring open-ended problems that probably will never be entirely resolved, or do you prefer exploring problems that offer a real chance of a practical solution? What implications might your answer have for a choice of majors?

5. Are you the artistic type who enjoys performing, creating, and viewing or listening to artistic works, or is art of relatively little interest to you? What implications might your answer have for a choice of majors?

6. Do you enjoy working with others, or do you prefer to work on your own? What implications might your answer have for choice of majors?

or frustration. Your school calendar will outline the process for academic appeals.

3. Some schools have an ombudsperson who assists students who feel they have been treated unfairly. The ombudsperson is generally a neutral mediator who tries to facilitate equitable solutions to disputes of an academic or personal nature.

> "Perseverance is not a long race; it is many short races one after another."
>
> Walter Elliott

4. Academic probation is a penalty imposed on students who have not met the academic standards of their program or major. This may involve sitting out for a year, taking remedial or make-up classes, or writing a letter or essay detailing your strategies for future success. If you are required to be on academic probation, ensure you use your time to its fullest advantage.

To avoid a failing grade in a course, consider withdrawing from it. Check your course calendar to find the withdrawal deadline. Remember—there may be consequences (student status or student loan) associated with these actions!

Dealing with Success Some people have as much trouble dealing with academic success as they do dealing with failure. As we first noted in Chapter 1, fear of success is a very real factor in some people's lives. They feel that somehow they're not worthy of success—that their success is a fluke and undeserved.

It's simply not true. We all deserve success, and when we achieve it, we should celebrate it. If you're doing well academically, it's not an accident; it's because you've worked hard and put your intellectual capacities to full use.

Success occurs because we want it to and because we've worked to make it happen. It can happen every day if we allow it. Success is not just reaching an endpoint, such as when we're handed our diploma. Success is a process. Any achievement that brings us closer to fulfilling our goals and dreams should be counted as a success.

> "Our deepest fear is not that we are inadequate. Our deepest fear is that we are powerful beyond measure. It is our light, not our darkness, that most frightens us."
>
> Marianne Williamson

But in the same way that we need to learn from failure, we also need to learn from success. We need to consider what we did and didn't do to achieve success. We need to think about how we might repeat successful behaviours in the future—such as using a study strategy that works for us—and how we can elaborate and extend the strategy to make the likelihood of achieving success even higher.

Finally, we need to keep in mind that life is not an either/or proposition; we're not either successes *or* failures. Even as we fail in one area, we succeed in others. And even as we succeed in one domain, other areas in our lives may not be going so well. Keeping success and failure in perspective is a critical aspect of doing our best in both academic and nonacademic realms.

Looking ◀◀ Back

How can I prepare for the academic choices that college or university demands?

- Making course choices involves finding out as much as possible about what your college or university has to offer. The school catalogue is the best initial source of this information.

- The most personal source of information and guidance in college or university are academic advisors, who have training and experience in advising students on courses, instructors, requirements, and regulations.

What is the best way to choose courses and ensure I'm getting the most out of my studies?

- In choosing courses, you should check out your selections with your academic advisor and then register for the courses. You should be prepared to choose different courses or sections if your initial selections are unavailable.

Speaking of Success

Dr. Anthony Brissett

Dental Assisting Diploma, George Brown Community College
B.N. Sc., George Brown Community College
M.D., Wayne State University

When Dr. Anthony Brissett began the Dental Assisting Program at George Brown College in 1986, he did not know that the career path he was embarking on would lead him to become a highly-skilled doctor specializing in otolaryngology (head and neck surgery), a well-trained surgeon practicing in several top American hospitals, a capable researcher with an interest in wound healing and scarring, a dedicated volunteer who provides cleft-lip and palate surgery to patients in developing countries, and an assistant professor and the director of the Facial Plastic Surgery Center at the prestigious Baylor College of Medicine in Houston, Texas.

As a high-school student, Anthony was not academically inclined, but his parents, first-generation Canadians, wanted him to attend college. So he enrolled in the Dental Assisting Program at George Brown Community College in Toronto, in large part because it was just a one-year program. While at George Brown, Anthony began to develop and mature personally and academically. He credits his courses and faculty at George Brown with providing a solid educational foundation and awakening his intellectual curiosity. After graduating from the Dental Assisting Program, Anthony completed the Nursing Program at George Brown and thought he would continue his education by enrolling in a

George Brown
The Toronto City College

Master's program in nursing. However, on the advice of his professors, he switched disciplines, and graduated from Wayne State Medical School with honours. From there he went to the celebrated Mayo Clinic in Rochester, Minnesota, to do his residency and then completed a fellowship in facial plastic and reconstructive surgery at the University of Minnesota in Minneapolis.

Anthony states that every step of the way his academic choices allowed him to gain more confidence, deepen his knowledge, to search for and meet new challenges, and to use his gift. The recipient of the 2002 Ontario Premier's Award for Health Sciences, an award given to distinguished alumni of Ontario community colleges, Anthony views his background in dental assisting and nursing as essential building blocks to his later academic and career success. In turn, he has demonstrated his appreciation for George Brown by establishing a scholarship benefiting dental assisting and nursing students.

While Anthony's academic and professional success is unquestioned, it has come with a high cost. Leaving his parents, siblings, friends, and immediate support group in Canada has been difficult but in the long run worthwhile, as he is now in a position to achieve satisfaction by contributing the most he can to society.

- You should verify that you have received your chosen courses, that the schedule of courses makes sense, and that your course schedule will help provide the number of credits needed to graduate.

- Be prepared to deal with errors during registration or to cope with the unavailability of courses that you need to take.

- Reflect on your postsecondary experience regularly, verifying that course choices, academic performance, personal growth, choice of major, and your overall educational experience are satisfactory.

How can I choose a major or program?

- Choosing a major or program first involves accepting a period of indecision, finding out more about yourself, seeking the help and advice of others, considering going beyond the traditional structure of your major or program, trying out unusual courses, and taking career plans into account.

How can I deal with academic failure and success?

- Failure and success are part of everyone's life.

- We need to learn to take responsibility for both our failures and our successes.

P.O.W.E.R. Portfolio

Choosing Your Courses and Major

1. Include a program brochure or course outline for your major in your portfolio, along with your course requirements, to show the academic and professional progress you are making. Your reflection could be an overall assessment of each course completed: what you learned, the biggest surprise, any disappointments, what you need to learn. Have projects, essays, assignments, and tests handy in case you want to include them later. This can be particularly helpful in the future, if you subsequently apply for advanced standing or prior learning assessment (PLA) for a different course or program.

2. Include your transcripts as you receive them. They demonstrate one (important) aspect of your progress to your final goal. As you compile your transcripts, note any patterns or trends. How do these trends relate to your choice of a program or major, or your readiness for your academic or career goals?

Resources

On Campus

The obvious choice for information about courses is your advisor. Sometimes your advisor will be associated with a general program, such as liberal arts; sometimes with a particular division or school, such as technology; or sometimes with a campuswide academic advising centre. Your course instructors also can often give good advice about what courses to sign up for. Finally, don't forget about your fellow students; they can be an excellent source of information about the most interesting and exciting courses. In fact, some schools publish students' course evaluations, which can provide valuable insights about particular courses and instructors.

In Print

Probably the most popular guide to careers is *What Color Is Your Parachute? 2004: A Practical Manual for Job-Hunters & Career-Changers*, by Richard Nelson Bolles (Ten Speed Press, 2003). In it you'll find ways to make decisions about choosing (and changing) professions, as well as ways to obtain a job.

On the Web

The following sites on the World Wide Web provide the opportunity to extend your learning about the material in this chapter. Although the Web addresses were accurate at the time the book was printed, check the P.O.W.E.R. Learning website, <www.mcgrawhill.ca/olc/power>, for any changes that may have occurred.

www.cdm.uwaterloo.ca
This career development eManual from the University of Waterloo contains a wealth of career development information, including self-assessment, occupational research, decision-making strategies for education and career, and career and life planning.

www.jobhuntersbible.com/intro/wciyp.shtml
Richard Nelson Bolles's site accompanies his book, *What Color Is Your Parachute? 2004: A Practical Manual for Job-Hunters & Career-Changers*, and contains a wealth of career information as well as links to most of the popular online tests.

www.workopolis.com/
Workopolis.com is Canada's biggest job site, with about 30 000 jobs posted daily. Users can create profiles, save résumés, track job applications, and create job lists.

www.macleans.ca/universities/index/jsp
Maclean's Guide to Canadian Universities 2004 presents up-to-date information about colleges and universities, including rankings based on student questionnaires and other criteria.

www.assessment.com/
MAPP, the motivational appraisal of personal potential, is an online career assessment tool that provides individuals with comprehensive information on motivations and links with matching careers, based on survey responses.

The Case Of...

No Clear Decision

As Tarik Chabar began his second semester of General Arts and Science at a large community college, he was still unsure of what to do. It was time to apply to a career program or to university, but Tarik couldn't seem to make up his mind what he wanted to do.

Tarik had thought seriously about several possibilities, including radiography, computer programming, and business purchasing programs, but nothing seemed to offer exactly what he was looking for. Part of the problem, of course, was that he *didn't* really know what he was looking for. In fact, Tarik was a lot clearer about what he didn't want to study than what he *did* want to study.

The clock was ticking, and Tarik felt lost. His parents offered many suggestions, but that just seemed to increase the pressure. And he knew that application deadlines were approaching and programs would be filling up. If he didn't make his own decision soon, circumstances might prevent him from making one he was happy with.

1. What seems to be Tarik's main problem in coming to grips with academic decision making?

2. How can Tarik's prior consideration of programs such as communications and business purchasing help him move closer to a decision?

3. How would you advise Tarik to make use of his understanding of what he doesn't want to study?

4. How can Tarik find out more about himself? Why is this important in choosing a community college career program or university major?

5. Do you think Tarik is taking this decision too seriously or not seriously enough? What advice would you give him about the importance of the academic decisions facing him?

Stress, Health, and Wellness

13

L ouis Denby's day began badly: He slept through his alarm and had to skip breakfast to catch the bus to campus. Then, when he went to the library to catch up on the reading he had to do before taking a test the next day, the one article he needed was missing. The librarian told him that replacing it would take 24 hours. Feeling frustrated, he walked to the computer lab to print out the paper he had completed at home the night before.

The computer wouldn't read his disk. He searched for someone to help him, but he was unable to find anyone who knew any more about computers than he did.

It was only 9:42 a.m., and Louis had an awful headache. Apart from that pain, he was conscious of only one feeling: stress.

Looking ▶▶
Ahead

Have you had days like Louis's? Are most of your days like his? Then you're no stranger to stress. It's something that all college or university students experience to varying degrees throughout their academic careers. In fact, almost a third of first-year college or university students report feeling frequently overwhelmed with all they need to do.[1]

Coping with stress is one of the challenges that postsecondary students face. The many demands on your time can make you feel that you'll never finish what needs to get done. This pressure produces wear-and-tear on your body and mind, and it's easy to fall prey to ill health as a result.

However, stress and poor health are not inevitable outcomes of college. In fact, by following simple guidelines and deciding to make health a conscious priority, you can maintain good physical and mental health.

This chapter covers the ways you can keep fit and healthy during—and beyond—college. It offers suggestions on how you can cope with stress, improve your diet, get enough exercise, and sleep better. It also will help you consider particular threats to mental and physical health that you're likely to face while you are in college, including alcohol and drugs, pregnancy, sexually transmitted diseases, and rape.

In sum, after reading this chapter you'll be able to answer these questions:

- **What is stress and how can I control it?**

- **What is involved in keeping fit and healthy, and why is it important for me to do so?**

- **What are the main threats to my health and well-being?**

- **What are the components of sexual health?**

Living with Stress

Stressed out? Tests, papers, due dates, job demands, roommate problems, child-care difficulties, financial hassles, relationship blues, political activities, committee work—it's no surprise that each of these can produce stress. But it may be a surprise to know that so can graduating from high school, starting your dream job, falling in love, getting married, and even winning the lottery.

Virtually *anything*—good or bad—is capable of producing stress if it in some way presents us with a challenge. **Stress** is the physical and emotional response we have to events that threaten or challenge us. It is rooted in the primitive fight or flight response wired into all animals—human and nonhuman. You see it in cats, for instance, when confronted by a threat. Their backs go up, their hair stands on end, their eyes widen, and, ultimately, they either take off or attack. The challenge stimulating this revved-up response is called a *stressor*. For humans, stressors can range from a first date to losing our chemistry notes to living through an ice storm.

Because our everyday lives are filled with events that potentially can be interpreted as threatening or challenging, stress is commonplace in most people's lives. There are three main types of stressors:

1. **Cataclysmic events** are sudden, powerful events that occur quickly and affect many people simultaneously. Tornadoes, hurricanes, and plane crashes are examples of cataclysmic events. Although they may produce powerful immediate consequences, ironically they produce less stress than other types of stressors. The reason? Cataclysmic events have a clear end-point, which can make them more manageable. Furthermore, because they affect many people simultaneously, their consequences are shared with others, and no individual feels singled out.

2. **Personal stressors** are major life events that produce a negative physical and psychological reaction. Failing a course, losing a job, and ending a relationship are all examples of personal stressors. Sometimes positive events—such as getting married or starting a new program—can also act as personal stressors. Although the short-term impact of a personal stressor can be difficult, the long-term consequences may decline as people learn to adapt to the situation.

3. **Daily hassles** are the minor irritations of life that, singly, produce relatively little stress. Being late for a class, receiving a tuition bill riddled with mistakes, and being interrupted by noises of major construction while trying to study are examples of daily hassles. However, daily hassles add up, and eventually they can produce even more stress than a single larger-scale event. Figure 13.1 indicates the most common daily hassles in people's lives.[2]

What Is Happening When We Are Stressed Out

Stress does more than make us feel anxious, upset, and fearful. Beneath those responses, we are experiencing many different physical reactions, each placing a high demand on our body's resources. Our hearts beat faster, our breathing becomes more rapid and shallow, and we produce more sweat. Our internal organs churn out a variety of hormones. In the long run, these physical responses

Stress
The response to events that threaten or challenge us

Cataclysmic events
Sudden, powerful events that occur quickly and affect many people simultaneously

Personal stressors
Major life events that produce stress

Daily hassles
The minor irritants of life that, by themselves, produce little stress, but that can add up and produce more stress than a single larger-scale event

Figure 13.1
Daily Hassles

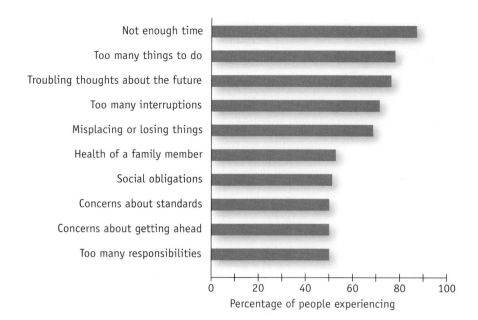

wear down our immune system, our body's defence against disease. We become more susceptible to a variety of diseases, ranging from the common cold and headaches to strokes and heart disease. In fact, surveys have found that the greater the number of stressful events a person experiences over the course of a year, the more likely it is that he or she will have a major illness (see Try It! 1, "Assess Your Susceptibility to Stress-Related Illness," on page 328).

Handling Stress

Coping

The effort to control, reduce, or tolerate the threats that lead to stress

Stress is an inevitable part of life. In fact, a life with no stress at all would be so boring and uneventful, that you'd quickly miss the stress that had been removed.

That doesn't mean, though, that we have to sit back and accept stress when it does arise. **Coping** is the effort to control, reduce, or tolerate the threats that lead to stress. Using the P.O.W.E.R. principles, we can ward off stress and actively deal with it.

Prepare: Readying Yourself Physically

Being in good physical condition is the primary way to prepare for future stress. Stress takes its toll on your body, so it makes sense that the stronger and fitter you are, the less negative impact stress will have on you. For example, a regular exercise program reduces heart rate, respiration rate, and blood pressure at times when the body is at rest—making us better able to withstand the negative consequences of stress. Furthermore, vigorous exercise produces *endorphins,* natural painkilling chemicals in the brain. Endorphins produce feelings of happiness—even euphoria—and may be responsible for the "runner's high," the positive feelings often reported by long-distance runners following long runs. Through the production of endorphins, then, exercise can help our bodies produce a natural coping response to stress.

If you now drink a lot of coffee or pop, a change in your diet may be enough to bring about a reduction in stress. Coffee, most soft drinks, chocolate, and a surprising number of other foods contain caffeine, which can make you feel jittery and anxious even without stress; add a stressor, and the reaction can be very intense and unpleasant. Simply reducing the amount of caffeine you take in can make you better prepared to deal with stress.

Eating right can alleviate another problem: obesity. Around 30 percent of Canadians between 20 and 64 are obese,[3] defined as having body weight more than 20 percent above the average weight for a person of a given height. Lest you think obesity is a problem only for older adults, experts estimate that 10 to 25 percent of all young adults have a weight problem.[4] Obesity can bring on stress for several reasons. For one thing, being overweight drags down the functioning of the body, leading to fatigue and a reduced ability to bounce back when we encounter challenges to our well-being. Also, about 30 percent of individuals who are 50 kg overweight have elevated blood pressure.[5] In addition, feeling fat in a society that acclaims the virtues of slimness can be stressful in and of itself.

Organize: Identifying What Is Causing You Stress

You can't cope effectively with stress until you know what's causing it. In some cases, it's obvious—a series of bad test grades in a course, a child whose behaviour at school is worrisome and causing you to miss classes, a job supervisor who seems to delight in making things difficult. In other cases, however, the causes of stress may be more subtle. Perhaps your relationship with your boyfriend or girlfriend is rocky, you are undergoing culture shock, or moving away from home was more difficult than you had expected and you have a nagging feeling that something is wrong.

Whatever the source of stress, you can't deal with it unless you know what it is. To organize your assault on stress, take a piece of paper and list the major circumstances that are causing you stress. Just listing them will help put you in control, and you'll be better able to figure out and apply strategies for coping with them.

Sources of Stress
1. Biology professor talks so fast that notetaking is nearly impossible
2. Difficulty paying rent this month.
3. Not enough time to study for Tuesday's psych test

1 Assess Your Susceptibility to Stress-Related Illness

Prepare: The purpose of this exercise is to determine the amount of stress in your life.

Organize: You will need the stress checklist below or online.

Work: Review the stressors on the checklist[6] and mark any that apply to you. Take each score for the items you checked. For items that occurred more than once, multiply the score for the item by the number of occurrences to maximum of four. Add up the total score for the items you checked. Read the following about interpreting your score.

Scoring:

If your total score is above 1435, you are in a high-stress period in your life and more likely to experience stress-related illness. A high score does not indicate you are sure to get sick but it does mean you should pay attention to dealing with stress. Ensure you get enough sleep, eat healthy foods, exercise, and ask for help when you need it.

Evaluate: Were you able to identify your stress level? What does your score indicate about the potential effect of stress on your life? What can you do about reducing your stress?

Rethink: Do you believe you can cope with your current stress levels? Do you need to rethink parts of your life to reduce stress?

87 Experienced the death of a spouse

77 Got married

77 Experienced the death of a close family member

76 Were divorced

74 Experienced a marital separation

68 Experienced the death of a close friend

68 Experienced pregnancy or fathered a pregnancy

65 Had a major personal injury or illness

62 Were fired from work

60 Ended a marital engagement or a steady relationship

58 Had sexual difficulties

58 Experienced a marital reconciliation

57 Had a major change in self-concept or self-awareness

56 Experienced a major change in the health or behaviour of a family member

54 Became engaged to be married

Work: Developing Effective Coping Strategies

A wide variety of tactics can help you deal with stress. Among the most effective approaches to coping are these:

* **Take charge of the situation.** Stress is most apt to arise when we are faced with situations over which we have little or no control. Take charge of the

53 Had a major change in financial status

52 Took on a mortgage or loan of more than $10 000

52 Had a major change in use of drugs

50 Had a major conflict or change in values

50 Had a major change in the number of arguments with spouse

50 Gained a new family member

50 Entered college or university

50 Changed to a new school

50 Changed to a different line of work

49 Had a major change in amount of independence and responsibility

47 Had a major change in responsibilities at work

46 Experienced a major change in use of alcohol

45 Revised personal habits

44 Had trouble with school administration

43 Held a job while attending school

43 Had a major change in social activities

42 Had trouble with in-laws

42 Had a major change in working hours or conditions

42 Changed residence or living conditions

41 Had spouse begin or cease work outside the home

41 Changed choice of major field of study

41 Changed dating habits

40 Had an outstanding personal achievement

38 Had trouble with boss

38 Had a major change in amount of participation in school activities

37 Had a major change in type and/or amount of recreation

36 Had a major change in religious activities

34 Had a major change of sleeping habits

33 Took a trip or vacation

30 Had a major change in eating habits

26 Had a major change in the number of family get-togethers

22 Were found guilty of minor violations of the law

situation and you'll increase your sense of mastery and reduce the experience of stress. For example, if several assignments are all due on the same day, you might try negotiating with one of your instructors for a later due date.

- **Don't waste energy trying to change the unchangeable.** There are some situations that you simply can't control. You can't change the fact that you have come down with a case of mono, and you can't change your performance on a test you took last week. Don't hit your head against a brick wall and try to modify things that can't be changed. Use your energy to address the situation as a problem to be solved: Seek out ways to improve the situation, not to rewrite history.

- **Look for the silver lining.** Stress arises when we perceive a situation as threatening. If we can change how we perceive that situation, we can change our reactions to it. For instance, if your computer science instructor requires you to learn a difficult spreadsheet program in a very short time, the saving grace is that you may be able to use the skill to your advantage in getting a job. (You can practise finding the silver lining in Try It! 2, "Look for the Silver Lining.")

Social support

Assistance and comfort supplied by others in times of stress

- **Talk to your friends. Social support,** assistance and comfort supplied by others, can help us through stressful periods. Turning to our friends and family and simply talking about the stress we're under can help us tolerate it more effectively. Contact your campus student life or counselling office for school, community, and professional social support resources.

- **Relax.** Because stress produces constant wear and tear on the body, practices that lead to the relaxation of the body might lead to a reduction in stress. Using any one of several techniques for producing physical relaxation can prevent stress. Among the best relaxation techniques are the following:

Meditation

A learned technique for refocusing attention and producing bodily relaxation

  - **Meditation.** Though often associated with its roots in the ancient Eastern religion of Zen Buddhism, meditation, a learned technique for refocusing attention and producing bodily relaxation, is practised in some form by members of virtually every major religion. Meditation reduces blood pressure, slows respiration, and in general produces relaxation in the body.

    How do you meditate? The process is actually rather simple. As summarized in Table 13.1, it includes sitting in a quiet room with eyes closed or focused on a point about 2 metres away from you and paying attention to your breathing. Though the specifics of what you do may vary slightly, meditation works by helping you concentrate on breathing deeply and rhythmically, sometimes murmuring a word or sound repeatedly.

Table 13.1

Methods of Meditation

Step 1	Pick a focus word or short phrase that's firmly rooted in your personal belief system or a neutral word like *one* or *peace* or *love*.
Step 2	Sit quietly in a comfortable position.
Step 3	Close your eyes.
Step 4	Relax your muscles.
Step 5	Breathe slowly and naturally, repeating your focus word or phrase silently as you exhale.
Step 6	Throughout, assume a passive attitude. Don't worry about how well you're doing. When other thoughts come to mind, simply say to yourself, "Oh, well," and gently return to the repetition.
Step 7	Continue for 10 to 20 minutes. You may open your eyes to check the time, but do not use an alarm. When you finish, sit quietly for a minute or so, at first with your eyes closed and later with your eyes open. Then do not stand for one or two minutes.
Step 8	Practise the technique once or twice a day.

2

Look for the Silver Lining

Prepare: The purpose of this exercise is to practise the skill of finding something positive—a silver lining—in potentially stressful situations.

Organize: You will need the list of example situations below or online. Add your own situations that are often stressful for you.

Work: Read each stressful situation and derive something positive, perhaps even humorous from each situation. Two examples are provided to help get you going.

Evaluate: How well were you able to develop positive responses to stressful situations?

Rethink: Do you think this strategy would help in future situations where you might feel overwhelmed by stress?

Situation	Silver Lining
1. Your car just broke down and repairing it is more than you can afford right now.	1. This is the perfect time to begin exercising by walking and using your bicycle.
2. Your boss just yelled at you and threatened to fire you.	2. Either this is a good time to have an honest discussion with your boss about your job situation, OR this is a good time to get a more interesting job.
3. You have two papers due on Monday and there's a great concert you wanted to go to on Saturday night.	3.
4. You just failed an important test.	4.
5. You're flat broke, you have a date on Saturday, and you wanted to buy some things beforehand.	5.
6. Your last date went poorly and you think your girlfriend/boyfriend was hinting that it was time to break up.	6.
7. Your parents just told you that they can't afford to pay your tuition next semester.	7.
8. You just got cut from a sports team or club activity you loved.	8.
9. Your best friend is starting to turn weird and seems not to enjoy being with you as much as before.	9.
10. You just realized you don't really like your academic major, and you're not even sure you like your school much any more.	10.

TRY IT! 3

www.mcgrawhill.ca/olc/power

Use Progressive Relaxation

You can undertake progressive relaxation almost anywhere, including the library, a sports field, or a classroom, since tensing and relaxing muscles is quiet and unobtrusive. Although the following exercise suggests you lie down, you can use parts of it no matter where you are.

1. Lie flat on your back, get comfortable, and focus on your toes.

2. Become aware of your left toes. Bunch them up into a tight ball, then let them go. Then let them relax even further.

3. Now work on your left foot, from the toes to the heel. Without tensing your toes, tighten up the rest of your foot and then let it relax. Then relax it more.

4. Work your way up your left leg all the way to your groin, first tensing and then relaxing each part. You may move up as slowly or as quickly as you want, using big leaps (e.g., the entire lower leg) or small steps (e.g., the ankle, the calf, the front of the lower leg, the knee, etc.).

5. Repeat the process for the right leg.

6. Now tense and relax progressively your groin, buttocks, abdomen, lower back, ribs, upper back, and shoulders.

7. Work your way down each arm, one at a time, until you reach the fingers.

8. Return to the neck, then the jaw, cheeks, nose, eyes, ears, forehead, and skull.

By now you should be completely relaxed. In fact, you may even be asleep—this technique works well as a sleep-induction strategy.

To vary the routine, play with it. Try going from top to bottom, or from your extremities in and ending with your groin. Or target any other part of your body to end up at, and take the most circuitous route you can think of.

– **Progressive relaxation.** Progressive relaxation does some of the same things that meditation does, but in a more direct way. To use progressive relaxation, you systematically tense and then relax different groups of muscles. For example, you might start with your lower arm, tensing it for five seconds and then relaxing it for a similar amount of time. By doing the same thing throughout the parts of your body, you'll be able to learn the "feel" of bodily relaxation. You can use the technique when you feel that stress is getting the better of you. (Use Try It! 3, "Use Progressive Relaxation," to experience progressive relaxation for yourself.)

• **Remember that wimping out doesn't work—so keep your commitments.** Suppose you've promised a friend that you'll help out on moving day and yourself that you'll spend more time with your children. You've also been elected to the student body governing board, and you've made a commitment to bring more speakers to campus. Now you are facing all the demands connected to these commitments and feeling stressed.

You may be tempted to cope with the feeling by breaking some or all of your commitments, thinking, "I just need to sit at home and relax in front of the television!" This is not coping. It is escaping, and it doesn't reduce stress. Ducking out of commitments, whether to yourself or to others, will make you feel guilty and anxious, and will be another source of stress—one without the satisfaction of having accomplished what you set out to do. Keep your promises.

E valuate: Asking Whether Your Strategies for Dealing with Stress Are Effective

Just as the experience of stress depends on how we interpret circumstances, the strategies for dealing with stress also vary in effectiveness depending on who we are. So if your efforts at coping aren't working, it's time to reconsider your approach. If talking to friends hasn't helped ease your stress response, maybe you need a different approach. Maybe you need to see the silver lining or cut back on some of your commitments. If one coping strategy doesn't work for you, try another. What's critical is that you don't become paralyzed, unable to deal with a situation. Instead, try something different until you find the right combination of strategies to improve the situation.

R ethink: Placing Stress in Perspective

It's easy to think of stress as an enemy. In fact, the coping steps outlined in the P.O.W.E.R. Plan at the right are geared to overcoming its negative consequences. But consider the following two principles, which in the end may help you more than any others with understanding how to deal with stress:

- **Don't sweat the small stuff . . . and it's all small stuff.** Stress expert Richard Carlson[7] emphasizes the importance of putting the circumstances we encounter into the proper perspective. He argues that we frequently let ourselves get upset about situations that are actually minor. So what if someone cuts us off in traffic, or does less than his or her share on a group project, or unfairly criticizes us? It's hardly the end of the world, and the behaviour of the other people involved in such situations reflects negatively on them, not us. One of the best ways to reduce stress, consequently, is to maintain an appropriate perspective on the events of your life, sorting out what is and is not important.

- **Make peace with stress.** Think of what it would be like to have no stress—none at all—in your life. Would you really be happier, better adjusted, and more successful? The answer is "probably not." A life that presented no challenges would probably be, in a word, boring. So think about stress as an exciting, although admittedly sometimes difficult, friend. Welcome it, because its presence indicates that your life is stimulating, challenging, and exciting—and who would want it any other way?

PREPARE

Ready yourself physically

ORGANIZE

Identify what is causing you stress

WORK

Develop effective coping strategies

EVALUATE

Ask yourself whether your strategies for dealing with stress are effective

RETHINK

Place stress in perspective

P.O.W.E.R. Plan

Eat right. Exercise. Get plenty of sleep.

Pretty simple, isn't it? We learn the fundamentals of fitness and health in the first years of elementary school.

Yet for millions of us, wellness is an elusive goal. We eat on the fly, stopping for a bite at the drive-in window of a fast-food restaurant. Most of us don't exercise enough, either because we feel we don't have enough time or because it's not much fun for us. And as for sleep, we're a nation in which getting by with as little sleep as possible is seen as a badge of honour.

> "The first wealth is health."
>
> Emerson

You can buck the trends, however; you can begin to eat properly, exercise effectively, and sleep better by following several basic rules.

Eating Right

- **Eat a variety of foods.** Strive to eat a range of different foods. If you make *variety* your goal, you will end up eating the right foods. Although many popular diets recommend reducing carbohydrates in favour of high-fat, high-protein foods, most nutritionists recommend eating a selection of foods that contain all the vitamins, minerals, and fibre a healthy body needs.

- **Eat plenty of fruits, vegetables, and grain products.** Enough said.

- **Avoid foods that are high in sugar and salt content.** Read labels on supermarket packages carefully and beware of hidden sugars and salts. Many ingredients that end in *-ose* (such as dextrose, sucrose, maltose, and fructose) are actually sugars; salt can lurk within any number of compounds beginning with the word *sodium.* Your best bet is to trust the nutrition labels that the Canadian government requires food manufacturers to put on their products.

- **Seek a diet low in fat and cholesterol.** The fat that is to be especially avoided is saturated fat—the most difficult for your body to rid itself of. Be especially careful to avoid trans fat, which is found in many processed snacks and junk food.

- **Less is more.** You don't need to walk away stuffed from every meal. Moderation is the key. To be sure you don't eat more than your body is telling you to eat, pay attention to internal hunger cues.

- **Schedule three regular meals a day.** Eating should be a priority—a definite part of your daily schedule. Avoid skipping any meals. Breakfast is particularly important; get up early enough to eat a full meal.

- **Be sensitive to the hidden contents of various foods.** Soft drinks and chocolate can contain substantial quantities of caffeine, which can disrupt your sleep and, along with coffee and tea, become addictive. Many cereals—even those labelled "low fat"—contain a substantial amount of sugar or salt. Pay attention to labels.

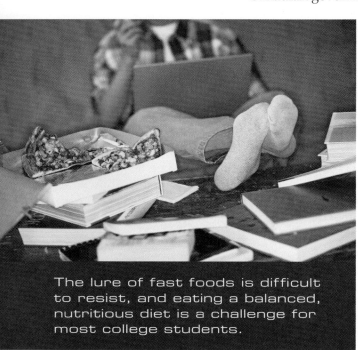

The lure of fast foods is difficult to resist, and eating a balanced, nutritious diet is a challenge for most college students.

- **Beware of eating disorders.** Between 1 percent and 4 percent of college- or university-age women, and a smaller percentage of men, suffer from an eating disorder. Those with *anorexia nervosa* may refuse to eat, while denying that their behaviour and appearance—which can become skeletonlike—are unusual. Some 15 to 20 percent of those with anorexia literally starve themselves to death. *Bulimia* is a disorder in which individuals binge on incredibly large quantities of food, such as a gallon of ice cream and a whole pie, but later feel so much guilt and depression that they induce vomiting or take laxatives to rid themselves of the food. Eating disorders represent serious threats to health and require aggressive medical intervention.

Making Exercise a Part of Your Life

Exercise produces a variety of benefits. Your body will run more efficiently, you'll have more energy, your heart and circulatory system will run more smoothly, and you'll be able to bounce back from stress and illness more quickly.

These students from Capilano College and the Royal Military College battle for the national soccer championship despite the snow. Intramural and varsity sports have the advantage of mixing regular exercise with an enjoyable social activity.

- **Choose a type of exercise that you like.** Exercising will be a chore you'll end up avoiding if you don't enjoy what you're doing.

- **Incorporate exercise into your life.** Take the stairs instead of elevators. Leave your car at home and walk to campus or work. Join an intramural team. When you're on campus, take the longer way to reach your destination.

- **Make exercise a group activity.** Exercising with others brings you social support and turns exercise into a social activity. You'll be more likely to stick to a program if you have regular workouts scheduled with a friend.

- **Vary your routine.** You don't need to do the same kind of exercise day after day. Choose different sorts of activities that will involve different parts of your body and keep you from getting bored.

One note of caution: Before you begin an exercise program, it is a good idea to have a physical checkup, even if you feel you're at the peak of health. This is especially true if you're starting an exercise program after years of inactivity. You also might consult a trainer at the gym to set up a program that gradually builds you up to more vigorous exercise.

Getting a Good Night's Sleep

Do you feel as if you don't get enough sleep? That's not surprising. Most college and university students are sleep deprived, a condition that causes them to feel fatigued, short-tempered, and tense. Insufficient sleep also leads to declines in academic and physical performance. You can't do your best at anything if you're exhausted—or even tired. Some scientists believe that long-term sleep debt could be a factor in the national epidemics of diabetes and obesity; in addition,

Stress is one of the prime hazards of the world of work. Consider these statistics from the Canadian Mental Health Association:[8]

- Workplace stress is the most common form of stress experienced by Canadians.
- Forty-three percent of all Canadian adults aged 30 and over feel overwhelmed by their jobs.
- Canadian workers view job stress as more prevalent than work-related injury or illness.
- Canadians are not alone. Job-related stress has been identified by the World Health Organization as a "worldwide epidemic."
- Not all stress is bad; without some degree of stress, people become bored and depressed. However, ill health can occur when our response to stress is not channelled properly.
- It is estimated that 40 percent of worker turnover is due to job stress.
- Job stress is a major factor in employee absenteeism. Statistics Canada calculates the annual cost of work time lost to stress at $12 billion.
- Workplace stress has been shown to cause backaches, migraines, and to lead to substance abuse, all of which contribute to poor job performance.
- Chronic stress can lead to hypertension, depression, and susceptibility to other common physical illnesses.
- Less obvious results of workplace stress are the feelings of frustration, anger, and hopelessness that affect stressed employees.

Consequently, considering potential stress should be an important consideration when choosing a profession.

MDS Nordion recently received a Healthy Workplace Award from the National Quality Institute for its first-rate health and wellness system. Two focuses of the program are encouraging employees to strike a better balance between work and family life, and stress reduction. The result is less attrition, fewer absences, less time lost to injuries.

inadequate sleep could weaken the immune system, leading to colds and other infections. To make matters worse, research studies in Britain have shown that prolonged sleep deprivation mimics a rapid aging process.[9]

Often the solution to the problem is simply to allow yourself more time to sleep. Most people need around eight hours of sleep each night, although there are wide individual differences. Realistically, there will be times when you are up late with your kids, spend the night away from home, lose track of time playing on the Internet until the wee hours, or have to pull an all-nighter. When you're behind on sleep, a nap can work wonders in boosting your alertness. A short nap can equal one hour of sleep you didn't get the night before![10] In addition to sleeping more, there are also some relatively simple changes you can make in your behaviour that will help you to sleep better. They include the following:

- **Exercise during the day.** Regular exercise will help you sleep more soundly at night, as well as help you cope with stress that might otherwise keep you awake.
- **Have a regular bedtime.** By going to bed at pretty much the same time each night, you give your body a regular rhythm and make sleep a habit.
- **Use your bed for sleeping and not as an all-purpose area.** Don't use your bed as a place to study, read, eat, or watch TV. Let your bed be a trigger for sleep.
- **Avoid caffeine after lunch.** The stimulant effects of caffeine (found in coffee, tea, and some soft drinks) may last as long as 8 to 12 hours.

- **Drink a glass of milk at bedtime.** Drinking a glass of milk before you go to bed will help you get to sleep. The reason? Milk contains a natural chemical that makes you drowsy.

- **Avoid sleeping pills.** Despite advertisements to the contrary, you're better off not taking sleeping pills. Although they may be temporarily effective, in the long run they impair your ability to sleep because they disrupt your natural sleep cycles. Alcohol is similarly ineffective.

- **Sleep in the dark.** Falling asleep with the lights or TV on can be unhealthy. Too few hours spent in darkness might boost cancer risk. Cancer researchers speculate that there might be a connection between the epidemic of breast cancer and hormone cycles disrupted by late-night light. For more information on breast cancer and its link to hormone cycles, check out <www.hopkinsmedicine.org/breastcenter/artemis/200111/feature.html>.

- **Don't try to force sleep on yourself.** It turns out that one of the reasons that we have trouble sleeping is that we try too hard. To follow this advice, try to relax when you go to bed—and don't try to go to sleep. If you're wide awake after 10 minutes or so, get up and do something else. Only go back to bed when you feel tired. Do this as often as necessary.

Staying Safe on the Job

Tim Hickman, a 21-year-old Fanshawe College student was killed in 1996, 10 days after an explosion at a London arena left him badly burned. He had been refilling an ice-resurfacing machine when it caught on fire and engulfed him in flames. The city, which was subsequently convicted of health and safety violations, has begun to rectify the conditions that resulted in Tim Hickman's death.

Dozens of young Canadians are hurt on the job every day and, as in Tim Hickman's case, some of those injuries result in death. New employees are especially vulnerable, with some accidents occurring within the first week of starting a job. If you have a part-time job, be aware of any concerns and make sure equipment operating instructions and emergency/safety procedures are explained to you. Make sure you are WHMIS (Workplace Hazardous Materials Information System) trained if you deal with hazardous materials.

For more information on young worker safety, check out the P.O.W.E.R. Learning Online Learning Centre at <www.mcgrawhill.ca/olc/power>.

Drug Abuse

For better or worse, drugs are part of our lives. It's virtually impossible to be unaware of the extent of the Canadian and international problem of illegal drug use, which involves millions of individuals who have used illegal substances at least once. Patterns of drug use and the ability to avoid abusing drugs are often established in college or university. These patterns can have a big impact on your academic career and your life, so it is a good idea to learn what you can now, before negative patterns of abuse, and in some cases, addiction, take hold.

Alcohol and Its Allure

The drug most likely to be found on college or university campuses is alcohol. It may surprise you to know that though it initially seems to raise your spirits, alcohol is actually and ultimately a depressant. As the amount of alcohol you consume increases, its depressive effects become more obvious. You've probably seen other negative effects. Drinkers show poor judgment, their memory is impaired, and their speech becomes slurred and eventually incoherent. If you drink enough, you'll pass out. And if you consume enough alcohol in a short period, you can die of alcohol poisoning.

The potential negative consequences of drinking have done little to prevent the use of alcohol on university and college campuses, many of which have pubs, bars, or licensed facilities in student activity centres. (To assess your drinking style, complete Try It! 4, "Personal Styles: Consider Your Drinking Style.") About 68 percent of Canadian university students describe themselves as regular drinkers.[11] The average university student in Canada has 6.5 alcoholic drinks per week.[12]

Some students drink even more and the extent of alcohol consumption can reach astonishing levels. According to a national survey of alcohol and drug use on Canadian campuses, 63 percent of Canadian university students had engaged in **binge drinking**, defined as having at least four (for females) or five (for males) drinks in a single sitting.[13] Around 38 percent reported binging on more than eight drinks.[14] Such heavy drinking doesn't just affect the drinker. Most college students report having had their studies or sleep disturbed by drunken students. Students in residence reported the highest levels of binge drinking;[15] the problem is enough of a concern that *substance-free* residences or *substance-free* floors in residences are growing in popularity on Canadian campuses.

Approximately 10 percent of Canadian adults are alcoholics or problem drinkers, and Canadian college and university students make up their fair share of the total.[16] **Alcoholics,** individuals with serious alcohol-abuse problems, become dependent on alcohol, experiencing a physical craving for it. They continue to drink despite serious consequences. Furthermore, they develop a tolerance for

Binge drinking

Having at least four (for females) or five (for males) drinks in a single sitting

Alcoholics

Individuals with serious alcohol-abuse problems who become dependent on alcohol and continue to drink despite serious consequences

---

Journal REFLECTIONS

College Drinking Experiences

Examine your own feelings about alcohol use by answering these questions.

1. Why do you think people use alcohol? Why do you use (or not use) alcohol?

2. What do you think the minimum age to legally drink alcohol should be, and why?

3. What is your opinion on people who only drink to get drunk? On binge drinking?

4. Have you ever suspected any of your friends or acquaintances of being alcoholics? Why?

5. Have you ever witnessed or been part of a scene in which drunkenness played a part in obnoxious behaviour? Rowdiness? Drinking and driving? Death? Violence? Abuse of others? What are your comments?

Personal Styles: Consider Your Drinking Style

Prepare: The purpose of this exercise is to help you assess your approach to drinking. Are you in control?

Organize: You will need the questionnaire below or available online.

Work: Be honest and answer the questions. Use the scale provided. Add up your answers to find a total score.

Evaluate: The lower the score the better able you are to control your alcohol consumption and use alcohol responsibly. If your score is over 40 you are likely to have problems controlling your use of alcohol.

Rethink: Is there a message in this exercise that you should change your drinking habits?

1 = Strongly disagree

2 = Disagree

3 = Neutral

4 = Agree

5 = Strongly agree

TRY IT!

www.mcgrawhill.ca/olc/power

	1	2	3	4	5
1. I usually drink alcohol a few times a week.					
2. I sometimes go to class after I've been drinking alcohol.					
3. I frequently drink when I am alone.					
4. I have driven under the influence of alcohol.					
5. I have used fake or borrowed ID to buy alcohol.					
6. I'm a totally different person when I am drinking alcohol.					
7. I often drink so much that I feel drunk.					
8. I wouldn't want to go to a party where alcohol wasn't allowed.					
9. I avoid people who don't like to drink alcohol.					
10. I sometimes urge others to drink more alcohol.					

alcohol and must drink increasing amounts to experience the initially positive effects that alcohol brings about.

The long-term consequences of high levels of alcohol consumption are severe. Heavy drinking damages the liver and digestive system, and can even affect brain cells. In fact, virtually every part of the body is eventually affected by heavy alcohol use.

Nicotine

Despite millions of dollars spent on anti-smoking education, bylaws prohibiting smoking in public venues, and graphic warnings on cigarette packages, smoking remains a significant health problem. Smoking causes lung damage and increases the risks of developing cancer, emphysema, and a host of other diseases.

Why do people smoke, when the evidence is so clear about its risks? They start to smoke for a variety of reasons. Smoking is sometimes viewed as a kind of initiation into adulthood, a sign of growing up. In other cases, teenagers see smoking as "cool," a view glorified by movies and television.

The problem is that, no matter what the reason a person tries a few cigarettes, smoking usually quickly becomes a habit because a major ingredient of tobacco—nicotine—is an addictive drug. An *addictive drug* produces a biological or psychological dependence. The absence of the drug leads to a craving for it that may be nearly irresistible.

Smoking cigarettes is one of the hardest addictions to break. Among the suggestions for quitting are the following:

- **Remain smoke-free one day at a time.** Don't think to yourself about not smoking tomorrow, or next week, or for the rest of your life. Instead, think of what you're doing as not smoking for the rest of the day. You can worry about tomorrow . . . tomorrow.

- **Visualize the consequences of smoking.** Visualize blackened, rotting lungs filled with smoke. Then think about the fresh, pink lungs that you'll have after you've stopped smoking.

- **Exercise.** The all-purpose antidote, exercise, will make you feel better physically and take your mind off smoking.

- **Use nicotine patches or nicotine gum.** "The Patch" and nicotine gum can provide enough nicotine to satisfy your craving for the drug, while permitting you to stop smoking. Physicians can also sometimes prescribe drugs that help reduce the craving for nicotine.

- **Avoid smokers.** It's nearly impossible to avoid the urge to smoke when others are lighting up. If you're trying to quit, stay away from people who are smoking.

- **Enlist the social support of family and friends.** Tell others that you're trying to quit, and accept their encouragement and praise.

- **Reward yourself.** Every few days, give yourself some kind of reinforcement for spending a period of time smoke-free. Go to a movie, buy a CD. Think about how you can afford these more easily since you aren't buying cigarettes anymore.

- **Join a quit-smoking program.** Many college and university health services hold periodic programs to help students who want to stop smoking. By enrolling in one, you'll receive the support of others who are in the same boat as you are.

- **Keep trying.** If after quitting you start smoking again, just consider that lapse as part of the process of quitting. Many people quit several times before they manage to quit for good.

Illegal Drugs

"Just say 'no.'"

If it were only so easy. Decisions about drugs are quite a bit more complicated than simplistic antidrug slogans would have you believe. They involve complex decisions about your body, peer pressure, and your personal values.

Several things are clear, however. Despite the prevalence of illicit drug use among college and university students—surveys show that approximately 30 percent of Canadian university students report using cannabis in the previous 12 months and 10 percent acknowledge using illicit drugs other than cannabis[17]—the benefits of drug use are difficult to enumerate. Apart from a temporary high, the advantages of using drugs are nil, and the use of illegal drugs is among the riskiest activities in which people can engage. Not only does drug use make you vulnerable to arrest, it also poses short- and long-term health risks. The escape from one's responsibilities that drugs provide is likely to make it even harder to later deal with those responsibilities—which aren't going to go away.

> "Every form of addiction is bad, no matter whether the narcotic be alcohol or morphine or idealism."
>
> Carl Jung

Not all illegal drugs are the same, and they produce widely varying effects and consequences. For information on the most common drugs and their effects, please go to the Online Learning Centre at www.mcgrawhill.ca/olc/power. But they all share a common result—a reduction in your awareness of what is happening around you and an escape from the realities of life.

People often fall into drug use without much thought. But doing so is still a personal choice. Preaching and slogans are not going to help you to make a sensible decision. You need to employ every critical thinking skill you can to determine exactly what you want—and don't want—to introduce into your body. Give some thought to why escape is attractive and consider seeking counselling instead. Allow yourself to consider the long- and short-term effects of drug use—both the physical effects as well as the potential effects on your own aspirations and dreams. Let yourself think about the legal consequences of drug use. A drug conviction can lead to expulsion from college or university and refusal by many employers to hire you. Furthermore, random drug tests are starting to become a part of corporate life in Canada, and your ability to get and keep a job may be placed at risk if you use drugs—even only occasionally.

Drugs that produce addiction, such as cocaine, methamphetamines, and heroin, present a further set of problems. The lives of people with drug addictions become centred on the drug. They enter into a pattern of alternating highs—when on the drug—and lows. During their lows, much of their thinking is focused on obtaining the drug and looking forward to their next high.

Addiction's Warning Signs Addictions to drugs—and alcohol—can begin subtly, and you may not be aware of the extent of the problem. Here are some signs that indicate when use becomes abuse:

- Feeling you need to be high to have a good time.
- Being high more often than not.
- Getting high to get yourself going.
- Going to class or work high.
- Missing class or work because you are high.

- Being unprepared for class because you are high.
- Feeling regret over something you did while you were high.
- Driving while high.
- Having a legal problem due to being high.
- Behaving, while high, in a way you wouldn't otherwise.
- Being high in nonsocial, solitary situations.
- Thinking about drugs or alcohol much of the time.
- Avoiding family or friends while using liquor or drugs.
- Hiding drug or alcohol use from others.

Any one of these symptoms indicates that you have a drug or alcohol problem. If you do have a problem, seek professional help. Addictions to illegal drugs or alcohol are extremely difficult to deal with on your own. No matter how good your intentions, few people can overcome the cravings brought about by an addiction to a particular substance without help.

Here are some places to which you can turn:

1. **College and university health services, counselling centres, and mental health centres.** Most schools provide services to help you overcome an addiction. They can evaluate the extent of the problem and refer you to the proper place for further help.

2. **Drug treatment centres and clinics.** Sometimes located in hospitals and sometimes independently run, drug treatment centres or clinics can provide help. You can also check your telephone book for a local listing of Alcoholics Anonymous or Narcotics Anonymous.

Sexual Health and Decision Making

Relationships, contraception, AIDS, rape—sexual health relates to a host of issues, involving not just your body but your heart and mind as well. In fact, it is often said that our most important sexual organ is our brain. It determines what we view as sexually arousing, and it's what we use to make decisions and choices about our sexuality.

Although the focus of the brief discussion of sexual health here is on strategies for protecting yourself (from pregnancy, sexually transmitted diseases, and rape), sexual decisions are also a reflection of your basic values. You can't make responsible decisions about sex without knowing what is important to you and how you view yourself. So you don't want to wait until a sexual encounter begins before thinking through your views of sexuality and what is and is not right for you.

Most campuses have health centres where students can see a nurse or doctor, access medical counselling, obtain birth control at reduced rates, or receive treatment, support, and information about issues such as abuse, date rape, and sexually transmitted diseases.

Preventing Unwanted Pregnancy

Abstinence

The avoidance of sexual contact

One and only one means of preventing pregnancy is totally effective. Don't have sexual intercourse. **Abstinence**, refraining from intercourse, only works, however, if you practise it without fail—something that many people find difficult. But it certainly is possible. Despite the folklore that insists "everybody's doing it," they're not. In fact, if you think critically about what others say about their sexual activity, you'll conclude that the possibility of misrepresentation of sexual activity is high.

Those who do want to have a sexual relationship can still avoid pregnancy. Many possibilities exist, including the following:

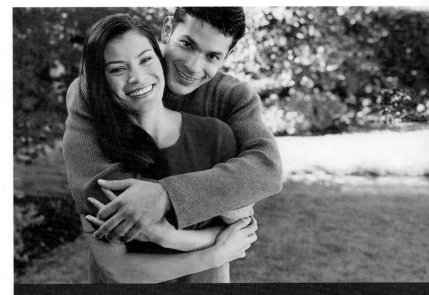

Relationships and sexuality raise substantial issues, involving your attitudes, beliefs, values, and emotions, as well as your body, in a complex intermix. Making responsible decisions requires that you know who you are and what's important to you.

- **Birth control pills.** Composed of artificial hormones, birth control pills are among the most effective ways of preventing pregnancy—as long as they are taken as prescribed. Except for women with particular medical conditions, the side effects are minimal.

- **Condoms.** Condoms are thin sheaths that fit over the penis. By preventing sperm from entering the vagina, they are highly effective in preventing pregnancy, if used properly and consistently. If they are positioned properly and are used with a contraceptive jelly that kills sperm, condoms are highly effective. Condoms, which can also protect against STDs, are readily available. A female condom is now available; although not as familiar or popular as other female contraceptive methods, it has the potential to be highly effective.

- **Depo-Provera injections.** A relatively new form of female birth control, Depo-Provera injections are long-lasting doses of progesterone that are given every three months. This contraceptive method is very effective (99.7 percent) and provides protection after 24 hours, but it does have some side effects that warrant investigation.

- **Implants**. One of the newest forms of birth control, Norplant implants work through a simple surgical procedure in which six tiny tubes are inserted into a woman's upper arm. Implants last for five years, preventing pregnancy for the entire time. With few side effects, implants are highly effective, but they are only practical for women who want to avoid pregnancy for extended times.

- **Intrauterine device, or IUD.** IUDs are small pieces of plastic inserted by a medical practitioner into a woman's uterus. Although highly effective, some have been found to produce unacceptable side effects, including infections and scarring that can make it impossible for a woman to get pregnant when she wants to.

- **Diaphragms and cervical caps.** Diaphragms and cervical caps are circular, dome-shaped pieces of thin rubber that a woman inserts into her vagina, covering the cervix. A sperm-killing cream or jelly must be used simultaneously, and the diaphragm and cervical cap must be removed after sexual intercourse. Although side effects are few, the risk of pregnancy is somewhat higher than with the other forms of birth control we've discussed; some 18 percent of women using them become pregnant. Diaphragms and cervical caps are prescribed by health care practitioners.

- **Contraceptive foam, jelly, gel.** These spermicides are most effective when combined with a condom, diaphragm, or other barrier method. When used with a condom, they are effective in preventing STDs. They are easily obtainable.

- **Contraceptive sponge.** The sponge, shaped like a large mushroom cap, is inserted into the vagina. It can be left in place for 24 hours, during which time it can be used for multiple acts of intercourse. Although it has few side effects, it has a failure rate of between 17 and 25 percent.

- **Emergency contraceptive pills.** Also known as the morning after pill, emergency contraceptive pills are taken within 72 hours of having unprotected sex. As a last resort, two doses of two pills (estrogen and progestin) are taken 12 hours apart. Severe nausea may result.

- **Rhythm.** The only form of birth control (besides abstinence) that involves no chemical or mechanical intervention, rhythm consists of refraining from intercourse during times in a woman's menstrual cycle when pregnancy is possible. With a failure rate of 20 percent, rhythm requires scrutiny of calendars, body temperature, or cervical mucus—all of which can be indicators of the time of the month to avoid intercourse.

- **Withdrawal and douching: ineffective birth control.** Withdrawal, in which a man removes his penis from a woman's vagina before climaxing, and douching, flushing the vagina with a liquid, just don't work. They should not be used for birth control because they are so ineffective.

- **Sterilization.** Sterilization is a surgical procedure that causes a person to become permanently incapable of having children. Vasectomies (for men) or tubal ligations (for women) are sometimes possible to reverse, but this method is not recommended for people who may decide to have children (or more children).

What You Can Do If You Are Pregnant

More than 40 percent of all pregnancies in Canada are unintended.[18] Usually unplanned pregnancies occur when contraception fails or people use it incorrectly. If you are one of the hundreds of thousands of Canadian women who unintentionally become pregnant every year, three options are available to you:

1. **Keeping your baby.** About half of unintentionally pregnant Canadian women keep their babies.[19] Not all unplanned babies are unwanted. But questions abound for the woman who is intending to keep her baby. Is the baby's father going to be involved in the child's life? To what degree? The baby is entitled to some financial support from the father, even if your relationship is over. Social assistance is an option for single parents; however, in Canada, 60 percent of single mothers and their families live in poverty.[20] Lifestyle, friends, relationships, and transportation are all subject to change when you become a parent.

2. **Adoption.** Although research indicates only about 2 percent of women in Canada choose to give up their babies for adoption,[21] it is an option that may be right for both you and your baby. New practices, such as open adoptions, allow birth mothers to choose adoptive parents for their child and permit ongoing contact.

3. **Abortion.** About 22 percent of pregnancies in Canada end in an induced abortion, a medical procedure that is legally available in all provinces and territories, except Prince Edward Island.[22] In 1995, almost 107 000 abortions were performed in Canada.[23] In 1995, 52 percent of all abortions in Canada were obtained by females between 20 and 29.

Twenty percent were obtained by women younger than 20. Three types of medical abortions are used, depending on how long the woman has been pregnant. Dilation and curettage (D&C) accounts for 90 percent of all medical abortions performed in the first 12 weeks of pregnancy. The dilation-evacuation-curettage (DEC) procedure is used after the 12th week, along with a late-term method, hormone-saline injection. The "abortion pill" RU-486, which is widely available in Europe, is currently undergoing clinical testing in Canada.

Medical abortions are medically very safe; however, emotional responses to abortion vary, depending on the woman and her values, religion, relationship with the child's father, and support systems. If you are contemplating abortion, you should carefully consider your psychological state and seek counselling and support if you need it afterward.

What You Can Do to Avoid Sexually Transmitted Diseases

Sexually transmitted diseases (STDs) threaten the general health, well-being, and reproductive ability of a sizable number of Canadians. It is difficult to determine how many Canadians have STDs, as many of the symptoms are mild enough to avoid detection (and reporting). While rates of chlamydia, syphilis, and gonorrhea are declining somewhat in Canada, viral STDs, such as herpes simplex, human papilloma virus (HPV), and HIV/AIDS are increasing.[24] For a list of common STDs, please go to the Online Learning Centre at www.mcgrawhill.ca/olc/power.

There are many varieties of STDs, although all share a similar origin: sexual contact. Depending on the type of disease, symptoms may include warts in the genital area, pelvic infection, painful urination, infertility, blindness, and even death.

The STD that has had the greatest impact in the past two decades is **acquired immune deficiency syndrome (AIDS)**. Although it started as a disease that most often affected homosexuals, AIDS quickly spread among heterosexuals. Some populations are particularly affected, such as intravenous drug users. Worldwide, more than six million people have already died from the disease. Some estimates suggest that 40 million people now carry the AIDS virus.

Although AIDS is the best-known STD, the most common is *chlamydia*, a disease that if left untreated can cause sterility in some victims. *Genital herpes* is a virus that appears as small blisters or sores around the genitals. Although the sores heal after several weeks, the disease can remain dormant and reappear periodically. Other STDs, although somewhat less common, also afflict millions of people.

It's no secret how to avoid AIDS and other STDs. Abstinence—the avoidance of sexual contact—is completely effective. However, many people are unwilling to make such a choice. Several alternative approaches, called "smart sex" practices, reduce the risk of contracting STDs. They include the following:

- **Know your sexual partner—well.** You should not have sexual contact with a person who is only a casual acquaintance. You want to know the person well enough to have a discussion with him or her in which you both talk about your sexual histories.

Sexually transmitted diseases (STDs)
Medical conditions acquired through sexual contact

Acquired immune deficiency syndrome (AIDS)
A lethal, sexually transmitted disease that causes the destruction of the body's immune system

- **Prevent the exchange of bodily fluids during all sex acts.** Avoid semen and unprotected anal and vaginal intercourse and oral sex.
- **Use condoms.** Condoms not only prevent the spread of AIDS and other STDs, but they also prevent pregnancy.
- **Be faithful to a single partner.** People in long-term relationships with only one other individual are less likely to contract AIDS and other STDs than those with multiple sexual partners.

Date Rape

We usually think of rape as a rare crime, committed by strangers. However, after the age of 18, 1 in every 4 women and 1 in 10 men will be sexually assaulted; 14 to 25 percent of female students will be victims of sexual assault during their university careers. Unfortunately, not only is rape surprisingly common, but rapists usually know their victims. The University of Alberta Health Centre reports that more than 80 percent of rapes that occur on university and college campuses are committed by someone the victim knows, and 50 percent occur on dates. Many of these assaults, categorized as **date rape,** happen during the first eight weeks of classes and most involve the use of alcohol. Between 15 and 30 percent of women attending university report experiencing acquaintance rape.[25]

What leads to rape? Most often, rape has less to do with sex than with power and anger. Rapists use forced sex to demonstrate their power and control over the victim. The rapist's pleasure comes not so much from sex as from forcing someone to submit.

In addition, rapes sometimes are brought about by the common—but untrue—belief that when people offer resistance to sex, they don't really mean it. If a man holds the view that when a woman says no to sex, she really means yes, he is likely to ignore the woman's protests that she doesn't want sex, resulting in rape. Some men may even believe that it is unmasculine to accept no for an answer, perhaps because they feel it is a rejection of them as men.

Whatever the causes, rape is devastating to the victim. Victims experience extreme anxiety, disbelief, fear, and shock. These reactions may linger for years, and rape victims may experience suspiciousness and a fear of entering into relationships.

Both men and women must be sensitive to the issue of date rape. Among the suggestions for reducing its incidence are the following:

- **Set limits.** Everyone has the right to set limits, and these should be communicated clearly, firmly, and early.
- **No means no.** When a partner says no, it means nothing other than no.
- **Be assertive.** You should never passively accept being pressured into an activity in which you don't want to engage. Remember that passivity may be interpreted as consent.
- **Communicate.** Partners should talk about their views of sexual behaviour and what is and is not permissible.
- **Keep in mind that alcohol and drugs cloud judgment.** Nothing hinders communication more than alcohol and drugs.
- **Be careful when you go to bars and parties.** Never accept drinks or opened cans from others or leave drinks unattended, as they can easily be spiked with date rape drugs, such as Rohypnol or GHB.

Date rape

Forced sex in which the rapist is a date or romantic acquaintance

Speaking of Success

Krista Bailey

Emergency Medical Technician Certificate, Saskatchewan Institute of Applied Science and Technology Emergency Medical Technician, Paramedic Diploma, Saskatchewan Institute of Applied Science and Technology

Determination and enthusiasm describe Krista Bailey and undoubtedly these characteristics help her save lives in her demanding career as a paramedic with Edmonton Emergency Medical Services.

Born and raised in Saskatchewan, Krista was the assistant aquatic director and senior guard at the Regina YWCA when a friend invited her to ride along on a shift with an ambulance crew. Krista was hooked and enrolled in the Saskatchewan Institute of Applied Science and Technology's Emergency Medical Technician (EMT) program.

One of her most memorable calls as an EMT involved a 2-year-old girl named Karlee Kosolofski, who survived after being found outdoors, frozen solid. Karlee was clinically dead when taken to the hospital, but the emergency medical treatment the girl received and her survival taught Krista to "never give up."

After four years of working as an EMT, Krista went back to SIAST to become a

paramedic, graduating in 1995. Her advanced standing as a paramedic gave her more opportunities to lead the calls she attended and to administer drugs and perform restricted procedures. In addition, Krista took on responsibilities as a field trainer and a relief supervisor.

In January 2001, Krista moved to Edmonton. She was drawn to the city for its active lifestyle. Krista appreciates the bike paths and opportunities to roller blade and run on her time off. However, Edmonton is also a larger centre with a much busier emergency medical service and because of Alberta's medical direction, the responsibilities of paramedics are greater and more comprehensive. Changing provinces meant becoming certified in Alberta, and Krista passed the exams with honours.

Shortly after beginning to work for Edmonton Emergency Medical Services,

Krista and partner, Justin Mazzolini, attended a call that was eerily similar to Karlee Kosolofski's case seven years earlier. A 13-month-old toddler, Erika Nordby, had been found frozen solid. Krista says she felt "a sense of peace" while dealing with Erika. "Everyone did their jobs and did them well." Erika not only lived, but she also exceeded all expectations of the medical team that treated her at the University of Alberta Hospital.

Krista, who is now a superintendent with Edmonton EMS, enjoys her job, as there is always a lot to learn. There are plenty of opportunities for in-service professional development, but formal education is on the back burner for the present, as Krista is beginning a new stage of her life as a wife and mother. Undoubtedly, Krista's calm and positive attitude will lead to continued success in all her important roles.

What is stress and how can I control it?

- Stress is a common experience, appearing in three main forms: cataclysmic events, personal stressors, and daily hassles. Excessive stress is not only unpleasant and upsetting, it also has negative effects on the body and mind.

What is involved in keeping fit and healthy, and why is it important for me to do so?

- For all people, keeping fit and healthy is both essential and challenging. It is vital to learn to eat properly, especially by eating a variety of foods on a regular schedule and by restricting your intake of fat, cholesterol, and salt.

- Exercise is valuable because it improves health and well-being. Choosing exercises that we like, making everyday activities a part of exercise, and exercising with others can help form the habit of exercise.

- The third key element of good health is sleeping properly. Good exercise and eating habits can contribute to sound sleep, as can the development of regular sleeping habits and the use of sleep-assisting practices.

- Coping with stress involves becoming prepared for future stress through proper diet and exercise, identifying the causes of stress in your life, taking control of stress, seeking social support, practising relaxation techniques, training yourself to redefine and reinterpret stressful situations, and keeping your promises.

What are the main threats to my health and well-being?

- One of the major threats that postsecondary students (and others) face is the improper use of drugs. The most commonly abused drug is alcohol, which is a depressant (despite an initial reduction of inhibitions and feeling of euphoria) and can lead to a physical or psychological dependence. Nicotine is the second most commonly abused drug.

- The use of illegal drugs presents not only potential dangers related to law-breaking and prosecution, but short- and long-term health risks as well. Drugs cause a reduction in awareness and involvement in life, and some drugs can be dangerously addictive.

What are the components of sexual health?

- Sexual health is as important as other forms of health. People must make their own individual decisions about their sexuality and how they will express it.

- Many forms of contraception are available, ranging from abstinence to surgical implants. Each form has different procedures, risks, and effectiveness.

- The incidence of sexually transmitted diseases (STDs) is high in Canada, with about 25 percent of the population experiencing an STD at some point in life.

- Rape is a surprisingly common crime, with most victims knowing the rapist—often in a circumstance known as date rape.

P.O.W.E.R. Portfolio

Stress, Health, and Growth

1. How do you deal with stress in your life? Is it by playing sports? working out at the gym? playing guitar? canoeing in wilderness preserves? practising yoga? Reflect on how your stress-management approach has helped you deal with the pressures of university or college. If you can describe *and* demonstrate how you manage stress in the fast-paced academic world, with multiple assignments, self-directed study, strict time frames, and critical evaluation, you may be able to convince an employer that you are ready for the pressures of a career! Consider including photographs of various activities, such as rock climbing, skiing, construction projects, gardens, or musical events to add variety and creativity to your portfolio.

2. Include a reflective analysis on the theme of health and wellness, including a personal assessment. Consider adding visual elements as well.

3. What training have you done or certificates and/or licences have you attained that would demonstrate your awareness of health and safety—WHMIS, CPR, first aid, bronze medallion, Smart Serve? Include evidence of these with a reflective statement on the importance of safety in various situations.

4. Create a PowerPoint presentation or poster session on some aspect of this chapter and include the disk in your portfolio along with a photograph and reflection.

Resources

On Campus

Your campus health service/medical provider is the first line of defence if you become ill. The staff can provide you with advice and often medical care. Furthermore, colleges and universities often have health education offices that help educate students on safer sex practices, on how to eat in healthier ways, and generally on how to increase wellness. Finally, schools sometimes offer stress reduction workshops to help students cope more effectively.

In Print

The title says it all: *The New York Times Book of Health: How to Feel Fitter, Eat Better, and Live Longer* (Times Books, 1998), by Jane Brody, provides an up-to-date, common-sense guide to living well.

Why Zebras Don't Get Ulcers: An Updated Guide to Stress, Stress-Related Diseases, and Coping (Owl Books, 3rd edition, 2004), by Robert M. Sapolsky, offers an entertaining guide to both the reasons we experience stress and ways of coping with it.

Sue Johanson's *Sex, Sex, and More Sex* (Regan Books, 2004) provides clear-headed, no-nonsense answers to some of the most frequently asked questions about sex, intimacy, and relationships. Readers of all ages and sexual orientations will discover that no question or topic is taboo for Canada's "sex lady."

On the Web

The following sites on the World Wide Web provide the opportunity to extend your learning about the material in this chapter. Although the Web addresses were accurate at the time the book was printed, check the P.O.W.E.R. Learning website, <www.mcgrawhill.ca/olc/power>, for any changes that may have occurred.

www.hc-sc.gc.ca/hppb/nutrition/pube/foodguid/index.html
Canada's *Food Guide to Healthy Eating* offers suggestions on healthy eating, vitamin supplements, and a food checklist.

www.uofaweb.ualberta.ca/healthinfo/
A comprehensive site on all aspects of student health concerns including interactive software on AIDS, alcohol, birth control, stress, STDs, and nutrition that can be downloaded.

http://canadaonline.about.com/aboutcanada/canadaonline/library/weekly/aa050997.htm
This Canada Online stress-management site gives lots of helpful information and links to a large variety of stress-busting sites.

www.campusaccess.com/campus_web/health/h3fit_expert.htm
Campusaccess has a fitness site with experts who will answer questions about bodybuilding, nutrition, vitamins, etc. It also links to the Campusaccess home page, which has many interesting sections relating to college life and postsecondary concerns.

www.mirror-mirror.org/eatdis.htm
This guide to eating disorders provides definitions, coping strategies, links to related organizations, and personal messages from survivors as well as information related to eating disorders.

The Case Of...

Grievous Bodily Harm

It started out innocently as a thank-you bash for volunteers after an all-day orientation event to raise money for charity. Andrea and her roommate, Jessalyn, both unfamiliar with their campus and both a little shy, went together for "mutual support."

The party was great—school spirit was high and people were so friendly. Andrea and Jessalyn gradually started mixing with other students from their own programs. Andrea was happy when the DJ started playing dance music, and danced steadily for about 45 minutes with a nice guy named Casey. As she drank the beer that Casey had brought her, Andrea waved across the room at Jessalyn. She was feeling a little light-headed and very relaxed.

The next morning, Andrea awoke in a strange bed, naked and feeling desperately sick. Beside her was a stranger. He said his name was Casey, said they'd hit it off at the party the night before and had come back to his place to continue to party—privately. Andrea just stared at him in disbelief. What was he talking about? Who was he? Why was she here? Where were her clothes? What time was it? What had happened to her?

As Andrea tried to get up and go into the bathroom, Casey started to touch her—he said she'd been a little unresponsive the night before, said he'd like to see a little more action. What was he saying ... that she had had sex with him? Andrea couldn't believe it; she was a virgin! Her face burning with embarrassment and tears filling her eyes, Andrea bolted into the bathroom, quickly dressed, and left, not saying a word. As she left the building, she realized she was in the residence beside her own. At least she'd be home soon.

As she let herself into her room, Jessalyn called out, "Hey, how are you? You left so suddenly with that guy—you must have really hit it off with him."

Andrea started to cry. "You saw me leave with him? You know I don't pick up guys at parties."

"Hey, An. I thought you really liked him. When you left, he was all over you, and you seemed okay with it," her roommate replied.

As she continued crying, Andrea sobbed, "You know me better than that, Jess. I wouldn't leave you without letting you know when I'd be home or where I was going. He says we had sex, but I can't remember a thing. I just want to have a bath, go to bed, and wake up knowing that this was just a bad dream."

1. What happened to Andrea?
2. What should Andrea and Jessalyn do now?
3. What were some warning signs that Andrea and Jessalyn could have tuned in to?
4. What should happen to Casey?
5. What is the school's responsibility in this situation?

Money Matters

14

hy do tours of Ottawa have to be boring? thought Derek Johnson as he picked up the Kilpatricks at their hotel. His parents, now living in Nanaimo, had asked him to show their friends around the capital district. Three hours later, the Kilpatricks told Derek that he was the best tour guide they'd ever had. A plan started forming. With summer and the heaviest tourist season coming up in a few months, perhaps Derek could skip looking for a job and go into business for himself.

With a $5,000 young entrepreneur loan from Industry Canada, Derek leased a passenger van and started squiring small specialty tours around Ottawa, up into the Gatineau Hills, and even to Algonquin Park. That summer he made enough money to pay next year's tuition, and he lined up enough business to pay the bills over the fall and winter. Derek was ecstatic—he made great tips; his tours were unique; his customers felt like VIPs. He took a few business courses and by the following summer, his organization and marketing were much improved. Derek was able to lease two vans, rent a small office, and hire another driver and tour guide. He discovered he liked being his own boss and that his young and fresh perspective on touring was a hit with customers.

Five years later Derek's firm, *Bytown Bus*, has served more than 300 000 visitors and he has a staff of 10 energetic, enthusiastic tour guides who are committed to providing the best and most entertaining tours of the Ottawa area. Derek doesn't drive the vans much any more—but he certainly enjoys driving his Lexus LX 470!

Looking ▶▶ *Ahead*

Money problems aren't often solved as readily as they were for Derek Johnson. And, even under the best of circumstances, our finances present us with challenges that affect many facets of our lives. Money often plays a large role in where we go to school, where we live, and what jobs we take. It is the source of many of our problems and much of our stress, forcing us to find a balance between what we need and what we want.

This chapter will show you how to manage your money. It begins by discussing the process of preparing a budget and identifying your financial goals—the basis for money management. The chapter goes on to examine ways you can keep track of your expenditures and estimate your financial needs and resources, and it discusses ways to exercise control over your spending habits and save money.

Education is one of the largest financial expenditures anyone encounters in life. Knowing the best ways to meet the costs of a postsecondary education—finding loans, grants, and scholarships—can give your finances a big boost and help you avoid graduating with thousands of dollars of debt. You will also learn what to do if your personal finances get out of control and how to stop the downward spiral of unpaid bills, defaulted loans, and unfavourable credit ratings. The chapter ends by suggesting ways to develop a financial philosophy.

After reading this chapter you'll be able to answer these questions:

- **What purpose does a budget serve and how can you prepare and stick to one?**

- **What help is available to pay for your higher education?**

- **What can you do if you fall into financial difficulty?**

Managing Your Money

Money management is a huge issue for Canadian postsecondary students. Most college students are worried about having enough money to complete their higher education. While over half of all students receive financial assistance from their families and almost half receive government funding (from bursaries, loans, or scholarships) the majority of Canadian students work in the summer to help pay for school, and 60 percent of students hold part-time or full-time jobs during the year to finance their education. However, the reality is that in 2003, six out of 10 students enrolled in community colleges anticipate graduating with debt; over 50 percent expect their debt loads will be $10,000 or more.

In addition to tuition fees and the costs of textbooks and other related school supplies that every postsecondary student expects to pay, almost one in five Canadian college students have dependants. Students with dependants, especially child dependants, know that almost everything about college is costlier—from housing to food to clothing to transportation to daycare expenses. It's no wonder almost 30 percent of Canadian college students are very worried about having enough money to complete school.[1]

> "Education costs money, but then so does ignorance."
>
> Claus Moser

If you have money concerns—and there's virtually no one who doesn't have at least *some* worries about finances—the solution is to develop a budget. A **budget** is a formal plan that accounts and plans for expenditures and income. Taking your goals into account, a budget helps determine how much money you should be spending each month, based on your income and your other financial resources. Budgets also help prepare for unexpected occurrences that would reduce your income, such as the loss of a part-time job or an illness, or for sudden, unanticipated expenses, such as a major car repair or needing to purchase a new computer.

Budget
A formal plan that accounts for expenditures and income

Although all budgets are based on an uncomplicated premise—expenditures should not exceed income—budgeting is not simple, particularly when you are a student. Several times during the year require especially large expenditures,

Keeping to a budget is a constant balancing act. For example, even though you know you'll need to purchase books at the start of each semester, you can't predict exactly how much they'll cost

Career Connections

Budgeting on the Job

If you've ever held a job, the salary you received was determined, in part, by your employer's budget.

Although they may not always be accessible to every employee, budgets are part of the world of work. Regardless of who the employer is—be it a small dry-cleaning store or the massive federal government—the organization undoubtedly has a budget outlining anticipated income and expenditures. Managers are expected to keep to the budget, and if their expenditures exceed what is budgeted, they are held accountable.

For this reason, the ability to create and live within a budget is an important skill to acquire. Not only will it help keep your own finances under control, but it will also prepare you to be financially responsible and savvy on the job—qualities that are highly valued by employers.

With e-business, e-banking, and e-trading, computerized finances are available to almost everyone in Canada. Numerous budgeting software applications are used by Canadian companies and you can get a head start by learning a software program and maintaining your finances on your computer.

> Entrepreneurship is the generator of most new jobs in Canada today. However, if you plan to start a business or buy a business, you need to create a business plan that includes a detailed budget. The Canada Businesses Services Centre has an Interactive Business Planner at: <www.cbsc.org/ibp/>. Similar versions are available online or on CD-ROM from most major banks.

such as the start of a semester, when you must pay your tuition and purchase books. Furthermore, income is erratic; it is often lower during the school year and higher during the summers. But a budget will help you deal with the ups and downs of income and expenditures, smoothing the curves and extending your view toward the horizon. Learning budgeting skills also helps prepare you for the world of work, of which budgeting is an important aspect, as discussed in Career Connections, "Budgeting on the Job."

Most of all, a budget provides security. It will let you take control of your money, permitting you to spend it as you need to without guilt because you have planned for the expenditure. It also makes it easier to put money aside because you know that your current financial sacrifice will be rewarded later, when you can make a purchase that you've been planning for.

Budgeting is very personal: What is appropriate for one person doesn't work for another. For a few people, keeping track of their spending comes naturally; they enjoy accounting for every dollar that passes through their hands. For most people, though, developing a budget—and sticking to it—does not come easily.

However, if you follow several basic steps—illustrated in the P.O.W.E.R. Plan—the process of budgeting is straightforward.

P repare: Identifying Your Financial Goals

Your first reaction when asked to identify your financial goals may be that the question is a no-brainer. You want to have more money to spend. But it's not that simple. You need to ask yourself why you want more money. What would you spend it on? What would bring you the most satisfaction? Purchasing a DVD player? Paying off your debt? Saving money for a vacation? Starting a business? Paying for college or university rather than taking out loans?

You won't be able to develop a budget that will work for you until you determine your short- and long-term financial goals. To determine them, use Try It! 1, "Identify Your Financial Goals," on page 358.

Organize: Determining Your Expenditures and Income

Have you ever opened your wallet for the $10 that was there yesterday and found only a loonie? Spending money without realizing it is a common affliction.

There's only one way to get a handle on where your money is going. Keep track of it. To get an overview of your expenditures, go through any records you've kept to identify where you've spent money for the last year—old cheques, rent and utility receipts, and previous college tuition can help you.

In addition, keep track of everything you spend for a week. Everything. When you spend $1.25 for a candy bar from a vending machine, write it down. When you buy lunch for $2.97 at a fast-food restaurant, write it down. When you buy a 49-cent postcard, write it down.

Record your expenditures in a small notebook that you carry with you all the time. It may be tedious, but you're doing it for only a week. And it will be eye-opening. People are usually surprised at how much they spend on little items without even thinking about it.

Finally, make a list of everything you think you'll need to spend over the next year. Some items are easy to think of, such as rent and tuition payments, because

Journal REFLECTIONS

My Sense of Cents

Answer the following questions about your financial sense.

1. How much money do you now have in your pockets and wallet? (Guess first, then look.) How close did you come? Explain how your answers reflect the importance of money in your life.

2. Do you know how much money you typically spend in a month on all expenditures, including food, lodging, and other items?

3. How much money do you estimate is needed each term for your college or university expenses, including tuition and books?

4. How would you rate yourself with regard to your ability to manage your money responsibly? What improvements are needed in this area?

5. What methods do you use to plan for future expenses? How effective have these methods been for you?

6. What are your short-term and long-term financial goals?

7. What immediate strategies would you use if you suddenly found yourself in a financial crisis and didn't have enough money to meet your obligations?

Working in a Group:
Identify Your Financial Goals

Prepare: The purpose of this exercise is to identify and organize your financial goals.

Organize: Use the planning tools provided below.

Work: Use the categories to identify and organize your short-term, mid-range, and long-range financial goals, Then use the tables provided in the text and online to estimate your expenditures and your estimated income for the next 12 months.

Evaluate: Were you able to construct a budget that matches your expenditures and income?

Rethink: Can you identify opportunities to use these tools in the future?

Short-Term Goals

What would you like to have money for in the short term (over the next three months)? Consider these categories:

Personal necessities (such as food, clothes, household supplies, day care costs, shelter, transportation, loan payments, debts, medical expenses):

Educational necessities (such as tuition, fees, books, school supplies):

Social needs (for example, getting together with family, friends, and others; charitable contributions; clubs; teams; entertainment):

Lifestyle improvements (for example, optional but desirable personal or educational tools, computer hardware and software, living space improvements, transportation improvements, clothing):

Other:

Mid-Range Goals

What would you like to have money for soon, but not immediately (three months to a year from now), but not immediately? Use the same categories:

Personal necessities:

Educational necessities:

Social needs:

Lifestyle improvements:

Other:

Long-Range Goals

What would you like to have money for one to three years from now? Use the same categories:

Personal necessities:

Educational necessities:

Social needs:

Lifestyle improvements:

Other:

STEP 2: Now put each of your lists in priority order, arranging items in each list across the categories.

Short-Term Priorities:

Mid-Range Priorities:

Long-Range Priorities:

After you've completed prioritizing your financial goals, consider these questions: What does the list tell you about what is important to you? Did you find any surprises? Would you classify yourself as a financial risk taker or someone who values financial security?

Working in a group, compare your priorities with those of your classmates. What similarities and differences can you find, and what can you learn from others' priorities?

To Try It! online, go to **www.mcgrawhill.ca/olc/power.**

Table 14.1

Estimated Expenditures for the Next 12 Months

Category	0–3 months from now	3–6 months from now	6–9 months from now	9–12 months from now
Personal Necessities				
Food				
Clothing				
Shelter (rent, utilities, etc.)				
Household supplies				
Transportation (car payments, gas, repairs, bus tickets, etc.)				
Loan and debt payments				
Medical expenses				
Childcare costs				
Other				
Educational Necessities				
Tuition and fees				
Books				
Computer costs				
Other				
Social Needs				
Relationships				
Clubs and teams				
Charitable contributions (church, food drives, donations, etc.)				
Presents (weddings, birthdays, etc.)				
Other				
Entertainment				
Movies and shows				
Trips				
Recreation and sports				
Eating out				
Gambling (lottery tickets, Pro-Line, etc.)				
Bars/Parties				
Lifestyle Improvements				
Educational				
Living space				
Computer				
Transportation				
Clothing				
Other				
TOTAL				

they occur regularly and the amount you pay is fixed. Others are harder to budget for because they can vary substantially. For example, the price of gasoline changes frequently. If you have a long commute, the changing price of gasoline can cause substantial variation in what you pay each month. Similarly, the cost of books varies considerably from one term to another. (Use Table 14.1 on page 360 to estimate your expenditures for the coming year.)

Determine Your Income Sources You probably have a pretty good idea of how much money you have each month. But it's as important to list each source of income as it is to account for everything you spend.

Add up what you make from any jobs you hold. Also list any support you receive from family members, including occasional gifts you might get from relatives. Finally, include any financial aid (such as tuition reductions, loan payments, or scholarships) you receive from your college or university. Use Table 14.2 to record this information. When you do, be sure to list the amounts you receive in terms of after-tax income.

Work: Making a Budget That Adds Up

If you've prepared and organized your budget, actually constructing your budget is as easy as adding 2 + 2. Well, not exactly, the numbers will be larger. But all you need to do is add up your list of expenses, and then add up your sources of income. In a perfect world, the two numbers will be equal.

But most of the time, the world is not perfect. Most of us find that expenditures are larger than our income. After all, if we had plenty of excess cash, we probably wouldn't be bothering to make a budget in the first place.

PREPARE

Identify financial goals

ORGANIZE

Determine expenditures and income

WORK

Make a budget that adds up

EVALUATE

Review the budget

RETHINK

Rethink financial options

P.O.W.E.R Plan

Table 14.2
Estimated Income in the Next 12 Months

Category	0–3 months from now	3–6 months from now	6–9 months from now	9–12 months from now
Wages				
Family support				
Financial aid				
Loan income				
Scholarship payments				
Other				
Interest and dividends				
Gifts				
Other				
TOTAL				

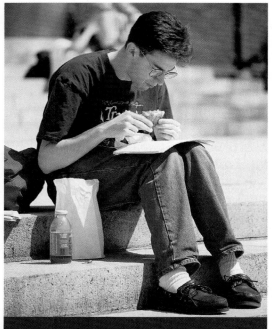

Bag it! One way to cut down on expenditures is to reduce everyday expenses, such as by making your own lunch, rather than grabbing a bite at a campus snack bar. Even small savings like this can add up fast.

If you find you spend more than you make, there are only two things to do: decrease your spending or increase your income. It's often easiest to decrease expenditures, because your expenses tend to be more under your control. For instance, there are many things you can do to save money, including the following:

- **Control impulse buying.** When you shop for groceries, always take a list with you, and don't shop when you're hungry.

- **Make and take your own lunch.** Brown-bag lunches can save you a substantial amount of money over purchasing your lunches, even if you go to a fast-food restaurant or snack bar.

- **Read the daily newspaper and magazines at the library.** College libraries subscribe to virtually every daily newspaper and magazine that you could want.

- **Check bills for errors.** Computers make mistakes, and so do the people who enter the data into them. So make sure that your charges on any bill are accurate.

- **Cut up your credit cards and pay cash.** Using a credit card is seductive; when you take out your plastic, it's easy to feel as if you're not really spending money. If you use cash for purchases instead, you'll see the money going out.

- **Make major purchases only during sales.** Plan major purchases so they coincide with sales.

- **Share and trade.** Pool your resources with friends. Car pool, share resources such as computers, and trade CDs.

- **Live more simply.** Do you really need a cellular phone or beeper? Is cable TV an absolute necessity? Is it really necessary to eat out once a week? Do you buy clothes because you need them or because you want them?

- **Do well in your classes.** One of the best ways to save money is to get good grades, because you avoid the hidden costs of poor performance. If you are forced to repeat a class because of a low grade, you'll have to take another course in the future as a substitute, and that may be an added expense. Doing well avoids the possibility of additional tuition costs.

There are as many ways to save money as there are people looking to save it. But keep in mind that saving money should not necessarily be an end in itself. Don't spend hours thinking of ways to save a dime, and don't get upset about situations where you are forced to spend money. The goal is to bring your budget into balance, not to become a tightwad who keeps track of every penny and feels that spending money is a personal failure. To help you get started, get a sense of your current style of saving money in Try It! 2, "Determine Your Saving Style."

Finally, it's important to remember that budgets may be brought into balance not only by decreasing expenditures, but also by increasing income. The most direct way to increase income is to get a part-time job if you don't already have one.

Many students work during school. Although it adds to the time-management challenges you will face, working does not mean that your grades

2

Personal Styles: Determine Your Saving Style

Prepare: The purpose of this exercise is to help you identify your saving style. Is it loose, nonexistent, or careful?

Organize: You will need the saving style scale below. It is also available online.

Work: Answer the questions and find and interpret your total score.

Evaluate: Does your saving style match your financial needs and your financial goals? If not, something needs to change. What changes can be made in your saving habits?

Rethink: Are you comfortable with how you mange your savings? Do you need to repeat this analysis periodically to ensure you are on track?

Read each of the following statements and rate how well it describes you, using this scale:

1 = That's me

2 = Sometimes

3 = That's not me

	1	2	3
1. I count the change I'm given by cashiers in stores and restaurants.			
2. I always pick up all the change I receive from a transaction in a store, even if it's only a few cents.			
3. I don't buy something right away if I'm pretty sure it will go on sale soon.			
4. I feel a real sense of accomplishment if I buy something on sale.			
5. I always remember how much I paid for something.			
6. If something goes on sale soon after I bought it, I feel cheated.			
7. I have money in at least one interest-bearing bank account.			
8. I rarely lend people money.			
9. If I lend money to someone repeatedly without getting it back, I stop lending it to that person.			
10. I share resources (e.g., CDs, books, magazines) with other people to save money.			
11. I'm good at putting money away for big items that I really want.			
12. I believe most generic or off-brand items are just as good as name brands.			

Add up your ratings. Interpret your total score according to this informal guide:

12–15: Very aggressive saving style

16–20: Careful saving style

21–27: Fairly loose saving style

28–32: Loose saving style

33–36: Nonexistent saving style

To Try It online, go to **www.mcgrawhill.ca/olc/power.**

will necessarily suffer. In fact, many students who work do better in school than those who don't work, because those with jobs need to be more disciplined and focused. In addition, a part-time job in an area related to your future career may prove to be helpful in getting a job after you graduate.

Considering part-time work is often a better strategy for dealing with budget shortfalls than taking out a loan. Because student loans are relatively simple to get, it's easy to use them as a crutch. Loans can be a help in an emergency or if you couldn't afford to attend college without them. If you do take out a loan, remind yourself: one day soon you'll have to pay it back, with interest.

E valuate: Reviewing Your Budget

Budgets are not meant to be set in stone. You should review where you stand financially each month. Only by monitoring how closely actual expenditures and income match your budget projections will you be able to maintain control of your finances.

You don't need to continually keep track of every penny you spend to evaluate your success in budgeting. As you gain more experience with your budget, you'll begin to get a better sense of your finances. You'll know when it may be possible to consider splurging on a gift for a friend, and when you need to operate in penny-pinching mode.

The important thing is to keep your expenditures under control. Review, and if necessary revise, your budget to fit any changes in circumstances. Maybe you receive a raise in a part-time job. Maybe the financial aid office gives you more support than you expected. Or maybe you face a reduction in income. Whatever the change in circumstances, evaluate how it affects your budget, and revise the budget accordingly.

R ethink: Reconsidering Your Financial Options

If all goes well, the process of budgeting will put you in control of your financial life. Your expenditures will match your income, and you won't face major money worries.

In the real world, of course, events have a way of inflicting disaster on even the best-laid plans:

- You lose your job and can't afford to pay next semester's tuition.
- Your roommate moves out and leaves you with an $800 phone bill. You don't have $800.
- Your parents, who have promised to pay for your education, run into financial difficulties and say they can't afford to pay your tuition any longer.
- Your car breaks down, and repairing it will cost $1,500. If you don't have a car, you can't get to campus. But if you pay for repairs, you can't afford tuition.

All of us face financial difficulties at one time or another. Sometimes it happens suddenly and without warning. Other times people sink more gradually into

Table 14.3

Steps in Dealing with
Financial Difficulties

Assess the Problem	Make a list of what you owe and to whom.
	Figure out a reasonable amount you can put toward each debt.
	Work out a specific plan.
Contact Each of Your Creditors	Start with your bank, credit card companies, and landlord.
	Explain the situation.
	Show them your plan to pay off debt.
See a Credit Counsellor	If you cannot work out a repayment plan on your own, visit a credit counselling service.
Stick to the Plan	Once you have a plan, make a commitment to stick to it.
	Your bank or creditor can help you identify a credit counsellor.

financial problems, each month accumulating more debt until they reach a point at which they can't pay their bills.

However it happens, finding yourself with too little money to pay your bills requires action. You need to confront the situation and take steps to solve the problem. The worst thing to do is nothing. Hiding from those to whom you owe money makes the situation worse. Your creditors—the institutions and people to whom you owe money—will assume that you don't care, and they'll be spurred on to take harsher actions.

These are the steps to take if you do find yourself with financial difficulties (also see Table 14.3):

- **Assess the problem.** Make a list of what you owe and to whom. Look at the bottom line and figure out a reasonable amount you can put toward each debt. Work out a specific plan that can lead you out of the situation.

- **Contact each of your creditors**. Start with your bank, credit card companies, and landlord, and continue through each creditor. It's best to visit personally, but a phone call will do.

When you speak with them, explain the situation. If the problem is due to illness or unemployment, let them know. If it's due to overspending, let them know that. Tell them what you plan to do to pay off your debt, and show them your plan. The fact that you have a plan demonstrates not only what you intend to do, but also that you are serious about your situation and capable of financial planning.

If you've had a clean financial record in the past, your creditors may be willing to agree to your plan. Ultimately, it is cheaper for them to accept smaller payments over a longer time than to hire a collection agency.

- **See a credit counsellor.** If you can't work out a repayment plan on your own, visit a credit counselling service. These are nonprofit organizations that help people who find themselves in financial trouble. Visit Industry Canada's Business and Consumer website for information about credit counselling services in your area at <**http://strategis.ic.gc.ca/epic/internet/ inoca-bc.nsf/en/ca01514e.html**>.

- **Stick to the plan.** Once you have a plan to get yourself out of debt, follow it. Unless you diligently make the payments you commit to, you'll find your debt spiralling out of control once again. It's essential, then, to regard your plan as a firm commitment and stick to it.

Credit Cards

"Congratulations! You've been preapproved for a Gold credit card! Just send us your signature on the enclosed authorization form, and we'll rush you your card."

Have you ever received such a letter in the mail? If so, you're far from the only one. Millions of people in Canada are regularly enticed to receive credit cards in just such a manner, and college or university students are especially attractive targets. In fact, during orientation or frosh week, several major credit card companies hold special promotions on campus in hopes of signing up new cardholders. In many cases, it doesn't even matter whether you have income; the mere fact that you're a postsecondary student is sufficient to win you approval to receive a card.

Credit cards are not necessarily bad. In fact, used appropriately, they can help get you through brief periods when you must make a purchase—such as a car tire to replace an unexpected flat—but temporarily don't have enough money to do so. But there are questions you should ask when deciding whether to get and use a credit card:

1. **Is there an annual fee?** Many cards charge an annual fee, ranging from $20 a year to $100 a year, although some are free. You need to determine if the advantages of the card are worth the cost of an annual fee.

2. **Do I need a credit card?** There are good reasons for getting a credit card, and bad reasons.

The Pluses of Credit Cards

- **Establishing good credit.** If you've ever owed money to a bank or your college or university, a computer file exists describing your payment history. If you have never missed a loan payment and always pay on time, you have a good credit history. If you haven't paid on time or have missed payments, your history has negative marks against it. Negative information can stay in a file for seven years, so it's important to establish and keep a clear credit history. Using a credit card moderately, never exceeding your credit limit, and paying on time will help you establish good credit.

- **Emergency use.** Few of us carry around enough cash to deal with emergencies. A credit card can be a life saver if we're on a trip and the car breaks down and needs emergency repairs.

- **Convenience.** Sometimes it's just easier to make purchases using a credit card. For instance, we can make purchases from catalogues over the telephone or on the Internet if we have a credit card. Furthermore, credit cards not only provide a record of purchases, but they also give us consumer protection should a product prove to be defective and we need a refund.

It's easy for most college or university students to get credit cards, and even easier to use them once they have them. The hard part comes later—paying the bills.

"Invest in yourself, in your education. There's nothing better."

Sylvia Porter

The Minuses of Credit Cards

There can be significant drawbacks to the use of credit cards. Potential problems include the following:

- **Interest costs can be high.** Unless you pay off your entire balance each month, your account will be charged interest. Here is an amazing statistic— if you use a credit card to purchase a $2,000 computer and make minimum payments at 18 percent interest, it will take 23 years to pay the balance. If you invested the same minimum payment amount, and invested it in a modest return mutual fund, 23 years later you would have nearly $40,000![2]

- **It's too easy to spend money.** Credit cards are so convenient to use that you may not realize how much you are spending in a given period. Furthermore, spending can become addictive or can be viewed as a recreational activity. In addition, the more credit cards students possess, the more their debt. The average debt of Canadian students possessing one credit card stands at $900, but rises to $1,600 among students with two cards, and $2,500 among students with three or more credit cards.[3]

- **If you're late in making your payments or exceed your credit limit, your credit rating will be damaged.** Credit card companies have long memories, and any mistakes you make will be reflected in your credit record for close to a decade. This may prevent you from buying a car or house in the future and jeopardize your ability to take out student loans.

Heed this advice: Even if you are in a serious relationship or would trust your roommates with your most prized possessions, *do not lend your credit or debit cards!* You are the one who is ultimately responsible for debts accrued in your name. It is not worth losing a friendship over bad debts. Be cautious with your credit cards!

Interest

Interest rates—the percentage of the unpaid balance you are charged on credit cards—vary substantially. Some interest rates are as low as 12 percent per year, while some are as high as 25 percent per year. If the rate is 25 percent, you may be charged $250 each year if you owe an average of $1,000. Furthermore, although some interest rates are *fixed*, meaning that they don't vary from month to month, others are *variable*, which means they change each month. How much they change is tied to various factors in the overall economy.

For instance, suppose you saw a $275 television set on sale "for a limited time" for $240. The $35 discount tempts you. The trouble is you don't have $240 to spare. But you do have a credit card—and you decide to buy the TV with the card and pay it off over time.

The advantages of this strategy are that you get the discount and have immediate use of the television set. The main disadvantage is that you will end up paying more than the $240 figure that you have in mind as the bargain price for the TV. In fact, depending on how high your credit card's interest rate is, how long you take to pay your bill in full, and how large each monthly payment is, you may wipe out most or all of the $35 savings that caused you to make the purchase in the first place. The more slowly you pay off the loan, the more money you pay for the television set.

For example, suppose you use a card with an annual interest rate of 12 percent, compounded monthly, meaning that the interest charge is applied each month, rather than at the end of the year—making the true annual rate 12.68 percent.

(Some cards even compound on a daily basis, resulting in a real interest rate that is even higher.) At the end of a year, assuming you pay $10 per month toward the $240 purchase, you will have paid $120 and still have $143.61 to pay. At the end of two years, you would end up paying $35 in interest on top of the $240 purchase price.

The 12-month calculation is illustrated in the first table below. To see how much of a factor the interest rate is, complete the second table, which shows the same purchase on a credit card with a 20 percent annual (approximately 1.67 percent monthly) interest rate, compounded monthly. (These calculations can also be figured automatically on several websites, including **<www.bankrate.com>** and **<www.quicken.com>**.)

Credit Card Payments: 12% Interest, Compounded Monthly (1% per month)

	Month 1	2	3	4	5	6	7	8	9	10	11	12
Unpaid Balance	$240.00	$232.40	$224.72	$216.97	$209.14	$201.23	$193.24	$185.18	$177.03	$168.80	$160.49	$152.09
Plus Interest of	2.40	2.32	2.25	2.17	2.09	2.01	1.93	1.85	1.77	1.69	1.60	1.52
Minus Payment of	10.00	10.00	10.00	10.00	10.00	10.00	10.00	10.00	10.00	10.00	10.00	10.00
Balance Due	$232.40	$224.72	$216.97	$209.14	$201.23	$193.24	$185.18	$177.03	$168.80	$160.49	$152.09	$143.61

Credit Card Payments: 20% Interest, Compounded Monthly (approx. 1.67% per month)

	Month 1	2	3	4	5	6	7	8	9	10	11	12
Unpaid Balance	$240.00	$234.01	$227.92	$221.72	$215.42							
Plus Interest of	4.01	3.91	3.81	3.70								
Minus Payment of	10.00	10.00	10.00	10.00	10.00	10.00	10.00	10.00	10.00	10.00	10.00	10.00
Balance Due	$234.01	$227.92	$221.72	$215.42								

Learn Your Credit History

Big Brother is alive and well, at least in terms of your credit history. If you've ever had a credit card in your own name, taken out a student loan, or sometimes just received an unsolicited offer for credit in the mail, there's probably a computer file describing who you are, where you live, and your financial history. It shows how big your credit lines are on every credit card you have, if you've ever been late on a payment, and a considerable amount of additional information.

Even worse—many people's credit histories are riddled with errors. That's why it's important to periodically check the record. To get a copy of your credit file, write a letter to one of the organizations listed below, stating you would like a complimentary copy of your credit report. Include your full name (including middle name), your date of birth, your current address, and any other addresses for the previous five years. You may include your telephone number, and social insurance number as well, but these are not necessary. You also need to include photocopies of both sides of two pieces of signed identification, like a driver's licence, credit card, or passport. Send the letter to Equifax Canada

Ltd., Consumer Relations Department, Box 190 Jean Talon Station, Montreal, Quebec, H1S 2Z2; or Trans Union of Canada, P.O. Box 228 LCD1, Hamilton, Ontario, L8L 7W2. For further information, call Equifax at 1-800-465-7166 or Trans Union at 1-800-663-9980.

Once you get your credit report, check it carefully. If you find any mistakes, contact the credit bureau and explain the error. They are legally responsible for investigating the report and correcting the file. It's also a good idea to check your file at least once a year.

Student Housing

While many Canadian college and university students live at home or in residence, a large number of students must or prefer to live independently off-campus. This has many advantages, such as providing an opportunity for additional self-responsibility, greater freedom, and more privacy, but there are a few factors that need to be considered to avoid financial difficulties.

Finding a Place Most colleges and universities have student-housing offices that offer information on both on-campus and off-campus housing. Housing listings are usually available online. If you are visiting your school's campus, bulletin boards often have ads by landlords, local families with rooms to let, and other students looking for roommates. Family friends, neighbours, and older students from your home town may have information about student housing, so word of mouth is an excellent way to learn about affordable housing near your college or university. Bear in mind that commercial apartment finders have direct or indirect fees that could make your apartment more expensive.

Location Finding a house or an apartment near your school may be very convenient, but it can also be quite expensive, as many owners count on renting to students and rents may be somewhat higher than for similar apartments not so close to campus.

Additional Costs Basic rent is only a part of what students need to consider when deciding on a house or apartment to rent. If utilities, such as heat, water, and electricity are not included in the rent, they may add a lot, depending on how the apartment is heated and how many showers you and your roommates take per day! Options, such as cable or satellite TV, Internet hook-up, and parking add to the total monthly bills and all the extra costs may add as much as 25 to 50 percent to your rent. In addition, landlords may require a 12-month lease when students may only need their apartment for eight or nine months of the year. Unless you can sublet your apartment, you may be on the hook for three or four months of rent over the summer.

Legalities Even if you know your roommates really well, make sure all occupants' names and signatures are on the lease. If your name is the only one on the lease, you may be responsible for any damage charges, the full rent, and any additional charges.

Be sure you give your landlord proper notice when you move out. Even if you have a lease, you should inform him or her in writing—depending on your province—30 or 60 days before leaving.

If you give your landlord first and last month's rent, you are entitled to interest on your last month's rent. Even though you may have to ask for this interest, your landlord is required to give it to you.

Some landlords require a security deposit in case damage occurs during the course of a tenancy. Report any damage you notice upon moving in, or you may be required to pay for repairs you are not responsible for. You are responsible for damage done by you or your guests; so be sure that parties don't get rowdy or out of hand.

If you have a dispute with your landlord or neighbours, contact your campus-housing mediator who can help resolve and offer advice regarding differences of opinion about leases, bylaws, rights, and responsibilities. If you have no housing mediator at your school, contact legal aid or a local law school to help you.[4]

Paying for Your Postsecondary Education

Tuition costs vary greatly from one program to another and one school to another, but they are substantial everywhere. In the past 10 years, tuition costs have just about doubled.[5] Tuition costs between $1,200 and $2,500 per year at the average community college or CÉGEP (depending on the province) and between $3,000 to $5,000 per year at the average university (although Quebec's and British Columbia's tuition fees are slightly lower). Professional programs, such as nursing or medicine, have higher fees. All schools have auxiliary fees, which can range from $200 to $700. Specific majors or programs may also include lab or extra fees, as well. In addition, books and school supplies may add several hundred dollars to your cost. Finally, if you live in residence, you can count on an additional $5,000 to $7,000, depending on whether you have a single or double room and the type of meal plan you choose. Living on your own, off-campus, can push that fee even higher.

Nothing about college or university is cheap. It takes enormous expenditures of three often-scarce commodities to attend a postsecondary institution: energy, time, and money. Many find that, of these, the easiest to find is—perhaps surprisingly—money. So many sources of aid for education exist that no one should feel that he or she can't afford a postsecondary education.

While it's not simple to get financial aid, it is a fact that if you are persistent, you can find many sources of funding for your education.

To find money to attend college or university, you will need to spend ample amounts of the other two scarce commodities: time and energy. The entire process of securing financial aid takes a considerable amount of preparation. You need to first identify potential sources of funds and then apply for them. You should assume the process will take from several weeks to as long as several months, depending on the type of aid you're applying for. The steps you need to take to find funding are summarized in the P.O.W.E.R. Plan.

Identifying the Different Types of Funding Available

Funding for college or university comes in three basic categories: loans, grants, and scholarships. Although each supplies you with funds for your higher education, they do so in very different ways.

- **Loans.** When you receive a **loan,** a bank, credit union, or other agency provides funds that must be repaid within a specified time. A loan carries a particular interest rate, which is stated as an annual percentage rate. The interest rate is the cost of borrowing. Think of a loan as renting money. As long as you have the use of someone else's money, you have to pay them "rent" for the privilege. Banks and other lending agencies make money through the interest they charge on loans, just as credit card companies do.

  For example, suppose a bank gives you a $5,000 loan that has an interest rate of 8 percent per year. Not only must you pay back the $5,000 over a specified period, but you must pay the bank interest of 8 percent on the balance that you owe on the loan. Obviously, the higher the interest rate, the more you are paying for the privilege of borrowing the bank's money.

  Three factors must be considered when you receive a loan: the stated amount of the loan (called the **principal**), the interest rate (stated as a percentage), and the length of the loan (referred to as the **term** of the loan). All three factors are important because they determine how much your payments will be when you pay the loan back.

Several kinds of loan programs exist for college and university students.

- **CSLP.** Although some students arrange student loans privately through their own banks, or set up student lines of credit, the Canada Student Loan Program (CSLP), sponsored by the federal government, is the most popular student loan program, because payments and interest are deferred until after you are out of school. Approximately 350 000 students in Canada receive subsidized loans every year. The Canada Student Loan is actually about 60 percent of the loan's total; a Provincial Student Loan accounts for the remaining 40 percent. You should know some of the details about the CSLP:

  - **Repayment.** You must start paying back your loan on the first day of the seventh month after your last day of school; however, interest is calculated starting the same month you complete school. You can calculate what your student loan repayments will be using interactive software at **<www.canlearn.ca/english/csl/hrdcloan/loanen.shtml>.**

    > "Interest works night and day, in fair weather and in foul."
    >
    > Henry Ward Beecher, author

  - **Interest relief.** People with difficulty repaying student loans have options; for example, you can apply for interest relief—a hiatus or break from loan payments for a short time (usually three months). People requiring additional relief can contact the National Student Loans Centre for information about other repayment options.

  - **Defaulting.** Defaulting on student loans occurs when you stop making or miss payments. This can lead to serious financial repercussions. One negative consequence is getting a bad credit rating, which can stay with you for a very long time and can affect your ability to buy a car, obtain a mortgage, or borrow money in the future.

- **Grants, bursaries, and scholarships.** These financial awards do not have to be repaid. Obviously, it's more advantageous to receive a grant, bursary, or scholarship than a loan. And not surprisingly, it's harder to qualify for these awards than for loans. Some **grants, bursaries,** and **scholarships**

Loan
Funds provided by a bank, credit union, or other agency that must be repaid within a specified time

Principal
The stated amount of a loan

Term
The length of time for which money is lent

Grant
An award of money that does not have to be repaid

Bursary
An award of money to a student based on need

Scholarship
An award of money to a student based on merit

are awarded by community service groups, labour unions, or individuals and families; criteria for receiving these awards may include financial need, merit, or specified field of study. Contact your financial aid office for information about awards that may be offered at your school. Amazingly, many scholarships and bursaries go unclaimed every year because students don't know about them.

In addition, the Canadian government has grant and scholarship programs that can help reduce the costs of paying for higher education for certain students:

- **Canada study grants.** These grants assist postsecondary students with special needs. These grants are targeted at students with permanent disabilities, high-need part-time students, women in certain doctoral programs, and student loan recipients who have dependants. Once you apply for your Canada student loan, you can submit your application for a Canada study grant at your school's financial aid office or your provincial or territorial student assistance office.

- **The Millennium Scholarship.** These scholarships, from the Government of Canada, are awarded on financial need; you must be eligible for a Canada student loan to receive this scholarship. Information about Millennium Scholarships can be obtained at your school's financial aid office.

Other ways of relieving the financial burden of your postsecondary education include:

- **Work-study programs.** Work-study programs provide student jobs in educational institutions. Typically, students work 10 to 12 hours per week in various capacities. Work-study placements may be tied to financial need and academic success. Contact your financial aid office for information on work-study opportunities at your campus.

- **Cooperative education.** Co-op programs are set up in many colleges and universities. Cooperative education provides opportunities for students to integrate periods of academic study with curriculum-related, productive work experiences. These programs allow students to test their skills, adjust to the work environment, and earn money.

Researching Possible Sources of Financial Aid

As you can see, several sources of financial aid are available. However, finding those sources can be time consuming. Your college or university financial aid office should be your first stop for researching sources of funding. The library and World Wide Web also contain many types of information about possible funding. A few sites are particularly useful: **<http://youth.hrdc-drhc.gc.ca/ythlink/sec1ind. shtml>**, a government website listing numerous awards, bursaries, fellowships, and scholarships, and the scholarship search websites at **<www.scholarships-canada.com/>** and **<www.studentawards.com/english/can/register.asp>**.

Whatever the potential source of financial aid, you'll be asked to bare your financial soul. There will also be forms galore. Before actually completing the forms, it will be important to gather the information you will need. If you are being supported by your parents, much of it may have to come from them, and they will have to complete some of the forms.

Keep track of deadlines! If you miss a deadline for applying for financial aid, you'll be out of luck; no exceptions are made. You'll just have to wait for another aid cycle.

Finally, make sure you know what your needs are. The typical costs of school include not only tuition but also fees, books, and supplies, as well as associated costs, such as transportation, housing, food, and childcare.

Applying for Financial Aid

It may seem that for every dollar in aid you get, there is a different line to complete on a complicated form. Prepare yourself for a blizzard of paperwork.

You need follow only two basic steps to receive financial aid:

1. **Apply.** To get a student loan, fill out an application form, which you can get at the financial aid office at the school you are applying to or at your provincial or territorial student assistance office. Some applications can be made online. Campusaccess.com has put together a detailed, informative section to make sense of all the different programs available to Canadian students. You can find information on financial aid programs, both federal and provincial, as well as scholarships at **<www. campusaccess.com/campus_web/educ/e2fin.htm>.**

2. **Wait.** It takes time for loan applications to be processed and financial aid decisions to be made. Apply 10 weeks in advance of the semester you are applying for. Be prepared to wait, and have contingency funding in place in case of administrative delays.

Show Me the Money: Building a Financial Philosophy

It's hard to forget the famous line from *Jerry McGuire,* the movie in which Tom Cruise plays a sports agent: "Show me the money." That direct statement—however crude—might be used to illustrate one financial philosophy: Life revolves around money.

Many would disagree. For instance, authors Vicki Robin and Joe Dominguez argue in their book *Your Money or Your Life*[6] that, while most people find money to be a controlling force in their lives and, consequently, their major source of stress, it needn't be. Yes, the authors concede, acquiring and spending money can become an obsession, and when this is the case the simple pleasures of life are lost. But Robin and Dominguez outline an alternative approach in which we reprioritize our values, live frugally, and ultimately achieve financial independence.

> "I'm so poor I can't even pay attention."
>
> Ron Kittle

Whether you choose to follow the path of Jerry McGuire or that of Vicki Robin and Joe Dominguez, the important thing is to develop your own personal financial philosophy. You can get a start in developing your financial philosophy by completing Try It! 3, "Discover Your Personal Financial Philosophy," which can help assess how money affects your life. It will help you consider the role that money plays in your life. How much does money motivate what you do? Are you interested in becoming rich, or do you tend to think more in terms of simply having enough to have a comfortable life, without lots of luxuries? What activities

3

🐾 Working in a Group:
Discover Your Personal Financial Philosophy

Prepare: The purpose of this exercise is to help you reveal your personal financial philosophy. What does money mean to you?

Organize: You will need the saving style questionnaire below, which is also available online.

Work: Answer the questions and find and interpret your attitude. After you have completed the questions, separate into small groups and compare your answers with those of other students.

Evaluate: Were you able to describe what money means to you?

Rethink: How would you use this information about your personal financial philosophy to improve your financial management or manage your money differently in the future?

A. Attitudes toward Money

	Strongly Disagree	Disagree	Neutral	Agree	Strongly Agree
1. Money is essential for happiness.					
2. Having money guarantees happiness.					
3. Money makes no difference to my happiness.					
4. More money equals more happiness.					
5. Beyond having enough to live modestly on, money doesn't make much of a difference.					
6. I frequently worry about money.					
7. I frequently daydream about having a lot of money.					
8. If I suddenly had to live on very little money, I could adjust easily.					
9. If I suddenly won a lot of money, I would go on a spending spree.					
10. If I suddenly won a lot of money, I would share it with my relatives.					
11. If I suddenly won a lot of money, I would give a large percentage to charity.					
12. If I found a substantial amount of cash in a bag, I would try hard to find its rightful owner.					
13. If I could carry only a briefcase full of $100 bills or my pet dog out of a burning building, I would take the dog.					
14. I plan to make a lot of money in my career.					
15. I plan to make only enough money to live in reasonable comfort.					
16. It's great to have money.					
17. Money is a necessary evil.					
18. Money is the root of all evil.					

B. Sources of Satisfaction

1. Which activities that you engaged in over the past five years have given you the greatest satisfaction?

2. How much money did those activities cost?

3. How would you spend your time if you could do anything you chose?

4. How much money would this cost each year?

C. Personal Financial Philosophy

Consider your attitudes toward money and the sources of your satisfaction. Sum up your personal financial philosophy here:

bring you the greatest satisfaction in life? Do those activities require a certain level of income?

Ultimately, consider how college or university relates to issues involving finances. Higher education is undoubtedly one of the biggest investments that you'll ever make. If you only think of it in terms of its eventual financial pay-off—getting a better job and leading a more affluent life—you'll be missing some central aspects of the process of educating yourself.

Speaking of Success

Murray Baker

B.A. (Honours), History, University of Western Ontario

Vancouver-based author, researcher, and speaker Murray Baker wrote his best-selling book, *The Debt-Free Graduate*, while working as the coordinator of first-year programs at the University of Western Ontario. With students and friends struggling to pay off loans, Murray saw the toll financial difficulties and stress levels associated with student debt take.

Now with yearly printings, *The Debt-Free Graduate*, which was written in Murray's spare time, has led to a new career for him. After its publication in 1996, Murray had requests for TV and radio interviews and invitations for speaking engagements. In 1997, he decided to pursue writing and speaking full-time, feeling he could make more of a difference in that role. Murray, who has just completed a U.S. edition of his book, has now given more than 200 interviews, and has written numerous articles for magazines and newspapers. In addition, he maintains a comprehensive website on student finances at **<www.debtfreegrad. com>**.

Financial advising may be a long way from being a history major; however, Murray says investing and finance always interested him and he pursued what had been a hobby to create a product he enjoyed that helped people. Murray believes there is significant transferability from his liberal arts education to his current career—particularly in the areas of researching, writing, speaking, critical thinking, and analytical reasoning. He says that while at Western he wouldn't have dreamed he'd end up as a professional speaker, but debating and analytical skills (developed during university seminars) have helped him in speaking on-air and in front of crowds.

Avoidance is one of the chief reasons students end up with financial problems, Murray believes. Student debt is a serious issue and sidestepping it gets students into a lot of financial difficulty. While he doesn't think every student can graduate debt-free, Murray believes all students can take control of their personal finances and reduce the debt they owe on graduation.

Murray is a strong advocate of proactive financial planning for students. The "get the loan, put it in the bank, and hope the school year is finished before the money runs out" approach to money management is ineffective. Murray recommends that students create budgets, and use them as road maps, avoiding consequences such as having to take on overly demanding part-time work, dropping out of school, or making forced errors, such as cash advances on credit cards. He also suggests students invest student loans in safe short-term investments, such as Canada Savings Bonds or GICs. Students can gain modest returns on their money (as opposed to little or no return in a bank account) and start to learn how to handle their finances. With this experience, students will graduate with sound financial knowledge, which will serve them well when they do start to earn money.

What purpose does a budget serve and how can you prepare and stick to one?

- Concerns about money can be significantly lowered through the creation of a budget by which expenditures and income can be planned, accounted for, and aligned with your goals.

- Budgets provide security by helping you control your finances and avoid surprises.

- The process of budgeting involves identifying your financial goals, keeping track of current expenses and estimating future expenses, and making the necessary adjustments to keep income and expenditures in balance.

What help is available to pay for your college education?

- Loans for education are available with reasonable interest rates and conditions, especially the ability to defer paying the loans back until after graduation.

- Grants and bursaries offer money without requiring repayment. They are harder to receive than loans because they are typically reserved for people with exceptional financial or other needs.

- Scholarships are usually awarded by colleges and other institutions based on either financial need or academic, athletic, or other abilities.

What can you do if you fall into financial difficulty?

- If financial difficulties arise, contact your creditors and arrange a plan for paying off the debt. If you need help in designing a repayment plan, nonprofit credit counsellors can help.

P.O.W.E.R. Portfolio

Money Matters

After completing Try It! 3, expand your thoughts into a submission for your portfolio. Your entry could be a reflective rationale, a poem, a motto, or anecdotes about your perspective on money. You could be artistic and create a collage to express your financial philosophy. Overall, your philosophy should be reflected in what you do, so try to provide some evidence for your entry. For example, Marc, who believes in *voluntary simplicity*, rejects the waste of *conspicuous consumption*. As proof of his philosophy, Marc can include a paper he wrote in SOSC255: Human Ecology, indicating the steps he has taken to live frugally; brochures and pictures of a *Simpler Living* conference he attended; and ways he and other concerned classmates have improved recycling on his campus. Jenn, on the other hand, believes money is a commodity that will grow and benefit those who deal wisely with it. She has participated in an investment club that finance students at her college started. She includes records of her dealings and a tally sheet showing the profits her group has made; a list of peer counselling appointments where she assisted fellow students with income taxes; and a financial report from the precision skating club she belongs to and for which she serves as treasurer.

Resources

On Campus

If you are receiving financial aid, you should know whether a particular office is devoted to the complexities of scholarships, loan processing, and other forms of aid. The personnel in the office can be very helpful in maximizing your financial aid package as well as in solving financial problems related to your schooling. If you have a problem with your finances, see them sooner rather than later.

In Print

David Chilton's *The Wealthy Barber: Everyone's Commonsense Guide to Becoming Financially Independent* (Prima Lifestyles, 1997) is Canada's best-selling book ever, aside from The Bible. *The Barber* offers the average person all the information needed to make a lifetime of good financial decisions.

Another excellent resource is Murray Baker's *The Debt-Free Graduate: How to Survive College Without Going Broke* (Career Press, 2000). The book is very helpful in preparing information for students about how to be financially fit.

On the Web

The following sites on the World Wide Web provide the opportunity to extend your learning about the material in this chapter. Although the Web addresses were accurate at the time the book was printed, check the P.O.W.E.R. Learning website, <www.mcgrawhill.ca/olc/power>, for any changes that may have occurred.

www.debtfreegrad.com/
A comprehensive site from Murray Baker with lots of information on student money matters, from banking to eating well on a budget. The site includes cost calculators, loan repayment schedules, and links to financial aid centres as well.

http://canadaonline.about.com/cs/educationfinances/
Education Finances in Canada has a list of numerous links on tuition, savings, student loans, RESPs, scholarships, and debt to finance a Canadian education.

http://canadaonline.about.com/od/budgets/index.htm
This is a very helpful Canadian site on budgets and personal financial planning resources to help in preparing a personal budget, managing money, and planning your future.

www.stretcher.com/index.cfm
The Dollar Stretcher is a website devoted to saving money that offers many helpful hints on how to cut costs.

The Case Of...

Overdrawn, Overwrought, and Over Her Head

Her life was a house of cards, and someone had just pulled one out from the bottom.

At least that's what it felt like to Tara Kenko. The month had started out badly when Tara found that she had made a mistake in her chequing account and had only $439, instead of the $939 she thought she had. After paying her share of the rent—$210— there wasn't enough money left to make her car payment. So she just put the bill aside, figuring that she'd take care of it later in the month when she got paid.

Things went from bad to worse two days later when her car refused to start. She had to have it towed to a mechanic, who told her that it would cost about $350 to get it fixed. She didn't have that, either, but she figured she could put it on her credit card even though her unpaid balance was already high. But later, when she went to pick up her car and pay for the repair, which turned out to be closer to $400 than the $350 she expected to pay, her card was rejected. She called the credit card company from the repair shop and was told that she had exceeded her authorized credit limit and that her card was frozen. Because the mechanic wouldn't let her take her car until she paid for the repairs, she was forced to leave it and catch a bus to campus.

The final straw came in her chemistry class. The instructor announced that students in the class would have to buy yet another book for the latest assignment. Having already spent $150 for books in that class alone, Tara was both angry and dismayed. She had no idea how she was going to find the money to pay for the book, let alone her regular car payment and the car repairs. She was in financial trouble, and she didn't know what to do.

1. What should Tara do now to start addressing her problem?
2. Can you suggest some approaches Tara can take to deal with the problem of the new book for her chemistry class?
3. How do you think the mistake may have occurred in Tara's chequing account? What advice would you give her to avoid a similar mistake in the future?
4. Given that Tara does not have a lot of leeway in her finances for multiple disasters such as the ones that befell her this month, what general course would you advise her to take as a way to plan her expenditures more effectively?
5. What steps might Tara take to decrease her expenses? What might she do to increase her income?

Endnotes

Chapter 1

1. The Conference Board of Canada. (2000). *Employability Skills 2000+*. The Conference Board of Canada, 255 Smyth Road, Ottawa ON K1H 8M7; Tel: 613-526-3280; Fax: 613-526-4857. [Online]. Available: <www.conferenceboard.ca/nbec>.

Chapter 2

1. Adapted from Middlesex Community College. (n.d.). *Modality Preference Inventory*. Middlesex Community College, 100 Training Hill Rd., Middletown, CT 06457. [Online]. Available: <www.mxctc.commnet.edu/clc/survey.htm>.

2. Adapted from Clark, D. (2000). *Learning Style Indicator: What Kind of Learner Are You?* [Online]. Available: <www.nwlink.com/~donclark/hrd/kolb.html>.

Chapter 3

1. Adapted, in part, from Ferner, J.D. (1980). *Successful Time Management*. New York: Wiley, p. 33.

2. Ibid.

Chapter 4

1. Farber, B.A., Brink, D.C., & Raskin, P.M. (Eds.). (1996). *The Psychotherapy of Carl Rogers: Cases and Commentary*. New York: Guilford Press; and Rogers, C.R. (1951). *Client-Centered Therapy*. Boston: Houghton Mifflin.

2. Dyer, G. (2001). "Visible Minorities." *Canadian Geographic*, 121(11), 44.

3. Nolan, M.F. (1997, April 26). "Tiger's Racial Multiplicity." *Boston Globe*, A11.

4. Tatum, B.D. (1997). *Why Are All the Black Kids Sitting Together in the Cafeteria? And Other Conversations about Race*. New York: Basic Books.

5. Statistics Canada. (1997). *Immigrant Population by Place of Birth, Showing Period of Immigration for Canada, 1996 Census*. [Online]. Available: <www.statcan.ca/english/census96/nov4/imm2a.htm>.

6. Tuckman, B.W. "Developmental Sequence in Small Groups," *Psychological Bulletin* (vol. 63, 1965).

Chapter 5

1. Pauk, W. (1974). *How to Study in College*. Boston: Houghton Mifflin.

2. Raloff, J. (2000, October 7). "Even Nunavut Gets Plenty of Dioxin." *Science News*, 158, 230. Copyright Science Service, Incorporated, 2000, October 7. Reproduced with permission of the copyright owner. Further reproduction or distribution is prohibited without permission.

3. 3M United States. (2001). *Articles and Advice: Minutes and Group Recordings*. [Online]. Available: <www.3m.com/meetingnetwork/readingroom/meetingguide_minutes.html>.

Chapter 6

1. Smith, M.U. (1992). "Expertise and the Organization of Knowledge: Unexpected Differences Among Genetic Counselors, Faculty, and Students on Problem Categorization Tasks." *Journal of Research in Science Teaching*, 29, 179–205.

2. <www.usu.edu/arc/online_learning_center/index.htm>.

3. Halpern, D.F. (1996). *Thought and Knowledge: An Introduction to Critical Thinking*. Mahwah, NJ: Erlbaum, p. 48.

4. Abel, T., Alberini, C., Ghiradi, M., Huang, Y.Y., Nguyen, P., and Kandel, E.R. (1995). "Steps Toward A Molecular Definition of Memory Consolidation." In D.L. Schacter (Ed.), *Memory Distortions: How Minds, Brains, and Societies Reconstruct the Past*. Cambridge, MA: Harvard University Press.

Chapter 7

1. Bransford, J.D., & Johnson, M.K. (1972). "Contextual Prerequisites for Understanding: Some Investigation of Comprehensions and Recall." *Journal of Verbal Learning and Verbal Behavior*, 11, 171–221.

2. Learning Disabilities Resource Community: Letter of Intent. (2000, July 19). Submitted to the Office of Learning Technology. [Online]. Available: <http://snow.utoronto.ca/initiatives>.

Chapter 9

1. Elbow, P. (1998). *Writing with Power* (2nd ed.). New York: Oxford University Press.

2. <www.techweb.com/encyclopedia/printDefinition?term=URL>.

3. From Petroff, L., & Teixeira, C. (2000). Portugal. Canada Heirloom Series Volume VII, Canada at the Millennium: A Trans-cultural Society. [Online]. Available: <http://collections.ic.gc.ca/heirloom_series/volume7/volume7.htm>.

4. From Richardson, C., and Friesen, J. (2004, May 9). "Buying an Essay Way Out," *The Eyeopener Online*: <www.theeyeopener.com/storydetail.cfm?storyid=786>.

Chapter 10

1. Higher Education Research Institute, University of California, Graduate School of Education & Information Studies. (1999). *The American Freshman: National Norms for Fall 1998*. [Online]. Available: <www.gseis.ucla.edu/heri/press98.html>.

2. Bottom Line: One Cliché is Absolutely the Worst (2004, March 25). [Online]. Available: <www.freep.com/features/living/cliche25_20040325.htm>. Retrieved: 2004, March 26.

3. Wydro, K. (1985). *Think on Your Feet: The Art of Thinking and Speaking Under Pressure*. Englewood Cliffs, NJ: Prentice Hall.

Chapter 11

1. Adapted from Halpern, D.F. (1996). *Thought and Knowledge: An Introduction to Critical Thinking* (3rd ed.). Mahwah, NJ: Erlbaum.

2. Ibid., and Bransford, J.D., & Stein, B.S. (1993). *The Ideal Problem Solver* (2nd ed.). New York: W.H. Freeman.

3. Adapted from Levy, D.A. (1997). *Tools of Critical Thinking*. Boston: Allyn & Bacon, p. 20.

4. Forer, B. (1949). "The Fallacy of Personal Validation: A Classroom Demonstration of Gullibility." *Journal of Abnormal and Social Psychology*, 44, 118–123.

Chapter 13

1. Sax, L.J., Astin, A.W., Korn, W.S., & Mahoney, K. (1990). *The American Freshman: National Norms for Fall 1999*. Los Angeles: Higher Education Research Institute, UCLA.

2. Chamberlain, K., & Zika, S. (1990). "The Minor Events Approach to Stress: Support for the Use of Daily Hassles." *British Journal of Psychology*, 81, 469–481.

3. Birmingham, C.L., Muller, J.L, Palepu, A., Spinelli, J.J., & Anis, A.H. (1999). "The Cost of Obesity in Canada." *Canadian Medical Association Journal*, 160, 483–486.

4. Obesity Canada. (2001). *Fact Sheet*. [Online]. Available: <www.obesitycanada.com>.

5. Myers, M.D. (2001). *Complications of Obesity*. [Online]. Available: <www.weight.com/complications.html>.

6. Source of checklist: Marx, M.B., Garrity, T.F., & Bowers, F.R. (1975). "The Influence of Recent Life Experience on the Health of College Freshmen." *Journal of Psychosomatic Research*, 19, 87–98 (Questionnaire on p. 97).

7. Carlson, R. (1997). *Don't Sweat the Small Stuff…And It's All Small Stuff.* New York: Hyperion.

8. Canadian Mental Health Association. (2001). *Ten Facts about Workplace Stress.* [Online]. Available: <www3.sympatico. ca/cmha. toronto/mhw4.html>.

9. Brink, S. (2000, October 16). "Sleepless Society." *US News and World Report.*

10. Ibid.

11. de la Hey, M. (2000). "Survey Highlights Problem of Binge Drinking at Canadian Universities." *Journal of Addiction and Mental Health.* [Online]. Available: <www.camh.net/ journal/journalv3no4/survey_ highlights_binge.html>.

12. Ibid.

13. Ibid.

14. Centre for Addiction and Mental Health. (2000). *First National Survey of Drug Use Among University Students Released by the Centre for Addiction and Mental Health Shows "Heavy" Drinking to be a Significant Concern.* [Online]. Available: <www.camh.net/ press_releases/can_campus_ survey_pr29300.html>.

15. Ibid.

16. Addiction Research Foundation. (1994). *Facts about… Alcohol.* [Online]. Available: <www.canoe.ca/ HealthReference/arf_facts1. html>.

17. Centre for Addiction and Mental Health. (2000). *First National Survey of Drug Use Among University Students Released by the Centre for Addiction and Mental Health Shows "Heavy" Drinking to be a Significant Concern.* [Online]. Available: <www. camh.net/press_releases/ can_campus_survey_pr29300. html>.

18. Childbirth by Choice Trust. (1999). *Fact Sheet: Unwanted Pregnancy.* [Online]. Available: <www.cbctrust.com/unwanted. html>.

19. Ibid.

20. Childbirth by Choice Trust. (1999). *The Economics of Contraception, Abortion, and Unintended Pregnancy.* [Online]. Available: <www. cbctrust.com/ECONOMIC. html>.

21. Childbirth by Choice Trust. (1999). *Fact Sheet: Unwanted Pregnancy.* [Online]. Available: <www.cbctrust.com/unwanted. html>.

22. Trouton, K., & Dzakpasu, S. (1998). *Fact Sheet: Induced Abortion.* [Online]. Available: <www.hc-sc.gc.ca/hpb/lcdc/ brch/factshts/inabor_e.html>.

23. Ibid.

24. Maticka-Tyndale, E. (1997). "Reducing the Incidence of Sexually Transmitted Disease Through Behavioural and Social Change." *Canadian Journal of Human Sexuality,* 6(2). [Online]. Available: <www.hcsc.gc.ca/hpb/lcdc/ publicat/cjhs/cjhs2.html>.

25. University of Alberta Health Centre. (1997). *Sexual Assault and the Law in Canada.* [Online]. Available: <www.ualber ta.ca/dept/ health/public_html/heathinfo/ SACan.html>.

Chapter 14

1. Millennium Scholarships press release: <www.millennium scholarships.ca/en/research/ archive>.

2. <www.rbcroyalbank.com/ agriculture/reference/risk_ management/risk_may_2001_ 001.html>.

3. <www. millenniumscholarships.ca/ en/foundation/publications/ archivepress/nov262001/>.

4. <www.canlearn.ca/ living/housing/clindex. cfm?langcanlearn=en>.

5. CanLearn Interactive. (2001). CanLearn Interactive. [Online]. Available: <www.canlearn.ca/>; and individual college and university home pages.

6. Dominquez, J., & Robin, V. (1993). *Your Money or Your Life: Transforming Your Relationship with Money and Achieving Financial Independence.* New York: Penguin USA.

Credits

p. 1 PhotoDisc/Getty Images

p. 4 Scott Markewitz/Getty Images

p. 10 Solstice Photography/Brand X Pictures

p. 15 NASA/Photo Researchers

p. 23 Michael Prince/Corbis

Pp. 27-28: The Learning Styles Modality Preferences Inventory, Middlesex Community College, available online at www.mxctc.commnet.edu/clc/survey.htm. Used by permission.

Pp. 32-33: Multiple Intelligence Inventory and the Eight Styles of Learning. Reprinted with permission of Gregory R. Gay, Learning Disabilities Resource Centre (LDRC) website at www.ldrc.ca

p. 36 PhotoDisc/Getty Images

p. 44 Cartoon: "Know Thyself." © The New Yorker Collection 1991 William Steig from cartoonbank.com. All Rights Reserved.

p. 47 Greg Gibson/AP Photo

p. 51 Courtesy Tom Currie

p. 57 JLP/Sylvia Torres/Corbis

p. 64 Getty Images

p. 74 PhotoDisc/Punch Stock

p. 79 Ed Bock Photography, Inc./Corbis

p. 80 Photo Credit: Karen Baer. Courtesy of Darryl Weeks, Outside Music

p. 85 Charles Gupton Photography/Corbis

p. 89 Royalty Free/Corbis

p. 92 Comstock Images/Alamy

p. 98 Tom Stewart/Corbis

p. 104 Sondra Dawes/Image Works

p. 108 Courtesy Jenny Zhang

p. 113 Ryan McVay/Getty Images

p. 116 Scott T. Baxter

p. 120 Raloff, Janet. (2000). "Even Nunavut Gets Plenty of Dioxin." *Science News,* Issue 15, p. 230. Reprinted with permission from *Science News,* the weekly newsmagazine of science, copyright 2000 by Science Service Inc.

p. 123 Robert Ullmann

p. 132 Photo Courtesy Kofi Boateng

p. 132 Logo of Niagara College. Reprinted by permission of Niagara College.

p. 137 McGraw-Hill Companies, Inc./Gary He, photographer

p. 142 Royalty Free/Corbis

Pp. 144-145 Exercise from Halpern, Diane F. (1996). *Thought and Knowledge: An Introduction to Critical Thinking,* 3rd edition, 48. Reprinted by permission of Lawrence Erlbaum Associates, Inc., Mahwah, NJ.

p. 160 Grace/Zeta/Corbis

p. 155 John Touscany/Index Stock

p. 156 Courtesy Elaine Hudson

p. 156 Logo of Nova Scotia Community College. Reprinted by permission of Nova Scotia Community College.

p. 161 Patrick Clark/Getty Images

p. 165 Excerpt from Bransford, J. D., & Johnson, M. K. (1972). "Contextual Prerequisites for Understanding: Some Investigations of Comprehension and Recall." *Journal of Verbal Leaning and Verbal Behavior,* 11, 717-721. Reprinted with permission of Academic Press.

p. 171 Mika/Zefa/Corbis

p. 182 Jose Luis Pelaez, Inc./Corbis

p. 184 Courtesy Rachel Trail

p. 184 Logo of University of King's College in Halifax. Reprinted by permission of University of King's College in Halifax.

p. 185 Patrick Clark/Getty Images

p. 189 Royalty Free/Corbis

p. 195 Pando Hall/Getty Images

p. 199 Royalty Free/Corbis

p. 207 Chuck Savage/Corbis

p. 211 Exercise adapted from The College Learner: How to Survive and Thrive in an Academic Environment, by Mark Renck Jalong, Mahoney Twiest, and Gail J. Gerlack with Diane H. Skoner. Englewood Cliffs: Merill/Prentice Hall. 1996. From <www.bucks.edu/%7especpop/Evaltest.htm>

p. 214 Courtesy Asta Kovanen

p. 214 Logo of the Okanogan Valley College of Massage Therapy. Reprinted by permission of the Okanogan Valley College of Massage Therapy.

p. 219 Ken Usami/Getty Images

p. 220 Royalty Free/Corbis

p. 222 Esbin Anderson/Image Works

p. 230 Didier Givois/Photo Researchers

p. 232 Michael Newman/PhotoEdit

p. 235 Exercise from http://writing. englishclub.com/ee/lth_shortessays.html.

p. 238 (top) Image courtesy of Seneca College Learning Commons (bottom) Royalty Free/Corbis

p. 239 Cartoon: © The New Yorker Collection 1998 Arnie Levin from cartoonbank.com. All Rights Reserved.

p. 240 Jose Luis Pelaez/Corbis (bottom) Screen image: Yahoo! Search: Animal Rights. Reproduced with permission of Yahoo! Inc. © 2005 by Yahoo! Inc. YAHOO! And the Yahoo! Logo are trademarks of Yahoo! Inc.

p. 252 Courtesy Shawn Thomson

p. 268 Courtesy of TSN The Sports Network

p. 268 Logo of Red River College of Applied Arts, Science and Technology. Reprinted by permission of Red River College of Applied Arts, Science and Technology.

p. 273 Matthias Kulka/Zefa/Corbis

p. 274 Royalty Free/Corbis

p. 276 McGraw-Hill Co., Inc./Gary He, photographer

p. 278 Superstock

p. 279 "The scale of tolerance-intolerance of ambiguity," Table 1 p. 34, in Budner, S. (1962). "Intolerance of ambiguity as a personal variable." Journal of Personality, Vol. 30, No. 7, pp. 29-50. Reprinted by permission of Blackwell Publishing, U.K.

p. 286, 285 Exercise adapted in part from Bransford, J. D., & Stein, B. S. (1993). The Ideal Problem Solver, 2/e. © 1993, 1984 by W. H. Freeman & Company. Used with permission. And adapted in part from Halpern, Diane F. (1996) *Thought and Knowledge: An Introduction to Critical Thinking,* 3rd edition, 48. Reprinted by permission of Lawrence Erlbaum Associates, Inc., Mahwah, NJ.

p. 290 Royalty Free/Corbis

p. 292 Courtesy Jeff Goplin

p. 292 Logo of The Northern Alberta Institute of Technology. Reprinted by permission of The Northern Alberta Institute of Technology.

p. 297 Stephen Wetstead/Corbis

p. 301 Royalty Free/Corbis

p. 308 CP Picture Archive (Phill Snel, Maclean's)

p. 311 CP Picture Archive (Jonathan Hayward, Canadian Press)

p. 318 Courtesy Dr. Anthony Brissett

p. Logo of George Brown – The Toronto City College. Reprinted by permission of George Brown – The Toronto City College.

p. 323 Karl Weatherly/Getty Images

p. 324 PhotoDisc/Getty Images

Pp. 328-329 Exercise from Marx, M. B., Garrity, T. F. & Bowers, F. R. (1975). "The Influence of Recent Life Experience on the Health of College Freshmen." *Journal of Psychosomatic Research,* 19, 87-98. Copyright 1975. Reprinted with permission from Elsevier Science.

p. 334 Steve Prezant/Corbis

p. 335 CP Picture Archive (Ian MacAlpine, Kingston Whig Standard)

p. 343 Digital Vision

p. 347 Courtesy Krista Bailey

p. 347 Logo of Saskatchewan Institute of Applied Science and Technology. Reprinted by permission of Saskatchewan Institute of Applied Science and Technology.

p. 353 Royalty Free/Corbis

p. 355 Tom Stewart/Corbis/Magma

p. 362 (top) Margot Granitsas/Image Works

p. 362 (bottom) PhotoDisc

p. 365 CP/Doug Ives

p. 366 Digital Vision/Digital Vision

p. 376 Courtesy Murray Baker

Index